Communication and Commerce along the Western Sealanes AD 400-800

Jonathan M. Wooding

BAR International Series 654
1996

Published in 2019 by
BAR Publishing, Oxford

BAR International Series 654

Communication and Commerce along the Western Sealanes AD 400-800

ISBN 9780860548430 paperback
ISBN 9781407349633 e-book

DOI https://doi.org/10.30861/9780860548430

A catalogue record for this book is available from the British Library

This book is available at www.barpublishing.com

BAR Publishing is the trading name of British Archaeological Reports (Oxford) Ltd. British Archaeological Reports was first incorporated in 1974 to publish the BAR Series, International and British. In 1992 Hadrian Books Ltd became part of the BAR group. This volume was originally published by Tempvs Reparatvm in conjunction with British Archaeological Reports (Oxford) Ltd / Hadrian Books Ltd, the Series principal publisher, in 1996. This present volume is published by BAR Publishing, 2019.

BAR
PUBLISHING

BAR titles are available from:

BAR Publishing
122 Banbury Rd, Oxford, OX2 7BP, UK
EMAIL info@barpublishing.com
PHONE +44 (0)1865 310431
FAX +44 (0)1865 316916
www.barpublishing.com

Contents

	Preface	iii
Chapter One	Sealanes and the Scholarly Terrain	1
Chapter Two	Introducting the Western Sealanes—Geography, Technology and Seamanship	6
Chapter Three	The Fifth Century—Continuity, Discontinuity and Cultural Change	22
Chapter Four	The Mediterranean and the Atlantic in the Sixth Century	41
Chapter Five	Gaul and the Western Sealanes in the Sixth Century	55
Chapter Six	Cargoes and Commerce between western Gaul and the Ireland in the Seventh Century	64
Chapter Seven	Routes of Maritime Trade in the late-Sixth through Eighth Centuries	93
Appendix One	Two Unsubstantiated Cases of Seventh-century Travel	105
Appendix Two	The 'Peninsular Road' Model	107
	Bibliography	108

List of Illustrations

p. 27—Fig. 1 Distribution of amphorae of Dressel types 1A and 1B (based on Gaillou 1984).

p. 28—Fig. 2 Late-Roman tablewares Argonne Ware, *Éponge* Ware (after Fulford 1978).

p. 39—Fig. 3 Distribution of Ogham stones in Ireland and western Britain.

p. 44—Fig. 4 Imported Mediterranean ceramics in western Britain and Ireland, PRS Form C: Mediterranean and western sealanes distribution.

p.58—Fig. 5 Iberian distribution of *Paleocristiana* pottery (after Molina, 241).

p. 75—Fig. 6 E1 rim forms.

p. 76—Fig. 7 E ware rim forms, E ware vessel forms.

p. 79—Fig. 8 E2 beakers from Herpes (Charente).

p. 80—Fig. 9 Possible E ware vessels from western France.

p. 85—Fig. 10 Glass vessels with combed decoration.

p. 86—Fig. 11 Glass vessels with 'chevron' decoration.

p. 89—Fig. 12 Glass cones: with horizontal sub-rim trailing; with 'lattice' festoons.

p. 90—Fig. 13 Glass vessels: with 'combed festoon' decoration; with optic decoration; with engraved decoration.

p. 91—Fig. 14 Possible parallels from the continent.

p. 99—Fig. 15 E ware pottery (map).

p. 100—Fig. 16 Glass vessels of 'Atlantic' type: British and Irish distribution.

p. 103—Fig. 17 Port sites discussed.

Preface

This book brings together historical and archaeological evidence to critique the thesis that there was regular long-distance communication and commerce along the Atlantic seaboard, over a period of four centuries, c. 400-800 AD, which is known variously as the 'early medieval', 'early historic' or 'early Christian' period. It pays particular attention to the evidence for direct maritime links of the continent with western Britain and Ireland—the existence of which is assumed in the studies of Zimmer, Crawford, Bowen, Ó Riordáin and Thomas, among others, but the exact nature of which has never been satisfactorily defined. New evidence, most notably finds of imported ceramics from western Britain and Ireland, has allowed us to go some way toward confirming the existence of such direct links and to reconstruct the routes of the voyages involved. It would be fair to say, however, that this process has yet to produce any consensus as to the scale, frequency and cultural impact of such contacts.

The complexity of the extant literature on this topic does not make its reassessment a simple task. Most secondary studies still exhibit a diffusionist approach, while the broader historical background has undergone substantial revision—especially our view of the role of the Irish in continental affairs. The societies along the Atlantic shores of Europe played a controversial role in the formation of the intellectual and religious culture of Europe in the early middle ages. The depth of Christian intellectual knowledge and the departure from religious orthodoxy in early medieval Britain and Ireland have been the subject of particular controversy. Data which suggest sources of overseas influence in the formation of insular Christian culture have inevitably been drawn into such debates. As we will see, however, this has had the unfortunate consequence of causing discussion of issues of communication and commerce to be relegated to the footnotes of studies of intellectual history—rather than their receiving the attention which they warrant in their own right. Treatment of communication issues in archaeological publications has not served to offset the lack of an historical debate. Two rather dated interpretive models, Zimmer's 'wine trade' and Crawford's 'western seaways' have almost by default continued to enjoy a widespread, if superficial, currency in the absence of a broad reinterpretation of the data for seaborne exchange.

The influence of diffusionist theories has also served to exaggerate the scale of western sealanes commerce beyond the limits of the evidence. We will see, however, that archaeological data, combined with a reconsideration of the historical sources, refute the diffusionist models and provide evidence for an episodic character and smaller scale for such long-distance voyages as took place along the western sealanes in the period AD400-800. This is not to say that the firm identification of some voyage events, using archaeological data, can be held to refute the existence of other, less archaeologically tangible, long-distance links which we might consider likely. Such data, however, can be used to identify the differing circumstances of individual episodes, and call into question the image of a regular backdrop of long-distance commerce which is ultimately drawn from these sources—and which acts as a *deus ex machina* in arguments concerning the transmission of culture.

The geographical area covered by this study is referred to throughout as the 'western sealanes', rather than the more commonly used 'western seaways'. It is not often appreciated that 'seaways' is a dated term with a specific sense in economic geography. A.C. Hardy's 1927 study of *Seaways and Sea Trade* in the twentieth century, for example, consciously eschewed the study of 'cargoes' in favour of the identification of 'trade flows' (Hardy 1927, ix). Crawford and Bowen adopted a similar, overly general, approach to the specific details of travel and exchange. The present work takes precisely the opposite stance to theirs, namely that any image of 'trade flows' in the traffic of the western sealanes in this period has been created by reading too much into the evidence for individual cargoes and events, especially by taking an insufficiently critical view of the chronology of the literary sources. My term, 'western sealanes', is intended as an alternative which, while deliberately evocative of the earlier discussions, hopefully conveys a sense of the need to study actual paths and individual episodes of travel, rather than sketching diffusionist models of cultural 'irradiation', or the existence of a 'maritime culture'. I am sure the term carries its own questionable implications, however, and few such general terms please everybody.

Discussion in this book focuses on the northern half of the western sealanes, with somewhat less reference to Spain and Portugal. In this it follows the previous studies of this topic, which are principally concerned with the cultural exchange which fuelled the growth of Christian civilisation in Ireland, Britain, and Gaul. Cases of links between Gaul and Spain and Portugal are discussed as fully as possible, but as my premise is that there is no natural unity to the western sealanes, I do not attempt to provide a comprehensive survey of all areas, at all times.

The first part of this book discusses the major theories in their historical context and traces their continuing influence upon more recent study. Chapter Two surveys the geographical and technological bases for the use of the western sealanes for long-distance travel and examines the sailing capacity of early mariners and their craft. Diffusionist models from prehistoric studies have been most influential in assessing the maritime capacity of early medieval peoples and polarities in the models presented can be extreme. Childe, on the one hand, could see the 'grey waters' of the western seas as being 'as bright with Neolithic argonauts as the western Pacific is today' (Childe 1946, 36). On the other hand, Murray can argue that 'however open the seaways as channels of prehistoric contact, conceptually water creates a barrier' (Murray 1991, 26-32). Both these models are too extreme. With respect to Childe's view it must be recognised that we are not in this case dealing with a maritime polity comparable to the Trobriand Islands, where the sea was fundamental to all communication. In response to Murray's statement, on the other hand, it may be noted that a hill, or a forest equally 'conceptually creates a barrier'. The conclusion from this analysis must be that the sea was simply one of the media of transport available to early medieval peoples, indeed one of the cheaper and less labour-intensive options. Where it was used, it was chosen above other media on account of a *combination* of economic, social and political, as well as technological, factors. The combination of factors varied from case to case. For this reason I have tried to make as full as survey as possible of the factors governing choices of vessel type and route.

Subsequent chapters deal with events of the fifth, sixth, seventh and eighth centuries. The material selected for study follows a simple enough plan. I have attempted to consider every explicit reference to long-distance travel by sea, as well as any case where direct maritime travel seems to be implied, such as where artefacts are found in a maritime distribution. This evidence is presented in a mostly chronologically-ordered discussion, though trying not to lapse into the type of generalisation which has characterised past study of this subject. Overseas traffic, though doubtless occuring throughout our period of concern, probably carried mixed cargoes, was of intermittent character, and cannot be easily drawn into an evolving model. A very much larger study will be needed to consider all the cases of cultural exchange which *might* have been achieved via seaborne contact along the western sealanes. For the time being, except in brief references, I have confined myself to the cases where I feel there is sufficient evidence to be reasonably certain of seaborne agency. There is much that this book can only touch upon. A full study of marine economy and local maritime traffic is a desideratum, not least because long-distance exchange is often integral with, and arguably less economically significant than, 'coastal' traffic. Literary sources such as the early Irish *Muirbretha ('Sea Judgements')*, Merovingian saints' lives and diplomatic sources, as well as archaeological data from sites such as Whithorn and Loughshinney—to name only two out of many—offer much scope for identifying cases of regional exchange and models for the role of marine industries in production. I hope to return to the study of these sources at later date. The present study, however, focuses principally on episodes of long-distance international contact. In showing this to be more discontinuous across the period AD400-800 than has previously been recognised we open up the potential for some aspects to be more finely dated, such as the importation events of imported ceramics, which in turn benefit the finer dating of evidence for local economy.

This book makes no claims for an especially exciting or innovative methodological basis. If it has any claims to originality of approach, it is perhaps where it advocates a full, critical, discussion both of textual and archaeological source material in the production of historical analysis. In this respect it must be seen as an unusually diachronic study, especially for my primary field of early medieval Celtic history, where much of the latest historical research is fixated on textual and linguistic issues (see, especially, Davies 1983, 67-8). The German positivist historians, who pioneered research into this topic and without whose enormous labours this subject would be much the poorer, accepted that *all* material, critically used, may be relevant to the answering of historical questions and I would concur with this. The archaeological and textual sources are used here in as critical a context as possible. Textual sources where possible are quoted in the original language and a translated appended—usually not my own, except where I feel particularly literal translation is required. I hope I have in all cases clearly acknowledged who the translator is. The discussion of imported ceramics and glass is based on extensive re-examination of the materials in 1988-9. Full corpuses are not provided here, however, as Dr Ewan Campbell will shortly publish comprehensive catalogues of these wares. I provide discussion of archaeological research issues on these wares, however, and I hope that other researchers will note my point that historical ideas underpin much of the supposedly 'archaeological' knowledge in this subject. The definitions of archaeology telling principally of economic and social matters, and history telling, often in more literary than actual terms, of the events of the great and the powerful, do not really define the use of the data made here. Divisions created by academic politics and fashion often lead to circularity of argument.

This book remains substantially the same as my dissertation of the same title, which I successfully submitted for the degree of PhD at the University of Sydney. Though it has been revised and expanded on some points, it still embodies many of the characteristic features of a dissertation, especially the focus on new evidence at the expense of attempting more general coverage. I am grateful to British Archaeological Reports for the opportunity to publish it, with all its faults, as a research monograph in its present form.

Over ten years of research, in several countries, I have acquired many debts for hospitality and helpful discussion. I would especially like to thank: Dr Lynette Olson, Professor Ian Jack and Dr Aedeen Cremin of the University of Sydney, Australia, for constant encouragement and assistance; the Commonwealth of Australia for a research scholarship; the University of Sydney for grants for travel to conferences and for research expenses. In 1987 I was fortunate to be able to spend six months at the Institute of Historical Research of the University of London, and to benefit from the facilities at the Institute of Archaeology and the British Museum. I would also especially thank Peter Hill, David Pollock and the Whithorn Trust, who made it possible for me to work on a site which was absolutely central to my interests, as well as providing much encouragement and assistance with my research. My other debts to museum, library and excavation staff in Britain, Ireland, France and Australia are too numerous to mention. Leslie Alcock, Anthony Bradshaw, Ewan Campbell, John Carey, Anne Clarke, Pierre-Roland Giot, Richard Heawood, Dafydd Kidd, Alan Lane, Kevin Murray, Oliver Padel, Philip Rahtz, Charles Thomas and Elizabeth Windsor, among many others, all provided encouragement at crucial moments, as well as help with specific matters. Edward James, Alan Lane and Carole Cusack made useful comments upon the text at an early stage, while Sue Youngs and Karen Jankulak read a draft at a late stage and provided invaluable comments. I accept full responsibility for all errors. Finally, support from my parents, Deirdre and Ted Wooding, and from my brother Robert saw me through many difficult times. Without their support it truly would not have been possible.

Chapter One

Sealanes and the Scholarly Terrain

The reader who approaches the study of the western sealanes in the early middle ages through the secondary sources is rapidly confronted by widely varying images both of the scale of maritime activity and the command which early mariners exercised over the conditions. On the one hand there is a general belief that these sealanes were traversed by large wine ships and a by a plethora of saints travelling in curachs and in trading ships. On the other hand some diffusionist theorists, in setting up such models of prolific activity, identify 'peninsular roads' and transhipment of goods overland—thus perversely arguing that fear of the open sea limited its use for communication and implying technical incapacity on the part of early mariners (Crawford 1936, 185ff; Bowen 1969b, 14; Miller 1978-80, 316-7; Thomas 1959, 101). The confused nature of this depiction owes much to the relatively limited nature of the evidence for actual voyages, combined with the 'all-or-nothing' character of polemical arguments. A balance cannot be found between the awesome character of the western seas and the mundane role that the sea is expected to play in polemical arguments against the theory of land-based diffusion. This book contends that such sweeping models are inconsistent with the evidence for actual voyages—as well as with what we know of the economy of post-Roman western Europe. Direct, long-distance travel along the western sealanes in the early middle ages neither shows signs of having emerged out of a pattern of geographically-determined diffusion, nor is it a direct continuation of Roman period exchange. Long-distance traffic over the period AD400-800 was intermittent in character and often governed by factors of economy, politics and personal relations. Choice of route was doubtless influenced by a combination of such factors—and it is only where political and personal links were sustained over episodes of a few years, or a few decades, that there was repetition of voyages along the same routes.

The western sealanes, more than any other part of Europe, have been a battleground for those who wish to emphasise the general role of the sea in the spread of culture. Though such debates were mostly enacted in the first half of this century, and their ideological basis is now at best only half-remembered, these diffusionist theories have left their mark in modern scholarship in indirect ways. Archaeologists working on imported ceramics found in western Britain and Ireland have consistently referred their results, directly or indirectly, to Heinrich Zimmer's theory of early medieval wine trading between Ireland and Gaul—in many cases without re-examining the historical basis of his theory (e.g. Ó Riordáin 1947, 45; Radford 1956, 69; Hodges 1977, 240-1; Alcock 1987, 89-90). Both Zimmer's 'wine trade' and Bowen's 'western seaways' have entered the scholarly discourse to the extent where use of these terms and concepts, even when clearly in debt to the models of Zimmer and Bowen, is often not even referenced to them. These models have attained the status of 'buckets' into which new evidence is simply dropped. In some cases of cultural history, the assumption of large-scale commerce or exchange promoted by Zimmer is used as a *deus ex machina* to explain why certain scholarly ideas and cultural motifs are found in early Christian Ireland (Smyth 1986, 203; Ó Corráin 1994, 18-19)—but not, say, in Anglo-Saxon England. The result of this has been that perceptions of the scale and intent of maritime activity along the western sealanes have been confused and made subservient to the need to explain cultural exchange, the scale of which may have no implications for the scale of maritime traffic. A constant backdrop of commerce has been created to explain the cultural development of early medieval Ireland and western Britain. New evidence has often only been taken to extend the existing models, rather than to put any limitations upon their scale. This has had the effect both of obscuring the evidence for change and development in the process of commercial exchange and of commodifying cultural ideas and artefacts. Latin literacy, Christianity and monastic ideas, as well as the material items needed for their practice, are perceived as further commodities in the pattern of exchange—the whole image being analogous to the spread of 'cargo cults'. That the ideas of one region or ethos became influential in Ireland or Britain is reduced to an accident of geography—overlooking the complexities of cultural change, and the internal forces which drive the acceptance or non-acceptance of new ideas.

So influential is the diffusionist model of the 'western seaways' in this topic, that we shall begin by confronting the tradition of diffusionist study of early medieval trade and communication between Britain, Ireland and the continent.

Zimmer's Thesis

In several studies published in the first decade of this century, Heinrich Zimmer (1902a; 1902b; 1909-10) pioneered a model of research into the development of early Christian culture in the Celtic world, proceeding largely through a study of its external contacts. The scope of this study, the greater part of which appeared posthumously as 'Über direkte Handelsverbindungen Westgalliens mit Irland im Altertum und frühen Mittelalter' in the proceedings of the Royal Prussian Academy of Science for 1909-10, was to have been a survey of the external contacts of Ireland and their cultural implications, beginning with the descriptions in Giraldus Cambrensis and tracing a receding continuum of contact along the western sealanes back to the time of the Phoenicians (Zimmer 1909-10; Meyer 1913b). Zimmer's death prevented the completion of this research and the broad thrust of his thesis was obscured by its subsequent reception and dissemination in English by Kuno Meyer—whose only real interest in Zimmer's work appears to have been in the contentious evidence, not overemphasised by Zimmer, for actual Gaulish *litterati* and mercenaries resident in fifth-century Ireland (Meyer 1910; 1913a).

That Zimmer was by training a comparative philologist, as well as the fact that only literary aspects of Zimmer's scheme were developed by Meyer and Vendryes (Meyer 1913a; Vendryes 1920, 19-24), has distracted attention from the fact that Zimmer's later writings all concentrate on what are essentially the concerns of nineteenth-century German positivist history. Zimmer's approach was characteristic of research being done in Germany at the time, for example by Bruno Krusch and Wilhelm Levison as a by-product of work for the *Monumenta Germaniae Historica,* which involved the editing of the Merovingian saints' *vitae* for positivist analysis and chronological and prosopographical work which in many respects has not yet been superseded (Krusch 1880; Ó Cróinín 1984; Harrison 1980; Gerberding 1987, 84ff). Seán Ó Lúing's (1994, 259) discovery that Mommsen was influential in Zimmer's appointment to the chair of Celtic in Berlin is highly significant in showing the closeness of Zimmer's connection with German historical positivism. Levison himself (1946) went on to develop the evidence for overseas exchange which this work uncovered into a study of links between England and the continent, on a markedly similar model to Zimmer's Celtic researches—if more limited in chronological scope. Levison's study, like Zimmer's, set up a model of commercially-driven communication to explain cultural links. The most obvious parallel to Zimmer's thesis, however, is in the later works of his contemporary Henri Pirenne. Pirenne argued for the cultural importance of what he saw as continuous patterns of commerce from antiquity into the middle ages in the Mediterranean—to set against those who saw isolation as the concomitant of the collapse of Roman rule. Zimmer's model—in contrast to that of Crawford and Bowen—argues for precisely the same pattern, with a taste for wine established in antiquity persisting into the middle ages as a continuous basis for trade.

These sweeping models were the product of an interest in the *minutiae* of diplomatics, at the expense of a critical view of the representative character of evidence. It is no coincidence that the evidence of imported eastern Mediterranean ceramics, in distinguishing different chronological phases in sub-Roman commerce, acts as a corrective not only to Pirenne's thesis, but also to Zimmer's. It is probable that both Zimmer as well as Pirenne—whose brief was to 'search... both in texts and in all the evidence available' (Lyon 1974, 266)—would have taken up the questions raised by these archaeological data, if they had lived to see them. Only Mayr-Harting (1972), however, following Levison's inspiration; and James (1982), following Mayr-Harting, really have taken up the agenda set by Zimmer's valuable and critical studies. If Zimmer's thesis had subsequently received as systematic an historical and archaeological critique as Pirenne's we might be in a much better state of knowledge concerning the overseas connections of early medieval Ireland.

The type of historical research done by the positivists gradually became less popular—historians on the Irish side seeing more long-term potential for documentary research into the cultural dimension of overseas exchange than for the study of actual commerce and travel. This left the analysis of the sea routes and voyages themselves to the geographers and, more recently, the archaeologists. In some ways this is a consequance of the piecemeal treatment of Zimmer's work, but it also reflects more more recent currents in 'Celtic' historiography (Byrne 1971a; Davies 1983). As we will see, a critique of theories of long-distance traffic along the western sealanes, like critique of the Pirenne's thesis, depends upon non-textual sources. Many 'Celtic' historians would see this as lying outside of their field of concern. Though Zimmer worked from texts, he put the contacts indicated by them into the foreground. Study of the archaeological data can now reveal information on the same contacts and Zimmer's researches, which uncovered material of outstanding importance, should not be judged the worse for a subsequent failure of others to refine and develop his model in full.

The gradual move away from the study of the primary evidence for commerce and travel also parallels the gradual decline of diffusionism. There is a tendency to attribute a messianic role to long-distance overseas links in the spread of culture—which serves to obscure the real interplay between contact and social change occurring within a society. This is, of course, no reason to abandon the study of these links altogether. Hillgarth is one who now would prioritise the cultural connection: 'perhaps this question of routes is, in the end, secondary... More crucial than the question of routes is that of reception' (Hillgarth, 1984, 13-14). Arguably both are important, and an understanding of the scale and character of each informs the study of the other. Processual approaches in archaeology have also tended to encourage a more complex view of the process of contact (Mytum 1992, 7-9).

Complex implications of cultural contact are easily seen in our period. For example, that maritime links existed between Britain and the Mediterranean in the early sixth century is beyond doubt. A fuller analysis of the evidence, however, sufficiently diminishes their scale to the point where they are unlikely to figure in the importation of many cultural influences (*contra* Crehan 1976). Nonetheless, the archaeological evidence must act as a corrective to those who would dismiss such contact altogether—as Raftery did only three decades ago (Raftery 1965, 199). Seventh-century Irishmen travelling to the continent could have done so by means of commercial shipping focused on the western Gaulish ports, just as Zimmer suggested. Archaeology now seems to confirm the existence of such voyages, previously accepted as an unproven factor (e.g. Riché 1976, 320). This does not immediately imply any 'natural' cultural link with western Gaul, however, as many of the Irishmen then went on to work in eastern Francia alongside Gaulish churchmen recruited from western Gaul (Hillgarth 1987, 311-12; Wallace-Hadrill 1985, 72-3, 143). The way in which the choice of route to the continent may have helped to determine their later theatre of their activity is therefore very complex, hinging on the question as to the role of the Irish in the western Gaulish church, and not upon simple landfall and regular routes of travel. It can only help our study of these complex processes, however, to clearly distinguish which way travellers actually *went*—even if this is only part of the process.

In summary then, the positivists, amongst whom Zimmer must be numbered, tended to see the links thrown up in hagiographical and diplomatic sources as glimpses of a larger, continuous, whole which served to facilitate cultural links over a long distance. More recent archaeological discoveries may be used to break down these perceived continuities into shorter-term patterns, often interrupted by political change. Some writers, such as Hillgarth, in taking up this agenda, downplay the need to assume direct links as a backdrop to exchange of knowledge between regions. Mayr-Harting (1972, 127), in his critique of Hillgarth also rightly observes that actual evidence is needed to postulate direct links. The positivists, like modern communications scholars (e.g. Cullen 1984, 18ff) saw actual evidence for transport as a significant factor in the mechanics of the dissemination of culture. It is important that we continue to focus and refine their models of exchange and contact with such new evidence as is now available.

The Western Seaways

The subsequent emergence of a school of archaeo-geographers, whom we will call the 'western seaways theorists', strongly influenced the reception of Zimmer's thesis. The notion of the sea as a 'highway' for the spread of early cultures was promoted by such diffusionists, as a reaction against the thinking of land-oriented geographers such as Sir Halford Mackinder. This backlash was a reaction against the imperialist flavour of land-based migration studies, though it was also fuelled by the fieldwork of Malinowski. Malinowski's encounter with Pacific cultures where deep-sea travel and exchange was common made much the same sensational and romantic impact upon European models of communication as Gaugin's Pacific paintings had made upon the salons of Paris. Such models exposed the fallacy of treating the sea as a natural barrier and the western seaways theorists rightly saw the role of maritime routes as undervalued by Mackinder. Doubtless also present, less strongly stated, was a reaction against the predominantly eastern-British orientation of Mackinder's model. Mackinder's approach emphasised the lowland east of Britain as the normal route of cultural influx into the British Isles (Mackinder 1902, 194ff; Bowen 1969b). Its origins may lie in Victorian fears of the sea, combined with an overemphasis on the example provided by the historic invasions of Britain by the Belgae and the Anglo-Saxons, which were lowland-based. Mackinder's model also reflected the diffusionist debates popular at the time, which emphasised migration of dominant peoples, rather than the spread of culture, and which tended to focus on land-based migration. The disappearance of such thinking from scholarly debate was appropriately hastened through its use by Haushofer in his theory of *Geopolitik*, which was taken by Hitler to legitimate German imperialism (Outhwaite 1957, 69).

O.G.S. Crawford and H.J. Fleure (famous for a range of studies of archaeology in terms of comparative anthropology: Peake and Fleure 1927-36), were amongst the scholars who formulated the response to Mackinder (Crawford 1912; Fleure and Roberts 1915) and the concept of the 'western seaways' thus evolved in the forefront of the diffusionist debate. The idea was especially taken up by Childe, one of the foremost proponents of diffusionism. Childe was to see these sea routes as being of primary importance for the cultural 'irradiation' of Europe (Cunliffe 1973, 17; Bowen 1969a, 79): 'their grey waters as bright with Neolithic argonauts as the western Pacific is today' (Childe 1946, 36). The 'western seaways' model also found support in the work of Sir Cyril Fox, continuing the archaeo-geographical work which he had commenced at Cambridge (Fox 1922). Aided by the cartography of Lily Chitty, he undertook the distributional studies which led to his influential work *The Personality of Britain* (1946). This set up a highland/lowland zone dichotomy, which integrated effectively with the 'western seaways' model insofar as the impenetrable character of the highland zone seemed to encourage the use of sea travel. The difficulties of penetrating the highland geography of western Britain also of course seemed to emphasise the unlikelihood of overland contacts from the east playing any seminal role in the cultural formation of the western zone. An important later consequence of this model was the briefly fashionable notion of the 'Irish Sea Culture-Province', a popular theme for colloquia in the late 1960s, which further emphasised the east-west division of Britain itself, by positing natural links between Ireland and western Britain (Shaw 1967; Moore 1969; Thomas 1972a; Graham-Campbell 1992: for critique of the idea: Savory 1973; Ryan 1973).

This debate, chiefly conducted with reference to prehistoric evidence, was integrated with the medieval when O.G.S. Crawford (1936) discussed as a whole the various geographical and distributional studies and analysed them in comparison with a series of early medieval voyages derived mostly from hagiography. In a final passage he compared his results to Zimmer's conclusions, stating that he had read Zimmer's work only *after* completing his paper (Crawford 1936, 200). This dramatic, superficial, citation has tended to obscure the fundamental lack of agreement between Zimmer and Crawford. The 'western seaways' theorists saw the Roman period as interrupting a long continuity:

> The spread of Roman power.....stabilised the eastern land routes and traffic flowed more and more to the continent across the Narrow Seas. The Western Sea routes were not to regain their vitality until the lowlands of south-eastern Britain were once again submerged by barbarian invasions (Bowen 1969a, 22).

Likewise, to Radford (1966, 25), the direct links between Britain, Ireland and the continent in the period AD400-800, indicated by imported ceramics, were a 'reversion to the pattern of 3000 BC'. Zimmer, conversely, saw antique traffic continuing into the middle ages. The models of Zimmer and the archaeo-geographers are in this respect fundamentally opposed. E.G. Bowen went on to develop the western seaways model along the lines laid down by Crawford, drawing frequent parallels between the early medieval period and prehistory (for the development of his thesis: Bowen 1944; Bowen 1954; Bowen 1969a; Bowen 1972)—while Childe was to term the megalith builders 'megalithic saints' (Cunliffe 1973, 27).

In most cases it is clear that the circumstances which govern post-Roman contact are unique to that period rather than a reversion to an earlier pattern of maritime diffusion. Moreover, it is worth noting that recent research has seriously questioned the central role of direct maritime links between the continent and the Irish Sea basin in prehistoric cultural diffusion (Ryan 1973). John Waddell's (1991-2) survey of prehistoric distributions around the Irish sea, for example, demonstrates just how strong the role of the shortest crossings has been in transmitting cultural ideas to Ireland, when compared with the possible role of seaborne distribution.

For the early middle ages, however, the sources chosen for comparison by the archaeo-geographers are not at issue so much as their methodology—though only a few cases drawn from saint's dedications and hagiography would now be accepted as evidence for travel and commerce in the period AD400-800 (O. Chadwick 1954, 187ff; laboured response in Bowen 1969a, 81-3; sensible comment in Laing 1975, 118-9). Also significant is that the work of Crawford and Bowen makes no notable analysis of either maritime or political factors—something barely defensible in a geographical approach. The only maritime model introduced by Crawford, that of locating 'peninsular roads', is mostly irrelevant (see below, Appendix Two). Whatever the value of their methods for theoretical geography, the work of Crawford and Bowen tells us nothing meaningful of the finer points of travel. It serves, rather, to suggest 'natural' routes of contact which often do not compare closely enough with actual travels—and which link a false model of prehistoric sea travel with historic activity in ways which obscure the differences and exaggerate the scale of the early medieval activity. Bowen's treatment of Crawford's map of sea-routes is a typical example. In recording a range of sea-routes implied by recent archaeological finds he simply superimposes them upon Crawford's map, affixing the comment that this evidence 'adds many details to the earlier maps of Fox and Crawford' (Bowen 1969b, 18). No effort is made to compare the data to discern whether the new data *invalidate* any of the earlier findings. By piling case upon case, uncritically, an image of many mariners, going every which where, is easily created.

Childe's comparison with Malinowski's 'argonauts' drew a strong image of prolific exchange activity into the early economy of the western sealanes, implying the economic context for a model of 'maritime culture'. This harmonised with the prolific image conjured up by the archaeo-geographers. The broad ideological brush with which these theories are sketched frequently obscures finer details which would show the comparisons to be false. The economy of the Trobriand Islanders, studied by Malinowski, involved short-distance sea travel as a matter of regular exchange between small islands and was not the same as long-distance voyaging between large landmasses. The comparison may be apposite to a region such as Dalriada, for example, but not to the western sealanes as a whole. The 'western seaways' theorists become very confused between local and long-distance traffic. Some of the erroneous elements of Crawford's thesis arise from the lack of such a clear distinction. For example, Crawford (1936, 195-6) interprets St Samson of Dol's crossing of Cornwall as use of a 'peninsular road' to avoid the voyage around Land's End (a superficially reasonable interpretation: though see below, 62-3; 107), but he also argues that St Patrick travelled *directly* from southern Ireland to western France and *thence* overland to the Mediterranean as another example of 'trans-peninsular' travel (Crawford 1936, 192-3). The point has been overlooked that differences of scale and distance require some refinement of methodology. If the route overland is so direct as to offset all the possible advantages of sea-travel, this is not the same as choosing the land route out of fear of the sea. And crossing Gaul is scarcely a 'trans-peninsular' journey.

Despite the often untenable generalisations of these theories, we should remain aware that diffusionist models are still very influential. Evidence for contact between the continent and the Irish Sea basin is still understood in terms of a wider model of 'maritime culture', in which regular commerce along the sealanes allow a constant alternative entry route for cultural influences upon Ireland, western Britain and Scotland. While most early medievalists would not go so far as Bob Quinn (1986) in following this model (which is strikingly reminiscent of the medieval Irish Milesian legends), there has been a basic acceptance of the assumption that maritime activity along the sealanes was prolific and represented a continuity from earlier ages.

My conclusions place strong limitations upon this model in terms of scale and continuity of activity. Serious criticisms are levelled at the case for fifth-century and earlier links between Ireland and the continent, a crucial element in the 'maritime culture' thesis. Indeed, the causal assumption that pre-existing commerce conditioned cultural contacts will be disputed. Such activity as there was must be understood in terms of a variety of political and economic circumstances, not natural connections upset by great events. The 'Irish Sea Province' is a particularly good case in point. Its general rejection has perhaps overlooked some cases which *do* seem to fit its model, notably distributions of pottery and glass imports (see below, 94ff), which are truly separate from comparable distributions in eastern Britain. These are chronologically specific to the late-sixth/seventh century, however, and to express them in terms of overarching geographical schemes would only serve to obscure their specific chronological context and their definite relationship to political differences, amongst other factors. The 'channels of intercourse' between Britain and the continent, far from being 'settled by nature and previous history', as Levison (1946, 5) would suggest, may be seen to restart in every era, or at least are reshaped under the impetus of identifiable events. Sixth-century contact with the Mediterranean can be linked to identifiable Byzantine interest in north-western Europe (Thompson 1980a, 498-507; Whitehouse 1992). Seventh-century Frankish interest in Ireland may be symptomatic of the Irish place in what Wood (1991, 13) has termed the 'world dominated by Franks' in that century.

Recent Perspectives

The evidence of artefacts, most notably ceramic evidence, has come to occupy centre stage in early medieval western sealanes studies since the 1950s. The ceramic evidence first achieved substantial notice in the excavations at Lagore and Garranes, where it was immediately linked to the 'wine trade' hypothesis of Zimmer (Ó Riordáin 1947, 70-1). Since Radford (1956) published his study of the imported pottery from Tintagel, Charles Thomas and a range of other archaeologists have rightly focused attention upon this material, which can be used to identify the overseas connections of Celtic Britain and Ireland and which also has the potential to refine insular archaeological chronology (Thomas 1976, 243). The literature relating to the identification of this material and its study will be fully reviewed in later chapters. These finds offer concrete examples of the types of links which the data studied by Zimmer and Crawford had seemed to indicate for the period AD400-800.

Studies from a historical perspective have been rare in the second half of this century. Lewis (1953, 271-2) and Doherty (1980, 67-89) have produced discussions of trade connections, still utilising Zimmer's references, though Doherty adds more from the Irish perspective and takes a critical view of all sources. J.F. Kenney's bibliographical study (Kenney 1929), contained many observations for a more politically-focused reassessment of Zimmer's thesis, which were finally taken up by Edward James in an excellent short study in 1982 (James 1982, 362-4; James 1977, Vol. 1, 220-58). James also fully embraced the example of Mayr-Harting, whose *The Coming of Christianity to Anglo-Saxon England* built on the approach of Levison in utilising commercial and literary evidence to create a model to explain the quality and diversity of the early medieval Christian culture of Anglo-Saxon England. In attempting to reassess the texts utilised by Zimmer, however, James rightly resorts to the evidence of imported ceramics, recognising the combined value of history and archaeology in critque of the models which Zimmer established. If subsequent critics—for example Hillgarth (1984, 14-16) and Duncan (1988, 70-1)—have pointed out that study along these lines is still inconclusive, this point only further necessitates the present study. The interpretation of the ceramic evidence has indeed been strongly influenced by the historical models, especially those of Zimmer, and we need to have some sensitivity to the interplay of historical and archaeological paradigms over the history of scholarship in this subject if we are to gain meaningful evidence from the archaeological data collected so far. Historians have not always recognised the richness of this relationship. The degree to which a scientific study such as the Peacock and Thomas 1967 paper on the petrology of E ware was dependent on a historical model still may not be fully appreciated (Wooding 1992, 2; Peacock and Thomas 1967, 39). This is not to say that this has been a negative influence. It will be demonstrated in the present study that scientific studies of glass require similar integration with non-scientific data to be meaningful outside of the technological-history paradigm (Sanderson, Hunter and Warren 1984; for alternative approaches: Campbell 1989b; Wooding 1992, 2-4).

The value of an integrated historical and archaeological approach may be set against the tendency to introduce new approaches into archaeological interpretation, which stem from non-historical bases, such as substantivist economic models (e.g. Hodges 1982). The application of such models to the archaeology of the western sealanes has been patchy. Hodges has attempted to identify sites in Ireland according to a substantivist typology (Hodges 1975, 19ff; 1989, 67), but often the criteria seem too vague. The assumption that islands are more likely to be trading sites, for example, is not so unquestionable that any island with imported artefacts must be assumed to be a major port. By contrast with the *emporia* of the North Sea basin, coastal sites with imports along the western sealanes do not reveal the sorts of long sequences which can allow us to be sure that trade was their *raison d'être.* Campbell and Lane, whose arguments command respect on the strength of their thorough revision of the database, argue for a dominance of secular sites over the trading system (Lane 1994), as does Thomas (1990). Substantivist terminology, however, introduces a peculiarly imprecise flavour to some arguments. Dunadd, which Lane convincingly depicts as an important exchange site, is represented as 'controlling' imports and production of prestige goods (Nieke and Duncan 1988, 17; Lane 1994, 109-112), but one is left wondering what the word 'control' actually means in this case. That valuable imports would need to come in under royal franchise is historically likely (see below, 68ff) and fits the archaeological distribution, as Lane (1994) demonstrates. Why a secular ruler would want to 'control' the importation of pigments used in manuscript painting (Lane 1994, 112), however, is not at all clear. The debate on exchange systems also carries with it the temptation to make evidence fit the narrow terms of the paradigm. Arnold (1983, 181-2) has rightly criticised the assumption that pottery is *per se* to be taken as an indicator of commerce—except where the pottery is unquestionably a container for traded goods. The latter is certainly true of the imported amphorae of the sixth century, for example, but not of E ware—which cannot be convincingly shown to be a container for trade goods (see below, 81).

The point which we have reached in this topic is one then where we see fresh evidence offering the potential to date and more clearly track the pattern of communication and commerce. The influence of external paradigms is strong, however, in ways which have somewhat confused the rather scattered data and our revision must remain conscious of this unusual mixture of data and theory.

Chapter Two

Introducing the Western Sealanes—Geography, Technology and Seamanship

Julius Caesar's account of his naval campaign of 56 BC against the Veneti of Armorica—our oldest surviving first hand account of western sealanes navigation—makes an apposite starting point for an introduction to the personality of the western sealanes. The modern scholar's perspective, like Caesar's, is underpinned by Mediterranean views of the role of technology and commerce—with Mediterranean ship technology having been adopted by northern Europe after the fourteenth century AD (Unger 1980, 234ff). For Caesar, the Atlantic was as fearsome an opponent as the Veneti themselves: 'because the difficulty of navigation on a vast and open sea, with strong tides and few—nay, scarcely any—harbours was extreme' *(summaque erat vasto atque aperto mari, manis aestibus, raris ac propore nullis portibus, difficultas navigandi: Bellum Gallicum* III.12, ed. & trans. Edwards 1917, 154-5). While parts of the Mediterranean, such as the Aegean, may be noted for their strong winds and storms, there are few appreciable tides to complicate sailing or to make landing a complex task: 'they [the Romans] could see that navigation on a land-locked sea was quite different from navigation on an Ocean very vast and open' *(ac longe aliam esse navigationem in concluso mari atque in vastissimo atque apertissimo Oceano perspicibant: Bellum Gallicum* III.9, ed. & trans. Edwards 1917, 150-1). Even during the summer—the time of Caesar's visit—the western sealanes are noted for unpredictable and shifting winds and for their wide tidal range.

Caesar, with characteristic adaptability, was able to develop new tactics to successfully complete his campaign *(Bellum Gallicum* III.12-15, ed. Edwards 1917, 152-9)—indeed, the British seas were to be the only theatre where compromise was regularly made in Roman methods of shipbuilding (Marsden 1972, 114-27).

Caesar's experiences set an example to the historian which needs to be appreciated in all its dimensions. The societies which have existed along the western sealanes have regularly navigated these forbidding waters, finding various technological solutions to the conditions. Initially disconcerting, the conditions command respect, but are not so terrifying as to compel travellers to go overland by preference, or to suppport arguments regarding the unsuitability of certain types of craft—such as curachs—for long-distance voyaging. At all times, however, the geographical factors render some choices of route and ship design more effective than others. Attention to the influence of individual factors may explain particular choices of route, location of port sites and of vessel design, which otherwise may seem arbitrary.

Throughout this, however, we need to remain conscious that the bulk of the evidence indicates a diverse and adaptable marine technology and capacity. This alone—begging questions such as whether the Celtic groups used wooden craft or whether the Germanic peoples knew the use of the mast and sail—is sufficent to indicate that most voyages of long or short distance were *possible.* This should not, however, lead us to the passive hyper-diffusionist conclusion that there must have been constant sea travel. Rather, it forces us to confront the actual range of factors—social, economic, political, cultural—which bring about the existence of long-distance communication.

The Western Sealanes: extent and general character

The western sealanes, for our purposes, are defined by the historical and archaeological evidence for traffic; and by previous historiography (also see above, iii). Bowen, after tracing the growth of interest in the 'western seaways' from an initial concern with links within British waters to a model including France and Spain (Bowen 1969b, 14-16), extended Crawford's definition of western seaways further to include the seas off the western coasts of the entirety of Europe. This is an area approximately 2,500 kilometres from the northern to the southern ends. The 'classic' quality of this definition is now even reflected in its use in a recent school text-book (Facts on File 1990, 1-26). Bowen would also extend the western seaways to include the Faeroes and even Iceland (Bowen 1972, 92ff) and Bullough, in a recent aside, refers to the Hebrides as being 'at the north-eastern extremity of the western Seaways' (Bullough 1982, 81). Lewis and Runyan, refer to 'a Celtic Atlantic thalassocracy... centring around the Irish Sea and Brittany and extending south to Coruña in Iberian Galicia and north to the Shetland and Orkney Islands' (Lewis and Runyan 1985, 15). Thomas more or less accepts this definition, though rightly noting the likely changes across time (Thomas 1990, 10-11), which would see the existence of links from one end of the sealanes to the other as only occasional and episodic. Over the four centuries upon which the present study focuses, there was indeed no consistent pattern of activity. For our purposes, however, we may follow Thomas's example and accept a working definition of the western sealanes as running from Gibraltar north to Dalriada. Only passing treatment will be given to Atlantic Ireland north of the Shannon mouth and to Scotland north of Kintyre. For reasons outlined in this study it will be contended that the latter areas really require separate treatment—as they appear not to have connected directly with the sealanes further south in any regular way. Before our period, the early Greek explorers of the Atlantic (c.325-100 BC) may have sailed westward around Ireland. Likewise after 800 AD, in the Viking Age, there was regular contact between north and south via such routes. In the period AD400-800, however, maritime activity to the west and north of Scotland seems to have been mostly separate from the western sealanes routes upon which the present study is focused.

It would seem to be fundamental that a study of sea travel along the western or northern sealanes should consider the influence of factors such as maritime topography and ship technology. It is surprising then that even a book entitled *The Northern Seas* (Lewis 1959) actually says little or nothing concerning the sea itself. Only a few studies—a somewhat speculative discussion of the distribution of megaliths (Davies 1946, 40-6), Warner's (1976) discussion of Roman material, McGrail's (1983) of cross-channel trade and Waddell's (1991-2) of prehistoric distributions—take serious account of the marine geography of the western sealanes. Information about maritime conditions of the western sealanes can be obtained from publications of the Admiralty Hydrographer and from the observations of actual mariners, present and past. The use of these modern sources of course raises questions as to whether the conditions of the twentieth century are comparable with those which obtained in the early medieval period. McGrail has addressed this point at some length (McGrail 1983, 303-4). There is evidence to suggest that conditions prior to circa 1300 were at times slightly warmer than in the present day. By the mid-first millennium AD, however, the most profound temperature changes were a millennium in the past, though we might assume an average of a week or two more of finer weather on a yearly basis and slight lessening of the danger of exposure in cold weather. Isotope levels in cores taken from the Greenland permafrost suggest that the period c.500-700 was slightly colder than the periods immediately preceding and succeeding it (Dansgaard *et al.* 1975, 25; Lamb 1977; Lamb 1992, 1-26), but the net difference from the present day may be accounted negligible. There is little other than indirect evidence for changes in air pressure. In the area of coastline changes there are probably greater discrepancies. The English Channel has been especially volatile in this regard. The estimated steady rise in sea level and rate of erosion in the latter region would imply the need for some care in using modern pilot manuals. Still any change would mostly be within the modern tidal range. Scilly is an exception, in part due to its individual terrain, which is susceptible to inundation on a scale not replicated even on the neighbouring coastline (Devoy 1990; Hawkins 1971; Tooley 1990).

The climate (Buchanan 1989; Coles and Black 1970; Cotter 1974; Hydrographer 1970; 1974a; 1974b; King 1893; Pryor 1988; Naval Intelligence Division 1941) of the western coasts of Europe is dominated by the Atlantic pressure systems. Simply, these are two pressure centres: the one high, in the vicinity of the Azores; the other low, in the vicinity of eastern Greenland. The former has dominance in the summer months, the latter in winter. Pressure is low over the continent in summer and the North-Atlantic low-pressure system weakens. The Azores high pressure centre becomes around 2 millibars higher and moves 2° further north with an extension east towards the Bay of Biscay. In the winter the North Atlantic low-pressure centre moves to 65° north latitude and pressure becomes higher over the continent, with an extension westward into the Atlantic from the Mediterranean. These pressure changes bring seasonal changes in weather patterns. Along the western sealanes, from Biscay northward, winds are chiefly from the south-west and west at most times of the year. North and east winds are at their most frequent in February, March, April and May. The frequency of gales is most profoundly affected by seasonal change in pressure system development. 80% of gales occur between October and March, the most severe in December and January. Most gales come from the south-west and west. For the west coast of Spain and Portugal winds tend more to the north and west in summer *(Penientes)* than further north. Swell in most regions of the western sealanes tends to follow the prevailing wind. Winds in the western Mediterranean in spring will often be easterly, known as the *Levanter*, favouring exit from the Mediterranean into the western sealanes. But in the Atlantic, *Vendevales*, south-westerly winds bringing bad weather and poor visibility, are common from November to April. These occur as far north as Galicia, but earlier in the season than in the south of Spain. In general, the intensity of wind and swell gradually increases as one travels north from Gibraltar.

The strong incidence of westerly winds makes coast-hugging particularly unsafe, except on the few eastward-facing coasts—which, conversely, have obstructive slack-water zones. Where the predominant wind is from off-shore, a vessel without the ability to sail effectively to windward runs the risk of being driven onto the shore either by strengthening of the wind, or upon the turning of the tide. As we shall see below, there is strong evidence that early medieval craft had next to no ability to perform to windward. Though obvious, it is still worth pointing out that the westward-facing coasts of the western sealanes are often peninsulas. Cotter (1974, 4) observes that the North Atlantic has a greater proportion of peninsulas than any other sea. The coastline of the Atlantic is indeed greater in length than that of both the other oceans combined (Outhwaite 1957, 48). Only the extreme ends of these peninsulas actually face west and on the south coast of such a peninsula a ship can be caught in a dangerous lee that will requires considerable sailing south and west to extricate itself, often in the face of a prevailing wind. Floodtide can often drive such a vessel, caught in this position, onto the shore. This is a form of 'embayment': whereby a vessel becomes landlocked, with either wind or tide obstructing its only path of exit. Openings in the western coasts are intensified in their dangers by a further factor. Directly facing the prevailing wind and swell, the English and Bristol Channels and the Bay of Biscay are subject to 'funnelling', especially the English Channel mouth. This phenomenon, caused by the narrowing-in of landmasses to either side, causes tidal patterns of great complexity and up to 20% strengthening of the wind. In the south of the Bay of Biscay the same phenomenon obtains. There the prevailing wind is northerly and a rugged coast faces it, with only a handful of safe harbours.

Tides are the most significant variable element in western sealanes navigation. Caused predominantly by the action of the Moon's gravitational effects upon the ocean, they are, however, significantly influenced by topography and the action of wind-generated currents. This aspect of the personality of the western sealanes was to fascinate Classical geographers (e.g. Strabo, *Geographica* III.3.3, ed. Dewing 1949, Vol.2, 66-7). Tidal streams are all but absent from the Mediterranean, where travel may in contrast involve sailing from peninsula end to peninsula end (Severin, *pers. comm.)* thus rendering any input of models from ancient Mediterranean navigation practices into the interpretation of northern European cases misleading. Peninsulas in the northern seas often divide tidal streams on different timetables and have, accordingly, an excessively volatile character. Nonetheless, tides are a regular variable factor in a region where most variations in marine conditions are only vaguely predictable. There is no doubt that early mariners must have been extremely conscious of, and knowledgeable concerning, tidal patterns. Tides in the western sealanes bring extreme changes in sea-level. Tides also begin to run at different times in different parts of the sealanes. A knowledge of the relative times of change of tides can be of great assistance to navigators. A mariner rounding the tip of Land's End, for example, having taken a favourable ebb out of Mount's Bay—leaving at half ebb—can pick up a nine-hour tide up the Bristol Channel (King 1893, 22).

Within the Irish Sea conditions have always affected the patterns of traffic. The tidal range within the zone exhibits great variety: less than 2m between Arklow and Wexford, but reaching between 6-8m along the Lancashire coast (Buchanan 1989, 3). Neither of these extremes is best suited to navigation for the mariner who wishes to work the tides. Where the tides are at their weakest, between Isle of Man and St John's Point on the coast of Ireland, the shallow waters yield exceptional levels of mackerel and herring (Buchanan 1989, 4), but navigation is hampered by slack water. Generally low wave heights along the east coast of Ireland make it more hospitable than the eastern shore of the Irish Sea, but these are accompanied by frequent shallows and sandbars between Wexford and Dublin (Buchanan 1989, 5). The tidal streams entering the Irish Sea from north and south meet at the Isle of Man, making it a logical staging-point for the mariner working the tides on a north-to-south voyage. In the north of the Irish Sea it is possible to work the tides flowing into the Clyde estuary. The tidal flow of the channel between Fairhead and Kintyre, however, is fearsome, being funnelled up to a speed of five knots (Buchanan 1989, 3).

In such strong tidal waters the tide is often the principal factor which affects planning for a journey. Progress against the tide can be negligible, except with the strongest of following winds. Ships stranded by the retreating tide could be prey for 'longshoremen', an extremely common form of piracy in all maritime societies.

The western coasts of Europe and the British Isles have a hazardous scattering of rocks and shoals. A frightening collection of shoals and offshore rocks exists off the western end of Brittany: Les Platresses and the submerged rocks of La Plate la Vielle, Île d'Ouessant and Île de Beniquet. There are strong tidal streams amongst these. Lands End, in Cornwall, also has dangerous rocks off the southernmost tip and in the northern lee, such as the Longships. There is no evidence that early medieval mariners actually used the routes close in around them leading into the Channel, though local traffic may well have done so. With detailed local knowledge it is possible, for example, to sail in a channel behind the main reefs of Ushant, sheltered from the offshore winds (Hydrographer 1974c; McGrail 1983, 321). Long-distance voyagers, however, are more likely to have given them a wide berth.

Shipping

The elements termed by Marx (1930, 172) the 'vascular systems of production', namely ships and containers, provide vital information about the capacity of overseas transport. Some attention is given to this topic in general books on early medieval trade and communication, though rarely comprehensively. Lewis (1959, 45-8) discusses ship types, as does Hodges (1989, 94-103) in another general survey, while Marcus integrates such data with a study of navigation techniques (Marcus 1980, 5-15; 100-18). Bowen, however, does not discuss any of these matters in depth. The situation is little better in general surveys of maritime history, however, with discussion of prehistoric and early medieval seafaring—the work of McGrail and Farrell being an exception—being characterised by an overly evolutionary approach and often uncritical treatment of sources.

It is easy to be too negative in making necessary criticism of the deficiencies of research into early northern European maritime history and in doing so devalue the very important contributions made by experimental archaeologists and amateur historians. Some of the deficiencies of the interpretations of maritime historians and archaeologists can be attributed to the treatment of their disciplines as arcane specialities, distinct from 'mainstream' history and archaeology (Bass 1966, 1-10; Haywood 1991, 2-5). It may not be fair to blame those working on individual and technical aspects for the failure of the broader disciplines to develop a humane view of the role of the sea in society. Maritime technology is a significant chapter in the transition from prehistory to the middle ages in northern Europe, yet it is rarely studied in connection with the broader paradigm of technological history (Maarleveld 1995, 4). Ships are by definition mobile, so technical innovations may move from one region to another in the fabric of maritime architecture. Changes in maritime technology may be indicators of fashions and influences in broader technological change, yet a tendency to see ship types as ethnically distinct and involving a separate technology may obscure this. For example, even though the influence of Roman designs may have been felt in Ireland from quite an early date, as evinced by early Latin loanwords for wooden ships, a recent find of a vessel of mortice-and-tenon construction from Ireland is confidently designated a 'Roman' ship, where it may be simply Roman influence upon native ship design (Brindley and Lanting, 1990, 10-11). Simplistic equations are made of particular ship types with particular ethnic groups—such as British and Irish Celts with curachs; Scandinavians with clinker-built craft. Such models of ethnic difference have given rise to convoluted arguments such as Bowen seeing the Broighter boat model as representing a skin-covered vessel (Bowen 1972, 187, caption to Plate 33) and Hodges's attempt to explain the wooden Utrecht ship as similar in shape to a curach (Hodges 1989, 97). The choice to use one of the available types of ship technology was doubtless more a matter of the appropriateness of the type to the function and its affordability to the persons wishing to use it (Unger 1980, 40-1, 253ff) than a matter of ethnic tradition. Some Germanic groups were clearly willing to use whatever vessels came to hand and to adapt to new techniques at need. Barbarian groups arriving on the shores of the Mediterranean quickly utilised captured craft e.g. in Aurelius Victor *De Caesaribus* XXXIII.3 (cited in Haywood 1991, 31) where Franks captured a fleet at Tarragona around 260 AD and raided the coasts of Africa. Haywood would even see ships from Pontus taken back to the Rhineland by escaping Franks in the 270s (Haywood 1991, 31). We must accordingly assume that there was a variety of maritime technology available at the close of the Roman period in northern Europe. Various types of craft might have existed in a given area, in use for different purposes.

The following discussion surveys the range of evidence for the types of vessels available along the western sealanes in the Roman and early medieval periods. Not all of the data surveyed here bear directly upon the thesis of long-distance communication outlined in subsequent chapters, but all these types of craft may have been involved in the redistributive exchange which is the concomitant of long-distance traffic. Moreover, a comprehensive survey of data on possible ship types is essential to bury, once and for all, some of the misconceptions regarding the range and capacity of various types of craft.

Celtic Ships

The study of seafaring amongst the Celtic peoples has mostly been conducted on a piecemeal basis. Debate has been preoccupied with what Farrell and Penny (1975, 19) have termed the 'inevitable argument about skin boats and wooden boats', which tends to overlook the evidence for a range of types of craft in use (Hornell 1946, 111-147; Marcus 1980, 3-32; Johnstone 1964, 277-8: for criticism, see De Courcy Ireland 1987, 38; Farrell and Penny 1975, 20). Critics of the preoccupation with curachs, however, have tended to dissipate their efforts in the thankless task of attempting to prove that the curach, a hide-covered boat, was not capable of the voyages described in early medieval Irish texts (e.g. De Courcy Ireland 1987, 38ff). A very few studies (Flanagan 1975, 3-8; McGrail 1987, 173ff) have recognised that the Irish evidence in fact makes clear that a variety of craft, mostly of wooden construction, were in use, doubtless for different types of activity and by different economic groups.

Many references which have been taken to refer to hide-covered craft very likely refer to wooden vessels. Where we have matter-of-fact references to a *duorum navicula transitorum* ('two-benched boat') in Dicuil (*Liber de Mensura Orbis Terrae* VII.14, ed. Tierney 1967, 74), or *vii sese* ('seven-benchers') in the c.seventh-century text *Senchus fer nAlban* (ed. Bannerman 1974, 42, 59-60), in use by ethnically Irish people, it is unlikely that these are curachs (*contra* Marcus 1953-4, 325; Johnstone 1974, 282).

Adomnán, writing in Scotland in the late seventh century, uses a variety of terms for ships, including *navis* (Adomnán, *Vita Columbae* I.4, ed. Anderson and Anderson 1961, 220), *longa navis* (Adomnán, *Vita Columbae* II.45, ed. Anderson and Anderson 1961, 452) and *barca* (Adomnán, *Vita Columbae* I.28, ed. Anderson and Anderson 1961, 264). The historicity of the material descriptions in Adomnán's text, which was written in Iona within only a century of the saint's death and which survives in a manuscript of early eighth-century date, is much greater than that of the majority of the Irish *vitae*—most of which survive in texts written at the earliest in the ninth century (and from later manuscripts still—Sharpe 1991, 9-12; Ó Caoimh 1989, 17-24). Another reliable seventh-century source, the Irish law text *Uraicecht Becc*, speaks in a similar range of terms: *long*, *bárc* and *curach* (*Uraicecht Becc*, ed. Binchy *CIH* 1978, 1615, 2280, 2332, for the three different recensions, which await a new edition).

The *longa navis* of Adomnán (literally 'long ship') is clearly a wooden vessel. Adomnán describes an incident 'when dressed timbers of pine and oak for a long ship were being drawn over land' (Adomnán, *Vita Columbae* II.45, ed. & trans. Anderson and Anderson 1961, 452). Old Irish *long* is evidently a borrowing from the Latin term *longa navis*. The use of this term for 'ship' was widespread, not merely confined to the Gaelic-speaking groups. The Middle Welsh word for ship is, likewise, *llong* (e.g. *Branwen uerch Lyr* I.18, ed. Thomson 1961, 1). Gildas, in sixth-century Britain, uses *longa navis* as cognate in meaning to the Germanic stem *cyul-* (*De Excidio* XXIII.3, ed. Winterbottom 1978, 97). *Longa navis*, in Latin, is used to describe a 'warship' (Ericsson 1984, 15) and the context in which it enters Irish may be the same. Carney would consider this a very early loan-word from Latin, on account of its appearance in the Leinster genealogical poems, along with probable pre-Christian Latin terms such as: *legión (legio)*, *míl (miles)*, *trebun (tribunus)* and others (Carney 1971, 69-70). These words suggest an imperial context and, all importantly, a comprehension of Roman conceptions.

So does the fact that a *longa navis* is made of wood imply that a *navis* must also be a wooden craft? The Andersons gloss the term as indicating a 'wooden ship', but in doing so they are at pains to correct Reeves's reading, and a manuscript variant, as *naves*—believing it to wrongly suggest a monoxylous (dugout) boat (Adomnán, *Vita Columbae* I.36, ed. Anderson and Anderson 1961, 282n). They also are perhaps unconsciously favouring the idea that *navis* alone indicates a non-wooden craft, but this is not certain.

Longa is obviously not a qualifier to specify 'wooden', hence what the more generic *navis* may be constructed of is ambiguous. The voyager Cormac's *navis* has a leather covering *(pellicum tectis:* Adomnán, *Vita Columbae* II.42, ed. Anderson and Anderson 1961, 444). This might imply it is a curach, or may refer to a canopy of leather, as *tectis* may mean a 'deck', as well as a covering for the hull. A boat voyaging such waters might certainly need a top cover. In the literary context, an eremitic voyage, a curach would seem likely. But when we recall that this episode is an early example of the *immram* genre (Carney 1963, 43), this ambiguous phrase may represent Adomnán's debt to a genre text in which a curach was specified. Elsewhere Adomnán describes curachs *(curuca)* with a specific lexical item and distinguishes them in the same phrase from *scaphae* ('skiffs': Adomnán, *Vita Columbae* II.45, ed. Anderson and Anderson 1961, 452). Adomnán occasionally qualifies *navis*, for example with *oneraria:* i.e. 'freight ship' (Adomnán, *Vita Columbae* II.3, ed. Anderson and Anderson 1961, 328; cf. Gregory of Tours, *HF* X.9, ed. Krusch 1885a, 492). The Latin usage of *navis* in the Mediterranean distinguished the merchant ship from the *galea* or long rowing vessel (Ashburner 1909, ciii), but it seems in the Irish case that *longa navis* conveys the sense of *galea*. There may be potential for further terminological debate in this evidence. That Adomnán uses *ratis* (raft) as cognate in meaning with *navis* (Adomnán, *Vita Columbae* 1.36, ed. Anderson and Anderson 1961, 282*n)*, however, reminds us that he is inclined to make elegant or metonymic usage of terms. It would seem safest to accept that *navis* is a generic term, and not a class of ship, and it can be used either of curachs or wooden ships.

Adomnán's *barca* (Adomnán, *Vita Columbae* I.28, ed. Anderson and Anderson 1961, 264) is the ship of visiting Gaulish sailors. The word is used only of their craft in Adomnán's text and seems therefore to imply some kind of distinction from indigenous craft. In the ninth-century Irish text *Tecosca Cormaic* it is seen in the context of a ship bringing imported goods *(Bárca do thocor i port, Allmaire sét:* 'inviting barcs into port, with treasures from over the sea': *Tecosca Cormaic* I, ll.25-8, ed. & trans. Meyer 1909, 2-3). The probability then is that the word specifically describes trading ships. When we consider that Adomnán certainly knew the writings of Isidore, the likelihood is that his definition here is taken directly from Isidore, who writes: *barca est quae cuncta navis commercia at litus portat (Etymologiarum Siue* XIX.19, ed. Lindsay 1911). The word itself may have a pre-Isidorian currency in Irish, however, as it is quoted in the Leinster genealogical poems (Carney 1971, 77), so we must be wary as to its vernacular meaning. The *bárc* of the *Uraicecht Becc* is implied to be a type built in Ireland, as the law relates to 'a builder of *ler long* ('sea-ships'), and *bairca,* and *curach'* (ed. Binchy *CIH* 1978, 1615, 2280 & 2332) who must obviously be resident in Ireland for the law to be relevant.

We see here wooden craft in regular use—both built in Ireland and sailed to the shores of Ireland. That these vessels were named by early Latin loan-words, such as *long* and *bárc*, may suggest, along with other evidence, that 'built' wooden boats, as opposed to logboats, proliferated under Roman influence (though this does not prove that they were previously unknown).

The curach is the preferred vessel in the texts that are known as the lives *(vitae)* of the 'maritime saints'. They are also the vessels used in the Irish writings known as the 'voyage' *(immram)* texts. The vast number of references in these texts have been taken to indicate that the curach was the most popularly used vessel in early medieval Ireland. The historical value of the evidence from these texts is questionable, however, as they are highly imaginative and often written well after the events they purport to depict. Particularly influential upon maritime history has been the *Navigatio sancti Brendani abbatis*—where St Brendan and his followers build themselves a curach to sail to the Paradise of the Saints in the ocean. This text is at least ninth-century, but has been argued to be as early as seventh-century, in date. It shares many episodes in common with the *immrama* and it is unclear whether they are hence earlier or later than the *Navigatio* (Selmer 1959, 10-11; Dumville 1988, 87-102).

The role of the curach in early medieval Celtic cultures has been exaggerated by the popularity of the *immrama* and the *Navigatio* as sources for hyper-diffusionist theories (eg. Ashe 1963, Severin 1978) and also by a range of circumstantial factors—such as the modern proliferation of the curach along Ireland's west coast. It is not often appreciated, however, that this has been a relatively recent phenomenon. Writers such as J.M. Synge (1919, 151) and Tomás Ó Criomhtháin (1929, 170) record that the curach's predominance since c.1850 is very likely as a reintroduction, to replace wooden 'luggers' and 'Seine boats'. Synge would attribute this to changes in the economy, which made smaller crews and cheaper vessels more desirable (Synge 1919, 152). Hence the predominance of the curach in Irish rural culture in the modern period need carry no implications that it was predominant in the past. Neither is there reliable evidence for its widespread use as a *seagoing* craft in antiquity. Avienus, Solinus, Pliny, Sidonius, Caesar and Lucan all make reference to curachs. Caesar's and Lucan's references, however, are only to use on inland waterways—while Strabo's reference (see below), is to the curach's use as an estuarial craft. Lucan refers to the use of coracles in Italy, on the Po, which he compares to their Ocean use by the Britons *(Pharsalia* IV.134, ed. Duff 1969, 184). When Caesar built coracles for use as river craft, modelled on those he had seen in Britain *(Bellum Civile* I.54, ed. Peskett 1914, 76-7) there is no suggestion that the curachs he was imitating were ocean-going craft. As we will see (below, 26), we must suspect that such descriptions of Celtic peoples putting to sea in curachs are interdependent.

There is probably no need to doubt that churchmen did use the curach for *peregrinatio* (Charles-Edwards 1976). *The Anglo-Saxon Chronicles* for 891 record how:

> þrie Scottas comon to Ælfrede cyninge, on anum bate butan ælcum gereþrum of Hibernia...se bat wæs geworht of þriddan hælfre hyde þe hi on foron...þa comon hie ymb vii niht to londe on Corn walum.

> (Three Irishmen came to King Alfred in a boat without any oars, from Ireland...The boat in which they set out was made of three-and-a-half-hides...and after a week

> they came to land in Cornwall: *Parker Chronicle* s.a. 891, ed. Plummer and Earle 1892, 82).

We may accept this text as a reliable witness to an actual event. Romantic associations may have attached to the curach concerning its use by the saints, and in view of the fact that some saints travelled in boats of glass or stone it is with care that we take at face value the evidence of the *vitae* for the types of ships used. The above episode is an event within the specific genre of sea-exile and pilgrimage. This is perhaps evinced in the detail of the number of hides from which the vessel was made (see Ireland 1991, 4-5; Mac Mathúna 1994, 335; Byrne 1932 , 97-102)—we have no evidence outside of this genre for its use as a descriptive term for the size of curachs. Literary discourse put a mystical value on ships covered in hides, evinced for example in the *Vita Brendani* and the (arguably Irish) Pseudo-Jerome commentary on Mark (Bischoff 1976, 81). This literary function of the curach may exaggerate its general role in early historic Ireland. In the *Vita Brendani,* St Brendan is prevented from entering Paradise until he returns in a wooden ship *(Vita Brendani* LXXI, ed. Plummer, 136; for textual tradition: Ó Caoimh 1989; Sharpe 1991, 390-1). In later-medieval tradition St Columba and his brethren first arrive at Iona in a curach which is symbolically buried. All voyages made by the saint in the more reliable *vita* of the saint by Adomnán, however, are in a *navis* (which may or may not be a curach, but is not distinguished as one: Adomnán, *Vita Columbae* I.1, ed. Anderson and Anderson 1961, 194—*contra* the sort of assumption in Johnstone 1962, 32: 'St Columba, of course, travelled from Ireland to Iona in a curragh'). At some point in the development of the hagiographic tradition the specifying of a curach must have come to be seen as particular to Irish eremitic symbolism, only as real as the symbolic commitment not to return to his homeland—which he does more than once. Until a full study is made of the priority of the texts in the voyage tradition we cannot rely upon them as witnesses to the regular use of curachs in monastic voyaging. Again we may note that a curach could be cheap to build (Hornell 1936, 9). If the *Navigatio* is any indicator of the reality of eremitic life, the fact that the brethren in the *Navigatio* build their own vessel may indicate that the curach was available to hermits who had no means to pay a boat builder.

Strabo describes the replacement of indigenous vessels with 'built' wooden ships in Spain as a consequence of Roman contact—a process which may serve as a comparative model for interpreting the process in the lands further north, such as Britain and Ireland, which later also came under Roman influence.

> διφθερίνοις τε πλοίοις ἐχρῶντο ἕως επὶ Βρούτου διὰ τὰς πλημυρίδας καὶ τὰ τενάγη, νυνὶ δὲ καὶ τὰ μονόξύλα ἤδη σπάνια

> (Up to the time of Brutus [136 BC] they [the Iberians] used boats of tanned leather, on account of the flood tides and shoal waters, but now, already, even the dugout canoes are rare: Strabo, *Geographica* III.3, ed. & trans. Jones 1949, Vol. 2, 76-7).

> Τοῖς ποταμίοις σκάφεσι πηκτοῖς μὲν τὰ νῦν, τὸ παλαιὸν δὲ καὶ μονοξύλοις

> (The river craft are now built, whereas long ago they were dugouts: Strabo, *Geographica* III.2, ed. Jones 1949, Vol. 2, 24—my translation).

Strabo's point is that there were indigenous traditions both of hide-covered craft and wooden craft amongst the Iberians. These came to be replaced by more elaborate wooden craft under Roman influence. As we will see below a similar range of elements can be found in late Iron Age Ireland, with logboats and curachs both in use. We would like to know, in both cases, whether the subsequent development of larger wooden craft was an expansion on the indigenous wooden designs (ie. an 'extended dugout') or a full adoption of Roman designs.

Literary and iconographic material may provide some clues as to the form and capacity of the curach and the wooden ship types. In the *Navigatio Sancti Brendani*, St Brendan and his brethren build a curach with the aid of iron tools:

> Costatum et columnatum ex silua, sicut mos est in illis partibus, et cooperuerunt illam coriis bounis [atque rubricatus] in roborina cortice. Et linierunt foris omnes iuncturas pellium ex butyro... Arborem quoque posuerunt in medio nauis fixam et uelum et cetera que ad gubernacionem nauis pertinent.

> (ribs and supports of wood, such as is customary in those part, and covered with ox hides, which were tanned in oak bark. They smeared the outsides of all the seams with grease..... They fixed a mast in the centre of the boat along with a sail and various items for steering the vessel—*Navigatio* IV, ed. Selmer 1959, 10-11).

The relationship of these details to modern curach-building is a subject for debate. There is only a small body of problematical evidence through which we may trace the descent of the modern curach from the medieval. In view of the conservative character of boatbuilding practice, however, which in the Germanic case shows similarities of practice and even dimension across hundreds of years, it is with reluctance that we should dismiss any similarities (Farrell and Penny 1975, 22-3). Nonetheless, it is fair to say that the argument that the modern curach may closely resemble the early medieval is worthy of detailed criticism.

References in a range of texts indicate that curachs were able to be sailed (e.g. Adomnán, *Vita Columbae* II.45, ed. Anderson and Anderson 1961, 452) evidently with a single mast and sail set in the middle of the vessel (hence the *Navigatio: in medio navis: Navigatio* IV, ed. Selmer, 11; *contra* Farrell and Penny 1975, 21 and now confirmed by Severin's experience). Severin's second mast is based on the fact that modern curachs traditionally have a mast in the bow (which he interprets as a legacy of an early foremast), but his arguments contradict the texts and at times are nonsensical (Severin 1978, 25). On the other hand, Severin has argued very convincingly that the reference to 'oak bark' in the *Navigatio* refers to a tanning process in which oak acids were used (Severin 1978, 27ff), indicating that leather rather than untanned hides (such as in Eskimo craft) were used. The alternative, that bark was placed between the frame and the skin, makes no appreciable sense. The outer skin was greased with fat or butter *(butyro)* in the *Navigatio* (IV, ed. Selmer 1959, 11), to make it watertight at the seams and to preserve the leather. Severin's use of wool grease is without textual support (Severin 1978, 27ff).

The excellent seagoing qualities of the well-balanced and flexible (also a quality frequently noted in Viking ships: Johnstone 1974, 72) curach would certainly be shared by its early medieval counterpart. Those doubters who have sought to dismiss the idea that the curach was suitable for Atlantic voyaging have clutched at straws. Severin in 1976-7 sailed his replica of a medieval curach from Ireland to America. There has been much criticism of this replica, mostly on account of points where he departed from the evidence to put in desired features, such as the second mast (e.g. O'Meara 1978). It does not follow, however, that the changes invalidate his work as evidence. The adjustments in design which he made (admittedly often on poor evidence), to compensate for an anticipated poor sailing performance of his craft, are offset by his lack of experience in sailing such a craft—most likely the shortfall in curach sailing ability in his crew *hampered* his vessel's performance. His performance statistics can be accepted as a pointer to the performance of such craft in the early medieval period. Some criticism of Severin's experiment is unreasonable and in it the critics of both his and Marcus' theses reveal a desire to assert the seaworthiness of wooden craft over skin boats (hinting at an impressionistic prejudice). Typical is De Courcy Ireland's citation of the following tiresome assertion: 'Dr Little...was no doubt nearer the truth in asserting that *oceanic* voyages from Ireland in the period under discussion, to be successful, would have needed a wooden ship' (De Courcy Ireland 1987, 39). The capacity of the curach to make long ocean voyages is surely not in doubt—but the evidence does not clearly demonstrate that long ocean voyages were made in curachs.

There has been much less exploration of the evidence for wooden vessels though we have some textual and iconographic evidence. What were the wooden ships like? Adomnán's *barca* was probably one of the continental types which will be discussed below—though there is evidence that Celtic and northern Frankish wooden ships may be interrelated. The Celtic Veneti, resident in Armorica in the later Iron Age, possessed wooden ships. It would be not unlikely that later wooden vessels built among their overseas Celtic neighbours would be of the same general class, though this is little more than speculation. The ships of the Veneti are described by Caesar:

> Carinae aliquanto planiores quam aestus excipere possent; prorae admodum erectae atque item puppes ad magnitudinem fluctuum tempestatumque accommodatae; naves totae factae ex robore ad quamvis vim et contumeliam perferendam transtra ex pedalibus in altitudinem trabibus confixa clavis ferreis digniti pollicis crassitudine...pelles pro velis alutaeque tenuiter confectae...Cum his navibus nostrae classi eiusmodi congressus erat, ut una celeritate et pulsu remorum praestaret, reliqua pro loci natura, pro vi tempestatum illis essent aptiora et accommodatiora.
>
> (Their keels were considerably more flat than those of our own ships, that they might more easily weather shoals and ebb-tide Their prows were very lofty, and their sterns were similarly adapted to meet the force of waves and storms. The ships were made entirely of oak, to endure any violence and buffeting. The cross-pieces were beams a foot thick, fastened with iron nails as thick as a thumb...Skins and pieces of leather finely finished were used instead of sails...When our own fleet encountered these ships it proved its superiority only in speed and oarsmanship; in all other respects, having regard to the locality and force of the tempests, the others were more suitable and adaptable: Caesar, *Bellum Gallicum* III.13, ed. & trans. Edwards 1917, 154-7).

Here, then, are wooden vessels built by a Celtic people. They are sufficiently different in design to the Roman craft that we may suggest that are one example of an expansion upon indigenous tradition. We can infer that they were double-ended. The solution to those extreme pressures of the sea which forced the curach builders (and the builders of Viking craft) to make a flexible vessel which would yield to the pressures of the sea, was in this case to build a boat so rigid that no combination of wind and tide could bend it at all. Most probably these vessels were carvel built, with closely-spaced frames (Haywood 1991, 17; McGrail 1983, 43-6). The prow and stern were so high that no sea could break over them (McGrail 1983, 43). We may note that this would have been a hindrance to the placing of oarsmen, with rowing points only really possible at the lowest point of the gunwale. A boat as heavy as this would be extremely cumbersome to row and Caesar notes their primary use of sails. The Veneti were principally a trading people and these vessels may have been mainly designed for cargo carrying. Traders rarely row their vessels over long distances as they do not carry unnecessary crew, needing the space for cargo and needing to keep overheads down. The ships of the Veneti would provide a considerable amount of dry space for cargo behind the high prow and stern.

Strabo tells us that the Veneti, 'do not bring together the joints of the planks'(οὐ συνάγουσι τὰς ἁρμονιας τῶν σανίδουν: Strabo, *Geographica* IV.4.1, ed. Jones 1949, Vol. 2, 234-5) from which we may safely infer that these craft were of carvel, not of mortice-and-tenon construction. The recent discovery of a wooden boat from Lough Lene, Co. Westmeath, however, does show the use of the mortice-and-tenon technique was known in the north at this time. The Lough Lene boat has been radiocarbon dated to the final centuries (c. 400-100) BC (Raftery 1994, 208-9).

The boat model from the first-century AD hoard of gold objects found at Broighter, Co. Derry in 1895 may provide some further clues. Its provenance has been considered very doubtful (Farrell and Penny 1975; Warner 1981; Bass 1972, 125 for illustration), but analysis of the gold content now seems to demonstrate its homogeneity with a La Tène collar found in the same hoard. If the hoard is not truly Irish, then it is very likely to be British and first century in date. The model is of a vessel of eighteen oars, one steering oar and a mast and sail. Farrell has estimated that the vessel depicted in the 18.4 cm model was around 17 metres in length, estimating on the basis of the relative size of oars and mast. The width of the model is hard to assess, owing to its having been crumpled at the time of discovery. The thwarts are a fair guide (if not to hull shape) and suggest a vessel 6 or more metres in width. The hull is double-ended and deep, along with its size making it unlikely to be a curach. Some of the arguments made by Farrell as to why it could not be a curach, however, are of doubtful relevance. It seems unlikely, for example, that a prehistoric model-maker would go to the trouble of modelling internal framework; so little can be made of its absence. Likewise the argument that modern Irish curachs have masts only in the forward part and small, triangular sails may only imply that the role of the sail has diminished as the curach became less involved in long distance voyaging. The evidence of the modern rig of a curach, often being fore-and-aft, is likely to be reflective of later changes. The Broighter sail is clearly square. Subsequent to Farrell's study, Severin has demonstrated that a curach can safely carry a mast amidships. This notwithstanding, there seems little about the model to suggest a curach. Is this then an ancestor of the *long*, or some other *navis?* If so, we may make some physical observations of value in assessing performance in seaway: it is broader than a Viking *langskip* and more bulbous, though reconstruction of the model has probably exaggerated this.

Gaulish/Frankish Craft

Remains of ships from the lower Rhine show an established tradition of large wooden seagoing vessels among the Franks from as early as at least the second century AD. These were sailing vessels, shallow of draught, with distinctive carvel construction, using heavy iron clench nails. It is regrettable that study on this topic is circumscribed by evolutionary arguments attempting to relate them to both earlier (the ships of the Celtic Veneti), and later (Frisian) traditions, which has resulted in them being referred to as the 'Celtic' class. It is equally likely that such craft were built by Germanic people.

This class of ships may or may not be ancestral to the principal vessels used in deep-sea voyaging by the Franks. They are clearly adapted to sailing in shoal waters and shallow rivers and their role may have been similar to that of the Thames barge of recent history, which mainly operated river and coastal trade—but which was untroubled to sail across or down the English Channel when a worthwhile cargo was on offer. Hence such vessels can cover both the role of local and deep-sea sailing vessels.

A range of ship finds suggests the predominance of this type of craft in antiquity. The second-century AD ship from Blackfriars in London, carvel built again with the characteristic massive timbers and clench nails (Marsden 1990), shows that the type was found on both sides of the Channel. The third-century ship find at St Peter Port in the Channel Islands shows the involvement of this type in traffic to western Gaul (Rule 1990; Gibbins 1995, 409-10). The Bruges boat, also of this class, is able to be partially reconstructed to show a vessel of some 16 metres in length (Marsden 1976). A mast survives from this vessel, and mast steps are found in most other cases.

Where Frankish warships are concerned, the possibility that a northern Germanic clinker 'longship' tradition may have existed in Frankish Gaul should be seen as unlikely in the light of the long pattern of contact between the Franks and the Roman Empire. Roman warships of the fourth century from Mainz show links with the native carvel traditions (Höckmann 1986, 390ff) as do Roman ships built in Britain (Marsden 1972, 114-24). Finally, the existence of captured ships from the Roman world is likely.

The vessel found in a dried-up branch of the Rhine at Utrecht may also exemplify northern Gaulish craft in the early middle ages. It is some 18 metres long and 4 metres in width. It is a shallow vessel, curved upward at both ends. It carried a light mast somewhat forward of amidships (Philipsen 1965). Dates from the timbers now are held to indicate a date of around 980 AD (Vlek 1987, 67). A comparison with the ships of the Veneti may not be far fetched, even allowing for a gap of nearly a millennium. Comparisons have been drawn with Carolingian coins from Quentovic and Dorestad, where boats with a similar curve to the Utrecht ship are depicted (Ellmers 1979, 11-12; Lehmann 1978, 239ff), though one should temper this argument, however, with the point that depiction of the ship on a coin can distort the shape in such a way as to exaggerate the curve at bow and stern. On the basis of a comparison with a more recently found boat of similar type from Waterstraat (near Utrecht) Vlek (1987, 139-40) has cast serious doubt on the possibility that these particular vessels were seagoing craft, but the existence of large, clinker built, craft in this region is still suggestive of further possible variety in river/coastal vessels.

Another category of Gaulish ships is probably Mediterranean in inspiration. The seventh-century shipwreck at Fos-sur-Mer, near Marseilles, is similar in style to a Roman trader. The hull is between 15 and 18 metres in length, with a beam of around 6 metres and a depth of 2 metres. It is shell built (in that the planks are nailed on from the outside) but some strakes have mortises and tenons, widely spaced (Reith 1985, 416). Hypothetical reconstruction has so far produced a round-bellied vessel, which may well be inspired by the assumption that the vessel is comparable to Roman styles of cargo vessels. Its capacity is estimated at around 50 tons, where the average Roman corn ship, by comparison, would have been between 130 and 60 tons (20,000-10,000 *modii*). The depth of the Fos-sur-Mer ship would link it to the ancient Mediterranean tradition.

Such a vessel find is of relevance to the study of the western sealanes. Though there is little evidence of Frankish activity passing around Spain, there is for the fifth through sixth centuries some possibility of an extension of western Mediterranean commerce into the Atlantic. The Fos-sur-Mer style of vessel was probably not well suited to such a voyage in that it is a very unwieldy style of vessel to easily negotiate the Straits of Gibraltar. The Fos-sur-Mer wreck may also at least be a pointer to the persistence of late-Roman style cargo vessels in this western province, not undergoing the evolution to smaller, more mobile craft taking place in the east (Van Doorninck 1972). It may offer pointers to a more general model for the west, that early medieval shipping may be a matter of continuing tradition from the Roman and pre-Roman past. We should always bear in mind that shipbuilding is often an aspect of local tradition which remains unchanged by population or administrative change. There is little specific evidence, anyway, that the Frankish element in western and southern Gaulish society exercised any role in seafaring.

Vandals, Visigoths and Suevi

None of these groups (unlike the Saxons) were maritime peoples before arriving on the western seaboard, unless we accept the doubtful arguments of R. L. Reynolds for a seaborne migration of the Suevi (Reynolds 1957). These groups most probably had some tradition of river-boat building. However the Roman edict of 419 suggests that the Vandals were ignorant of shipbuilding and forbade any citizen from teaching them, on pain of death (Musset 1975, 56). Evidently, this measure had little effect, as the Vandals were soon at sail both in the Mediterranean and the western sealanes, where Hydatius records Vandal pirates in the Atlantic (see below, 29). Likewise, as noted above, the Gothic king Euric recruited Gallo-Roman naval commanders, such as Namatius, to protect his coasts from the Saxons. It is clear that the Goths and the Vandals simply appropriated local shipping for their purposes.

For Spain and Portugal, there is little apart from anthropological evidence, beyond the statements of Strabo regarding the replacement of traditional logboats and curachs after the Iron Age (see above, 11). Strabo also notes the number of Roman vessels voyaging to the region (see below, 26), which presumably provided a model for these new craft, though wooden boatbuilding traditions from western Gaul are another possibility as trade out of the Garonne grew under Roman influence (see below, 25). Filigueras has assembled evidence from anthropological sources which points to both Germanic and Mediterranean influences in the early medieval shipping of Spain (Filigueras 1979). In particular there is a tradition of clinker building around the Douro, which he attributes to the Suevi. Some features of hull design in indigenous Portuguese and Spanish craft still built in the twentieth century have also been compared to the 'Celtic' class though this is a less convincing case (Filigueras 1977).

Saxons

The role of the Saxons in western sealanes navigation is not entirely clear, though recent studies by Michael Jones (1993) and John Haywood (1991), have sought to critically re-examine the divergent sources on Saxon seafaring. Sidonius mentions Saxons being present as seaborne pirates off the coast of western Gaul in the fifth century AD and they have a continued presence in the sixth century (see below, 29). There they may constitute one of the groups involved in western sealanes commerce (certainly we find them working for a Frankish merchant— Gregory of Tours, *HF* VII.46, ed. Krusch 1885a, 365-7) as they lived on islands at the mouth of the Loire from where they seem to have visited the Garonne estuary (Sidonius, *Epistolae* VIII.9, ed. Anderson 1936 & 1965, Vol. 2, 446-7).

The type of vessels used by these Saxons is not certain. Gildas describes the ships of the Saxon invaders of Britain using the Germanic stem *cyul-* ('keel': *De Excidio* XXIII, ed. Winterbottom 1978, 97), the only Anglo-Saxon term used in his writings, which he equates with *longa navis*. These 'keels' would certainly have been wooden craft, built in the clinker tradition with overlapping strakes. The Nydam ship (c.300 AD), a double-ended craft of oak, twenty seven metres long by three broad, found in a bog near Schleswig in 1863, may be closely ancestral to this type (Haywood 1991, 63-6). Later in time, the Viking ships are a product of the same lines of evolution. The Nydam ship has no sail and Brøgger and Shetelig have popularised the view that this is symptomatic of a Germanic ignorance of the use of the sail prior to the Viking period (Haywood 1991, 62-75). Gildas might be thought to imply, however, with his comments upon the Saxon's arrival with *secundis velis (De Excidio* XXIII, ed. Winterbottom 1978, 97) that 'keels' could be sailed. Jones has critically reassessed this terminology, favouring the rhetorical interpretation (Jones 1993, 31ff). The terminology must still give the reader pause. We should note, however, that in the strong wind and tide of the northern seas wind is as much a factor in rowing as it is in sailing. A vessel being rowed can often make no progress at all into a strong wind. Gildas' phrase may well sit within this context. If the keels of Gildas's time were to be sailed they would have to have been built with higher gunwales than the Nydam ship evinces.

When we consider Saxons raiding the Atlantic coast, however, it is hard to see them doing so in rowing vessels—which may be why this side of their activities has been neglected (Haywood 1991, 23ff). This oversight seems very much to reflect a desire to create a monolithic technology for the northern Germanic groups, based solely upon mastless, clinker-built vessels and, moreover, the desire to slot every find into an evolving typology from sewn wooden boats to clinker-built craft (Crumlin Pedersen 1978; Cameron 1982). We must question the lack of plurality of this picture, based as it is on a handful of ship-finds. Haywood's conclusion (1991, 1ff), that the historical and archaeological circumstances which have seen the survival of a handful of wooden vessels in Scandinavia have unduly weighted our view of northern European maritime history towards a too limited picture, is by no means wide of the mark.

Sidonius makes two references to Saxons which have been previously noted, but not fully explored (Wooding 1988b; Jones 1993, 43-46). A reference to hide-boats is in the earlier of the two, as part of a catalogue of barbarians in the *Panegyric on Avitus*, dating from early in 456, when Avitus was emperor in Rome:

> Aremoricus piratam cui pelle salum sulcare Britannum ludus et assuto glaucam mare findere lembo:
>
> (the Armorican region too expected the Saxon pirate, who deems it but sport to furrow the British waters with hides;

> cleaving the blue sea in a stitched boat', *Panegyric on Avitus* ll. 369-71 ed. & trans. Anderson 1936 & 1965, Vol. 1, 150-1).

This equation of Saxons and skin boats occurs in all exemplars of this text (ed. Luetjohann 1887, 212).

The second reference, dating from after Euric's accession in 466, is in a letter to Sidonius' friend Namatius. Namatius was an admiral in the service of Euric, engaged in patrolling the coasts around Bordeaux:

> Inter officia nunc nautae, modo militibus litoribus Oceani curvis inerrare contra Saxonum pandos myoparones... exercent ad illos naufragia, non terrent est eis quaedam cum discriminibus pelagi non notitia solum, sed familiaritia. nam quoniam ipsa si qua tempestas est huc securos efficit occupandos, huc propisci vetat occupaturos, in medio fluctuum scopulorumque confragosorum spe superventus laeti periclitantur:
>
> (discharging the duties now of a sailor, now a soldier were roving the winding shores of Ocean to meet the curving vessels of the Saxons... Shipwreck, far from terrifying them, to them is training. With the perils of the sea they are not merely acquainted, they are familiarly acquainted; for since a storm whenever it occurs lulls into security the object of their attack and prevents the coming from being observed by victims, they gladly endure dangers amid billows and jagged rocks in order to achieve a surprise (*Epistolae* VIII.6.13-14, ed. & trans. Anderson 1936 & 1965, Vol. 2, 430).

There are several important questions here. The first is whether the vessels in both passages are the same—i.e. is *myoparone* a word for a a skin-covered craft? It would greatly aid our critique of those who see the panegyric reference as a poetic licence if it could be shown that, to Sidonius at any rate, Saxons consistently sailed in such vessels. Secondly, what was Sidonius's source for this information? Can these sources be brought to bear on this issue? *Myoparone* is a rare and largely poetic word, of Greek origin. Its associations are with piratical activity (e.g. Cicero, *Verrine Orations* II, 1, ed. Greenwood 1976, 231). Isidore of Seville saw it as descriptive of coracles, though here he might be drawing upon Sidonius:

> Mioparo quasi minimus paro. Est enim scapha ex vimine facta, quae contecta crudo coreo genus navigi praebet ; quales utuntur Germanorum piratae in Oceani litoribus vel paludibus ob agilitatem. De qualibus Historia 'Gens', inquit, 'Saxonum, mioparonibus, non viribus nituntur, fugae potius quam bello parati' (*Etymologiarum Siue* XIX.1, ll. 20-22, ed. Lindsay 1911).

Are the *myoparones* of the Saxons actually coracles? A lot depends upon the interrelationship of the texts, but some speculations can be made. To Isidore of Seville *myoparones* were of the genus *coreo*. The Saxon use of *myoparones* is supported by a quotation, not identified in Lindsay's edition, which is from Hegesippus:

> genus hominum perhibetur et praestans ceteris, piraticis tamen myoparonibus, non uiribus nititur, fugae potius quam bello paratum (Hegesippus, *Historiae* V.150, ed. Ussani 1932, 320).

That Sidonius would write on practical matters from a largely literary basis is unsurprising and Jones (1993, 43-6) rightly warns against any attempts to take his words at face value. Sidonius's panegyric description echoes the image in Avienus (see below, 26)—there associated with Celtic peoples. There is little doubt that Sidonius knew this text, or another text with the same source as Avienus. There are two words in common (*pellis, salum*) and they are central to the image created of hides travelling through the salty sea.

All this is of crucial relevance when we consider the degree to which later writers were to quote these earlier descriptions of the Atlantic and its peoples. It can be shown as probable that most Classical references to British and Irish peoples in sea-going coracles are interdependent, in many case using sources which underlie Avienus's description. This is problematical for the assumption of coracles being a solely British phenomenon, as Avienus's source was almost certainly talking about Spain, not Britain, with the Roman acceptance that skin boats are British being one of the bases for misreading the text, even in antiquity, as concerning regions further north (Hawkes 1977, 19-22; below, 26).

Saxons might have exploited the particular qualities of the skin boat (just as Caesar did—see above, 10) in their Atlantic raids. In their occupation of marshy islands as a base, some of which Gregory of Tours locates in the Loire, the shallow draught and easy landing ability of coracles could have been a great asset. Whatever our scepticism, Marcus's silent emendation of Sidonius's Saxons to 'Irish' is totally unacceptable (Marcus 1953-4, 313; 1980, 8). Jones's excellent discussion of the complexities of the rhetoric of Sidonius and Gildas still follows the implicit agenda of Brøgger and Shetelig in attempting to dismiss evidence which does not fit the basic thesis that Saxons did not know the use of sails. We must see discussion on this topic as having been too narrow minded.

Mediterranean Craft

The evidence of imported ceramics on Irish, western British, Spanish and Portuguese sites, which clearly arrived by sea through the Straits of Gibraltar, implies a presence of Mediterranean ships on the western sealanes in the sixth century. As will be discussed further on, voyages originating in the Aegean, but taking on further cargo at Carthage (or some other Tunisian site), are most likely (see below, 41ff). We should remain open-minded as to whether the ship was of eastern or western Mediterranean origin, but the bulk of the *cargo* was certainly loaded in the east.

If an eastern Mediterranean ship was used, the ship found at Yassi Ada in Turkey, a Byzantine cargo ship wrecked around 625 or 626, provides a suggestive comparative model (Bass and Van Doorninck 1982). It contains large quantities of the two main classes of amphorae found on western sealanes sites, as well as the same North African tableware. Though maybe three-quarters of a century later than the dateable British finds, it is possible that a craft of this type was involved in mid-sixth-century voyages to the western shores of Europe. The Yassi Ada ship differs from Roman and late Roman craft in being small: 20.52 metres in length and especially narrow: only 5.22 metres in beam (beam to length ratio 1:4). It is quite deep: 2.25 metres (Bass and Van Doorninck 1982, 86). It was constructed of cypress (keel and posts), elm (frames) and pine (planking—Bass and Van Doorninck 1982, 160). Th construction method varied from the Roman technique in that the ship was only mortice-and-tenon joined up to the waterline. Above that point the planks were nailed directly to the frames (Bass and Van Doorninck 1982, 58-63). It was a faster ship, of lighter timber and cheaper to build than its Roman period counterpart. It is at once slightly longer, narrower and deeper than it western Mediterranean counterpart at Fos-sur-Mer. Its capacity was around 40 tons. Its depth in the water would give it good windward performance and its single (probable) lateen sail, greater manoeuvrability (Van Doorninck 1972, 135). These changes are most likely the adjustments necessary for a transition from capitalised, bulk commerce in controlled waters, to entrepreneurial luxury, or semi-luxury, trade in waters now harbouring many hostile elements. Bass notes that 'if our ship seems too lightly timbered, we should remember she was not an Atlantic courier. In fact, she was probably not intended for heavy weather at all' (Bass and Van Doorninck 1982, 84). Scholars of the Atlantic sealanes should be careful not to take this comparison at face value. In good weather this vessel would perform effectively in Atlantic swells, though for regular navigation of tidal waters it would need to be stronger. There are strong winds (for example the *Meltemi)* and currents in the Aegean and any ship built for those conditions could negotiate the sea route which took the Mediterranean wares to the Atlantic coasts (below, 51ff).

We may conclude that a range of types of ships were in use along the western sealanes in the early middle ages. The predominant types involved in trade were probably Celtic and Roman derivatives, corresponding generally with Ellmers's 'Celtic' class—though we should remain open-minded as to which more modern traditions they relate to. The evidence of Strabo can be accepted as indicating a transition from dugouts and curachs to larger 'built' wooden vessels in Spain as early as the last centuries BC—and the Broighter boat also suggests that 'built' wooden ships were in use in the Irish Sea in the first centuries AD.

Smaller vessels in use included vessels of dugout and curach type, doubtless continuing quite ancient traditions. Romantic aspects of the use of curachs obscure our understanding of the scale of their involvement in western sealanes traffic, but they are certainly present in Britain and Ireland for coastal use and may have survived in some continental contexts even into the early middle ages. In the Irish Sea basin the references to ships involved in local travel do not usually specify curachs, though they are seen towing logs in the *Vita Columbae* (Adomnán, *Vita Columbae* II.45, ed. Anderson and Anderson 1961, 452). All the traditions of the 'maritime saints' and their use of curachs should be regarded as historically doubtful. We should accept that personal choice and a range of economic factors were often responsible for design selection and leave behind the evolutionary and determinist arguments which have promoted the image of populations in thrall to singular technologies.

Seamanship

Seamanship is perhaps the least measurable factor in the study of long-distance voyaging. The will and ability of mariners to sail over long distances, through forbidding conditions, is easily underestimated and can sometimes only be reconstructed by impressionistic speculation. Some basic assumptions are necessary, however, before further analysis. In the absence of firm evidence to the contrary, it is advisable to assume that early medieval mariners were capable of sailing most, if not all, possible routes along the western sealanes. We should put aside the key assumption of the hyper-diffusionists—namely that a failure to make certain voyages demonstrates an incapacity to do so—and follow the example provided by McGrail, of considering issues of seamanship as factors to take into account, in assessing the elapse of time in voyaging certain routes, and in considering the ease of use of one route over another.

Many of the inferences which can be made regarding the practice of seamanship by early medieval mariners arise directly from the limitations of the terrain. When we consider both the prevailing winds and the coastal features, for example, it would appear that sailing by hugging the coast on the westward-facing shores of the western sealanes would have been an especially dangerous approach to long-distance voyaging. We should assume that early medieval mariners probably had a healthy fear of such shores—artefact distributions examined in later chapters provide no evidence to the contrary. There can indeed be no question that western sealanes mariners would have been well accustomed to sailing out of sight of land. To cross from Gaul to Cornwall by the shortest western sealanes route, at an average speed of around 2.5 knots—which McGrail calculates as an average speed for an early medieval vessel, considering both windward and downwind performance (McGrail 1983, 300)—would involve spending around 20 hours out of sight of land. Even though McGrail's speed estimate may be a little slow for the wooden ship types, depending as it does on the performance of Severin's replica curach to voyage from the Loire estuary to the Scilly Islands (a more likely actual voyage) at twice McGrail's estimate would still leave the mariner out of sight of land for around 12-15 hours, which is assuming optimum visibility. Off the west coasts of Britain the Admiralty Pilot warns 'At sea rain can be expected...on twenty days per month in winter and fifteen days per month in summer' (Hydrographer 1974b, 16). Sea fog is also common along the sealanes when a westerly blows over cold water. These factors reduce visibility and make reliance on coastal marks even more difficult. As noted above, however, summer visibility in Spain and Portugal is much more dependable.

It is most likely that western sealanes voyagers navigated out of sight of land by dead reckoning: through orienting their vessel as it left shore and estimating the distance covered. Leeway slippage, average speed and other variable factors would be reckoned through observations of the boat's performance. 'Steering by run of the sea' is a common practice in northern navigation: to maintain the ship's position by steering a consistent angle across a prevailing swell pattern. Nineteenth-century Shetland fishermen were able to follow a prevailing swell even through distracting surface currents (Walton 1974, 10). A knowledge of regional currents would enable the mariner to detect the proximity of land even in fog. Only the combination of fog with a storm, or with calm, would result in the mariner being disoriented (what the Icelandic texts term *hafvilla*—Marcus 1955, 601-5).

That much of the land bordering upon the western sealanes is highland territory would have been advantageous to mariners wishing to avoid the dangers close in to land: McGrail notes that headlands thirty metres in height can be seen from a distance of eleven and a half nautical miles: and headlands sixty metres in height, from as far as sixteen and a half nautical miles. At five hundred metres they are visible from a distance of twenty-five nautical miles (McGrail 1983, 311). The headlands of Cornwall and Brittany are high enough to be seen from well out at sea and have prominent cliffs (Personal observation 1987; Naval Intelligence Division 1941, 113). The mountains of Cantabria in the north of Spain make a good landfall for a vessel heading southward, being between 900 and 2,100 metres. This is a considerable aid to navigation, as the north coast of Galicia is very poorly served with harbours. Travelling northward to Ireland, the Wicklow mountains of Ireland's south east make another good landfall. Around the Irish Sea, the Isle of Man, north Wales, south Wales and the Mountains of Mourne are all visual aids to navigation. In the north of the Irish Sea it is possible to be in sight of south-west Scotland, Man, Ulster and Kintyre all at once.

Much debate on seamanship may obscure what was probably mostly achieved by observation and instinct. We may presume that early medieval mariners had some knowledge of navigation by use of the celestial bodies, certainly in use for direction finding and it seems likely that the Scandinavians of the tenth century had knowledge of latitude reckoning (Marcus 1980, 109-14)—though the prevalence of fog and rain make the use of these methods impossible for much of the time. Early medieval mariners would possibly also have had knowledge of the flight patterns of migratory birds and of which birds indicated a proximity of land (Hornell 1946, 142-9; Marcus 1980, 114-5). There is no evidence or likelihood that such mariners would have possessed the magnetic compass. It is possible that they used sounding-leads for checking depth and seabed composition, as these were known in the ancient Mediterranean (Herodotus, *Histories* II.5, ed. Godley, I, 280), and find mention in Icelandic texts after the thirteenth century (Marcus 1980, 108). The application of leads is limited without detailed knowledge of the area to be navigated, however, and is mainly only used to determine position relative to *known* details of seabed composition and depth (cf. Herodotus, *Histories* II.5, ed. Godley, I, 280), which in the modern era are marked on charts. At its simplest it can also be used to warn a mariner of dangerous shallows while entering a harbour or river mouth, but this is less of an issue for shallow draught vessels, where an oar is usually sufficient for testing for safe depth of water. The massifs underlying the Atlantic islands sometimes provide shallow waters many miles offshore. Mediterranean ships navigating the Atlantic, however, may have used them to test harbour or channel depths, as these vessels were likely to be deeper than northern European craft.

Regular man-made navigation marks were probably not in use in this period, though Rutilius *(De Reditu Suo* ll.457-62, ed. Duff and Duff 1932, Vol. 2, 804) notes their continuing use in the Mediterranean. Some man-made structures may have played a navigational role. Structures on headlands or islands might serve as navigation marks. In Cornwall in the medieval period small chapels were often built on headlands, for example at St Ives and Zennor. One, at Carn Brea, was definitely maintained as a 'beacon hermitage' (with a tithe called *byckenage* payable by local fishermen in the fourteenth century—Pool 1964, 26ff). Whether or not similarly located early medieval chapels were built deliberately for this purpose, it is possible that they performed the same function from the mariner's point of view. The presence of an early burial ground in Tintagel churchyard may have interesting implications in this connection. The medieval church itself is listed as a prominent navigation mark even today (Hydrographer 1974b, 33; Novakowski and Thomas 1990, 1-8; 25-7). The early medieval burial ground on Lundy also appeals as a similar conjunction of a good navigation mark with an early Christian settlement.

A feature of sailing practice which limits the movement of vessels is pilotage. A vessel entering unfamiliar waters is limited in where it can operate by the extent of its knowledge of the local conditions and the lie of the land. It is usually assumed that operators of foreign ships arriving in region would put in to shore at some point to take on a local pilot or gain directions, or presumably would bring with them some person from their own region who had knowledge of the route. Several early medieval texts refer to the profession of 'pilot' *(gubernator* though we should note that this term might also mean simply 'steersman': Adomnán, *Vita Columbae* II.41, ed. Anderson and Anderson 1961, 436; Asser, *Life of Alfred* XCI, ed. Stevenson 1904, 77).

No sea routes should be considered unusable by early medieval vessels. Maritime data do not answer questions in such an absolute way. Regularly used routes, however, often will be explicable in terms of convenience of navigation and areas where on archaeological or textual evidence we may suspect vessels did not venture may often be inconvenient of access. Some imagination is needed in treating this material. There must be a distinction between local and long-distance traffic and their respective levels of operation. There are also undoubtedly regional and commercial distinctions. For example the series of voyages around the Inner Hebrides which are mentioned by Adomnán's *Vita Columbae* and in the *Annals of Ulster* (for totals see Bannerman 1974, 149-50), in a country united only by sea, represent a level of acceptance of the need to navigate dangerous waters which was probably unique in Britain at that time—and a technology and practice well-adapted to it. The case of a possibly owner-operated Mediterranean ship entering the Bristol Channel, very far from home, however, is quite another. The presence of a local pilot on board might be of some benefit (if there was not a language problem), but even so the ship would be unfamiliar to that pilot, while the master might be suspicious of groundswell and tides (not known in the Mediterranean) and accordingly very cautious. A Gaulish ship arriving at Kintyre would not be incapable of sailing north to Iona or Dunollie, but the maritime obstacles might be sufficient to discourage the attempt, considering the alternative destinations to the east of Kintyre, such as Dunadd and Dumbarton.

The best time of year to navigate the western sealanes is between April and August, at which time the weather is at its finest and most predictable. Gales are at their lowest frequency during this season. These seasonal differences are particularly pronounced in Portugal and Atlantic Spain, where there is virtually no summer cloud, but in winter, almost permanent cloud cover. It is difficult to imagine early medieval mariners attempting voyages between November and March. However we should take note of the writings of Dicuil who records the sojourn of Irish monks in Iceland, voyaging there in February and returning in August (Dicuil, *Liber de Mensura Orbis Terrae* XI, ed. Tierney 1967, 74). The return date is logical, being near the end of the viable sailing season. The earlier date is a little less likely: as in winter, especially in January, there is a strong likelihood of gales off the south-east of Iceland. Unique maritime reasons for leaving on this route early in the season, however, can be adduced. The motivation of ascetics to sail in February, however, may not have been shared by commercial sailors. Probably February was not a normal sailing month. This evidence nonetheless teaches us to be wary of underestimating what early medieval mariners would accept as possible in this regard. In several texts reference is made to the need for a favourable wind to leave a harbour. Egbert, for example, was waiting for such a favourable wind in an Irish harbour (perhaps Waterford—see below, 68), when his ship was wrecked (Bede, *HE* V.9, ed. Colgrave and Mynors 1969, 478). St Samson of Dol was delayed by the need to wait for a favourable wind to travel from Ireland (perhaps Howth) to Wales (*Vita Samsonis* XXXVIII, ed. Fawtier 1912, 134). The importance of favourable winds is also stressed in the *Vita Columbae* (I.1, I.18, II.15, II.45, ed. Anderson and Anderson 1961, 196, 244, 356, 452) and a range of other texts. The 'favourable wind' is a very common topos in hagiography and it would be unwise to take any incident in this context at face value. The common formula involves the saint being a person capable of raising a favourable wind when no one else can, thus elevating him above others. The frequent reference to this factor, however, still demonstrates it to be a major concern in western sealanes navigation. In the navigation of the northern seas a favouring breeze is crucial. The windward performance of early medieval craft was poor. Various factors account for this. For a vessel to perform well to windward requires it to possess certain key design features. Firstly it must displace sufficient space to present a barrier to leeward slipping, or possess a keel or leeboard/centreboard structure to fulfil the same role. It must also be of sufficient mass to stay down in the water and broad enough to maintain its balance sailing across the wind. Severin's experiments with his curach *Brendan* in 1976-7 showed it to perform very poorly to windward. It was able to sail only to within 6 points of the wind and, being an extremely light craft, made of lightweight materials it lost an average of 2 points to leeward while this closely hauled (Severin 1978, 290; McGrail 1983, 300). A second important range of factors relate to the sail itself. A square sail is not an efficient instrument for windward sailing, but there is no evidence that fore-and-aft style sails were in use by this period. The yard on the Broighter Boat and the evidence of the Viking Age vessels all point to square sails being the only type in use in northern Europe before the early modern period. A square sail tends to concede ground every time the vessel changes tack. With a fore-and-aft sail the boat can be 'brought about' by pointing directly into the wind and pulling the sails across. In a square-rigged vessel, the boat must be 'gybed' at the end of each tack, by turning the boat so that wind passes around the stern (otherwise the sails blow back and can break the mast). Often during this manoeuvre the boat is blown backwards. The square sail does not, either, present a very efficient shape to the wind unless the vessel is running with the wind directly astern. An episode in the *Vita Columbae,* in which a favourable wind is raised by miraculous intervention, indicates that the sailors would row until such time as they are able to raise up the 'yards cross-wise' *(antemnas crucis),* i.e. at a right-angle across the mast (Adomnán, *Vita Columbae* II.45, ed. Anderson and Anderson 1961, 454-7). Finally, a long, narrow boat is most unsuitable to windward sailing, as turning the boat is made difficult by the length of the keel. A *longa navis,* we might speculate, must then have been primarily a rowing boat, like the Viking longship. In strong tidal waters, in any event, a vessel with poor windward performance will make little progress against the tide. Even with a favourable wind, progress can be poor. It is likely then that navigation of the western sealanes depended upon waiting for a favourable wind and tide, the latter predictable, but not the former. Few questions of sailing with seasonal winds would enter the picture, once north of Spain—as they are simply not predictable in the more northern latitudes of the western sealanes.

Rowing *(remigo)* is certainly referred to, however, though we must be careful to consider the implications arising from its use. Both in economic terms and from sheer practicality it must be assumed that oars were only used when sail was impracticable. In the northern seas there appears to have been no adaptation of ships to make them actual weapons of war (unlike, say, the Mediterranean galleys with fitted rams). The favouring of oars in a warfare context would chiefly be for manoeuvrability. A notable person being conveyed in style might also have carried sufficient oarsmen to be propelled by their force. In most cases, however, the implication is simply that oars were used to enter or exit harbour (for example in the *Vita Columbani* XXIII, ed. Krusch 1902, 97) or to escape danger (Adomnán, *Vita Columbae* I.19, ed. Anderson and Anderson 1961, 246). Again, in a craft only carrying a small crew, progress against the wind is often impossible under oars, though they are useful in travelling with the tide. Mostly it is simpler to await the change of wind and/or tide.

Replica craft are our principal source of evidence for speed estimates. Severin's replica curach made an average performance of 2 to 3 knots in a average day's run of 40 miles and speeds could sometimes be as high as 7 to 12 (Severin 1978, 289-90), though we must take account of his anachronistic second sail (Severin 1978, 25). Magnus Andersson's Gokstad replica averaged 10-11 knots over the same route (Johnstone 1974, 72), again with an anachronistic second sail. Performance statistics for experiments with *knörrs* are not yet available, but would be more comparable with ships of the 400-800 period on the western sealanes (they would be likely to be lower than Andersson's figures). It is likely that wooden vessels would average higher than curachs, being heavier and hence less prone to leeway slippage and able to sail closer to the wind. Severin's curach could sail within 6 points of the wind, but slipped 2 to leeward (Severin 1978, 290). Andersson's vessel had a slippage of around 1 point (Johnstone 1974, 72). McGrail rightly points out, however, that the presence of a foresail might improve windward direction by as much as point, so within 7 points of the wind might be the real limit. McGrail's conclusion is that an average daily performance for all pre-Viking craft is unlikely to have been above 2.5 knots (McGrail 1983, 300) which might put the average for light wooden craft around 3-4 knots daily, with an average 60-70 miles elapsed per day. The optimum may be estimated as 6-7 knots. A ship such as the Yassi Ada craft, by comparison, with a deeper hull and possibly fore-and-aft sail, would have appreciably better windward performance.

A distinct difference between the northern and southern traditions is in the area of displacement and tonnage. Northern shipping was circumscribed by the need to negotiate tidal estuaries and by a lack of deep harbours. Hodges, for example, associates the relocation of many harbours after the ninth and tenth centuries with the increasing depth of ships (Hodges 1989, 97-8). The creation of more effective harbours and dredged channels in recent times has led to the abandonment of less sheltered and convenient harbours, which is one of the reasons adduced by Alcock for the rise of Glasgow at the expense of Dumbarton, which had previously been the head of navigation (Alcock 1981, 159). Severin's 12 metre curach replica was only 5 tons, while the Broighter archetype might have been 20 to 30 tons. The Yassi Ada ship, by comparison, was around 40 tons and the Fos-sur-Mer 50. The latter two would have been more limited in landing potential. They could use deep harbours, if such were available. Otherwise they would have landed most effectively on a beach at the turn of tide, where they would either lay over on one side or use supports ('legs') to stand the vessel upright. They would have been less easily able to negotiate an estuary.

Our understanding of the factors governing landing sites and the navigational criteria required for them is one of the most poorly developed aspects of this subject. It is of course at the point of making land, not during the voyage on the open sea, that the greatest dangers will threaten the mariner—at the point of landing the mariner's movement is restricted by: the surrounding (and underlying) land; the climatic complexities created by the effects of the shore upon wind and sea; and the legal questions governing the right of mariners to land and exchange goods or disembark passengers.

McGrail has defined a set of basic criteria for portsites in Iron Age northern Europe, which will be quoted here as a text for discussion, as they are broadly applicable to a post-Roman environment. The landing site must have:

> Nearby natural features (headlands etc.) which make a good landfall and can be readily distinguished. The approach must be well-defined and useable, almost regardless of wind-direction, and the landing-place itself should have an aspect such that it is sheltered from the predominant wind and swell. A moderately sloping beach of sand, shingle or mud where the boat can easily take the ground is also to be preferred (McGrail, 1983, 311).

These criteria do not take account of possible man-made navigation aids such as lights and channel markings, but, as stated above, the presence of these in either the pre- *or* post-Roman environment of the western sealanes is difficult to discern. It is best to assume that natural features played a primary role. A harbour such as Padstow in Cornwall, for example, may be one of the best in its region today, but it has extensive shoals and is dangerous without local knowledge. It may have been a quite inconvenient estuary in which to unload a ship without its current retaining walls and quays compared, say, to the controversial harbour at Tintagel, where steep cliffs overhanging the bay make quite useful winching-points (and were so used in the last century: Thomas 1986, 6). Such a judgement, however, must also take account of the likely nature of the ships involved and their degree of acquaintance with the terrain. A Mediterranean ship with a heavy, cumbersome cargo of amphorae seems to have come to Tintagel instead of putting into the Camel estuary (see below, 52), whereas St Samson of Dol used the latter harbour on his shorter-distance, voyage from Wales (see below, 62), in a local ship of surely much lower tonnage than those coming from the Mediterranean.

Even with geographically appropriate ships, in a region with such strong winds and tide there would always have existed a need to cope with potential disaster, especially when close to land. The western sealanes are a severe testing ground. On the one hand, as McGrail observes, this may have bred a somewhat casual attitude: evinced, he feels, in Sidonius' comments on the Saxons' casual attitude to shipwreck (McGrail 1983, 303). The surviving commentaries upon the no longer extant Old Irish *Muirbretha (Sea Judgements)* describe the fate of the cargoes of wrecked ships and the dues to be paid by the proprietors of the voyage if a vessel 'came consigned to a certain person, and it was not into his land they happened to be driven, but into the land of another' *(in tan tainic fo thomus duine airithi hi 7 ni 'na lesc lama-sin fein dorala iat s a ferann duine aile 'na comocus:* ed. Binchy *CIH* 1978, 315). These provisions highlight the degree to which the old sailors' adage 'the trouble begins when you get near land' holds true. This is a point which few landlubbers writing about this region appreciate. Sailing practice of the Viking Age saw the development of a sailing technique *(sigla til brots)* whereby a storm-driven ship could make land without loss of crew or cargo, but at the expense of the ship (Marcus 1980, 103-4):

> Var þá engi annarr til en stefna á land upp...sigldu þá til brots ok kómu at landi við Humru mynni; þar heldusk menn allir ok mestr hluti fjár annat en skip; þat brotnaði í spán.
>
> (There was no other course but to steer onto the shore...they sailed onto the shore and came to land at the Humber mouth; all the men and other goods on board were rescued, but the ship broke up: *Egils Saga* LIX, ed. Nordal 1933, 177).

Modern Irish curach sailors use a similar technique (Marcus 1953-4, 312) and such vessels and sailing techniques would have existed also in early medieval Ireland. It may be this sort of practice that the *Muirbretha* reflects. The experience of Egbert, who while waiting for a favourable wind to leave Ireland, was struck one night by a storm of such violence that his ship was left 'lying on her beam ends among the waves' *(atque oportunos aliquot diebus uentos expectarent, facta est nocte quadam tam saeua tempestas, quae perditas nonnulla ex parte his quae in naui erant rebus:* Bede, *HE* V.9, ed. & trans. Colgrave and Mynors 1969, 478-9), though with part of her stores salvageable, is further illustration of the problems of wind, tide and unpredictable weather in conjunction. These conditions are the hallmark of the western sealanes. Sinking in deep water is less often mentioned. A rare example is *Annals of Ulster* s.a. 737:

> Felbe filius Guaire Mael Rubi, .i. heres Crosan, in profundo pilagi dimersus est cum suis nautis numero xx.ii.
>
> (Failbe son of Guaire, heir to Mael Rubh of Applecross, drowned in the great depth of the sea with his sailors, numbering 22': ed. & trans. MacNiocaill and MacAirt 1983, 190).

Stranding by an ebb-tide (rather than the deep-sea storm in the story of his Biblical namesake, Jonah), was sufficient adversity to bring about the release of St Columbanus:

> Cum iam remigera arte, prosperantibus zepheris, navis ad alta pelagi tenderit, undarum moles obvenit navemque ad litus redire coegit planoque terris solo depulsam reliquid, collectuque in sinibus aequor quievit.
>
> (When they were rowing the ship on a course for the sea, with a favourable wind, a massive wave met their ship and drove them back onto the shore where they remained, as the wave drew away quietly to the channel: Jonas, *Vita Columbani,* I.23, ed. Krusch 1902a, 97-8).

Terminology may, however, be imprecise. In an episode in Gregory of Tours's *Historia Francorum,* Waroch's ships sink en route to Belle Île:

> Warocus in insulis fugire cupiens cum navibus oneratis auro argentoque vel reliquis rebus eius, cum alta maris coepissent commoto vento, dimersis navibus, res quos imposuerat perdidissent.
>
> (Waroch was fleeing to the islands in ships laden with gold, silver and his other possessions; a violent storm blew up, the ships sank, and all his property was lost: *HF* X.9, ed. Krusch 1885a,492).

Thorpe would translate *dimersis* (a common medieval form of *demersis*—also found in Adomnán) as 'founder' (Thorpe 1974, 557), which would imply a simple overwhelming of a ship by waves. These are especially notorious waters for shoals, however, and as Waroch escapes the shipwreck with only loss of cargo he actually may have been driven aground.

Alongside these geographical hazards, however, were hazards of a human character, which may have caused greater concern. Piracy was common in the fifth century, when Saxons roamed the sealanes off the western coast of Gaul and the Channel mouth and Vandals were sighted off the coast of Spain. Still, in such an environment people and cargoes were probably safer out in ocean than close to land. In 585, for example:

> Navis, quae de Galleis in Galliciam abierant, ex issuo Leuvieldi regis vastatae sunt, res ablatae, hominis caesi atque interfecti nonnuli captivi abducti sunt.
>
> (Certain ships which were sailing from Gaul to Galicia had been looted on the orders of King Leuvigild, their cargo stolen, their crews wounded or even killed, and some of their men taken captive: *HF* VIII.35, ed. Krusch 1885a, 404; trans. Thorpe 1974, 469).

In the *Vita Wilfridi,* Wilfred's ship was blown aground in the land of the South Saxons and the mariners faced robbery at the hands of the locals *(Vita Wilfridi* XIII, ed. Colgrave 1927, 26). Such piracy could be aided by the laws of salvage. The notorious 'sharks' of nineteenth-century Britain boarded accidentally-stranded boats before the tide could refloat them and then claimed a percentage of their value as if they were shipwrecks under the law. Though the sources do not attest directly to the existence of such operators, the Old Irish *Muirbretha* (see above, 20; below 68-70) appear from the surviving commentaries upon them to have defined the legal liability of being driven onto someone else's land and would open the way for such practice. An incident in *Laxdæla Saga,* where embayed mariners must be brought before the king to determine whether their cargo is forfeit, though dating from well after our period, still illustrates the point that foreign mariners feared the precise liabilities defined under Irish maritime law *(Laxdæla Saga* XXI, ed. Einar Ól. Sveinsson 1934, 54).

The opportunity for free movement which was offered by the sea is hence an important factor. In the Roman period, traders bringing goods from the Mediterranean to southern and western Britain, and the reverse, operated via land routes across Gaul to the north and west coasts; and thence by sea to Britain. In the sixth century AD goods from the eastern Mediterranean came by a longer route, via the Straits of Gibraltar and touching only upon Portugal and Spain. Reasons for the new choice of route might be easily enough found. Gaul, by the sixth century, was no longer ruled by the same powers as controlled the eastern Mediterranean. A Byzantine mercantile expedition, crossing the territory of a Frankish ruler, as citizens of an empire which was seeking to expand right to his borders, might not be warmly welcomed and might pay heavy dues. Currency paid to a Frankish king, or even trade with Frankish merchants, would enrich those outside the empire, which might not please the Byzantine ruler (Lewis 1978, V, 140). Foreigners were often subject to political investigation. That Mediterraneans were treated with suspicion in the Frankish kingdom even in the seventh century can be seen in the incident where Bishop Hadrian, accompanying Theodore of Tarsus to Britain in 668, was imprisoned by Ebroin who 'suspected him of having some mission from the emperor to the kings of Britain, which might be directed against the kingdom over which at that time he held the principal charge' (*Hadrian autem Ebrinus retinuit, quoniam suspiciabatur eum habere aliquam legationem imperatoris ad Brittaniae reges aduersus regnum, cuius tunc ipse maximam curam gerebat*, Bede, *HE* IV.1, ed. & trans. Colgrave and Mynors 1969, 332-3).

Nonetheless, it might be wrong to overstate the neutrality of the sea. Substantivist studies have tended to treat the sea, and especially islands offshore, as separate from the land in political definition and to treat the shore as a boundary between the two. The shore is not a national boundary in modern politics, neither was it so in the early middle ages. In early Irish law the waters up to 'nine-waves' offshore constituted, if not 'territorial' waters, at least a statutory limit to jurisdiction (see below, 69). Exemption from internal penalties was only attained by passing beyond this limit. This is sufficient evidence to note that the sea was not considered separate from, but included within, a broader definition of society. Fishing, beachcombing and trading all were subject to law and royal jurisdiction. When Cormac Ua Liatháin was sailing the western shores of Scotland, St Columba is supposed to have been sufficiently concerned for his potential safety to need to negotiate protection from the King of Orkney (see below, 106)—even in such little-explored waters, they were still inclined to feel that they were within the scope of defined polities. If we are looking to explain why Mediterranean traffic to Britain in the early middle ages did not follow the prehistoric routes across Gaul we must also consider that, political factors aside, the sea is a medium for *direct* traffic. The economic circumstances which supported 'down-the-line' traffic in prehistory; a cumbersome overland network in the Roman; and which encouraged direct trade of less bulk and more speed in the sub-Roman era, were all subtly different. While diffusionist and substantivist studies have encouraged the inclusion of the sea in interpretations of the spread of culture, they have not entirely facilitated a humane inclusion of sea-travel in our broader picture of society and economy.

We may draw the following conclusions from the material surveyed in this chapter. The western sealanes as defined by past scholarship encompass waters with a wide variety of climatic and environmental conditions, which contrast with the relative regularity and predictability of the Mediterranean environment. The cultures along the shores of the western sealanes brought a range of technological solutions to the problems presented by these conditions. With poor records and the amateurism of maritime historiography, our understanding of the character of these solutions is still limited. The study of the shipping and seafaring of the northern seas in antiquity and the early middle ages is still in a very limited state and deserving of more treatment than is possible here. The data relating to the Atlantic Celtic and Saxon groups considered here, along with the material discussed in Haywood's recent study of the late-antique sources for Germanic seafaring, serve at least to demonstrate the narrow character of the debate to date, which has above all failed to include seafaring fully into broader definition of society and stubbornly refused to recognise the diversity of the technology involved—though the last word remains to be said on most critical points. It remains to stress that a most important outcome of recognising the capacity and diversity of early medieval seafaring technology and technique is to bury the hyper-diffusionist fallacy: we should not be asking 'where could these people travel', but 'where *did* they travel. Technical capacity then becomes a factor in an equation, rather than being mistaken for a reason for travel.

Chapter 3

The Fifth Century—Continuity, Discontinuity and Cultural Change

Fifth-century sources unequivocally depict a time of great change in western Europe. St Patrick, Prosper, Sidonius and Hydatius, among others, have all left contemporary accounts of Atlantic Europe in the fifth century which indicate a high level of piracy, political change and Christian missionary activity. The historian examining the history of transport faces the following questions in the light of such events. Did trade and communication carry on without reference to such change and instability? Or did maritime piracy and migration totally change the character of seaborne communication? We might imagine a scaling down of interregional exchange or, conversly, as Roman control over the land declined and smaller states emerged, the sea might possibly have become *more* important as a means of communication, by reason simply of its ability to bypass borders and hostile lands.

Both Zimmer and Pirenne, discussing the Atlantic and the Mediterranean respectively, argued for a continuity of long-distance seaborne commerce, starting in the Roman period and continuing, uninterrupted, into the middle ages. Their interpretations downplayed the disruption to all exchange caused by the fifth-century migration and piracy. While their models have mostly passed out of popularity, on account of the obvious evidence against a continuity of commodity exchange on the scale permitted by widespread Roman control, it might be said that the 'capitalist constant' has come in again at the backdoor, in the form of an image of continuous traffic on a smaller scale. The following comment by Thomas is an excellent example of the problem and will be quoted here as a text for discussion:

> Small ships that could carry jars and mortaria and perhaps wine in little casks could of course carry people—people like Patrick in the fifth century, Columbanus in the sixth, let alone the merchants from the land of the Franks and the occasional Frankish mercenaries who brought their swords with them. That Christians, in the early fifth century including pilgrims on their way to the Levant, could have travelled this way is certain; and it is in the highest degree probable (Thomas 1981a, 271).

This comment embraces material from different centuries—Mediterranean and Gaulish ceramic groups from western Britain and Ireland; the 'Frankish' metalwork from Lagore; and Zimmer's 'wine trade' all under one model. In fairness to Thomas, it must be said that he is not blind to changes which occurred from century to century, as many of his other studies demonstrate (e.g. Thomas 1990, 11-14). In supporting a cultural thesis in this case, however, he is content not to minimise the continuity of the pattern, observing that: 'traders always prefer to ignore both politics and war' (Thomas 1981a, 300). Cases such as Leuvigild's sacking of captured ships (see above, 20-1) and the Irish laws on distraint regarding flotsam (see below, 68) would suggest that traders could afford to ignore neither politics nor war. Thompson also suggests continuity from century to century:

> there is evidence for substantial seaborne trade between Gaul and Galicia in the later sixth century and we shall find some facts easier to account for if we assume that this trade was already flourishing in the fifth century (Thompson 1982, 143).

Patterns indicated by texts and imported artefacts are treated here by Thompson as likely to be continuous—even if the evidence is discontinuous—if they fit the cultural connection required. On the one hand we must admit that such assumptions are in many respects quite reasonable. The evidence which will be discussed in the following chapters suggests that small-scale commerce was both normal and may be assumed to exist at most times across the period AD400-800. On the other hand, there are times when discontinuity in long-distance traffic is clearly identifiable and our clearest evidence, such as imported ceramics, must be seen to testify to long-distance exchange events which would not be likely to have occurred across the whole of this period.

It will be demonstrated that direct links between Ireland and Gaul are unlikely in the fifth century and earlier. Thompson's Gaul-Galicia link will be seen as slightly more likely, if without any solid evidence. We will see that the direct Mediterranean connection which brought ceramics to early medieval sites in the Celtic west is also likely to have been absent from the fifth century—even trading links between the western Mediterranean and Portugal are doubtful. Ceramic distributions, the dating of which for the fifth century are now on a much firmer footing, show that the western Mediterranean was by no means in continuous contact with the east in the sub-Roman period. The fifth century is a clear hiatus, which Pirenne overlooked, because he relied upon circumstantial similarities between the pictures provided by fourth and sixth century accounts of east-west commerce.

What is the cause of the fifth century discontinuity? The activities of Germanic pirates on the western sealanes are likely to be partly responsible, but we should not exaggerate by implication the likelihood that commercial voyaging would have occurred on a larger scale in the absence of such piracy. Changes in population and government occurred on a wide scale in the fifth century. In the centuries which followed, there is little evidence of the emergence of long-term commercial patterns. Rather, we have evidence of spasmodic and heterogeneous long-distance exchange, with different economic bases in different cases. This point has mostly been lost, and quite clear evidence for the structure of such exchange overlooked, in the rush to identify continuous patterns.

This chapter must tackle a rather diverse range of topics, to establish what are mostly negative points. As continuity across several millennia is asserted by the 'western seaways' theorists we should begin by briefly tracing the pattern in the centuries prior to the fifth century AD, to demonstrate the more or less complete lack of evidence for direct voyages from the continent to western Britain and Ireland prior to the fifth century AD. We will then proceed to examine such evidence as exists for the use of the western sealanes in the fifth century. Finally, we will look at the case advanced by Zimmer for a continuity into the early middle ages of a commercial pattern commenced in antiquity. We will see that the distinction of fifth-century activity is an important preliminary to understanding the context of the much more substantial direct continental links of Britain and Ireland in the sixth and seventh centuries. It also is important if we are to gain a clear idea of the differences in sea-use occasioned by the Frankish and Visigothic expansions.

Traffic Prior to the Fifth Century

The western sealanes enter history in the reports of Mediterranean mariners, who ventured north from Phoenician and Greek colonies in the western Mediterranean. Unfortunately the accounts of these writers have mostly been lost and we access them only through later writers, which has been the cause of much confusion of interpretation. The voyage of Pytheas, c.325 BC, was the first definite account of a voyage to Britain and Ireland, and was probably connected with Alexandrian interests in northern Europe, ultimately never realised (Hawkes 1977). There has been a tendency in the modern era to accept the testimony of accounts supposedly derived from Phoenician sources, suggesting an early interest in Britain as a source of tin (Hencken, 1930; Kenney 1929, 118-38; Hawkes 1984, 211-33; Penhallurick 1986, 123-131). Tin mines in Spain, however, rather than Britain, are the more likely terminus of any Phoenician voyages. It should also be noted that Greek writers were wont to claim Phoenician precursors at many sites of Greek activity in the west and most such claims are, accordingly, to be regarded as questionable (Aubet 1993, 167-70).

Later classical and medieval written accounts often describe the western sealanes in terms of a discourse derived from these earlier accounts. When we find Strabo writing of the tides of the western sealanes (Strabo, *Geographica* I.1.8, ed. Jones 1949, Vol. 2, 16-19; III.3.3, ed. Jones 1949, 66-7), or even Dicuil as late as the ninth century discussing pack-ice north of 'Thule' (Dicuil *Liber de Mensura Orbis Terrae* XIII, ed. Tierney 1967, 74-5), they are making reference, directly or indirectly, to Pytheas' lost periplus *Περὶ του Ὠκεανου* ('concerning the ocean'). References to Atlantic voyaging in Caesar and Sidonius, and even those sixth- and seventh-century Byzantine authors who describe tin as a 'British' product (discussed below, 46), must be understood in terms of knowledge of earlier writers.

The fourth-century and earlier accounts come from direct voyages from the Mediterranean. In the final centuries BC, however, there was a gradually escalating commerce conducted into the Atlantic from northern and western Gaul, under Roman stimulus. This commerce seems to have brought Cornish and Spanish tin to Roman markets. The reputation of Cornwall for tin in this period may have caused the identification of the ancient 'Cassiterides', from the earlier sources, with Britain and Ireland. As we will see the Cassiterides were probably in Spain. This represents the beginning of a confusion of Spain and Britain which colours history and geography right up to the medieval period and beyond.

Information gathered, formally and informally, in the process of the conquest of western and northern Europe by Rome informs classical geography in the first century BC onward, though it is mixed in with the earlier sources. Diodorus Siculus *(Historical Library* V.22, ed. Oldfather, Vol. 3, 156-7) describes a trade in tin from *Belerion*—identified by Ptolemy as Land's End—through a trading centre on a tidal island, *Ictis* to the coast of Gaul and overland to the Mediterranean. The identification of *Ictis* must remain controversial (Hawkes 1984, 211-33). The powerful Venetic people of Armorica in the time of their defeat at the hands of Caesar (56 BC), 'had a large fleet plying between their own ports and Britain' (Caesar, *Bellum Gallicum* III.8, ed. & trans. Edwards 1917, 146-9). The Veneti would most likely have operated the western sealanes end of the tin trade, which seems to have declined by the time of the Roman occupation of Britain and this seems now to be confirmed by archaeology (l'Hour 1987, 113-31). It is not clear whether it was Caesar's invasion which itself brought about the cessation of the trade, by destroying the Venetic fleets, though Strabo suggests that Venetic resistance was based on a desire to prevent Roman competition (Strabo, *Geographica* IV.4.1, Vol. 2, ed. Jones 1949, 234-5).

Though trade between the western coast of Gaul and the south coast of Britain continued throughout the Roman period, no evidence exists that the Veneti traded into the Irish Sea basin. O'Kelly's attempts to identify 'cliff castles' of a Venetic type in Co. Cork rested on the barest of typological evidence, as he himself admitted (O'Kelly 1952-3, 32-4). Classical sources seem to indicate that the Gauls had no knowledge of Ireland. When Caesar questioned merchants for details regarding Britain before setting sail in 55 BC he found:

> Quae omnia fere Gallis erant incognita. Neque enim temere praeter mercatores illo adit quisquam, neque eis ipsis quidquam praeter oram maritimam atque eas regiones quae sunt contra Gallias notum est. Itaque vocatis ad se undique mercatoribus neque quanta esset insulae magnitudo, neque quem usum belli haberent aut quibus institutis uterentur, neque qui essent ad maiorum navium multitudinem idonei portus, reperire poterat.

(Almost all these matters were unknown to the Gauls. In fact, nobody except traders journeys thither without good cause; and even traders knew nothing except the sea-coast and the districts opposite Gaul. Therefore, although he summoned to his quarters traders from all parts, he could discover neither the size of the island, nor the number or strength of the tribes inhabiting it, nor their manner of warfare, nor the ordinances they observed, nor the harbours suitable for a large number of ships: *Bellum Gallicum* IV, ed. & trans. Edwards 1917, 204-6).

Caesar is known to have had contacts with more than one western Gaulish seafaring group, at least the Veneti, and 'Gallic ships conscripted in Poitou, Saintonge and other subject areas' *(Gallicisque navibus, quas ex Pictonibus et Santonis reliquisque pacatis regionibus convenire iusserat: Bellum Gallicum* III.11, ed. & trans. Edwards 1917, 153). If western Gaul and the Irish Sea were in contact during this period it would be surprising if Caesar could learn nothing from such seafarers apart from details of the south coast of Britain. There is no question of the capacity of the Veneti to make voyages into the Irish Sea. They appear from Caesar's account to have been excellent seamen, with ships well equipped for western sealanes travel (Caesar *Bellum Gallicum* III.13, ed. Edwards 1917, 154-5). But there is simply no evidence that they did. The Roman networks, which followed the Veneti in trade along the western coasts of Gaul, also seem to have totally excluded Ireland.

Tacitus's (98 AD) description is informed of the 'approaches to its (Ireland's) harbours from commerce and the reports of merchants' *(...aditus portusque per commercia et negotiatores cogniti:* Tacitus, Agricola XXIV, ed. Hutton 1914, 211). The *Geography* of Ptolemy provides an extensive list of place names from the Irish coast, which seem to have been collected in the last centuries BC. These indicate observers who had travelled the east coast, as well as the south and west coasts as far as the Shannon mouth (Mac an Bhaird 1991-2). It is more than likely these names represent the knowledge that Tacitus describes. These names are at their greatest concentration on the Leinster and Munster coasts of Ireland. Whether or not this carries any implications for other evidence of Roman contact, such as the distribution of Roman finds and the evidence of ogham for early Latin literacy in this region, must remain an open question. What should be stressed, most of all, is that nothing in the distribution of Ptolemy's place-names, even those from the Atlantic coast of Ireland, suggests a source for this information in Gaulish, rather than British based voyages. The prevailing winds (south-westerly), facilitate a broad reach (i.e. sailing at right-angle to the breeze) to Britain in both directions. The example of the ogham distribution shared between the same area of south-west Ireland and Dyfed in Wales, is ample testimony to a likelihood of such a link with Britain.

The details which classical writers give from the first century AD onwards reflect a continuing *lack* of input from direct sea voyages along the western sealanes into the Irish Sea. The mistaken orientation of Ireland and Britain to the continent, which placed Ireland between Britain and Spain, was never corrected, which we might imagine would have occurred if anybody had made the voyage from the continent to Ireland. Pliny, for example, gives only the distance of the shortest crossing from Britain. He provides no details concerning the distance from Ireland to Gaul (Pliny, *Naturalis Historia* IV.16, ed. Rackham 1942, 198). He does, however, provide accurate distances for the southern coast of Britain in relation to Gaul. Tacitus notes that Ireland is easily accessible from the seas off Gaul (Tacitus, *Agricola* XXIV, Hutton 1914, 211). In the same passage, however, he describes it as lying between Britain and Spain, which would put it unrealistically near to Gaul.

If there was trade around the shores of Britain and Ireland, none of the maritime geographical data passing back to geographers served to correct the various cartographical errors which emerged in the orientation of northern and western Britain and Ireland in relation to the continent. This adds to the impression that only the short crossings were being used in the Roman period. A range of writers from Caesar through Strabo even to Procopius suggest that the coast of Ireland lies opposite Spain and the Aquitaine (Tierney 1976, 257-65; Killeen 1976, 207-15). Classical writers were to remain in ignorance of the orientation of Ireland in relation to the continent. It was to give rise, probably via Orosius and Isidore, to the Milesian legends of medieval Irish tradition, which used the false belief that Ireland was only just out of sight of Spain to explain the earliest settlement of Ireland as being from Spain (Macalister 1938-56). This legend has both directly and indirectly influenced the notion of the 'western seaways' school that there were early direct links with the continent. It has also led to more far-fetched, hyper-diffusionist, arguments for cultural unity along the western seaboard (Quinn 1986).

It is with some reservations that we should accept that the sources of Graeco-Roman geography and cartography give any more than a general indication of the range of routes involved in commercial contact between Britain, Ireland and Gaul. Earlier details were worked into a cartographical tradition where they were distorted by Greek geometric models. A writer as early as Tacitus seems to be working from maps which show the sorts of distortions evident in the (later) work of Ptolemy (Baumgarten 1984, 195ff). The texts of Pytheas, Philemon, Timaeus, Marinus and Posidonius have been lost and the early date of the underlying sources of Avienus's *Ora Maritima*, crucial in Hencken's influential reconstruction of early Irish Sea trade routes (Hencken 1932, 168, 181ff), is now much debated. Avienus's work is said to depend on earlier sources (Murphy 1977, v-vi): a Greek *'Massiliote Periplus'* as well as a commentary, but doubts now attach to whether this was an otherwise unknown *periplus*, or whether Avienus's work is derived totally from known authors.

It is not clear whether many voyages were conducted by the Romans along the sealanes of the Irish Sea basin. The 'circumnavigation' of Scotland described by Tacitus, for example, seems only to have involved sailing to Cape Wrath from the east and turning back (Tacitus, *Agricola* XXXVIII, ed. Hutton 1914, 236). That mariners were chiefly making east-west voyages from Britain to Ireland seems most likely (Tacitus, *Agricola* XXIV, ed. Hutton 1914, 211). Voyages on a north-south line are not recorded.

The detail in the works of Strabo and Avienus can be re-examined in the light of archaeology. Strabo (c. 64 BC-19 AD) describes a range of trading links between western Gaul and the south of Britain, by way of the southern part of the western sealanes:

> Τέτταρα δ' ἐστὶ διάρματα οἷς χρῶνται συνήθως επι την νησον ἐκ τῆς ἠπείρου, τὰ ἀπὸ τῶν ἐκβολῶν τῶν ποταμῶν, τοῦ τε Ῥήνου καὶ τοῦ Σηκοάνα καὶ τοῦ Λέιγηρος καὶ τοῦ Γαρούνα.
>
> (There are only four passages which are habitually used in crossing from the mainland to the island, those which begin at the mouths of the rivers - the Rhenus [Rhine], the Sequana [Seine], the Liger [Loire], and the Garumna [Garonne]: Strabo, *Geographica* IV.5.2, ed. & trans. Jones 1949, Vol. 2, 253; for discussion see Cunliffe 1984, 24-36).

Zimmer (1909a, 363-400) maintained that this trade from the Garonne and Loire most likely took in Ireland as well as Britain, but we should note that Strabo definitely does not mention Ireland in this connection. Moreover where he does mention Ireland, elsewhere, it is only in most erroneous terms (Strabo, *Geographica* IV.5.4, ed. Jones 1949, Vol. 2, 258-9). We should also note, with Richmond, (Richmond 1958, 144) the sparseness of evidence for western Ireland in the geography of Ptolemy. And we must always be conscious of the confusion of Roman sources regarding the orientation of Ireland to the continent.

Both Tacitus and Ptolemy cite merchants as their major source, Ptolemy providing more detail of the inland regions than Tacitus. Tacitus's merchants seem to have stopped at boundary trading sites, rather than penetrating the interior. These voyages clearly favoured the east and south coasts. The likelihood that all these Roman, and immediately pre-Roman, contacts with Ireland were from Britain is also confirmed by the lack of the sorts of prestige goods, notably amphorae, found in the Channel trade network. The western sealanes traffic described by Strabo is separate and seems to follow the same pattern described by Diodorus in connection with tin trading: with goods being shipped along the Gaulish rivers to and from the Mediterranean (Gaillou 1984, 3-23). A range of archaeological evidence seems to confirm the lack of involvement of Ireland in such traffic emanating from Gaul. The distribution of the amphorae of Dressel types 1-4 and related imports arriving in Britain during the late second through the first century BC relates to the pattern of contact described by Strabo which brought 'grain, cattle, gold, silver and iron...hides, slaves and dogs' (σῖτον καὶ βοσκήματα καὶ χρυσὸν καὶ ἄργυρον καὶ σίδηρον..... δέρματα καὶ ἀνδράποδα καὶ κύνες —Strabo, *Geographica* IV.5.2, ed. & trans. Jones 1949, Vol. 2, 254-5) back to the continent, presumably in return for the contents of the amphorae and related cargoes. The distribution of the amphorae (Peacock and Williams 1986, 87-106), and their discovery in Channel shipwrecks (Rule 1990, 49-56), again indicate voyages between Channel ports and western Gaul, though this activity does not proceed into the Irish Sea. Other recent archaeological finds may relate to this traffic. A shipwreck from Ploumanac'h, discovered in 1983, contains a range of lead ingots including some bearing inscriptions of the north and eastern British Iceni and Brigantes. The link again is obviously via the English Channel, not the Irish Sea (l'Hour 1987, 113-31; Gaillou and Jones 1991, 51-60 for a balanced view). It may be important to note the central role of Brittany itself in this traffic. The idea that the Loire and Garonne mouths were acting as feeders to Britain depends upon our reading of Strabo, and he, it must be remembered, probably thought of the western shores of Britain as lying just off the mouths of these rivers. What we can be sure of is that there was extensive trade all along the western and northern shores of Gaul which had little, or nothing, to do with the western zone of Britain.

Fulford has mustered evidence from distribution of late-Roman tablewares of the fourth century to support a continuation of this pattern of commerce. *Céramique dite à l'éponge* is the most relevant of these finds, as a distributional study implies a western Gaulish origin (Gaillou, Fulford and Clement 1980, 265-78), with the distribution extending to southern Britain in the fourth century AD. Concentrations of finds are in Dorset, Hampshire and Sussex, with a scatter of finds in Kent, Devon and the head of the Bristol Channel. This would clearly indicate a seaborne importation around Brittany, with a major landfall in the Solent. Fulford (1978, 58-69) and Thomas (1981b, 4) have suggested further landfalls in the Bristol Channel, which they suggest 'prefigures' the D and E ware importations. A distribution of the ware in Cornwall or South Wales, however, would be needed before the Bristol connection is explicable as anything more than an overland distribution from the Channel ports. Finds of Argonne ware in Gloucestershire, Shropshire, north Wales and eastern Ireland seem, likewise, good evidence of such an overland path from the Channel, though further identifications and discoveries may change this picture, which is so far only based on a limited series of finds. In this connection we should note Gildas' references to 'the Severn...along which luxuries from overseas used to be brought by ship' (*Sabrinae...per quae eidem olim transmarinae deliciae ratibus vehebantur, De Excidio* VII, ed. & trans. & trans. Winterbottom 1978, 90), though it is not clear whether this implies contact with the continent through the mouth of the Bristol Channel. In any event, by the mid-sixth century—allowing that Gildas's floruit is only with caution located in that time—the Bristol Channel, at least, had seen the voyages which brought in the sub-Roman Mediterranean wares (though Gildas is equally likely to be harking back to a Roman period image). In any case, as Gildas also suggests that the sea all about Britain is 'uncrossable' (*intransmeabili*) apart from the crossing to Calais (Gildas, *De Excidio* III.1, ed. Winterbottom 1978, 89), he may be indicating an internal network only.

The northern end of Roman period traffic thus seems to have excluded direct contact with the Irish Sea. When the sixth- and seventh-century voyages were made from Atlantic Gaul into the Irish Sea basin this was a new development, not a continuity of Roman and pre-Roman traffic. In Roman and pre-Roman Gaul the river routes seem to have been oriented towards overland traffic, not simply as feeder routes to take material inland from a maritime network, though undoubtedly they also would have filled such a role. Such overland activity is notably less frequent in an early medieval context (James 1977, 220), and certainly less often involves the types of bulky goods traded in the Roman period. This pattern, then, undergoes a break in continuity. In the sixth century, overland traffic of Mediterranean goods through eastern Gaul was to continue intermittently. Where contacts by sea from western Gaul into the Channel continued (James 1977, 221ff), however, they no longer carried goods from the Mediterranean.

The work of Avienus (c. 400 AD) has had an influence on theories of western sealanes disproportionate to its reliability, on account of its use by Hencken to assert the existence of contacts between Cornwall and Ireland as part of the tin trade and related long-distance trade focussing on Cornwall and Armorica. As we have seen, there is nothing in Strabo's discussion, or in the evidence of archaeology, to suggest an involvement of Ireland in this network: the distance between Ireland and Cornwall is not great, but there is no evidence.

Hencken's theory depends on an acceptance that Avienus's work is based on a *periplus* from antiquity which reflects an actual ocean voyage from the western Mediterranean as far as Armorica.

> Sub huius autem prominentis vertice sinus dehiscit incolis Oestryminicus, in quo insulae sese exerunt Oestryminides laxe iacentes et metallo divites stanni atquae plumbi, multa vis hic gentis est, superbus animus, efficax solertia, negotiandi cura iugis omnibus, netisque cumbis turbidum late fretum et beluosi gurgitem Oceani secant non hi carinas quippe pinu texere et acere norunt, non abiete, ut usus est, curvant faselo(s), sed rei ad miraculum navigia iunctis semper aptant pellibus corioque vastum saepe percurrunt salum. Ast hinc duobus in sacrum, sic insulam dixere prisci solibus cursus rati est. Haec inter undas multa[m] caespitum iacet, propinqua rurus insula Albionum patet.
>
> (Under the head of this promontory, the Oestrymnic bay lies open for the natives. In it the islands called Oestrymnides stretch themselves out. They lie widely apart and are rich in tin and lead. There is much hardiness in the people here, a proud spirit, an efficient industriousness. They are all constantly concerned with commerce. They ply the widely troubled sea and swell of monster-filled Ocean with skiffs of skin. For these men do not know how to fashion keels with pine or maple. They do not hollow out yachts, as the custom is, from fir trees. Rather they always marvellously fit out boats with joined skins and often run through the vast salt water on leather. But from here, there is a two-day journey for a ship to the Holy Island - thus the ancients called it. This island, large in extent of land, lies between the waves. Again the island of the Albiones lies near: Avienus *Ora Maritima* ll. 94-112, ed. & trans. Murphy, 8-9).

These men 'constantly concerned with commerce' make a colourful counterpart to Childe's 'neolithic argonauts' (see above, 3), but this is a very vague text upon which to rest any serious argument. There is good reason to question the idea that Avienus's text represents the core of a real sailing manual, as well as the idea that the *Albiones* have anything to do with Albion. The tin-mining and hide-covered boats fit equally well with an Iberian, rather than British, connection. Hawkes has quite rightly questioned the distances involved and has stressed that in terms of the distances described in the text the tin-producing Oestrymnides are better identified with some point on the Iberian coast (Hawkes 1977, 3ff; Penhallurick 1986, 127-8). The detail on skin boats and dugouts is close to that of Strabo's on Iberia (see above, 11), the description of a lack of dugouts then is easily explained as a distinction of the Oestrymnides from other parts of Iberia. A people called the *Albiones* lived in Galicia. Finally, that the Oestrymnides are a 'two day journey' from Ireland would be better explained by the usual classical error regarding the orientation of Iberia to Spain.

Both the writings of Strabo and Avienus describe traffic from the western coast of Spain through the Straits of Gibraltar into the Atlantic:

> ἅπασα δ' ἡ ἐμπορία πρὸς τὴν Ἰταλίαν ἐστι καὶ τὴν Ῥώμην, ἔχουσα τὸν πλοῦν μέχρι τῶν Στηλῶν ἀγαθόν, πλὴν ἔι τίς ἐστι περὶ τὸν πορθμὸν δυσκολία καὶ τὸν πελάγιον τὸν ἐν τῇ καθ' ἡμᾶς Θαλάττῃ. διὰ γὰρ εὐδίου κλίματος οἱ δρόμοι συντελοῦνται, καὶ μάλιστα τῷ πελαγίζοντι· τοῦτο δὲ πρόσφορόν ἐστι ταῖς ἐμπορικαῖς ὁλκάσιν. ἔχουσι δὲ καὶ οἱ ἄνεμοι τάξιν οἱ πελάγιοι.
>
> (But all the foreign trade of the country is carried on with Italy and Rome, since the voyage as far as the Pillars is good, except, perhaps, for a certain difficulty in passing the strait, and also the voyage on the high seas of Our Sea. For the sea-routes all pass through a zone of fair weather, particularly if the sailor keeps to the high seas; and this fact is advantageous to the merchant-freighters. And further, the winds on the high seas are regular: Strabo, *Geographica* III.2.5, ed. & trans. Jones 1949, Vol. 2, 30-1).

Strabo also describes the redistributive traffic along the river systems (Strabo, *Geographica* III.2.4, ed. Jones 1949, 28-9), servicing this exchange. The goods involved are: 'grain and wine... olive oil... wax, honey and pitch... Kermes... salted-fish and wool': σιτόν τε καὶ οἶνιος... και ἔλαιον... κηρὸς...μέλι καὶ πίττα... καὶ κόκκος ταρικεία... μᾶλλον—Strabo, *Geographica* III.2.6, ed. & trans Jones 1949, 32-3) and a range of minerals (Strabo, *Geographica* III.2.8, ed. & trans. Jones 1949, Vol. 2, 38-41).

In the first century AD the early forms of Dressel amphorae appear in Portugal, paralleling their appearance on the northern arm of the western sealanes. Later imports are rarer, with the manufacture and distribution of later amphorae series in Portugal itself being taken to indicate a flourishing of local production in wine and other luxury goods at the expense of imports. As Alarcao observes, the study of Portuguese amphorae abroad might be indicative of movement in the opposite direction (Alarcao 1988, 88), but such evidence is only slowly becoming available. Italian fine wares were common in Portugal in the first century, but fell away with the establishment of the local sigillata industry. That these were mostly products of Arezzo, Pozzuolli and the Po may be suggestive of their having been part of the same traffic

Fig. 1
Distribution of amphorae of Dressel types 1A and 1B (after Gaillou).

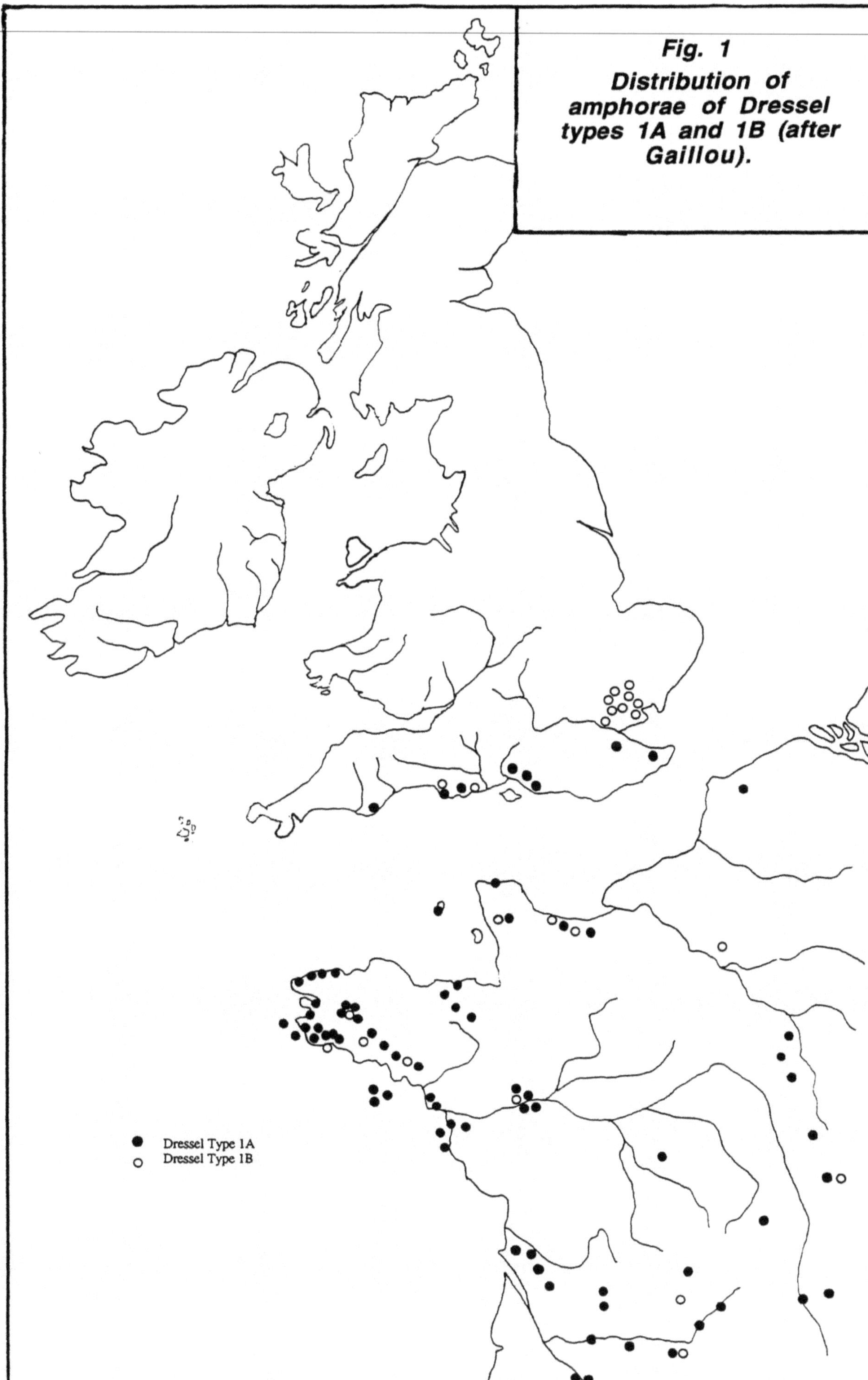

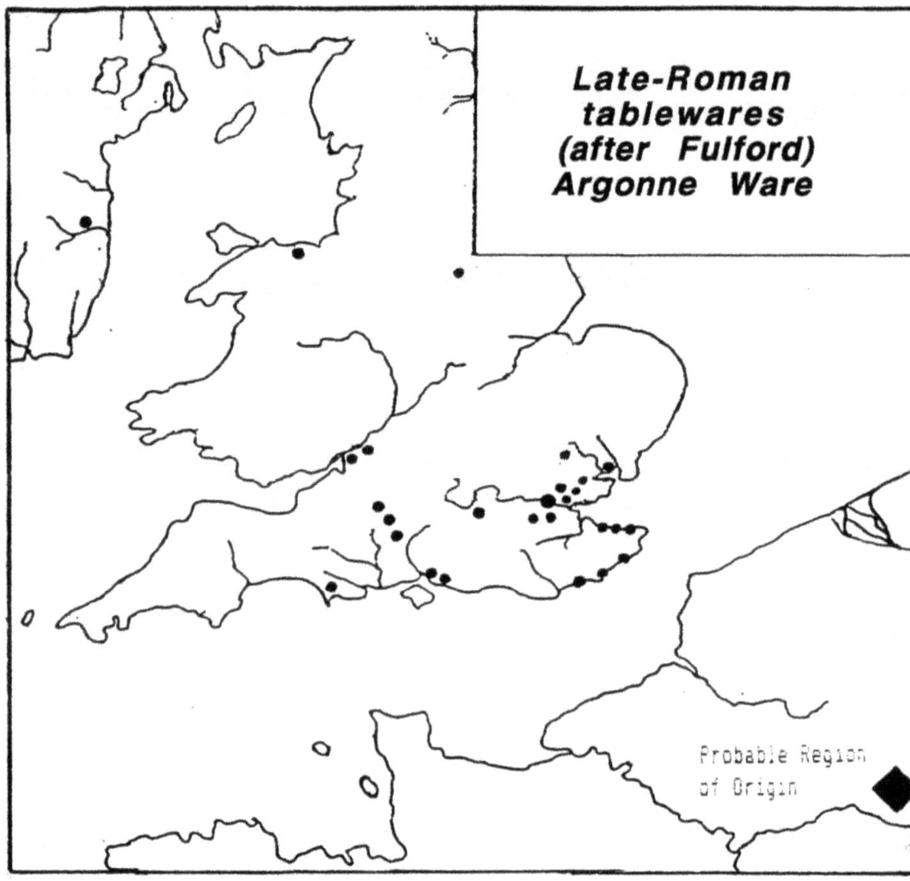
Late-Roman
tablewares
(after Fulford)
Argonne Ware
Probable Region
of Origin

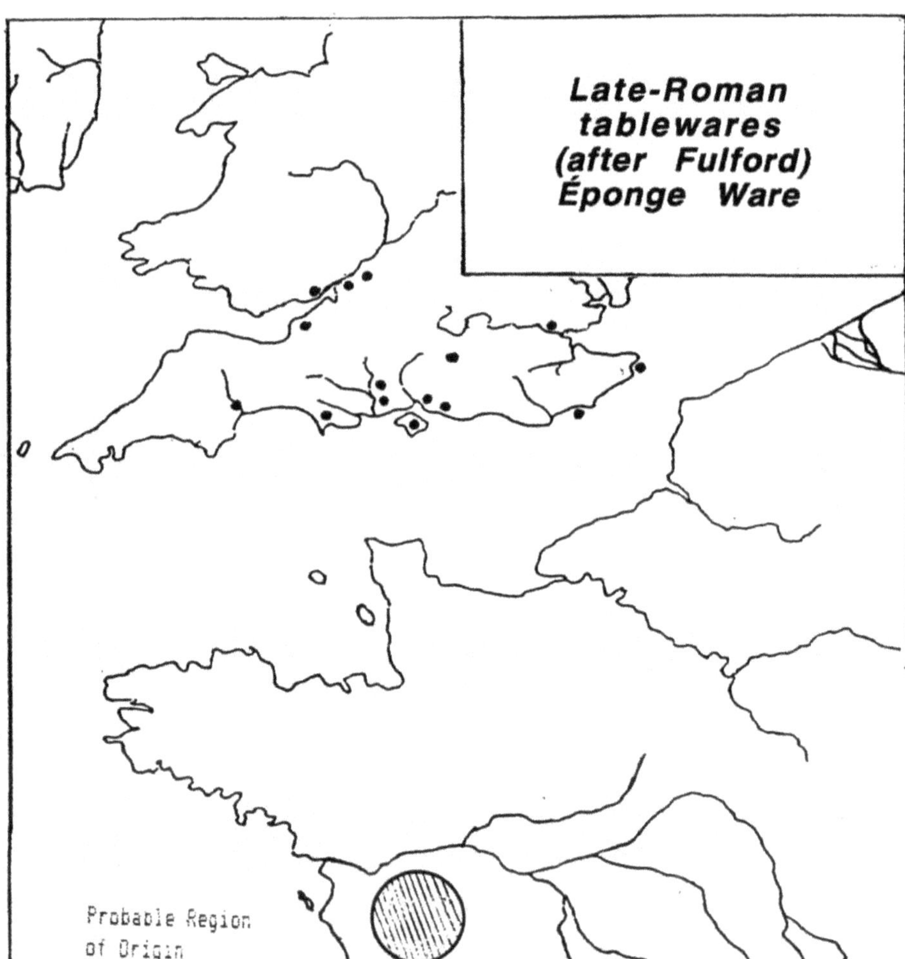
Late-Roman
tablewares
(after Fulford)
Éponge Ware
Probable Region
of Origin

Fig. 2

across Gaul described above in connection with Britain, in that they are from a region of Italy in close proximity to the eastern end of the overland route, but this is not any more likely than a maritime distribution. In the third century the appearance of Byzacena (Class 34) amphorae from North Africa may be noted (Cardoso 1978, 63-78). At the same time importation of African Red Slipware (hereafter ARS) begins to dominate western Iberian assemblages, continuing through to around 450 AD. Something of a hiatus may be identifiable in the importation after this point, with common fifth-century types not being found. It is also to be noted that our evidence for fifth-century sites in Portugal is limited, albeit this is in part a reflection of the crucial diagnostic value of ARS itself. Despite the long held belief that later ARS finds at Conimbriga were datable to the last phase before the destruction of that city in 465, it is now clear that these finds are evidence of later occupation, which is itself a warning against readily accepting historical chronology in site dating, though historical sources support later occupation anyway (Thompson 1982, 213). A short second period of importation is now identifiable, contemporary with the influx of Phocaean Red Slipware (henceforth PRS: Hayes 1972, 462; Hayes 1980, 521; but ignore his dates in the light of Fulford and Peacock 1984, 114; Prieto 1984, 540-8). The ARS forms found in this phase are almost identical with a narrow chronological range found on western British and Irish sites. This importation is certainly by way of the Straits of Gibraltar and is no earlier than the last quarter of the fifth century and most probably later still (see 41ff).

It would obviously be of some significance if we could identify the date when communication shifted from the river routes across Gaul to the direct route via the Straits of Gibraltar. Some of the series of ARS may have been entering Spain and Portugal by way of maritime distributions through the Straits of Gibraltar as early as the third or fourth century (Hayes 1972, 423). A Class 49 (Amalgro 54) amphora from Bordeaux (Keay 1984, 656) is just as likely to have arrived this way as through an overland network. Further distributional study will doubtless refine these issues, though we should be clear that tablewares alone are not a good guide to direct maritime contact in the absence of larger objects such as amphorae, which are far less likely to have been portaged across the Meseta.

When, in the mid-fifth century, Germanic piracy became particularly rife on the western sealanes, Vandal pirates raided Spain, presumably from a base in North Africa by way of the Straits of Gibraltar. Hydatius describes such Vandals off the coast of Galicia in 445:

> Vandali navibus Turonio in litore Gallaeciae repente advecti familias capiunt plurimorum.
>
> (Vandal ships suddenly appear at Turonium on the coast of Galicia and many households are depleted: Hydatius, *Chronicon* n. 131, s.a. 445, ed. Mommsen 1894, 24; also see Haywood 1991, 60).

This was undoubtedly the *Turonium*, near Tuy, mentioned in the sixth-century *parochiale* of Galicia (*Ad Tudensem ecclesias que in vicinio sunt: ...9. Turonio*, ed. David 1947, 43). The inspiration behind the voyage is difficult to assess. Tranoy (1974, Vol. 2, 83) prefers to believe that these were Heruls, not Vandals, but again as with the Saxon raids we should be wary of such assumptions that long-distance voyages were unlikely. If Hydatius says they were Vandals, we need better grounds than these for doubting his judgement. Certainly it would be a considerable voyage from Africa. An embassy from Africa had been to Galicia in c. 458, though whether this had any connection with the earlier raids must remain an open question (*legati Gothorum et Vandalorum pariter ad Suevos veniunt et revertuntur*: Hydatius, *Chronicon*, n. 192, s.a. 458, ed. Mommsen 1894, 31). This Vandal activity requires further consideration in the light of the changes occurring at this time in western Mediterranean trade. Did the well-established late-Roman African trade with Iberia give way to piracy? Pentz has argued that the Vandals did nothing to interfere with the escalating import traffic from the east into Africa (Pentz 1992, 1-7), but they may have been responsible for a disruption to trade westward in African products. Purely Atlantic activity, such as Herul piracy on the Iberian coasts, would be less likely to disrupt traffic from the Mediterranean.

Raids and the Fifth-Century Migrations

The Atlantic piracy of the Heruls, Saxons and Vandals also remains a much neglected topic, though pleasingly now given suitable treatment by Haywood (1991, 23-50). The crucial question for our purposes is the effect this activity had on trade and communication patterns in the fifth and following centuries. Did Saxon and Herul piracy disrupt extant trading activity in the fourth and fifth centuries? Did Frankish and Visigothic conquest of western coastal regions bring a new control of existing trading activity, such as it was? The Visigoths seem to have quickly drawn upon shipping resources to protect the coastline, just as Caesar had done four centuries previously. Sidonius, however, suggests that some of these recruits came from the ranks of the Saxons and Heruls themselves, as well as Gallo-Romans such as Namatius, who were not necessarily regular mariners. Whether invading groups became involved in trade is another interesting question. Saxons were resident in the area near Tours in c.584, most likely they are the descendants of the Saxons in this area in the previous century. That they are found working with a merchant of Tours trading with Orléans in 585 (see below 31) may imply a general involvement in mercantile activity, but there is no proof that this has any maritime link. In the case of the *Britanni* who made their way down the sealanes to Brittany and Galicia, the involvement in exchange may be more likely. The simple migration pattern of these groups bespeaks a maritime capability sufficient to cross the English Channel and the Bay of Biscay. Presumably this continued to be utilised in coastal traffic, if not continuing contact with Britain.

In Iberia continuity remains more likely, especially in the light of the limits of Visigothic interest outside of the Meseta, though we may note that Leuvigild was quick to interfere with maritime traffic at the time of his conquest of the Suevic kingdom (see above, 21). We should also note the depredations of the fleets of Iberia during successive barbarian invasions (Haywood 1991, 30-1).

Raids by seaborne Celtic and Germanic groups upon the northern shores of the sealanes occured from the third century onwards. Initially these were by groups such as the Scots, Picts, Saxons and Heruls, which had a developed maritime capability. They were to remain the most numerous in western sealanes raiding into the fifth century. The Scots, Saxons and Britons later became seaborne colonists. Some of these groups are part of migration patterns which begin before, and finish after, the fifth century. For the sake of convenience they will be discussed primarily at this point. In part this is to recognise that they figure in the disruption of the previous pattern, which has its most profound effect on maritime traffic in the fifth century. By the sixth century most groups had ceased raiding and some had formed colonies in the areas they had previously raided. Further conquest and migration in the sixth century seem mostly to have followed on lines commenced, and into areas established, in the fifth. For example, by the sixth century the Breton migration is no longer really settlement, but exchange of people from Britain to another region which has an established British population. Church councils in Gaul and Spain (see below, 59) show that British groups maintained separate identities where they settled abroad. Gregory of Tours provides more than one example of early fifth-century migrants who continued to see their identity as distinct. The implications of ongoing contact between colonists and their ethnic homelands are often underappreciated. An early medieval colony might be established by refugees, but remain in regular contact with its homeland and even be the focus of royal intervention from that homeland. This was later to be the case in Scandinavian Iceland, for example. We are not sure as to the basis of the foundation of Dalriada, of which the name, meaning 'portion of Riata', discounts the legend of the individual Fergus Mór and his eponymous sons (Bannerman 1974, 121-3) and implies corporate foundation by the Dál Riata in Ireland. We are at least clear that ongoing contacts were maintained and periodic attempts to control Dalriada from Ireland accompanied this process (Bannerman 1974, 18, 157-70). There are at least hints that Brittany was under the aegis of Dumnonia for some of the sixth century, also, though the sources which suggest this have considerable problems (for useful discussion see Padel 1981a, 72-3).

Let us now look closely at where these raiders and colonists went. The Irish and the Picts are listed as seaborne raiders by Gildas and earlier writers, though it is uncertain whether the Picts ever raided the western coasts of Britain. Whatever seaborne commerce there was along the shores of the Irish Sea was presumably disrupted by this activity. Irish colonists certainly made their way to western Scotland and Irish migration to Dyfed is undoubted (Richards 1960; Coplestone-Crow 1981-2). Ogham stones also testify to an Irish influence in North Cornwall and Gwynedd, though this is not so clearly a migration as those to Dyfed and Dalriada (Thomas 1972a).

British migrations are on a considerable scale, doubtless in the form of Gildas' refugees who 'headed for lands overseas' (*alii transmarinas petebant regiones: De Excidio* XXV, ed. & trans. Winterbottom 1978, 98). There were evidently direct refugee migrations in the face of Saxon conquest, though we should not discount previous links which might have existed between Armorica and the south west of Britain. Anthemius is also said to have brought some British mercenaries to Gaul to fight Euric (Jordanes, *Getica*, Mierow 1915, 118; Sidonius, *Epistolae* VIII.6, ed. Anderson 1965, Vol. 2, 418ff). The migrations are dateable to at least the 460s from the writings of Sidonius (*Epistolae* III.9.2, ed. Anderson 1965, Vol. 2, 36-7) and from the signature of the 'British bishop' at the First Council of Tours in 461 (Haddan and Stubbs 1878, 72-3). We should be wary of the assumption that the existence of a separate diocese of Britons (see Morris' note to Winterbottom's edition of Gildas) is any indication as to how recent its establishment was. The existence of a separate diocese of British in Spain for some time should be noted in comparison. Suggestions that the migration went also to Normandy are less certain, where they are based on the *Bretteville* group of names (Morris 1977, I, 89), which might just as easily indicate Norman period translocation of Bretons (though admittedly this usually involved the abandonment of vestiges of Breton ancestry, Davis 1976, 36ff). A group certainly seem to have made their way along the sealanes to Galicia, though they do not appear in the sources until the sixth century (see below, 59). The evidence of Procopius is controversially held by Thompson to suggest a further, sixth century, migration (Thompson 1980a), but the likely reality is that persistent migration occurred throughout the fifth and sixth centuries and we should be wary of setting up simple causal relationships with any single event.

The Saxons are understood to have been raiding off Britain as early as the fourth century and in Armorica by 287 (Haywood 1991, 23ff). Historians have tended to overemphasise the eastern British end of their activity, with its lasting political consequences, at the expense of their other activities, some of which certainly took them into the western sealanes. The Saxons are a persistent presence in northern and western Gaul onward into the sixth century, not simply as raiders, but as settlers. Gregory of Tours, for example, describes Saxons as settled on the Loire where, as early as the reign of Childeric I, they were attacked by the Franks on islands between Saumur and Angers (Gregory of Tours, *HF* II.19, ed. Krusch 1885a, 65). The word 'Saxon' admittedly might have been used by late-Roman writers as one of a number of generic terms for 'barbarian' (Haywood 1991, 4), but we should regard this as a dangerous assumption and follow Haywood in accepting statements of ethnicity at face value, unless there is real cause to do otherwise. As we have seen, the presence of Saxon raiders seems to have inspired the Gothic rulers of Bordeaux to take steps to maintain a naval force to counteract their raids. Namatius was one Gallo-Roman recruited by Euric in this connection around 466. As Sidonius writes to him in reply to a message from Saintes, we may presume that Saintes was a base for Namatius' activities. M.E. Jones has cast doubt upon Sidonius's real knowledge of the Saxons, and even sees fit to dismiss the existence of the messenger from Saintes (Jones 1993, 40ff; Sidonius, *Epistolae* VIII.6, ed. Anderson, Vol. 2, 428). However the existence of Saxons as raiders in the Bay of Biscay, perhaps from bases on the Loire, need not be doubted. G.J. Marcus's correction of 'Saxons' in Sidonius' *Panegyric to Avitus* to 'Irish' is not acceptable (see above, 15).

In the sixth century a group of Saxons living near Bayeux were mobilised by Fredegund (*HF* X.9, ed. Krusch 1885a, 492) and Saxon involvement in the foundation of the emporium at Quentovic in north-east Gaul seems undoubted (Wood 1983, 18-19). Archaeological investigation has also added details to this picture. Saxon objects, such as saucer brooches of sixth-century date, have been identified on sites in Normandy (Lorren 1980) and the site of Herpes, in Charente-Maritime (western France), has also produced square-headed brooches of undoubtedly Saxon type with Style One animals of sixth-century date (now in the British Museum Delamain Collection: Kidd 1989, 105-6). Finds such as this raise interesting questions, however, which deserve more attention than they have received in recent scholarship.

The evidence for raiding and settlement raises a series of issues. Undoubtedly any claims for continuity of usage of the western sealanes through the sixth century are affected by this evidence. The Saxons and the Irish came to settle regions where first they had raided, just as the Vikings were to do some three to four centuries later. Whether these settlements (like those of the Vikings) were a result of a direct transition based on political and social developments at home, or the simple expansion of raiding bases into colonies, cannot be determined. The British, on the other hand, are portrayed as reluctant migrants by Gildas (*De Excidio* XXV, ed. Winterbottom 1978, 98). The Vandals only took to raiding by sea after reaching the Mediterranean. An aspect of continuity might be seen in the continued presence of the two clearly more active maritime groups in commerce in the sixth and seventh centuries. Irish ships are seen in traffic to the continent in the seventh century (*Vita Filiberti* XLII, ed. Levison 1910, 603). Saxons are seen working for a merchant involved with transporting wine by riverboat between Orléans and Tours in the sixth (*HF* VII.46 1885a, ed. Krusch 1885a, 365-6). The presence of Saxon objects in south-west Gaul in the sixth century may also imply Saxon maritime links. British maritime activity seems less present after the migration period, though British vessels visit Noirmoutier in the *Vita Filiberti* (XL, XLI, ed. Levison 1910, 603).

The raids and migrations of the fifth century must be considered to have had other effects. The nature of settlement along the shores of the western sealanes may well have changed. Conimbriga, for example, was destroyed by the Sueves (Hydatius, *Chronicle* n. 241 [s.a. 468], ed. Mommsen 1894, 34). The abandonment of this site, however, is now seriously in doubt (see below, 45). Presumably other towns extended their fortifications in the face of raids. The evidence for significant use of a coastal site such as Tintagel, in the region of Cornwall with the clearest evidence for Irish activity, may be in some way linked with the activities of Irish raiders or migrants. A network of Irish contacts may even explain why ships called there in the fifth/sixth century. Considerations of this kind are important in understanding the limited picture of fifth-century activity.

The weight of political change in the fifth century makes it a logical point at which to seek change in western sealanes activity, or a starting point for a new pattern. That there would be radical change in the maritime pattern should not be seen as inevitable. Nor was it inevitable that change had to follow the collapse of Roman government in north-western Europe. Often central political change makes little change to private shipping activities. This must remain an even stronger caveat for marginal areas of the empire than it does for the Mediterranean. In other cases, maritime activity may have been evolving with the changing pattern of late Roman politics: in a period in which so much ethnic relocation occurred, we should be wary of asserting any continuity of use of routes if we are not sure if the people using them are ethnically the same as their precursors.

Roman period communication had favoured overland traffic through Gaul, both for persons and goods. As Africa came to play a greater economic role, and Rome a politically less significant one, this perspective shifted somewhat, with African products going directly by sea to western Iberia. In the north-east of Europe, however, overland traffic persisted, with Class 45 amphorae and African tablewares still travelling northward to eastern Britain overland. A fifth-century decline in most distributions finds some textual corollary in accounts of piracy at sea and migrations overland. We cannot know how much traffic continued to use western Gaulish or Irish Sea ports. We can stress the lack of evidence for voyages from Gaul to Ireland, though tablewares such as *éponge* pottery *may* indicate voyages from western Gaul to the Bristol Channel in the fourth century.

For international travellers the fifth century brought definite changes of priority. A writer such as Rutilius Namatianus characterises changing attitudes. Writing about a voyage from Italy to Mediterranean Gaul in 416, he notes that he is travelling by sea because the land is politically unstable:

> Postquam Tuscus ager postquamque Aurelius agger, perpessus Geticas ense vel igne manus, non silvas domibus, non flumina ponte coercet, incerto satius credere vela mari.
>
> (Since Tuscany and since the Aurelian highway, after suffering the outrages of Goths with fire and sword, can no longer control forest with homestead or river with bridge, it is better to entrust my sails to the wayward sea: Rutilius, *De Redito Suo* I, ll. 37-42, ed. & trans. Duff 1932, 766-7).

It is not Rutilius's choice of mode of transport which we should see as characterising the era. A few decades later the Mediterranean might have become more dangerous than the land. It is the *basis* of his choice which is significant. No longer is one method of travel chosen simply for reasons of relative economy or convenience. It is safety which is the primary factor. Rutilius implies that he would, in the normal way, have travelled by land. We would assume then that persons in the fifth century would maintain continuity of practice of travel where possible. Hence it is not until late in the fifth century, when all vestiges of

Roman control over the sub-kingdoms of Gaul have declined with the Frankish takeover, that use of the overland routes begins really to give way in favour of the sea. The same is probably true Britain, with early fifth-century travellers to and from Ireland probably still travelling through Britain. Once the pattern has seriously altered, however, direct sea travel becomes more in evidence. By the late sixth century we can definitely state that a churchman such as St Columbanus would more likely have travelled by sea from Ireland directly to Gaul—though a century later, after the setting up of new links after the Synod of Whitby he might have gone via Anglo-Saxon England. It is impossible to identify the sorts of clear discontinuities in practice which some would like to see in the fifth century. Fifth-century societies went through several phases of change in which Roman political models declined by stages. And fifth-century travellers were not automata, but made choices, as Rutilius demonstrates. On the western sealanes the choices may have been more limited compared with the range of Mediterranean transport facilities. In the absence of fourth-century shifts of route in the north, this would suggest a persistence of Roman patterns until political circumstances made them unviable: especially where we can see the seas becoming especially dangerous through piracy.

Zimmer, Wine and Christianisation

Behind the uneven picture of fifth-century history we can discern significant cultural events taking place: the spread of Christianity to Ireland and western Britain, and the acquisition of literacy alongside. Investigation of the character of these acquisitions, to identify the routes by which they were spread, would seem to offer potentially important detail on communication and commerce along the western sealanes. The fact that the sources are often ambiguous seems to have encouraged attempts to locate earlier and later movements within the *terra ignota* of the fifth century. Ireland, for example, had by the fifth century experienced foreign contact and the spread of Christianity and literacy for more than a century. In archaeology, too, the fifth century has been treated as something of a dumping-ground for the beginning and ending of chronological sequences. There is now little evidence to suggest that any of the imported ceramics found on western British sites are any earlier than the very late fifth century. In particular, E ware should never have been associated with the fifth century, and was so only largely on the basis of an association with Zimmer's historical model (Thomas 1976, 254). The imported Mediterranean wares seem to experience a hiatus in the west precisely in the fifth century (see below, 45-6). Zimmer however, along with his literary executor Kuno Meyer, put the fifth century at the centre of debates concerning the spread of foreign culture to Ireland—though they were concerned to date some processes of contact to even earlier centuries. Zimmer's basic thesis will be reviewed now.

The core of Zimmer's thesis, which concerned the arrival of Christianity and Christian culture in Ireland, was a study of Ireland's trading connections with other European regions, his conclusion being that Ireland was in close contact with Gaul in the fifth century and earlier. A measure of the impact of this theory was that Kenney ranked the Gaulish connection ahead of all other potential influences in the creation of a Christian culture in Ireland (Kenney 1929, 159). This link, which Zimmer saw as having its origins in the Roman period, was seen to be in the form of a regular trade built around large cargoes of wine. These conclusions were not reached from a basis purely in economic history, but were necessitated by what Zimmer saw as inescapable conclusions as to the scale of classical influence in Ireland by the sixth and seventh centuries, and the particularly Gaulish character of the heresies and more orthodox movements, such as monasticism, which found root in early medieval Ireland.

That the study of trading links can provide insights into the potential routes by which culture may be spread, and the dates at which scholars and texts could travel, is a sound enough approach. Zimmer's thesis tended to play down links with Britain, however, and assert too early a date for direct contacts with Gaul. The latter now cannot convincingly be shown to begin before the mid-to-late sixth century. Even though the attendant cultural thesis has largely been discredited, however, Zimmer's wine trade is still looked to as one of the major means by which cultural influences were disseminated. Indeed, the idea that a trade in wine was the primary cargo in western sealanes traffic in the early medieval period has been taken up by nearly every scholar concerned with this topic.

Zimmer had a particular interest in proving the existence of direct contacts between the Bordeaux region and Ireland as early as the fifth century, on account of a now generally discounted theory of the origins of the classical tradition in Ireland. This theory was fuelled by a note in a Leyden manuscript referring to an exodus of scholars from the continent, following the invasion of the Huns, Goths and Alans:

> Sub quorum vastatione omnes sapientes cismarini fugam ceperunt et in transmarinis videlicet in Hiberia [sic] et quocumque se receperunt maximum profectum sapientiae incolis illarum regionum adhibuerunt.
>
> (At the devastation of those all the wise men on this side of the sea took flight and in the lands overseas, that is Hiberia and wherever they went, greatly increased the wisdom of the inhabitants of those regions: text in Müller 1866, 389).

I have translated *sapientes* literally here as 'wise men'. 'Learned men' is the more common translation made of this text, but this may be prejudiced by Zimmer's theory that they were *rhetorici*, rather than, say, the men wise in government (the loss of whom would have been indeed lamented in fifth-century Europe). The manuscript text is a discursive entry in a glossary, of mostly different character to this entry, in a manuscript (Leyden Voss. Lat. F.70, f.79) no earlier in date than the eleventh or twelfth century. The text does not refer to any departure point for the exodus. Zimmer inferred this to be Bordeaux. His argument rested upon the references to the Bordeaux rhetorician Ausonius in Latin texts of debateably Irish origin (e.g. *Hisperica Famina* ll. 41, 58, 92, 117, 273, ed. Herren 1979a, 66-73; 84) and the possible (now discounted) Aquitanian origin of the grammarian Virgilius Maro Grammaticus, whom medieval tradition ascribed to Toulouse (Zimmer 1910a, 1031-98—this view of Virgilius is amusingly put into the mouth of Umberto Eco's character William of Baskerville, in *The Name of the Rose:* Eco 1984, 311-13). Zimmer also placed undue emphasis upon what he saw as the general trading significance of Bordeaux, which he compared in a dramatic passage to the Hamburg of his own era (Zimmer 1909c, 591), so as to establish the likelihood of operating sea routes by which the refugees might have travelled to Ireland.

Zimmer's methods were very critical and comprehensive by the standards of his era, but obviously more positivistic than would be the case today. In the tradition of his era, exemplified by his contemporary Mommsen, Zimmer sought to make a comprehensive assembly of sources and dissect them. The relative chronological value of the sources escaped him, however, while the volume of the references which he uncovered exaggerated the scale of activity between Ireland and Gaul. The Leyden glossary entry is six or seven centuries after the event, without any intervening textual tradition, and must be held to be inadmissable as evidence as a result. The fact that the glossary's *Hiberia* is not *Hibernia* oddly enough might be its sole claim to authenticity (Kenney 1929, 142—but also see now: Jung 1995, 221-3): it is the form used by St Patrick *(Confessio* XVI, ed. Hood 1978, 25) and close to that used by St Columbanus *(Epistolae* II, ed. Walker 1957, 22) and Isidore of Seville (Baumgarten 1984, 193). Even so, in a medieval manuscript it is far more likely to be an error, or, less likely, a very learned high medieval forgery. The whole passage has the air of having been written by some ingenious medieval scholar, literally a precursor of Zimmer, to explain how classical learning arrived in Ireland early enough to produce master scholars by the eighth century. Zimmer's expansion of its testimony itself raises sufficient problems. Zimmer took Virgilius Maro Grammaticus to be the fifth-century 'Virgilius Moro' referred to by Ennodius *(Opera,* ed. Vogel 1885, 242). Michael Herren's researches have demonstrated the grammarian's indebtedness to Isidore of Seville—hence his *floruit* cannot have been as early as the fifth century (Herren 1979; Herren 1970). Doubt has even been cast upon Virgilius' real links with an Irish milieu, though some Irish influence seems undeniable (Law 1982, ch. 4). Paralleling this has been a decline in the belief in an early presence of advanced classical scholarship in Ireland. The Irish achievement is seen as founded in energetic research abroad, based on a sound grammatical approach, rather than any extensive text-based learning in Ireland (James 1982, 372ff—but now see Smyth 1986, for a contrary view).

Zimmer's earlier work also involved a maritime contact model and likewise emphasised a link with western Gaul. The same critical facility which Zimmer applied to non-contemporary sources in the *sapientes* thesis, he used to brilliant effect on this topic. Zimmer was one of the first scholars to take issue with the unscholarly acceptance of the role of St Patrick in the conversion of Ireland, seeing the model favoured by scholars in his era as overemphasising the role of one individual and following the propaganda of Armagh (Zimmer 1902a, 117ff). Again, however, he overemphasised the Gaulish connection.

Those who have made sensible criticism of Zimmer's use of the source materials have still seriously understated the weakness of the case for wine trading. Perhaps we see here the influence of the tastes of modern people obscuring their vision of the tastes in the past. We know, from Adomnán, that in Ireland in the sixth and seventh centuries, wine was 'necessary for the most holy mysteries' *(Ad sacrosancta misteria necessarium vinum: Vita Columbae* I.1, ed. & trans. Anderson and Anderson 1961, 196—also second reference to same episode at II.1). The early church in Ireland must have been obtaining wine for the mass by some means. We cannot overlook Bede's *(HE* I.2, ed. Colgrave and Mynors 1969, 20) comment that the vine does grow in Ireland (even though Giraldus was later to state the opposite: see below, 34).

Wine for the Mass would not need to have been of high quality and wine being poured into water in the chalice was part of early Irish liturgical practice, as evinced by the *Stowe Missal (Fin iarum arhuisque hicaelech: Stowe Missal,* ed. Warner 1906 & 1915, 37). On this basis it cannot have amounted to a trade in its own right. Wine is listed in the commentaries upon the *Muirbretha* as only one of the goods which might be found in the cargo of a wrecked ship (see below, 70). It is accorded no especial status in the laws. Only a handful out of the corpus of surviving Old Irish legal texts make reference to wine and these are commentaries referring to the one tract: the lost text *Muirbretha* ('Sea Laws'). Hence there is only one actual legal reference and there it was in the context of a likely ship's cargo, of equal status with a range of other goods (see below, 68-70).

In saints' *vitae* there are as many miracles of turning water into ale, as there are water into wine (e.g. *Vita Brigidae* VIII.2, trans. Connolly and Picard 1987, 16). In the Irish Laws the drinks of secular men of high status were more likely to be mead or ale (Binchy 1981, 3-6), though when dealing with the Irish Laws there is a potential for deliberate archaism. Hence we must be wary of the fact that the goods described might be more likely those which are traditionally of value—i.e. a newly acquired aristocratic taste may not be seen as a traditional symbol of legal status. We must adopt a critical view of the chronology of Irish legal texts, but it is worth noting that the *Críth Gablach* describes ale as a king's drink. It is neither one of the canonical texts, being unglossed and separate from *Senchus Mar,* and of reasonably certain date. References to the Saxon invasion of 684 *(Críth Gablach* l.523, ed. Binchy 1940, 21; xiv; however see Kelly 1989, 264 for possible conflation of the text) and *Cáin Adomnáin* (c. 690: *Críth Gablach* l.524, ed. Binchy 1940, 38: xiv), provide a *terminus post quem* and indicate that it was intended to relate to contemporary situations (Charles-Edwards 1986). Jonas, writing in a continental Irish milieu in the late-seventh century, observes that the Irish, like most north Europeans, prefer ale to wine as a beverage (Jonas, *Vita Columbani* I.16, ed. Krusch 1902a, 82). Even for the king described in the ninth-century *Tecosca Cormaic,* though wine and mead are expected at his court as signs of his ability to attract goods from overseas (*Tecosca Cormaic* 1, l. 44, ed. Meyer 1909, 4-5), it seems that 'not banqueting without *ale*' (*nírba ólchobrach cen cuirm: Tecosca Cormaic* 11, l. 6, ed. Meyer 1909, 18-19), was most important in maintaining one's reputation.

There are references in Irish sagas to Gaulish wine being consumed in high status contexts and involved in gift-giving and exchange between high status persons. A good example is in *Tochmairc Emire*, where Forgall Manach comes to Conchobar's court disguised as an ambassador from Gaul, bringing gifts of wine and gold objects (ed. Meyer, 443; Vendryes 1920). These material descriptions in Ulster Cycle literature, however, must be regarded as having no historical value before the eighth or ninth century AD, the date around which their language shows them to be written. Jim Mallory's statistical study of references to metal values in the Ulster Cycle showed that one third of references were to silver, a metal effectively unknown in pre-Christian Ireland. This questions the received wisdom that they are a 'window on the Iron Age' and adds to the growing suspicion regarding the other 'Celtic' images in these stories (Mallory 1987; *contra* Jackson 1963). The references to wine probably reflect the values of an audience of the 800s or 900s who had by then developed a genuine taste for wine, or perhaps some deliberate creation of an 'heroic age' image. Likewise what we may make of the reference, to the death of Muirchertach Mac Erca in the early medieval equivalent of a butt of Malmsey must remain an open question, as it is ascribed to a date which is just before the period for which we accept the annals as likely to be contemporary witness, and is hence likely to be a later addition (*Annals of Ulster* s.a. 534: *Demersio Muirchertaig filii Erce .i. Muirchertaigh mc. Muireadaidh mc. Eoghain mc. Neill Naoighiallaigh in dolio pleno uino...*: ed. MacNiocaill and Mac Airt, pp.70-1). Reluctance to abandon the idea of a widespread taste for wine amongst any early Celtic group may be attributed to the seductive quality of Diodorus Siculus' clichéd remarks on the Celtic taste for wine. There is certainly no evidence, however, that the stories of the native cycles reflect any actual state of affairs before 700 AD. The law codes, which are earlier in language than the sagas, depict tastes in alcohol which are the opposite of the above. This distinction between the sources needs to be made.

If Zimmer's wine consumption model were to have any merit, we would have to suppose a taste for wine amongst the Irish probably acquired through 'prestige goods' exchange with the Roman world. The absence of literary evidence for Roman period links of Ireland with the continent, and the absence of archaeological finds of the early Dressel series of amphorae from Ireland, must firmly discredit this idea. Reliable references to wine consumption outside of church services only occur in the *Paenitentiale Cummeani (Inebriati igitur vino: Paenitentiale Cummeani*, ed. Bieler 1963, 110—this text is probably mid-seventh century). But even there the context is consumption by churchmen, in connection with church activities.

Zimmer assumed that wine consumption existed on the same scale in Ireland in the Roman period, or earlier, as in the high middle ages. To serve this taste, he then proceeded to assume the existence of a commodity trade on something of the same scale as in the high middle ages. Here he seems to have conflated the references to the activities of the Veneti, the trade out of Bordeaux into the Channel in the Roman period and a variety of references to early medieval traffic. His failure to recognise the differences between the activities described in the various accounts is not so blameworthy: the archaeological clues to assist in this were not available to him and, unlike many of his successors in this field, he at least quoted most examples accurately and discussed them at length. We cannot, either, criticise his positivistic treatment of texts. The serious methodological flaw in his work is that he stressed a continuity by arguing backwards across time. His study of the wine trade begins with a citation of the familiar passage from Giraldus Cambrensis in the twelfth century:

> Vina tamen transmarina ratione commerti tam habunde terram replent, ut uix propaganis prouentusque naturalis in aliquo defectum percipias.
>
> (Imported wines, however, conveyed in the ordinary commercial way, are so abundant that you would scarcely notice that the vine was neither cultivated nor gave its fruit there: Giraldus, *In Topographia Hibernie* 2, ed. O'Meara, 121; trans. O'Meara 1982, 35).

This model is then pushed back over a scattering of sources to suggest the continuity of this trade pattern over most of the first millennium. It need hardly be said that this treatment of Giraldus' comment as a model fails to take account of the circumstances of medieval commerce. Wine trading between Ireland and France was predicated upon the development of south-west France as a producer of wine, at the expense of other, subsistence, production. Irish voyages to France depended in that period upon a demand for grain and hides in France—French ventures to Ireland upon capital provided by Italian bankers (O'Neill 1987, 44ff). These factors are extremely unlikely to have obtained on this scale in the economy of pre-800 Europe. Zimmer's large scale, single cargo, model was too much driven by his cultural thesis.

The wine trade and *sapientes* must be totally rejected, except insofar as there is little doubt that wine was traded, but not as a 'wine trade'. Zimmer's intensely diffusionist cultural model is also simplistic, seeking a wholesale transplantation of foreign scholars to explain the high quality of early Irish learning. Not surprisingly, it was principally taken up by non-Irish scholars such as Meyer and Vendryes.

With the removal of the wine trade thesis and the *sapientes* from serious consideration, the evidence for a seaborne link between Ireland and Gaul in the fifth century becomes virtually non-existent. There is no maritime reason which should be adduced for this—the question is simply historical and economic. Such links had not previously been maintained with Ireland and there is no evidence that any began in the fifth century. There was considerable influence of the Gaulish churches upon the growth of the church in Ireland, which may be a separate matter to the basic dissemination of Christianity. As we will see, in every case the intermediary of the British church is likely to be involved. Not only is it unlikely that even a Gaulish churchman such as Palladius would have travelled directly from Gaul to Britain, we must also accept that his presence in Ireland argues for no link between the Gaulish and Irish churches that is independent of Britain.

No Irish are commemorated in continental sources or monuments, but travellers from Britain are commemorated in fifth-century cemeteries. A Dumnonian woman was buried in Dalmatia in 425, and a Tolosanus *Britannus natione* was buried in Arles, sometime in the mid-400s (Knight 1981, 57). The spread of such fifth-century lapidary formulae as *hic iacet* to western Britain can be explained by these links: this is, as Knight (1981, 57) has emphasised, a quite separate matter to traffic along the lines of Zimmer's model. Only selected formulae are borrowed, which suggests the input of individuals who have been resident in individual parts of Gaul, rather than a comprehensive contact with the Gaulish tradition. .

Palladius, a bishop of Gaulish birth, was sent in 431 to organise the Christian communities in Ireland *(Ad Scottos in Christuom credentes:* the Irish who believed in Christ: Prosper, *Chronicon* s.a. 431, ed. Mommsen 1892, 473). We cannot overemphasise the importance of this definite statement as to the existence of pre-Patrician Christianity in Ireland. Here the often doubtful question of whether the appointment of a bishop implies earlier Christian presence is explicitly answered by the text. The Gaulish origin of Palladius, however, has been overemphasised (Mytum, 1992, 40; Thomas 1981a, 301). That his mission was as an extension of Germanus's activity against Pelagianism in Britain, cannot be in doubt (Charles-Edwards 1993, 7-8). The conjunction of the dates alone is suggestive. In the *Contra Collatorem* (c.434) Prosper also links the events, noting that Leo 'having ordained a bishop to the *Scots,* zealously worked to keep the Roman island catholic, having also made the barbarian island Christian' *(ordinatio Scotis episcopo, dum Romanam insulam studet servare catholicam, fecit etiam barbarum Christianem: Contra Collatorem* XXI, ed. Migne PL 1846, 271). St Jerome described Pelagius as 'heavy with Irish porridge' *(praegravatus pultibus Scothorum:* see Wooding 1988a, 12-17), if nothing else, conceptually linking the Pelagian problem in Britain to Ireland. Pope John's letter to the northern Irish bishops (640) a century later is still rebuking them for following Pelagian doctrines (Bede, *HE* II.19, ed. Colgrave and Mynors 1969, 200-1). The British links of the anti-Pelagian mission, however, are crucial. Palladius was in Ireland to fight a heresy that the *British* were also following. No uniquely Irish connection with the Gaulish church is being followed here. In travelling to Ireland for the same purpose as Germanus did to Britain, Palladius was almost certainly acting on information from British informants or from Germanus himself. There is hence every likelihood he would have followed Germanus' path to Britain, rather than have sailed directly to Ireland. Muirchú, in the seventh century, explicitly states that Palladius died in Britain, *en route* back to Gaul (Muirchú, *Vita Patricii* VI, ed. Hood 1978, 64), but the source of this information is unknown and there is no reason to believe that it is independent.

No discussion of accounts of western sealanes navigation can be complete without consideration of the case of St Patrick, who was an eyewitness to travel along the western sealanes. Born in Britain, he was captured by pirates:

> Annorum eram tunc fere sedecim. Deum enim verum ignorabam et Hiberione in captivitate adductus sum cum tot milia hominum.
>
> I was then about sixteen years old. I did not know the true God and I was taken into captivity in Ireland with so many thousands: *Confessio* I, ed. & trans. Hood 1978, 23, 41).

Little may be gained by rehearsing the arguments regarding the date or birthplace of Patrick—the reader is referred to the massive literature on these topics. Neither of the two sets of annalistic dates (e.g. *Annals of Ulster* s.a. 431 & 2, 461, 492, 493, ed. MacNiocaill and Mac Airt 1983, 38-9, 46-7, 54-5, 55-7), nor the attempts to date the Coroticus who is the addressee of Patrick's *Epistle* (Thomas 1979, 86, 93), inspire any confidence. We may simply observe that Irish tradition puts him later than Palladius.

Patrick definitely travelled on the western sealanes and as Thomas has rightly said: 'any evidence of 5th-century travel is desirable' (Thomas 1979, 82). The route of his journey remains unclear. To quote Thomas again, from his 1990 study of links between Gaul and the Irish Sea:

> Patrick, a Briton, narrating in his *Confessio* how as a lad he escaped from slavery in the north of Ireland (this in the late 430s) and from some point on Ireland's southern coast sailing in a ship to—I believe myself—the north coast of Armorica (Thomas 1990, 3).

Thomas' statement is a very frank summary of the problem: the route taken by Patrick really comes down to a matter of opinion. The problem lies in the ambiguity of Patrick's own words. Patrick himself simply states that his escape after six years in captivity was to a port 'not near at hand but perhaps two hundred miles away' *(et non erat prope, sed forte habebat ducenta milia passum:* Patrick, *Confessio* XVII, ed. & trans. Hood 1978, 26), from whence he took a ship abroad (Patrick, *Confessio* XVII-XVIII, ed. Hood 1978, 26). Some details are provided. The ship's master and crew are pagan (Patrick, *Confessio* XVIII, ed. Hood 1978, 26). Patrick converses with them. This does not assure us that they are Irish—they might also be British, or Gaulish. Patrick, from his Latinity, seems likely also to have been a Latin speaker (Mohrmann 1961, 3) and could most likely make his way in all three tongues. It is tempting to suggest that the crew's paganism makes them less likely to have been Gaulish. The cargo of the ship is unknown. Traditionally favoured was a less likely manuscript variant *canes* over *carne* to allow the idea that the cargo was Irish wolfhounds *(et bene refecti et canes [carne] eorum repleti sunt: Confessio* XIX, ed. Hood 1978, 26). This was taken to extraordinary lengths by Crawford (1936, 193), who explained this as an unusual 'direct' voyage to 'Gaul', without taking the supposed peninsular road over Cornwall:

accountable to the difficulties of travelling overland with dogs! Thomas would suggest 'the attractive notions about exports of Irish wolfhounds...ought to be relegated to folklore' (Thomas 1990, 16). Perhaps this is a trifle extreme if we are contemplating commerce in general: Strabo and Symmachus both indicate that a continental market for British and Irish dogs had existed (Symmachus, *Epistolae* II.77, ed. Seeck 1883, 65), and hunting did not end with the Roman period, even if circuses did. However, Thomas' stricture is entirely appropriate for the Patrick legend.

Further details have been interpreted either too imaginatively, or too literally. Patrick states:

> Protinus navigavimus. Et post triduum cepimus et viginti octo dies per desertum iter fecimus, et cibus defuit illis et fames invaluit super eos
>
> (We set sail at once. Three days later we made land and wandered through a wilderness for twenty-eight days, and they ran out of food and a hunger overtook them: *Confessio* XVIII-XIX, ed. & trans. Hood 1978, 18-19).

Most interpretations of this have been too literal, considering the unspecific nature of the comments. Let us accept, for the sake of argument, that Patrick travelled overland from somewhere in the north of Ireland to a port in the south—the most common interpretation. Three days sailing may have taken him to Britain or to Gaul. At an average speed of three-to-five knots this could fit a voyage to Gaul. It may agree with Patrick's comment which follows: 'And again a few years later when I was in Britain with my kinsfolk they welcomed me as a son and asked me earnestly not to go off anywhere and leave them at this time after the great tribulations which I had been through' *(et iterum post paucos annos Brittanniis eram cum parentibus meis, qui me ut filium susceperunt et ex fide rogaverunt me ut vel modo ego post tantas tribulationes quas ego per tuli nusquam ab illus discederem: Confessio* XXIII, ed. & trans. Hood 1978, 27). We must be wary in our interpretation of this comment, however, in that it could be easily taken to mean that he had made his escape to Britain initially and then was referring ahead to a time when he was again in Britain.

In his *Epistola* (XIV, ed. Hood 1978, 37) Patrick professes knowledge of Gaulish customs, while the *Confessio* vaguely supports the later traditions of a sojourn in Gaul by Patrick:

> Unde autem etsi voluero amittere illas et ut pergens in Brittanniis - et libentissime paratus eram quasi ad patriam et parentes; non id solum sed etiam usque ad Gallias visitare fratres et ut viderem faciem sanctorum Domini mei.
>
> (And even if I wanted to part from them and head for Britain: and I would have been only too glad to do so, to see my homeland and family, and not only that, to go on to Gaul to visit the brethren to see the face of my Lord's holy men: *Confessio* XLIII, ed. & trans. Hood 1978, 31).

He would expect to travel onward to Gaul via Britain. The fact that his family home lay on this route does not lessen this point. Even so, these words must not really be taken to prove a Gaulish sojourn. As Herren observes (Herren 1989, 81-2; also Dumville 1993, 26), Patrick consistently contrasts the positive qualities of Gaulish Christianity against the weakness of the British. That he professes knowledge of Gaul is proof of his espousal of an ethos of Gaulish origin, not of his having been in Gaul, especially as his view is an idyllic one. *Fratres* is a term with a spiritual context which need not imply actual acquaintance. Indeed the expressed desire to look upon the faces might even imply that he had not before done so.

Turning now to the detail in Patrick's account, we must observe the serious danger in taking literally any of Patrick's numbers *(contra* Thomas 1979). After three day's voyage he wandered twenty-eight days in a 'wilderness'. Elaborate arguments have been made to the effect that this was Brittany, but this seems a little ingenuous. It is hard to imagine anywhere where one could wander in a wilderness for twenty-eight days in early medieval western Europe and it is conceivable that this episode and the great length of time involved are allegorical, something analogous to the Biblical ordeal in the wilderness. His captivity was for six years (Patrick, *Confessio* XVII, ed. Hood 1978, 26). After thirty years he is persecuted (Patrick, *Confessio* XVIII, ed. Hood 1978, 28). Many years later he is captured for sixty days (Patrick, *Confessio* XXI, ed. Hood 1978, 27). The blessed lady of Irish birth who becomes a 'virgin of Christ' takes six days to decide (Patrick, *Confessio* LXII, ed. Hood 1978, 31). Multiples of three are strongly in evidence. Twenty-eight is not a multiple of three, though added to the three day's voyage (allowing for the landing and first day in the wilderness to be the same) it becomes thirty. This sort of argument is profitless, however, except insofar as Patrick is writing for edification, not as a guidebook, and there is no more reason to take the wilderness story literally than to accept the details in a more metaphysical miracle story. Finally, we may contrast Patrick's care to locate some episodes in Britain with his lack of precision with regard to the wilderness story. There seems, then, no specific landfall which can be determined from Patrick's escape. Even Muirchú, it must be noted, places St Patrick's stay in Gaul at the terminus of a separate journey (Muirchu, *Vita Patricii* IV & VI, ed. Hood 1978, 63-4). Patrick is one of our earliest first hand reporters of travel on the western sealanes, but we must conclude that little of the detail of his account can be of much use to us. One item is worthy of note. In a harbour Patrick could find a ship's crew to carry him abroad.

The above discussion has no doubt said nothing which can be regarded as adding to an already overworked debate. We may conclude, however, that the case for Patrick's direct voyage to the continent is based on no definite evidence–only some highly ambiguous passages, an espousal of admiration for Gaulish practice and some confusing, probably allegorical, measurements of distance and time.

Sources other than literary texts were introduced very early into this topic with Christian Sarauw's (1900, 7) study of loan-words into early Irish. Recent work on the topic of early literacy and its implications has revived interest in this evidence (Stevenson 1989; Harvey 1987; McManus 1983). The loan-words and Sarauw's typology were taken up by O'Rahilly and Jackson (O'Rahilly 1942,

42-5; Jackson 1953, 122-48) to defend the idea of continental and other contacts. O'Rahilly followed Sarauw in separating Latin loan-words into two putative strata which he equated with the respective activities of Gaulish and British missions. The strata were defined on the criteria of their treatment of Latin phonemes and labelled by the convenient contrast provided the phonemic substitution in forms of the same name: *Cothrige/Pátraic*. O'Rahilly contended that the *Cothrige* stratum reflected the introduction of words by speakers of classically pronounced Latin where post-vocalic /c/ and /t/ were spirantised: 'this class of loanwords can only have been introduced by the Palladian missionaries, educated Gauls and Italians of the fifth century, who had preserved in their speech the classical values of the Latin consonants' (O'Rahilly 1942, 43). He contrasted this with the more obviously British origin of the latter group. This judgement very probably reflects Zimmer's theory of the presence of *rhetorici*. In fact current studies of Gaulish and Italian Latin in the fifth century (McManus 1984, 182) show that these were no more classical in these values than British (McManus 1984, 188). Anyway, why should we assume that all of Palladius's party were Gaulish, even if he was?

In a well-argued study Damien McManus (1984, 179-96) has firmly buried the supposed dichotomy: explaining the words as gradual borrowings across time, with adaptation occurring to different degrees as comprehension of Latin varied. Words which suggest acquisition prior to the loss of final syllables or the first appearance of lenition (Sarauw's phonological criteria were very selective) can be linked to various stages of linguistic evolution in Ireland, whereas the previous bipartite model necessitated their consideration as a group within a limited chronological phase. What must be stressed in this case is the confusion caused when a use of linguistic data to defend or expand historical evidence, or at least to integrate with it, is confused with linguistically derived conclusions. McManus makes this clear. Further as Harvey (1985, 1-9) observes, Jackson tied his chronology to quasi-historical dates, coming obviously unstuck on using 432 as a benchmark for the Patrician mission (Jackson 1953, 142). The method was not unsound, but the historical errors do invalidate the conclusions derived from them and this is rarely appreciated by the non-linguist.

A range of evidence not available to Zimmer comes from the archaeological side. These data offer the opportunity to date and provenance voyages in and out of Ireland, though this evidence too has been subject to attempts to use it to prove direct continental connections. The evidence for Roman contact with Ireland is small in quantity. Dermot Bateson and Richard Warner have identified two basic groups of Roman imports: the first dating from the earliest centuries AD; and the second centring on the fourth century. The latter group is consistently associated with the raiding period, while Warner has defined the former group as arriving by a variety of means, with a Roman agency for some made likely by finds such as the typically Roman cremation burial at Stoneyford (Warner 1976, 274; Bateson 1973, 21-97; Bourke 1989, 56-7). Warner distinguishes these contact phases by asserting the lack of third-century objects in Ireland (Warner 1976, 267-70) and he is followed in this by Laing (1985, 269-70). This bipartite division may be misleading, however, insofar as it allows the sort of dichotomy to be set up that has been seen in the case of the loan-words. That the later group of imports reflect a much more extensive contact need not be doubted, nor need we doubt that it relates to the direct contact of which the raiding is a part. But the earlier 'group' may reflect escalating casual contact over a range of time, for which no discontinuity is necessary to distinguish them from later activity.

Perhaps more crucial to the present study is the need to establish the routes of arrival. The Roman material in Ireland falls into three geographical groups which are taken to reflect three maritime connections. The northern group of artefacts reflects ongoing Iron Age links between Scotland and northern Ireland (Warner 1983, 161-87). The Scotland-Northern Ireland route is the shortest crossing point to Ireland: hence we should not be too quick in following Thomas in making modern comparisons highlighting the continuing importance of the Dublin-Holyhead route. The dominance of this link today reflects the political turmoil of Northern Ireland, the south-western political focus of modern Britain and, above all, the roadbuilding of Thomas Telford. Finds in the vicinity of Leinster might be logical in terms of the natural crossing from Gwynedd, but the objects from Leinster sites might also be explained by voyages from further north. The southern group of finds, scattered across Cork, Waterford and Tipperary, are the crucial group to explain in terms of western sealanes travel. Such has been the power of the Zimmer and 'western seaways' theses that most discussions have still been keen to highlight a continental origin as being equally likely as a British to explain the presence of Roman objects in southern Ireland (Stevenson 1989, 132). The considerable links between southern Ireland and Dyfed, however, provide an impressive testimony to west-east contacts, rather than the supposition that the south coast of Ireland would look naturally south to the continent. One subject worthy of greater attention is the number of Roman finds from the valley of the Barrow—including the Stoneyford finds and the Loch Lene boat—and the corresponding concentration of ogham stones in that region. There is nothing here to reflect a continental connection over a British one.

The existence of a predominant link between the very south of Ireland and Dyfed is clearly seen in the distribution of the ogham alphabet. This is a lapidary alphabet derived from Latin alphabetical classificatory models of the type characterised by the fourth-century grammarian Donatus (McManus 1991, 23-8), though Carney is probably correct in asserting that it derives from grammatical discourse which gave rise to Donatus' scheme, rather than from Donatus himself (Carney 1975, 56). The question of its place of origin is unclear, but around 4/7 of the total distribution is concentrated in counties Kerry, Cork and Waterford, with another 2/7 in Cornwall and Gwynedd and, most particularly, Dyfed (we should follow McManus in excluding Pictish oghams from this picture, on account of their obviously later nature, both in the forms used and, more significantly, their alignment on the stones, McManus 1991, 9). The ogham stones date from the fourth through sixth centuries AD (McManus 1991, 40-1). This is still a matter of some debate, but we should be aware that the colonial occurrences, our principal concern here, are perhaps the best dated as many have bilingual inscriptions of late-fifth/sixth century date (McManus 1991, 78ff). The function of the stones remains unclear, especially in the pagan context, but the commemorative function is central and appears harmonious with Christian activity in the British examples (McManus 1991, 43).

The distribution of ogham is by no means all maritime, and we should be wary of using the finds in Co. Kerry to argue maritime links with Cork—it is the idea which moves, not the stones. Where the alphabet is used on the eastern rim of the Irish Sea, however, it is clear we have evidence of maritime reflux between specific parts of Ireland and their colonies. McManus's clear statement is worth quoting:

> the distribution in Britain corresponds more or less in frequency to that of the respective areas in Ireland from which the colonists who brought it across the Irish Sea probably set forth, being minimal (if non-existent) in Scotland as in the adjacent area of north eastern Ireland whence Argyll was settled in, or around, the fifth century, and maximal in south-west Wales colonised by Irish settlers from the south east around the fifth century (McManus 1991, 45-7).

Inscriptional evidence thus shows clear divisions between northern and southern Ireland, as well as the northern and southern zones of the Irish Sea. Inscribed stones in the ogham alphabet are rarer in northern than in southern Ireland. Where they occur on the eastern rim of the Irish Sea basin, they are confined to areas no further north than a Dublin/Gwynedd line. The concentrations in Counties Kerry, Cork and Waterford in Ireland, Dyfed and Gwynedd in Wales, the southern tip of the Isle of Man, and the area around the Camel estuary in Northern Cornwall may be said to circumscribe a maritime province excluding for the most part the northern maritime zone of the Irish Sea. It will be noted that there are maritime reasons, both in terms of available winds, currents and visibility of landmasses that encourage the northern lands to at times look more naturally to each other, than to lands south of a Dublin-Gwynedd line (see above, 8).

We must continue to emphasise the idea that contact between Ireland and Britain during the Roman and sub-Roman period may serve to explain most importation of culture from further abroad. In the case of ogham, and the concentration of Roman finds in the Barrow Valley, we may be looking at cultural contact which comes from the Bristol ports or maybe Chesire or Lancashire. But the role of the shortest crossing, from southern Scotland to Northern Ireland, should not be underrated in its importance, as it is by the 'western seaways' school. John Waddell (1991-2, 29-40) has emphatically demonstrated that it was a major route of cultural exchange in earlier prehistory and this may also be true for the Roman period. St Patrick's northern British origins remain controversial (Thomas 1979, 83-4), but the presence of an early nucleus of Christianity at Whithorn has been confirmed by Peter Hill's excavations (Hill 1987, 1989, 1990, 1992), as well as the undoubtedly pre-seventh century 'Latinus' stone (Thomas 1992). It has become an apposite cliché to observe that it could well be the Galloway region which Tertullian is referring to in his comment that in his day (209 AD) Christianity penetrated 'even those British regions unreached by Rome' *(Brittanorum inaccessa Romanis loca, Adversos Judaeos* VII, Haddan and Stubbs, *CEDRBI*, Vol. 1, 11). From Whithorn it is a very short crossing to Ireland. The Gaulish chimera has tended to focus attention upon Christian activity in Leinster. While the south remains a highly possible location for early Christian communities, it must be emphasised how poor the evidence is. The evidence for the activity of the followers of Palladius in the Wicklow region is not reliably early (Bowen 1969a, 112-3; Thomas 1981a, 304; Sharpe 1989, 376-99). The early Christian communities were possibly in the north and if any likely offshore connections are to be sought, the nearby early community in Galloway is perhaps a more likely connection than southern Irish links with the continent.

This chapter has considered two largely separate continuity models which contend that traffic along the western sealanes in the period AD 400-800 was a continuity of ancient patterns. It has found in the negative in both cases. The first model posits the idea that patterns of western sealanes traffic from the continent northward to Britain and Ireland have prevailed since early prehistory. The second model argues that, regardless of the prehistoric pattern, tastes for Roman commodities such as wine or oil had been developed in western Britiain and Ireland, which lasted into the post-Roman period and were sufficently developed to support a direct seaborne traffic to the western zone.

That neither the prehistoric artefactual evidence nor the Roman period sources indicate direct traffic to Britain from the continent must be seen to negate the first model, though this does not in any way prove that no such voyages were ever made—the technology available was certainly suitable to the task.

The issue of lingering Roman values and tastes is more complex and less easily dismissed, as we cannot pretend that both imperial and Christian Roman ideas are not present in the political and religious life of post Roman Britain and Ireland. Thomas is inclined to play down the Roman legacy:

> The argument that several centuries of Romanitas imbued the collective race-instinct of the native British with a taste for unfamiliar luxuries, a taste that could not be met after the economic collapse postulated in the early 5th century, is not only a trifle naive but implies both a penetration of Roman manners and a degree of everyday continuity far beyond the evidence (Thomas 1988a, 11).

There is an element of conscious self-criticism here: throw-away lines on consumer tastes have characterised archaeological reports on the ceramic evidence, those of Thomas no less than others (see above, 22). Goods such as wine and oil had probably only trickled into western

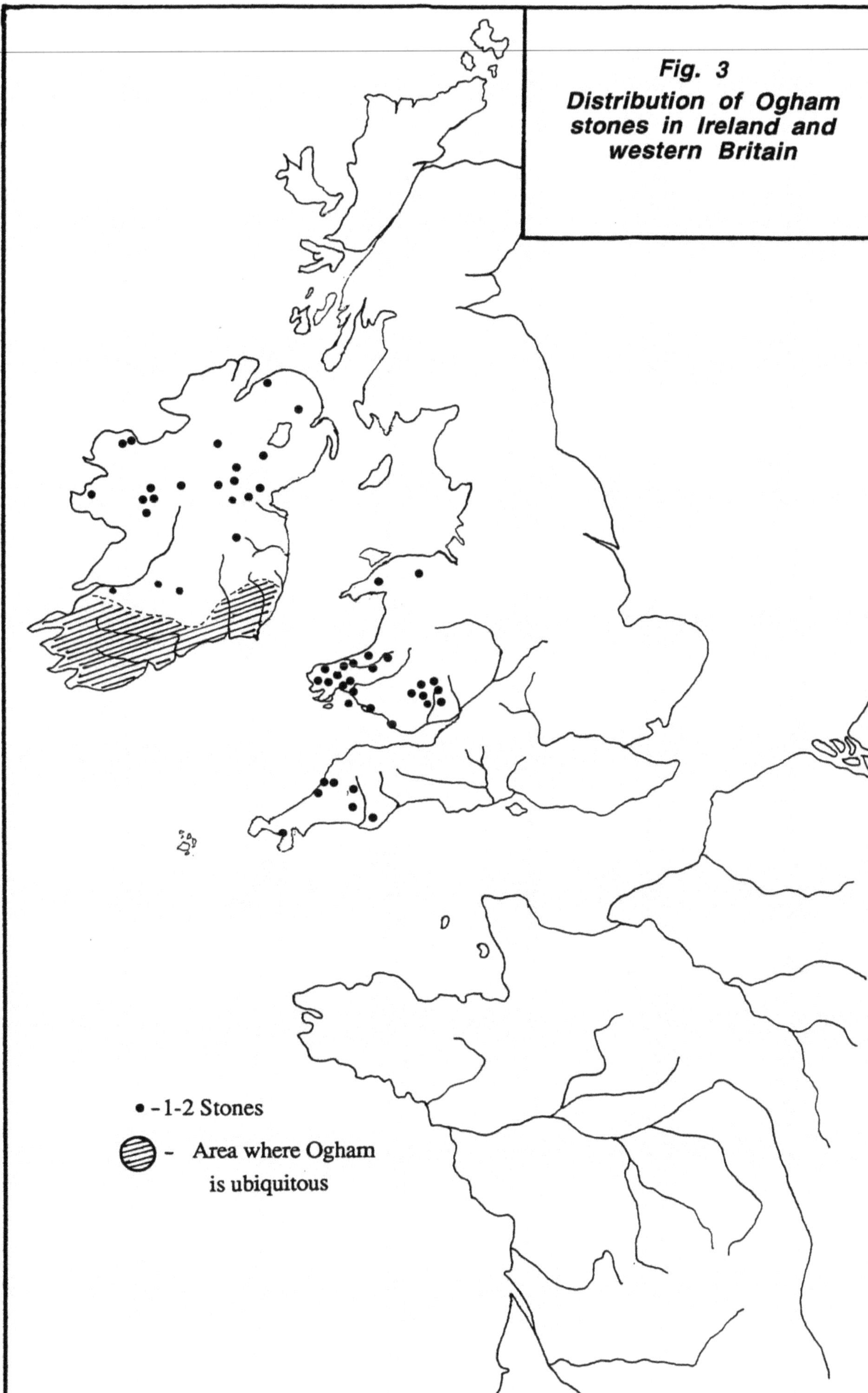

Fig. 3
Distribution of Ogham stones in Ireland and western Britain

Britain as prestige goods associated with sporadic exchange. In the post-Roman period a market might still be found for them, but it quite likely was a different market. Wine and oil have uses in church ritual and celebration. If this is a continuity of *Romanitas* then, as Columbanus said of the Irish church, it owes more to the legacy of the Rome of Peter and Paul than to that of the empire (Columbanus, *Epistulae* V.11, ed. Walker 1957, 48-9). Gildas is conscious of the importance of wine and oil as images of prosperity (we may also recall here the Roman discourse which saw these items as universally appealing to barbarians, as evinced in various late-Roman laws: Thompson 1982, 10-11), but the evidence of Irish sources puts little value on them in a secular context. There seems, likewise, no justification for following Laing in seeing the obvious Roman models behind penannular brooches, hanging bowls, hand-pins, finger rings, bracelets and combs as evidence of deep, politicised, Romanisation of Irish society (Laing 1985, 262-8). These objects need not have had any Roman value by the time they reached Ireland through the filter of northern British 'buffer' kingdoms. That these types of objects continued to be made on both sides of the Irish Sea reflects continuing contact between east and west, rather than a separate, strong legacy of *Romanitas* on each shore established exclusively in the Roman period. In this case the notion of an 'Irish Sea province' (see e.g. Alcock 1969, 63-5) is more convincing than the isolation model, but the emphasis must really be on the shortest links between neighbouring landmasses, rather than a 'maritime culture province'.

While the sixth- and seventh-century ceramic imports into western Britain and Ireland show some indications of regular trade, there is no evidence of the regularity or the scale seen in Roman period Atlantic traffic, described for example by Strabo, or in the high medieval traffic between France and Ireland described by Giraldus Cambrensis. Both these trades, cited by Zimmer as continuous with early medieval western sealanes traffic, served markets with wholly different scales of demand to early medieval Britain and Ireland. In the Roman period the market was in eastern Britain, where the tastes of *Romanitas* were far more in evidence; in the high medieval instance the context is cheap commodity movement between France and an Ireland restricted in its market by English trade regulation (O'Neill 1987, 44ff). In other words, continuity models are illusory and cause us to forget that commerce and exchange are driven by tastes and demands in each era, for which economic bases evolve that are largely unique to that era.

Chapter Four

The Mediterranean and the Atlantic in the Sixth Century

In the Mediterranean, the very late fifth or early sixth century saw a short resurgence of commerce and communication between the Greek east and the Latin west. The degree to which this exchange was discontinuous with earlier activity, in all theatres, is now clear from archaeological evidence. Eastern Mediterranean ceramics only reappear in the early sixth century, after a gap of around a century, on sites in Africa, Italy and Spain. This break in continuity clearly indicates that commerce was disrupted by fifth century events. The textual data are neither specific enough in reference, nor so comprehensive, as to indicate this discontinuity, which is why Henri Pirenne could read references to the arrival of eastern luxuries in sixth-century Frankish sources as indicating a continuity of east-west exchange from the Roman period, overlooking intermittent discontinuity, and seeing the persistence of *mare nostrum* oblivious to political change (Pirenne 1939; Havighurst 1978; Hodges and Whitehouse 1983). *Mutatis mutandis,* Zimmer's thesis of a similar continuity of Atlantic activity through the fifth century is also unlikely. The same ceramic evidence which is used to question Pirenne's model is crucial in the study of sixth-century activity in the western sealanes. Around the early 500s, the Byzantine thrust into the western Mediterranean extended west in a brief *floruit* of direct traffic of eastern Mediterranean goods into the western sealanes, as far as Portugal and Britain. The evidence for this activity, in the form of finds of imported Mediterranean pottery along the Atlantic seaboard, is of primary importance to the study of western sealanes traffic as a whole, despite the fact that its chronological range is narrow and its involvement with cultural transmission doubtful. The historical background to this brief connection may be significant, hinting at a strong Byzantine interest in northern Europe.

There is, as we have seen, evidence for Roman period voyages through the Straits of Gibraltar, carrying goods from North Africa to Atlantic Spain and Portugal. Identifiable sixth-century activity along this route, however, is of a separate character. The distribution of Mediterranean pottery in western Britain and Ireland from late fifth or early sixth-century sites makes it possible to specify that the vessels entering the Atlantic began their voyages in the eastern Mediterranean. The very limited textual evidence relating to this Atlantic *floruit,* though by itself of little value, is supportive of the evidence of the ceramics in supporting the eastern Mediterranean agency.

That we can establish only a narrow chronological range for such Atlantic activity does not diminish either its relevance to western sealanes traffic, or to the study of the wares in general. The narrowness of the *floruit* is in fact advantageous for establishing a benchmark for insular chronology. The selection found on Atlantic sites informs our understanding of the ways in which certain wares overlap in chronology in the Mediterranean as well as which combinations may make up whole ships' cargoes.

The imported wares have been widely discussed in Ireland and Britain since the 1940s (Ó Riordáin 1942, 134; Ó Riordáin 1947, 70-1). A widely used alphabetical classification was established by Radford (1956, 59-70) and was taken up and developed by Thomas (1959, 15-22; 1981b, 89-111; 1976, 245-55). The potential of these finds for refining the chronology of western sealanes sites understandably attracted the most attention initially, as these wares are found in the context of long sequences in Mediterranean contexts and are sometimes dateable by coin evidence. This provides a datum-line of some importance for the anumismatic archaeological chronology of the Irish Sea basin. Discussion to date has not entirely neglected the implications of the finds for social or economic history, though historians with such concerns have not made as much use of this evidence as they might. Such considerations are important, as it is easy to date the individual wares to a wide time-frame. A consideration of the group as an integrated whole, however, a historically likely scenario, suggests a much more limited importation event. This is also a defensible model archaeologically.

The bulk of the Mediterranean imports in the Irish Sea basin are found in the south, especially in the south-west peninsula of Britain. Only scattered finds have been made in Atlantic Portugal and Spain to date, but this is a misleading statistic as there is less published excavation of early medieval sites in Iberia than in Britain and Ireland, and excavated material probably awaits identification. Ewan Campbell (forthcoming 1996) suggests that: 'what is important about this distribution is that the number of vessels from British and Spanish sites is of the same order of magnitude even though the Spanish sites are closer to the source of the pottery' and this may well turn out to be the case, as it is certainly true as regards the range of types present. There will be further evidence from Portugal and Spain, however, and we must bear in mind that if the traffic was commercial in nature, rather than a specific political mission (see below, 47), the British finds may be isolated speculations arising from a much larger traffic with Atlantic Iberia.

The finds fall into two broad functional categories: amphorae and tablewares. These can be further subdivided into different classes of these types of vessels. A brief listing of these types will now be made:

Tablewares

PRS: Phocaean Red Slipware (Late Roman C; generally corresponding to previous British Class Ai). This class is made up of bowls and dishes in a soft orange-red fabric. A thin, darker red, slip usually covers the inside and outside surfaces. Stamped decoration (often on a Christian theme) is sometimes found on the base and the rims are often rouletted (Hayes 1972, 456-8, 463; Hayes 1980, 525-7; Thomas 1981b, 6-7). The British finds firmly identified are predominantly of Hayes' Form 3, with a few from Tintagel, which Thomas suggests are of Form 10. The finds from Portugal are likewise of Form 3 (Prieto 1984, 540-8). A kiln site with Form 3 wasters is known from Phocaea in western Turkey, so an origin in Asia Minor is likely (Langlotz 1969, 380). The general date range of this type in the western sealanes fits within the short western Mediterranean *floruit* of the ware: late-fifth to mid-sixth century. Form 10 may be earlier in the fifth century, in which case the model proposed below would suggest that either these are misidentified or are residual vessels which had already had a long life as fittings on board a visiting ship.

ARS: African Red Slipware (Late Roman B; generally corresponding to previous British Class Aii). The western sealanes finds are of bowls in a darker, harder fabric than PRS with a wash on the external and internal surfaces, similar in colour to the fabric. They are rouletted on the rim, but otherwise undecorated (Campbell 1988A, 124; Hayes 1972, 460, 464; Hayes 1980, 484-523). No kiln site has yet been found, but increasingly it is clear that the origin point is somewhere in the vicinity of Tunisia. The identified western British finds are of Hayes forms 81, 88, 91, 99, 103 and 104. This same collection of later forms is generally paralleled in Portugal, but there is a sequence of earlier forms. Earlier forms appear in Roman contexts in eastern Britain (Bird 1977), but this earlier activity is clearly unrelated. Date range is variable, according to forms. British examples are early sixth century.

'Eastern Mediterranean Coarsewares'. Recently identified amongst the Tintagel finds these consist of bowls and amphorae, with seven different fabrics so far identified. Mica inclusions would suggest an eastern origin (Hartgroves and Walker 1988, 24-5).

'Tunisian Tableware'. A mid- to dark-brown tableware found at Tintagel. Similarities between these pieces and coarsewares from Tunisia in the Reading University collections have so far been noted (Thomas, *pers. comm.)*. As with the above group, various sherds in the amphora category 'B Miscellaneous' are likely to be of this type, unnoticed because of a lack of formally distinguishable features.

Amphorae or Storage Jars

(Numerical classes are as in Peacock and Williams 1986. These will hopefully now become standard. There is, as Thomas has commented, something 'grotesque' about the use of the British labels in a Mediterranean context and the plethora of other names for these wares makes comprehension difficult).

CLASS 43 (British Class Bi). Globular, two handled amphorae with distinctive 'comb' decoration in a band at shoulder point, sometimes spreading out to additional bands below. The neck is usually splayed and the base has a basal knob. The coarse fabric can appear to come in varying colours and compositions, though such differences may well be post-depositional (common in unglazed wares). The Mediterranean evidence suggests, on distributional grounds, an Aegean origin, though Rumanian kilns may also have existed (Peacock and Williams 1986, 182-4). One kiln site has been found in Southern Greece (Munn 1985, 342-3), but this is unlikely to be the only one. Greek letters are often etched on Mediterranean examples. British finds often carry etched graffiti (see below). The date range is between the fourth through seventh centuries, though there are earlier and later forms. In the Atlantic context, however, there is no reason to look beyond the period late-fifth through sixth and on typological grounds none are identifiable as post-sixth century (see below).

CLASS 44 (British Class Bii). Narrow, thin walled amphorae with sharp ribbing over length; widely spaced at middle of the body, closer at the shoulder and base. Red painted Greek characters (dipinti) occur on the shoulder of many Mediterranean examples. Date range is from the fifth to seventh centuries in the Mediterranean (Peacock and Williams 1986, 185-6).

CLASS 45 (British Class Biv). Western sealanes finds of this type are of the (later) two handled form, where there is enough of the vessel surviving to determine this. The one-handled form also occurs in Britain, however, so only the finding of the shoulder provides absolute certainty of post-Roman date, though any western British find is, on distributional grounds, likely to be of the two-handled type. Tall narrow amphorae tapering to a narrow foot. The fabric is hard, with a very distinctive deep red/brown colour and micaceous. The vessels have thin walls with light external ribbing. Egypt and Asia Minor have been proposed as sources for the ware. Peacock and Williams favour the latter on petrological grounds (Peacock and Williams 1986, 188-9). These vessels have a wide date range in Mediterranean contexts (first through seventh centuries) though the two-handled type is only common in the fifth century onward.

CLASS 49 (AMALGRO 54, British Class Bvi). Cylindrical, spoutless amphorae with a small everted rim and tapering at the bottom to small, flat base. The vessels have small loop handles and groove decoration on shoulder and base. The fabric is brown and sandy with a greyish core and limestone inclusions. Thought to be from Gaza. Fourth to sixth-century date (Peacock and Williams 1986, 198-9; Thomas 1981b, 16).

CLASS 34 (AFRICANA II, British Bv, 'Byzacena'). Cylindrical amphorae, a metre or more in length, with a pointed toe and collared rim, of buff to brick red fabric with a pale slip. Provenance is determined by name stamps (on Mediterranean finds) which suggest a central Tunisian origin. Dating is up to the end of the fourth century, but probably continues into fifth (Peacock and Williams 1986, 155-7; Thomas 1981b, 15).

B MISCELLANEOUS (formerly Biii). A collection of untyped sherds. Of sherds previously attributed to this class, many have now been identified firmly as belonging to known classes. The remainder are mostly African and eastern Mediterranean amphora sherds in coarse fabrics (Hartgroves and Walker 1988, 24-5).

When British finds of these wares were first identified as being of Mediterranean provenance it was natural enough to assume that they would represent evidence of continuing contact with the coasts of Gaul and that the wares had been carried by way of the same river routes across Gaul as had been active in the Roman period (Radford 1956, 68-9). Fieldwork by Bernard Wailes in the 1950s, however, showed these wares to be absent from western France and the negative evidence continues to confirm this. The absence of finds has continued far beyond the point where it can be attributed to a simple failure of French archaeology to discover examples. Where would we expect to find the wares if the overland routes were being used? Centres such as Bordeaux, Orléans and Tours have all seen extensive exploration and related late-Roman wares are known from these sites. We would not now expect PRS or class 43 amphorae to exist unrecognised in those centres.

Bernard Wailes found parallels for the tablewares in Portugal (Wailes 1963, 36-46) and this evidence was interpreted as attesting to the existence of sea traffic around the Iberian peninsula and through the Straits of Gibraltar, bypassing the overland routes through France. The matter largely rested there for more than a decade. Thomas, who with Wailes conducted much of the early research on the Mediterranean wares in Britain, focused attention on investigating the Mediterranean leg of this activity before attempting any deeper analysis of their socio-economic context in Britain (though he has recently returned to this topic—Thomas 1988a, 7-25). It might be argued that the latter is an historical, rather than a strictly archaeological, problem. The role of the imported wares as diagnostic fifth- and sixth-century artefacts was of primary interest to excavators. Historians seemed to shy away from the material as it does not seem to have much corresponding documentary testimony and, further, did not reveal the expected connections with Gaul. Certainly, in the context of the spread of religious or artistic culture it only seemed to link up with a school of 'Mediterranean influence' thought which had cast a largely misleading and unscholarly obstacle in the path of the discernment of real cultural links (Raftery 1965, 193-204).

Even so, the phenomenon of direct connections with the Mediterranean must be of interest to historians. From the historical standpoint the following questions need to be answered. By precisely which route did these wares reach Britain? What was the chronological range of the maritime ventures which brought them? What was the nationality of the seafarers? Was this direct traffic from the Mediterranean? Were the wares transhipped at any point? Finally, why did these voyages take place? Are they due to commercial, or other impulses? Thomas addressed these questions briefly in 1982 and again in 1988 (Thomas 1988a, 10ff), while Leslie Alcock (1987, 89-92) has made a recent attempt to answer some of these questions in the context of a reassessment of Dinas Powys. Having ruled out the likelihood of these wares having travelled overland through Gaul (where we might be dealing with a more 'down-the-line' traffic, or traffic in much smaller individual cargoes of amphorae than are implied by direct voyaging), grouping the imports into potential ships' cargoes becomes necessary and this problem is tackled by both Alcock and Thomas. Whether we accept the minimalist view espoused by Thomas, involving no more than two or three hypothetical ships, or the more expansive model of Alcock, who believes that the finds are more likely to have trickled in as part of heterogeneous cargoes, all arguments begin with the assumption that these wares were part of shiploads assembled in some foreign centre.

The separation of tablewares and amphorae for classification purposes, as is commonly done (Thomas 1981b, 6ff), can obscure more meaningful groupings. Whatever the character of the voyages involved in this activity, it is clear that the tablewares were a lightweight accompaniment for substantial amounts of amphorae. An important distinction in examining these finds is between eastern Mediterranean tablewares and amphorae, on the one hand, and the African tablewares and amphorae, on the other. The African group is very much smaller than the eastern Mediterranean: forming only around 20% of the entire assemblage of Mediterranean finds in western Britain and Ireland (Thomas 1988a, 12), but the greater part of this 20% is the African tablewares, which would have formed a much smaller part of ships' cargoes than the amphorae. This makes it unlikely (*contra* Alcock 1995, 84) that the cargoes were transhipped in Africa—whence we would expect a much higher African component. It is not yet clear whether a similar quantitative breakdown occurs at Conimbriga. Comparisons with the Portuguese quantities could be informative on the question of whether entire eastern Mediterranean ships' cargoes were at least reaching Portugal.

Another question is whether to group the wares as to date. The distribution of Mediterranean wares in western Britain and Ireland, despite being widely dispersed throughout the Irish Sea basin, represents a limited selection of artefacts which were ubiquitous in the Mediterranean at varying times, but which overlap within a narrower chronological range. Some of these, such as the class 43 amphorae, have been found in widely varying chronological contexts in the Mediterranean and offer problems for finer dating. The point is that none of the amphorae are confined to a limited dating bracket, therefore dating each individual type does not help answer the question of the date of their arrival in Britain (e. g. Mytum 1992, 253-7; Miller 1979-80, 317). The collection of finds needs, rather, to be treated as an entire assemblage and the *proportion* of each type of ware compared to proportions at sites producing quantities of these wares in dateable contexts. The Avenue du Président Habib Bourguiba and other sites in Carthage (Fulford and Peacock 1984; Riley 1981, 85-124)

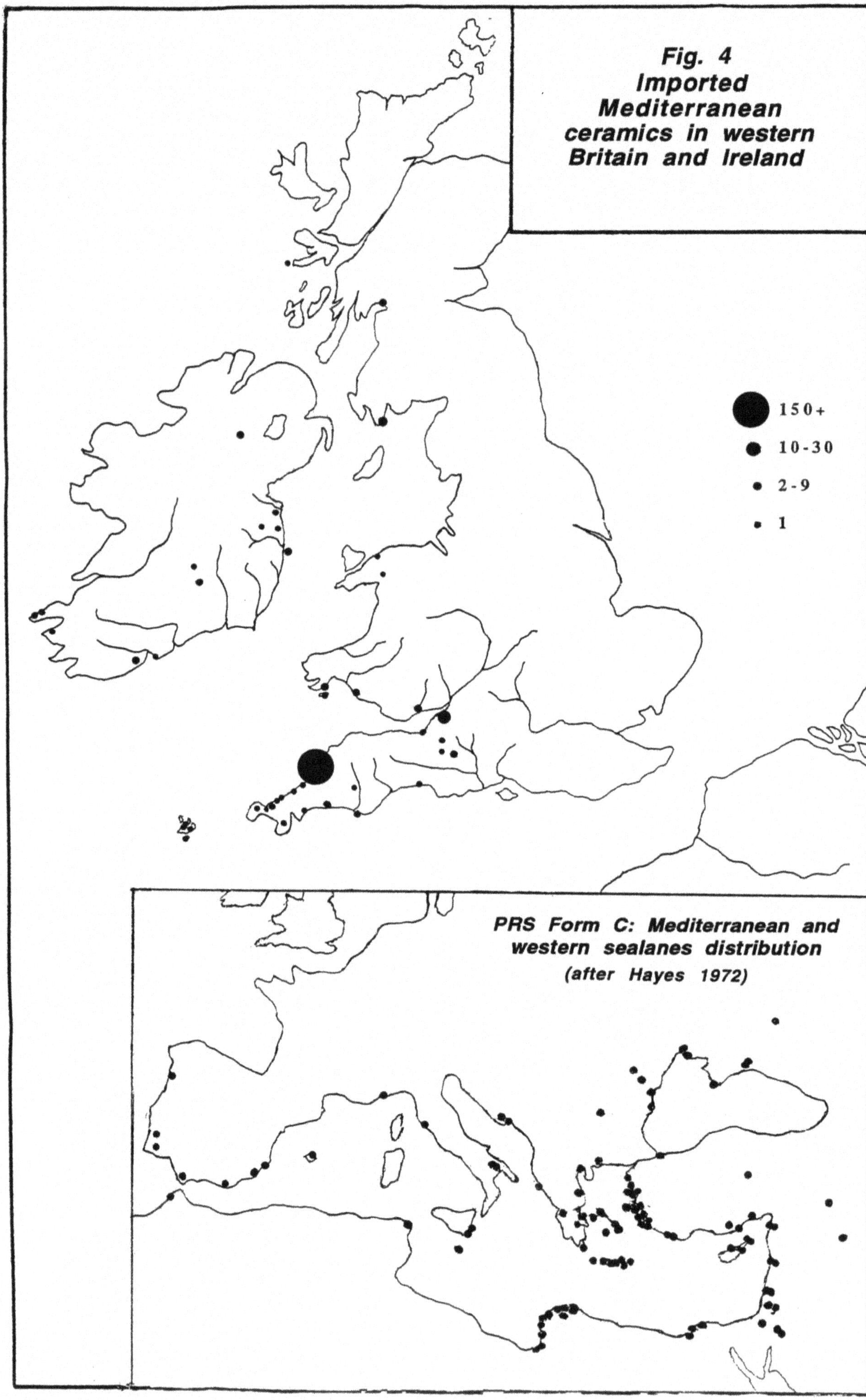

Fig. 4 Imported Mediterranean ceramics in western Britain and Ireland

and the comparative material from Rome discussed by Fulford (1989, 1-6) offer an informative basis for such comparisons.

That the Class 43 and 44 type amphorae are contemporaneous must be seen as unquestionable. Beyond this point there is little agreement. As with the topic of glass studies (see below, 84) a type of oral tradition has fuelled suspicion of the c.500 dating provided for these wares by Thomas and others. The wide date-range of Class 44 in the Near East has been taken as indicating a likely irreducible date-range for the imports (M. Ryan, *pers. comm.;* Alcock 1995, 84). The late-fifth-century date ascribed to some ARS imports has also been held to indicate *two* chronological horizons on British sites—one late fifth and another early sixth century—each of these being seen to reflect separate voyages or sets of voyages (e.g. Mytum 1992, 252-3; Miller 1979-80, 315).

The variety amongst the imports is a red herring. Of course when looking at this evidence through a positivist model, we might see material evidence of a developing pattern of contact stretching over a century or more. The Class 34 amphorae may be early fifth century, as might be some of the PRS. The Class 45 and 49 amphorae are certainly more common in the fifth century and some of the African Red Slipware pieces were dated by Hayes to the late fifth century. Or, alternatively, we might suggest that earlier contacts brought in only the putatively earlier African material (ARS and Class 34 amphorae), to be followed by contacts bringing eastern Mediterranean material. The fact that African wares were reaching Portugal in the fifth century could be used to support this developing model. Hayes' initial dates for the ARS forms found in Britain have been disputed, however, as they depend too much on the historical chronology of the destruction phase at Conimbriga. The series found in Britain may be as late as sixth century, taking account of Mediterranean evidence. To be wrong about Conimbriga is, anyway, to be wrong about Britain, as the later series at Conimbriga indicates that it was part of the same network which was bringing the wares to Britain.

Thomas, in his 1981 study, drew attention to the previous occurrence of ARS in Britain (Thomas 1981b, 4). This importation clearly ceased a century or more before the sub-Roman importations began, however, and their greatest concentration is in south-east Britain (Bird 1977). Forms 2, 3, 5, 6, 8, 9, 23, 32, 48, 50, 52 and 67 are the earlier types represented and are totally exclusive of the early medieval British group. As they most likely indicate overland distribution through Europe, any suggestion of a connection between these and the later finds of ARS may therefore be discounted. Fulford dismissed this possibility as long ago as 1979 (Fulford 1979, 127-8). There are, likewise, amphorae of Classes 45 and 49 in late Roman Britain, but these are in a clear eastern British province and their progress to Britain is traceable overland through eastern Gaul/Germany (Peacock 1977, 295-300; map in Peacock and Williams 1986, 189).

At the Carthage Avenue du Président Habib Bourguiba site, in the horizon c.375-450 AD, Classes 44, 45 and 49 are the predominant eastern Mediterranean types present. Eastern Mediterranean types only account for 8% of amphorae found. ARS is extremely common in that horizon. By the 475-500 horizon, however, 24% of the amphorae found are eastern Mediterranean in origin: Class 44 being the most common, but half of the total being of 45, 49 and Palestinian types. In the c.475-500-533 horizon this eastern Mediterranean proportion remains the same, but with 45, 49 and Palestinian types declining, and 43 becoming more common. Class 44 also increases. PRS type 3 is also present for the first time around 500 (Fulford and Peacock 1984, 260). The c.475-500-533 bracket is thus statistically a close parallel with the combined British assemblages, with the weight upon the post 500 period. There must be no doubt that the majority of voyages to Britain fall into this range. If the types of wares which were commonest at an earlier date were part of earlier shiploads we must assume that they would be commoner in the British assemblages. They are not.

We will now turn to the dateable tablewares. The dates for all of these have undergone some revision on the basis of the analysis of the material from Carthage. The British finds of ARS are now all more likely to fall between c.475 and 550 AD. Previously, forms such as A103 and 104 had been dated to the later fifth century, on account of the supposed desertion of the Conimbriga site, following a destruction phase which was identified with the 465-8 date provided by chronicle evidence (see above, 31). Of the Conimbriga pieces, forms 91 through 104 fall into a bracket c.500-550, with only forms 56, 67 and 76 being possibly earlier (and 76 can be as late as c.500). Fulford has indeed noted that most of the commonest fifth century forms are absent from Conimbriga (Fulford and Peacock 1984, 114). Form 84, however, is found elsewhere in Portugal. This is generally thought to be fifth century, though its absence in any quantity from Carthage means that dates are less readily refinable. The later Conimbriga material mostly falls into a markedly similar range to the British and Irish pieces and is separated from earlier ARS distributions in Iberia by nearly the entirety of the fifth century. Class 44 amphorae, moreover, are found at Conimbriga, seeming to strengthen the parallel with the British assemblages (Keay 1984, 655). The overwhelming number of pieces are thus from forms consistent with the idea of an early to mid-sixth-century horizon. The A81 from Tintagel could, accordingly, be an erroneous identification and earlier forms from Conimbriga may be accounted residual from the earlier Portuguese *floruit* of ARS. The western sealanes assemblage of tablewares can easily be made consistent with the chronologically limited model thus postulated.

The chronological evidence seems to demonstrate that the sixth-century voyages to Portugal and Britain by Mediterranean ships constituted a very short episode. We may not completely deny the possibility of voyages, slightly earlier or later, which are lost to history because they did not carry pottery. The possibility of this is diminished, however, when we consider the ubiquity of pottery in Mediterranean enterprise over a much wider period. It might be argued that coin, likewise, is ubiquitous and not found in Britain. The movement of coin, however, is far more subject to regulation than the movement of pottery. Ireland and western Britain did not use coin anyway (the possible finds of Byzantine coins in Ireland should be

ARS forms found on British and Portuguese Sites, New Dates from Carthage (page references are to Fulford and Peacock 1984):

Form (after Thomas 1981b)	Earliest Floruit
104c.	500 (pp. 73 &109) c.525-
103B	c.500 c.500-75.
99	c.500 (pp.71) c.525-35 ditto Conimbriga
96	c.525-75 (pp. 69)
91C	525-550 (pp. 63-5)
81	Early 5th.
67	360—425-50 (Can be confused with 103)

(PRS Form C latest: c.530—(Fulford and Peacock 1984, 87)

discounted as their context does not prove contemporary importation: Bateson 1976, 177-8). We can also emphasise the consistency of the evolving model for the contacts which are demonstrated by the ceramic evidence, with the British finds being a clear extension of a larger ceramic assemblage in Portugal, which is itself again an extension of a larger western Mediterranean assemblage.

Having established the chronological basis of the ceramic finds, we will see how we may fit this evidence into the historical context of the sixth century, before proceeding to reconstruct the voyages and cargoes involved. The eastern Mediterranean element in the western Mediterranean is a quantifiable intrusion, running parallel with, and slightly preceding, the increasing eastern presence of the era of Justinian (Pentz 1992, 1-7). The considerable historical implications of this activity for the understanding of Justinian's Reconquest are beyond the scope of this study to explore. The underexplored evidence for Byzantine interest in Britain during this period, however, certainly seems relevant to the study of these wares, as Fulford (1989) has highlighted.

Most attempts to find literary witness to this Byzantine-British connection have focussed on an episode in the *Life of St John the Almsgiver*, of which rather too much has been made. The episode occurs in a seventh-century (post 641) hagiography of St John of Alexandria (trans. Dawes and Baynes 1948, 216-18: ed. Delehaye, *Analecta Bollandiana* 45, 30-33, but Dawes and Baynes use a broader range of recensions). The story concerns a sea-captain 'fallen upon evil days' to whom St John gave a ship of the church and a cargo of twenty thousand bushels of grain (Dawes and Baynes 1948, 216). The ship, a *δρόμον*, 'runner' (ed. Delehaye, *Analecta Bollandiana* 45, 31), was blown by a violent tempest and after twenty days reached Britain, where there was a great famine. The *πρώτος τῆς πόλεως* ('chief man of the city') then offered the captain one nomisma for each bushel, or a return cargo of tin (*κασσίτερον*: ed. Delehaye, *Analecta Bollandiana* 45, 32). The tin was accepted, but when the sea captain returned to the Mediterranean he found that the tin had miraculously become silver (Dawes and Baynes 1948, 218).

This story is obviously literary in tone and frequent selective use of its detail at face value has been unjustified. In a text of this type it is not unreasonable to have a ship being driven to a far off place by storm, with minimal reference to actual geography, so this motif certainly has no power to suggest how Britain and the eastern Mediterranean actually came into contact again in this period. The idea that British people would have coin to exchange is anachronistic. The text is also frequently misquoted: it does not suggest trade with Galicia, as Lewis claims (1978, 146) and does not describe how 'the fleets of the patriarchs of Alexandria sailed to Cornwall in the early seventh century'! (Brown 1971, 156).

The story also has an obvious antecedent. In Herodotus is the well-known story of Colaeus of Samos, who was struck by an east wind while en route from the Aegean to Alexandria and ended up being blown through the Straits of Gibraltar to Tartessus. From here he brought back a valuable cargo which enriched him and the people of Thera (Herodotus, *Histories* IV.152, ed. Godley 1926, 352-3). The similarity of these stories makes it very likely that Herodotus has influenced Leontius. This does not affect the possibility that Britain and tin were synonymous in the discourse of Byzantine literate culture. It further underscores the point, however, that our accounts of Atlantic Europe are usually deeply interwoven with early Classical detail concerning the Atlantic, which often passes the notice of readers looking only from a medieval perspective. Stephanos of Alexandria (floruit 610-640) talks of *ἡ βρεττανίκη μετταλος*, which must have been a commonplace for tin (Penhallurick 1986, 10). Whether this is informed by Classical or more recent knowledge is not clear, but is worth remembering that Leontius and Stephanos would have been men of book learning. Taken in conjunction, however, the two sources do indicate a discourse in which tin was seen as a British product, around a century after real Byzantine ventures may have been reaching Cornwall. If 'British metal' was a literary commonplace for tin in the Byzantine world, as a legacy at least of Classical knowledge, we should not rule out the possibility that such discourse may even have *inspired* the initial idea of Byzantine voyages to Britain.

Another set of references can be partly explained as derivative of Classical writings, and in other respects as imaginative, but they still raise more significant questions of Byzantine interest in Britain. One statement in the *Anekdota* of Procopius is plain enough at first sight:

> Toὺς δὲ βαρβάρους ἅπαντας οὐδένα ἀνεὶς καιρὸν χρήμασιν ἐδωρεῖτο μεγάλοις ἑῴους τε καὶ ἑσπερίους πρός τε ἄρκτον καί μεσημβρίαν, ἄχρι ἐς τούς ἐν Βρεττανίαις ᾠκημένους
>
> (He [Justinian] never ceased pouring out great gifts of money to all the barbarians, both those of the East and those of the West, and those of the North and to the South, as far as the inhabitants of Britain: Procopius, *Anekdota* XIX.13, ed. & trans. Dewing, Vol. 6, 232-3).

Britain here is clearly cited in a superlative sense, to emphasise an outstanding folly of Justinian. The fact that it is the only location explicitly cited in this passage, however, is significant. From archaeological analysis we can now (*contra* Thompson 1980a, 505) be much surer that voyages to Britain could have been taking place, at least only a few decades prior to Procopius' account. There are, however, various problems with equating the episodes in his texts with the actual voyages. Some obvious points of detail may be noted. The *Anekdota* specifies the sending of money offshore and the contact which brought in the pottery was evidently anumismatic. While Procopius may be generalising here, we must set this detail in the context of the real concern in eastern Europe and Asia regarding inflation, through the flow of currency offshore (Lewis 1978). The detail of 'money' most likely suggests the sending of tribute to England, where money was valued, rather than Celtic Britain, but the possibility that the contents of the amphorae may have been a corresponding non-monetary tribute, to an anumismatic zone should not be ruled out.

In the context of his writings, the information Procopius gives regarding Britain is small in quantity, and at best confused, but its context suggests that it occupied a greater degree of his attention than the quantity of data given might suggest. As Thompson (1980a, 504-5) observes, Procopius' discussion of Britain in *Gothic Wars* VIII.20 takes the form of a lengthy digression in a discussion primarily concerning eastern affairs (also see Ward 1968), though we may not go so far as Thompson does (1980a, 504) in imagining Procopius stopping in mid-pen stroke, as it were to include some 'hot news' from the north. Procopius makes reference to actual persons who had been to north-western Europe in a passage concerning how the souls of the dead are ferried from the continent to *Brittia*, which he notes was common knowledge in Constantinople because of the presence there of people who had actually taken part in this activity (Procopius, *Bellum Gothicum* VIII.20, ed. Dewing 1914-35, Vol. 1, 252-3). There is not a lot which can be made of such a fantastic story, but the *Anekdota* reference to barbarians 'streaming from all the Earth into Byzantium' (Procopius, *Anekdota* XIX.14, ed. & trans. Dewing 1914-35, Vol. 6, 232) supports the argument that there was considerable mid-sixth century communication between northern Europe and Constantinople (Thompson 1980a, 505). That the *Brittia* reference describes activity focusing on the Rhineland, however, may probably indicate that these travellers have come down the Danube, rather than their being mariners who had made the voyage along the western sealanes.

More pertinent is the general interest in Britain evinced in Byzantine sources. We are told that Belisarius offered Britain to the Goths:

> 'καὶ ἡμεὶς δὲ Γόθους Βρεττανίαν ὅλην ξυχωροῦμεν ἔχειν, μείζω τὲ παρὰ πολὺ Σικελίας οὖσαν καὶ 'Ρωυαίων κατήκοον το ἀνεκαθεν γεγενημένην
>
> 'And we on our side permit the Goths to have the whole of Britain, which is much larger than Sicily and was subject to the Romans in early times' (Procopius, *Bellum Gothicum* VI.6, ed. & trans. Dewing 1914-35, Vol. 3, 344-5).

This comment, reflecting a rather unrealistic offer perhaps, may demonstrate a real future intent to conquer Britain on the part of the Byzantine forces. In this case we might regard the voyages which brought in the amphorae as possibly being reconnaissance missions in the same way that Pytheas's seems have been for Alexandrian interests, around nine centuries before. Trade and geographical investigation play a direct role in the expansion of imperial complexes and, confronted with such historical and archaeological evidence for a direct Byzantine interest, however slight the evidence may be, this possibility must remain in our minds. In general we may note that the Byzantine role in Northern affairs is worthy of more attention. The comparability between Byzantine burials and some royal graves in Anglo-Saxon England and Francia have long been noted, but insufficiently explored (see, for a timely reminder, Whitehouse 1992, 123). The western British connection is earlier in date, and more direct, but the principal point is simply that Britain was very much within what the Byzantine authorities regarded as their sphere of interest—a point sometimes lost upon western medievalists, by whom the Greek-speaking eastern empire is often treated as a separate matter.

Western sources also imply eastern Mediterranean maritime links, this time with Atlantic Spain. Of particular interest are the *Vitas Sanctorum Patrum Emeretensium*, written near Mérida around the 630s, and supposedly concerning events c.560-600. In the *Vitas* eastern Mediterranean merchants visit Mérida in eastern ships. *Negotiatores graecos in navibus de orientibus* are described as coming to the coast of Spain *(advenisse atque Hispaniae litora contigisse)* and thence to Mérida *(Vitas Sanctorum Patrum Emeretensium* IV.32, ed. Garvin 1946, 168). Whether the merchants came by land or by water from the coast is not specified. It is probable that they sailed up the Guadiana, however, as Mérida had been a river port in the Roman period and doubtless continued to be so (Collins 1980, 203-4). Considering the geographical obstacles to an overland journey from the Mediterranean, there can be no question that these merchants had travelled from the Atlantic coast, having first negotiated the Straits of Gibraltar. It is pleasing to note that 'merchants' rather than simply seafarers are specified and that they are said unequivocally to be of eastern Mediterranean origin. The text may be reasonably accepted as describing a state of affairs remembered in the region—being written locally and so soon after the events described. The fact that 'Greek merchants' are described as having entered the western sealanes must have implications for our interpretation of eastern Mediterranean artefacts on Atlantic sites in Spain, Portugal and Britain and might allow us further to assume that the voyages which brought them there were often mercantile in character and involved not middlemen but actual Greek *negotiatores.* The British finds might of course be secondary distributions from Spain or Portugal. The archaeological evidence suggests otherwise, however, as will be explored below.

In *De Viris Illustribus*, Isidore describes St Martin of Braga's journey to Galicia:

> Martinus, Dumiensis monasterii sanctissimus pontifex, ex Orientis partibus navigans, in Gallaeciam venit.
>
> (Martin, saintly priest of the monastery of Dumium, sailed out of eastern parts, and came to Galicia: *De Viris Illustribus* XXXV, ed. Migne, *PL* 83, 1100).

We know from Gregory of Tours that Martin was a Pannonian by birth and that he left Pannonia to visit the sacred places of the east *(nam hic Pannoniae ortus fuit, et exinde ad visitanda loca sancta in Oriente properans: HF* V.37, ed. Krusch 1885a, 243). This might imply that these were the 'eastern parts' from which he came to Galicia, rather than Pannonia itself. It seems, however, that Isidore is ignorant of Martin's exact origins so 'out of the east' (which might include Pannonia) is perhaps all the phrase can be taken to indicate. Gregory of Tours also states unequivocally that Martin travelled by sea to Galicia *(De Virtutibus Sancti Martini* I.12, ed. Krusch 1885b, 144-6). Gregory wrote after 573, so we may presume the events of Martin's voyage from the east are as early as the 560s: Isidore would suggest sometime in the reign of 'Theodemir', c.551-565 (for the problems of dating this episode, Thompson 1980b, 83ff). The two writers, then, are in agreement that Martin voyaged out of the Mediterranean to Galicia and that this event occurred in Gregory's case only a decade or so before he wrote, and in Isidore's a little over half a century. This combined testimony, so close to the event, must carry some weight as evidence. The fact that the two writers do not name the same king at the time or tell quite the same story might be seen as reason to treat this episode as of doubtful reliability. On the other hand, the fact that they do not agree on every detail assures us of the independence of the two accounts, to which we might add the considerable evidence of Gregory's knowledge of Gaulish travels to Galicia and the fact that he definitely met one traveller from Galicia (see below, 57).

In conclusion to this survey of the possible literary relations of the voyages indicated by the ceramic evidence, we may conclude that the episode of Martin of Braga's voyage need not be slotted into the same model as the Mediterranean wares. An exceptionally important character may well charter a ship for an unusual voyage. The details of the *Vitas Patrum Emeretensium* and of Procopius, however, seem to indicate a Byzantine interest in the western sealanes which is wholly relevant to the ceramic evidence and suggests that the activity may have both commercial and political impetus behind it. The problem in this case remains one of causation. The British and Irish finds may be explained as a simple enough extension of the growth of Byzantine activity in the Western Mediterranean in the early sixth century. The focus on the story in Leontius has tended to obscure the sound evidence for Byzantine connections as far as Atlantic Spain and Portugal, from where Britain is nowhere near as exotic a destination as it may be from the Levant. This does not, however, explain why ships went as far as Britain. Atlantic Spain may still have been linked with Mediterranean trade patterns. To reach Britain, on the other hand, involved a voyage across the open sea, as well as possible language barriers. We will return to this point below.

It first must be considered whether the specific mechanics of the voyages themselves and the vessels and locations involved can be reconstructed. Can we consider that the Mediterranean wares all were imported as part of definable cargoes and can we safely assume that their context on the Atlantic sealanes is as a regular extension of Mediterranean distributions? A great deal of debate has surrounded our ability to quantify the activity involved and adapt it to shipping and cargo models.

Alcock, Thomas, Campbell and the author have all discussed the amphora finds in comparison with the shipwreck at Yassi Ada in Turkey, drawing differing conclusions as to its comparability. This ship was a Byzantine cargo ship, with a cargo of some 900 amphorae of mostly classes 43 and 44, though these are later types than those found on British sites and the shipwreck's date of around 625 AD is at least a century later than the *floruit* of the British finds. The usefulness of this shipload of similar amphorae in providing a model for the interpretation of the British finds was appreciated two decades ago (L. Olson, *pers. comm.)*, but detailed discussion of the shipwreck waited upon full publication of the finds and it has been further slowed by the fact that Bass researched the comparative forms seemingly without reference to the work being done by Peacock, Fulford and Williams.

Alcock, Thomas and Campbell all, for differing reasons, accept a lower level of compatibility between the Yassi Ada model and the British assemblages than will be argued here, their doubts based on what they see as a greater variety of forms seen among the British finds than is found in the Yassi Ada assemblage. This leads Alcock and Campbell to conclude that the amphorae arriving in Britain are part of diverse cargoes, rather than a small number of concentrated shiploads of amphorae, while it leads Thomas to assert that a small number of very mixed shiploads of amphorae were arriving. It will be suggested here that the diversity at Yassi Ada is probably underestimated. It is also likely that the above scholars misinterpret each other on the point at which the British assemblage is more diverse than the Yassi Ada, namely, whether the diversity is between the types (i.e. class 43, 44, etc.) or the sub-types present—i.e. different decoration forms, sizes, etc.

Alcock has expressed the strongest doubt that the imports are part of regular Mediterranean cargoes (Alcock 1987, 90-3). His interpretation is based in part upon comparisons with the cargo composition of the shipwreck from Yassi Ada. The predominance of the Classes 43 and 44 at Yassi Ada argues for a basically comparable cargo to those which went to Britain, where Classes 43 and 44 make up 90% of identifiable amphora finds. There are differences. In Britain Class 43 makes up around 35% of total finds and Class 44, 54%. At Yassi Ada the ratio is 12%:71%. There may be good reason not to overemphasise the similarities, as the Yassi Ada voyage is a century later and working within the east. Nonetheless, its comparability as a mixed, bulk cargo of amphorae, made up of predominantly two types, the same as predominate in Britain, seems compelling.

Alcock, however, considers the wide range of forms *within* these two classes displayed by the combined British and Irish assemblage to differ from the model provided by Yassi Ada. The Yassi Ada assemblage contains a limited range of variants of Classes 43 and 44 (Bass and Van Doorninck 1982, 156-9), but Bass's analysis of the Yassi Ada amphorae identifies different forms of each class. Most of his analysis is conducted by sample, however, rather than quantification and this alone may obscure some of the variety present. In the sample which he has published, however, there is certainly variety to be observed. The class 44 types vary between 50.5 and 41.1 cm. in height, with considerable range in mouth and shoulder size, and varying proportion in the spacing of the ribbing (Bass and Van Doorninck 1982, 157). Six published illustrations in Bass' report show principal variant forms. Class 43 amphorae exhibit a similar range of variation in height (Bass and Van Doorninck 1982, 159). Decoration of the latter is much more standardised, with the majority (fifty out of a sample of eighty) having a single band of decoration around the shoulder (as do the British types). Still, some vessels have marked variation in shape and decoration (Bass' sub-type *2b:* Bass and Van Doorninck 1982, 156-7). The question is, then, whether this variety in form is of the order of that which Alcock has noted amongst the British finds. Firstly, it should be noted that Alcock's histogram for the British finds matches Bass' figures for class 43 quite closely, where the majority are of one form: Bass' sub-type *2a* (with the band of decoration around the collar). This is the ubiquitous form on British and Irish sites. The class 44 comparison, however, is the crucial one. The principal basis for determining variant forms that the present writer can discern amongst the British finds is decoration (e.g. the distribution of bands and other markings on the body of vessels). The decorative range at Yassi Ada in this respect seems as great as that in Britain. The class 44 finds at Yassi Ada are far more varied than the class 43. Again the evidence of Yassi Ada and the British/Irish assemblage is superficially consistent. Alcock *(pers. comm.)* explains his concern as being that while the variety in the British assemblage is no greater than in Bass's series, the same range is seen in a very much smaller number of finds in Britain. If this is so, only a very full publication of the Tintagel material is likely to clarify this problem to the point where comparisons can be made with Yassi Ada. The obvious difference in period between Yassi Ada and the British finds must be noted—perhaps standardisation increased across time. But more likely the context of the Yassi Ada find would explain greater standardisation, with the amphorae on board coming from a probable Black Sea kiln, where the variety of forms was more limited.

Thomas is inclined toward the opposite of Alcock's view: that the forms of Classes 43 and 44 in the British assemblage demonstrate that the wares formed the cargo of at most one or two ships, though he endorses Alcock's argument concerning the variety present (Thomas 1988a, 12). It seems, however, that he appreciates Alcock's argument as stressing the variety of types (i.e. class 43, 44 etc.) present and not the variety *within* types, so this agreement may be based on a misapprehension (it is noticeable that Thomas does not cite Bass directly).

> The close similarity in the vessels, notably among the B amphorae, found at all these sites suggest that they may have formed a single cargo. If so, it was a mixed bag, put together for potential customers to whom the absence of a homogeneous batch or order was not a point of any relevance (Thomas 1988a, 12).

Thomas thus seems to see the basic classes as fairly uniform in their British occurrence (with which I would concur), but the substantial presence of Class 45, 49, 34 and miscellaneous types as the point of departure from the Yassi Ada model. This is certainly true: though there are types other than Class 43 and 44 at Yassi Ada, they are in much lower proportion than in Britain. In the light of the Carthage assemblage and its evidence, we may see the Atlantic voyages as occurring at a time when earlier amphora types were giving way to classes 43 and 44 in international exchange. Hence the half-dozen or more classes present may be accounted to this overlap, the transition having ceased at the time of Yassi Ada (where, anyway, we would not expect the African additions to the cargo). We must not overlook the chronological and regional difference of Yassi Ada in its use as a model for comparison.

Some further features of the diversity of the Yassi Ada assemblage should be appreciated. Other parts of the ship, especially the 'galley area' also contained a range of minor tablewares and miscellaneous amphora finds (Bass and Van Doorninck 1982, 184). One of these (P79), interestingly enough, was a class 43 of the standard sixth-century type found in Britain. Another (P74) is a class 45 (Bass and Van Doorninck 1982, 184). Clearly such amphorae, not carried as a principal cargo, could remain in use for a century or more beyond their general *floruit*. Another area of interest is the discovery of reworked amphora sherds at Yassi Ada which were found to constitute stoppers for the standard cargo amphorae (Bass and Van Doorninck 1982, 160-1). Generally these were of the same fabrics as the amphorae themselves and were sealed in with pitch or resin. The writer can recall having seen such pieces among the British assemblages in the past (without realising their significance). At least one is published, a Class 44 disc from Congresbury in Somerset (Rahtz 1974, 110, Fig. 3, no. 20). This roughly worked piece, some 7 cm. in diameter compares very closely with the Yassi Ada pieces, which average between 5 and 7 cms in diameter. This evidence, it should be noted, again reinforces the idea that the insular amphorae assemblages are consistent with normal Mediterranean cargoes. An amphora at Congresbury clearly arrived with its stopper in place (hence with its contents, likewise), the stopper not being of an easily reinsertable type. In a few cases such residual use of old amphorae, and amphora sherds as stoppers, might partly explain variety amongst the decorative forms on British finds. These finds are also of obvious importance in site chronology. Where the stoppers are found they are a likely indicator of the first opening of the amphorae, which may well have had a residual use as storage jars. The stoppers, sealed in with wax, would not have been amenable to easy access and hence are less likely to have remained in use for such secondary purposes. Alcock has noted a repaired amphora in the assemblage at Cadbury (Alcock 1995, 84), which would have been unable to hold liquid—though it is not clear whether this repair was previous or subsequent to its being brought to Britain. He is right to stress, however, that dry goods might equally have been carried in such a container even in Mediterranean contexts.

Campbell, also, does not accept that the Yassi Ada model is appropriate to the British evidence. He cites the existence of other Mediterranean shipwrecks where such pottery is found as a much more minor element of cargoes (Campbell 1996 forthcoming; Parker 1984, 99-114). If we are to follow these views we might be looking at dozens of voyages. One can only say that the narrowness of date range of the tablewares must be appreciated here and that the amphora types do not range so widely in form as to suggest a long period of activity. If a dozen or more voyages were involved, they span no more than a few decades. Such maximal views must also be considered in their broader context. It is more natural in archaeological terms to err on the side of assuming plurality, which may be contrasted with the reductionist tendency of historians (see below, 81), but the archaeological views do not exist in a vacuum. The desire to see sustained contact with the east may reflect unease at the notion that the voyages could have no significant cultural impact. This will be discussed further below.

Alcock strongly questions our ability to quantify the cargoes: especially to minimise the activity on quantitative grounds. Calculating from on site experience, he estimates that the recovery rate of vessels might be less than 0.2% (Alcock and Alcock 1990, 138-9). We should concur with Alcock (Alcock and Alcock 1990, 138-9) that on-site experience inclines to the view that most Class 43 vessels are represented archaeologically by one or two sherds only, though he observes that at odd sites, such as Dinas Powys (to which we may add Derrynaflan, where the sherds were concentrated in a ditch: R. Ó Flóinn, *pers. comm.)* most of the sherds come from one vessel. This, as he himself observes, makes a contrast with attempts to estimate site frequency from sherd numbers through application of statistical methods at selected British sites (Alcock and Alcock 1990, 138-9).

The question is obviously a matter which requires that we measure the number of vessels recovered (regardless of the number of sherds) and compare this to the relative quality and quantity of excavation area, but such things can only be measured in impressionistic terms, as we will see. We might start by taking the Yassi Ada total as a model to estimate quantities from: 900 amphorae. The current British total of classes 43 and 44 is, at a rough estimate, around 160 vessels (Thomas 1988a, 12; updating Thomas 1981b, 10-13; also recent finds from Derrynaflan and Whithorn). This is around 18% of a ship's cargo, using Yassi Ada as a model. If we remove from these figures the large totals from Tintagel and Congresbury the total for the remaining sites is around 65, or 7.2 % of a cargo divided among some 30 sites. Postulating then that we might have found as much as 60%, say, of the total material at Congresbury and Tintagel, we will postulate a figure of 70-80 vessels for these two sites combined, or around 8% of a cargo. Superficially, then, the evidence does not yet preclude the single-ship model. On the other hand, however, Thomas estimates that the scale of excavation at Tintagel may be as low as 10% of the potential area, which would justify the conservatism of Alcock's estimate. Whether all areas will produce the scale of material so far found is debatable. The area excavated by Radford on the island is outside of the early medieval settlement area—which recent research would suggest lies directly under the castle. Radford's site may be a rubbish dump for the main settlement. On the other hand, amphora sherds seem to have been found in every recent excavation on the site. The fact that these have become increasingly focused on more likely sites of activity, such as the harbour (Bowman 1991, 23) and the churchyard (Novakowski and Thomas 1990, 1-4, 14-15) only slightly diminishes the ubiquity of the material in discovery patterns.

No evidence as to quantity so far gives reason to imagine that any site in the north of the Irish Sea basin will produce finds on the same scale as those in the south, though the finding of four different classes (43, 44, 45 and 49) at Whithorn is intriguing. Many of the Cornish finds have been only been surface finds of stray vessels. The unexcavated sites which produced these may produce large totals. But we should also note the increasingly broad range of its distribution. The accompanying distribution map (p. 44) shows the sites and proportions of wares so far excavated (a distinction is not made between individual types in view of the fact, as explained above, that the wares are likely to be contemporary and different cargoes are probably not distinguishable from different selections of types). Finds from Clogher (Co. Tyrone), Cashel (Bennett 1994, 73) and Derrynaflan (Co. Tipperary) Inishcealtra (Co. Clare), Baile na bhFionnúrach (Co. Kerry—1994 find sighted by the author), Dumbarton (Dumbartonshire) and the recent find of several vessels at Whithorn (Wigtownshire), have extended the distribution markedly in the last decade. The distribution still seems to be focused on the Irish Sea, however, with only relatively small quantities coming from inland sites such as Cashel, Derrynaflan and Inishcealtra, but with larger totals from waterside or near-coastal sites such as Dalkey Island and Whithorn (though the latter two sites, it must be noted, were larger scale excavations than the former). The northern end of the Irish Sea also has clearly fewer than the south. This might be good grounds for not following Thomas in considering the more northerly finds as part of the voyage of a Mediterranean ship (Thomas 1988a, 20). It seems as likely that they are more local redistribution from the south-west, upon which the distribution clearly centres. Brittany is another question. A definite piece of Class 44 amphorae has been found at Île Lavret, Brêhat (Giot and Querre 1985, 95-7) and this must give pause. The idea of a voyage into the Channel mouth is supportable by finds as far west as High Peak and Bantham in Devon (the latter clearly a coastal trading site to which the finds did not travel overland: Fox 1955; Pollard 1966). The early medieval archaeology of Brittany is so poorly known that major find sites must not be ruled out.

What cargoes were involved? Two models of commerce must first be considered. If *negotiatores* were regularly pushing into the Atlantic, the idea that a few ships might proceed on a speculative voyage to Britain is plausible. Such a trip might have brought back any suitable cargo. The second model, usually taken for granted in discussions of this topic, is the idea that Britain was singled out as a destination: the core of the return cargo being alluvial tin, melted into ingots. This heavyweight cargo would be a logical replacement for the full amphorae. Evidence for early medieval tin-working in Cornwall has been mustered by Penhallurick in his recent, comprehensive, survey. Collation of these data, however, does not bring immediate rewards for those seeking to tie the Mediterranean imports to tin-working areas. But if we follow Thomas in extending analysis to take in all areas worked in antiquity, rather than the one or two definite early-medieval sites out of a potentially much larger number, we may conclude that more than one potential landing place of the Mediterranean wares was close to tin working sites (Thomas 1988a, 14). Ingots of worked tin are attested in early medieval contexts, at Prah Sands giving radiocarbon dates to the seventh century (Penhallurick 1986, 234).

Are there other likely export goods? Campbell suggests other metals, citing in particular traces of British lead from Carthage (Campbell 1996 forthcoming), but presumably these could be recycled from the Roman period. We should accept his point, however, that tin is not the only possible element, and any supplementary goods may be carried once a major cargo has rendered the voyage profitable, even if they are goods that are available more close to home. Goods such as honey or leather are also possible and quite able to survive intact a voyage of a couple of months. Anyway some goods might be sold on the return journey, not carried all the way back to the eastern Mediterranean. The ships may indeed have 'tramped' their way back.

Of the outward cargoes we should note the Yassi Ada example, where the cargo space is dominated by the amphorae and their contents. This contrasts with the small proportion of the cargo space which the Gaulish ceramics of the seventh century would have occupied in any ship. Even so, heavy goods might not have been the most valuable element in the cargo. The amphorae may have been a ballast for a valuable cargo of spices, or other valuable goods of light weight.

What was in the amphorae? The usual conclusions are wine (classes 43 and 45) and oil (class 44). Residue analyses on Mediterranean examples are only at an early stages (Condamin 1976; Hartgroves and Walker 1988, 26-7), however, and nuts, fish sauce, even nails, are all possible. Gregory of Tours records wine of Gaza being brought to the west (*HF* VII.45, ed. Krusch 1885a, 348)—the amphorae of class 45 are often linked with this traffic. One presumes a market for wine could be found. Oil, however, is not even listed as a likely ship's cargo in the commentaries on the *Muirbretha* (see below, 68-70), so we may need to consider it less likely.

The economic basis of the activity is another vexed question. The presence of Greek merchants at Mérida might make entrepreneurial trade plausible, though we may doubt that Mediterranean entrepreneurs had any advance knowledge as to the sorts of surplus that potentates in western Britain and Ireland might use to pay for imported luxuries. Perhaps the initial motivation was not trade at all, but attempts to secure allegiance from the northern neighbours of the Franks. We must remain completely open-minded on this point. We cannot be sure that the ships were manned by Greeks, only that they had been loaded in the eastern Mediterranean. The various excavations around the Mediterranean are bringing to light possible parallels to the graffiti and dipinti on the western sealanes amphora finds. These may in time tell us something of the ethnicity of the traders (Bass and Van Doorninck 1982, 161-2; Thomas 1981b, 13-14; Fulford and Peacock 1984, 141-54). It is fair to say that the presence of both Latin and Greek in these might be seen to detract from the homogeneity model suggested above. On the other hand, we have little or no knowledge of the mixture of races which might be in a Byzantine ship's crew, let alone among stevedores. Modern ship's crews are frequently international in mix and we should note the evidence of eastern Mediterranean graffiti on the Gaulish ship from Fos-sur-Mer (*World Atlas of Archaeology* 1985, 110). Thomas concludes that the medium of communication between the merchants and their customers must have been Vulgar Latin. The Latin graffiti may be seen as adding weight to this, though we perhaps should not follow Thomas in highlighting the incidence of sites with Latin memorials and other Christian remains as being more likely landing points (Thomas 1988a, 19-21).

There seems no doubt that the ship/s which reached the Atlantic had travelled from a base in the eastern Mediterranean, with only a stop in Africa where it/they took on more goods, without unloading the principal cargo. If the goods had been transhipped to other vessels, we would expect a greater admixture of types, including African amphorae—though a few of these may be present (Hartgroves and Walker 1988, 24-5). A voyage from the Aegean or Alexandria represents a voyage in the vicinity of some 5,000 kilometres (10,000 for a return trip). The voyage may have been accomplished in more than one sailing season, though we may make a case for a voyage over a single season being more than possible. At 2.5-3 knots average speed the return journey would take not much less than 3 months sailing time, allowing for short stops, but not for a longish stay in Britain to change cargoes. As has been discussed above, the high proportion of eastern Mediterranean ceramic vessels in the insular assemblage gives us no reason to suppose that the major cargoes of the ships were exchanged *en route,* though clearly more goods were taken on in North Africa, or some other place in receipt of African wares.

Reynolds has commented on the small quantity of eastern Mediterranean wares in Valencia, including an absence of PRS (Reynolds 1984, 474-5) during its sixth century *floruit,* while noting the regularity of imports of African amphorae (Reynolds 1984, 475) from the third through sixth centuries (Simon Loseby, *pers. comm.*, has noted a similar pattern at Marseilles). This may provide some clues as to routes of voyages. Southern Spain naturally enough looks to Africa, which is part of the same trading province. A ship coming east from Constantinople, however, and perhaps looking for a market away from the main catchment of African products, need not be expected to have travelled as far north as Valencia, whereas PRS is found at Alicante (Reynolds 1984, 475), which would tally with a voyage taking a direct route to the south of the Balearics (the direct route to Valencia is obstructed by the latter islands). Currents of around 1-3 knots along the southern shore of the Mediterranean favour only an eastern voyage, so on its outward leg a vessel would more likely follow the northern shore westward from Alicante. African coarsewares from Tintagel suggest that a landfall in Tunisia was almost certain *en route*. Some delay would be likely here, however, as the possibility of a favourable exit wind from Tunisia in May-September is less than 10% for a vessel travelling westward. The frequent easterly winds *(Levanter)* from Spring through to Autumn, however, would favour the voyage westward into the straits.

The boundary between the Mediterranean world and the western sealanes is no arbitrary historical construct. A vessel seeking to enter the Atlantic faces a difficult voyage against an incoming surface current of around six knots. This current is the consequence of the small number of watercourses flowing into the Mediterranean, which replace less than 30% of the amount of water lost through evaporation. On the return voyage, both the current in the straits and along the southern shore of the Mediterranean would assist a quick passage homeward.

Once in the Atlantic, the prevailing winds from April onward are north-westerly until one is north of Galicia. As in the Mediterranean, these tend to be consistent through summer months, with the frequency of gales after April becoming very low indeed. Visibility is good in summer months, with cloud cover over Iberia being virtually non-existent. The coast is low-lying from north of Granada through to Galicia, however, which would make recognition of landfalls difficult. On the other hand, a vessel making a long tack away from land stands little danger of disorientation through losing sight of celestial marks.

Imported Mediterranean pottery in Portugal and western Spain suggests landfalls in the vicinity of the Tagus and Mondega. More specific landfalls are not yet known. Gregory of Tours and Isidore of Seville also suggest a voyage by Martin of Braga from the Mediterranean to Galicia, which in this era might indicate either the north or west coasts of Iberia, even perhaps the Duoro estuary.

No evidence exists that the vessels put in to shore anywhere between Iberia and Cornwall. We have already looked at potential political reasons for this, with Byzantine interests excluding the Franks. Some maritime support for this exclusion may also exist in the fact that an exit wind from the Bay of Biscay is below 30% likelihood for a vessel travelling north, and the bay is notorious for storms. Local knowledge in Galicia presumably included an understanding of the route required to cross the Bay of Biscay and of the Ushant landfall as a landmark *en route*. It is difficult to imagine mariners undertaking a voyage directly to Britain all the way out of sight of land and it is doubtful that intellectual knowledge of the orientation of the landmasses was accurate enough to make this possible (see above, 24). The Admiralty Pilot warns that 'The NW coast of Brittany.. is encumbered by dangers' (Hydrographer 1974c, 26). These lie between 10 and 14 miles offshore and comprise reefs and islands. There is a particular danger of being set by the flood tide onto the shoals SE of Île d' Ouessant (Ushant). 'The area between Île d' Ouessant and the mainland SE is encumbered by islands, reefs and shoals, which it is imprudent to approach without local knowledge' (Hydrographer 1974c, 215). North of Galicia the chances of a fair wind in summer are around 60%, though this will tend to be south-westerly and may present problems for entering the Celtic Sea. For the return journey, the chances of a fair wind are only around 30%, increasing as one proceeds south of Cape Cornwall, but this, also, is inclined to be westerly.

A primary landfall in the Tintagel region seems certain. Others in Munster, Dyfed and Somerset are also possible. Whether these voyages went further north than the Celtic Sea is uncertain. Finds north of this point are scattered and may be attributable to secondary distribution. The Isles of Scilly are a quite likely first landfall. Apart from the archaeological evidence, the relatively weak tidal streams around the islands and consistent, if shallow, ground around them contrasts with the dangerous shoals and groundswell off Cape Cornwall. For a vessel proceeding from the south-west into the Celtic Sea, proximity to Cape Cornwall brings the danger of being driven into the Channel mouth. Again Scilly is a preferable landfall. Miller has suggested, however, that Munster was a landfall for ships from the south and this, too, has some of the same advantages (Miller 1978-80, 315). If we allow for the presence of more than one ship we need not consider that the same first landfall was made each time.

We may distinguish the maritime circumstances of the western part of the Bristol Channel from the east, which may explain the prominence of Tintagel in the distribution. West of Padstow, Lundy and St Govans the tidal streams are influenced by the set of the tide into the St George's Channel. The Admiralty Pilot also warns that between Cape Cornwall and Hartland Point:

> A groundswell is usually present and this renders the coast unsuitable for anchoring and makes access to the small inlets and harbours difficult and, at times, impracticable (Hydrographer 1974b, 27).

The Pilot advises that 'Land can safely be made between Hartland and Trevose' (Hydrographer 1974b, 31), though we should note that this is partly on account of the presence of modern lighthouses. The Pilot also recommends that Trevose Head (71 metres) is a good landfall, on account of its distinctive profile (Hydrographer 1974b, 27 & 31). In good weather this is visible from around 15-18 nautical miles. The surrounding country is lower, causing it to stand out. The headlands of the Rumps and Tintagel are also distinctive. The Pilot further highlights Tintagel church as a landmark (Hydrographer 1974b, 33). While the present church is only high medieval in date, we should note the evidence for earlier activity on the same site, especially the seeming burial ground from the 1990 excavations (Novakowski and Thomas 1990, 4 & 13). Along this stretch of coast the swell sets vessels SW toward the land, but the influence of groundswell seems to be less threatening. All of this does tally interestingly with the seeming selection of Tintagel as a major landfall. We should also take note of Sir Richard Grenville's positive assessment of the anchorage:

> this baye is all fayer sandy grounde good to ancor in and thear is neuer lesse then five fathoms of water at the loeste ebbe, shepes may ryed here all wyndes exsept the northewest (Thomas 1988d, 46).

The shoals 12 miles NW of Cape Cornwall would require a wide berth. On leaving Scilly, soon after high water, a vessel would face a tidal stream setting E. at first (+0130 —+0530 Dover) and then NE. (+0600 — -0500). Working the tides would thus be necessary along this stretch. At turn of tide a vessel heading east may face a SW (-0430 — -0030) tide (Hydrographer 1974d). At 2.5 knots Scilly to Padstow would take around 24 hours. We cannot discern whether voyages along this route would have travelled in stages, stopping in at land overnight, or would have taken the NE set of the tide to achieve an offing and not put in again until east of Padstow. The presence of Mediterranean pottery in the bays of Padstow and St Ives might imply landfalls at these points. These, only surface finds so far, may be secondary redistributions, however, perhaps from Tintagel itself. The imported Mediterranean wares are, anyway, so ubiquitous along this coast that there are many sites which may or may not be primary stopping places. On the other hand, it would be naive to assume that all such sites were primary stopping points for mariners without local knowledge. Further finds will hopefully clarify the picture. We should note, however, that both the major harbours on this coast are encumbered by shoals and groundswell which, while their size renders them valuable as harbours today, may not have made them attractive to early medieval vessels, apart from local traffic. The eminence to the north of St Ives has a medieval chapel, probably of the 'beacon' type (see above, 17), but it is not established whether there was earlier activity on this hill.

There is a danger of attributing a determinist role to simple maritime factors, without knowledge of the mariners' actual respect for such factors. Their influence in a case such as this, however, where the mariners are probably foreign to the region, is, accordingly, likely to be very high. We must suppose that a vessel from abroad making for Tintagel probably did not do so accidentally, hence a local pilot (obtained in Scilly?) or some local knowledge may have been involved. At this point we must ask: did the ship come to Tintagel because it was accessible, or because it was a distribution point for the desired product? If the desired product was tin, one presumes it could have been obtained elsewhere on the coast. The scatter of finds of Mediterranean imports along both coasts also suggests that the ships' cargoes could have found a receptive market elsewhere. A combination of factors is likely to be responsible, in which the maritime convenience of the site, almost entirely discounted by scholarship, is likely to have been a major factor.

Thomas' map of distributions from putative centres in the Bristol Channel is mostly very convincing (Thomas 1988a, 17). Tintagel is an inescapable choice. There must also be little question that all the Somerset finds are distributions from the north coast, with the quantities from Congresbury making a landfall in the Yeo estuary. The proximity of this point to Glamorgan, however, makes questionable whether there would need to be a separate progress to take in Dinas Powys.

At this point we may note that a primary voyage to the south-west is all that may be taken for granted. The contrast between the northern and southern occurrences within the Irish Sea basin is considerable. North of a Dublin/Gwynedd line, the wares occur exclusively upon sites which are politically in the highest category: Whithorn, Iona, Dumbarton and Clogher. In Cornwall, the context can be more humble: the very small enclosed site of Trethurgy and casual finds such as at St Michael Carhayes, St Ives and Padstow are not uncommon. This perhaps diminishes the likelihood of a voyage north of Dublin, and likely enough of a voyage north of Cornwall. Where goods are ubiquitous finds this suggests a ready availability. Where only very high status sites are in possession of such goods, the cargoes in question may be smaller scale. More will be said about these sites and their context in Irish Sea traffic in Chapter Seven, where comparisons with E ware and glass distributions may be brought to bear.

The scale of pottery finds in Britain and Ireland is now sufficient to make the single ship theory unlikely, though more than a few years of activity would also seem unlikely. This will be discussed further below. The most satisfactory model would be a few ships over a few years, maybe the same ship visiting a few times, or a few ships at one visit.

There is a great deal more to be learnt about this episode in sixth-century maritime exchange. We should note the following likely conclusions: that the voyages (we are safest in assuming more than one) were a short-lived episode of direct contact between the eastern Mediterranean and western Britain, exclusive of western Gaul. The causes remain a mystery, but the voyages *do* extend known distributions of eastern goods in the western Mediterranean and contemporary discourse shows Britain, rather than Gaul, may have preoccupied Byzantine interests.

The historical importance of the traffic (especially in establishing archaeological chronology) may not lie in it having any interventionist role in cultural development. Vague chronological parallels are sometimes made which hint at a desire to show a stronger physical impact at the British end than is really possible or necessary. Such cases include: associations with the spread of monasticism (Haseloff 1987, 45); bubonic plague (Morris 1965, 145-85: British and Irish outbreaks are, however, only recorded in chronicles which are likely to be derivative of foreign sources: *Mortalitas Magna in qua pausat Mailcun rex Genetodae, Annales Cambriae* s.a. 549, ed. Morris 1978, 85; *Mortalitas magna in qua isti pausant...*, AU s.a. 549, ed. MacNiocaill and Mac Airt 1983, 76-7) and even leprous human bones of from Tean, in Scilly (Thomas 1985, 198; Hart 1989, 261-9). Of the latter, which have been taken as the remains of an actual traveller from the Mediterranean, we should note, *contra* Thomas, that leprosy was not necessarily confined to the Mediterranean in the sixth century (AU s.a. 571, ed. MacNiocaill and Mac Airt, 1983, 86-7; Peate, 1974-6, 361-3; Gregory of Tours, *De Virtutibus Sancti Martini* I.11, ed. Krusch 1885b, 146; *Concilia Galliae* A. 511-A695, ed. de Clercq 1963, 156, 233).

The desire to see these long-distance links as explaining the spread of Christian culture, would seem to beg far more important questions than it answers. Neither the appearance, nor disappearance, of these links should be in any way attributed with a major impact upon society or economy, in view of their potentially limited nature. At best they dissuade us from seeing Britain and the eastern Mediterranean as really worlds apart, but to attribute to them a major role in the spread of culture, even if they were much more substantial, is to imply a form of cargo cult model for the spread of belief—as if momentary commercial links between two suitable regions were explanation enough of the process.

Thomas's idea that the cross-inscribed dishes played a role in spreading cross-forms is more supportable, as the known use of imported dishes over a period of time is what would be required, not the hypothetical presence of cultural practitioners. *Contra* Haseloff, however, we should not place too much emphasis on the contacts as having potential to date the spread of less tangible artistic influences (Haseloff 1987, 45), however satisfying the chronological comparisons may seem.

The sixth-century imports provide an interpretative problem which mostly arises from confusion as to the types of information provided by archaeology and history. As a relatively securely dateable, short-term exotic import group, the Mediterranean wares constitute a significant *datum* for a region which, in the absence of coins, has a relatively insecure archaeological chronology in the early medieval period. In this we may compare its role to that played by Roman period artefacts in the setting up of chronologies in Indian and African archaeology. These wares cannot have played any major role in the economy of Britain and Ireland. Gildas's reference (above, 25) to a past in which wine and oil were luxuries which were brought along the Severn may refer to the events which brought in the Mediterranean wares, or just as likely to events long past. Even so, the value of these imports as aristocratic symbols of *Romanitas,* even if considerable mustering of local resources was made to exchange for them, was probably just that: as symbols only. That amphorae were transported considerable distances to royal sites inland, such as Clogher, Cashel and Cadbury, in no way detracts from such a model. The activity would still have only enriched or depleted the coffers of a few individuals.

Such a conclusion does not entirely vindicate those critics who have observed that too much attention has been given to the imports (Griffiths 1992b; Hill 1992a). Without the imports as diagnostic artefacts we would not have most of the archaeological evidence which we possess for early medieval economy on the shores of the Irish Sea—that is, we would not be convinced that a good deal of it was early medieval in date. The real problem is the false equation that sees archaeological evidence as primarily evidence of settlement and economy. Objects such as the amphora stopper of eastern Mediterranean type, immediately recognisable from comparisons with Bass's Yassi Ada report, have been overlooked in Britain because of a tendency to slot imports into a 'resource/raw material/redistribution' paradigm, in which the 'reworking' of artefacts for redistribution is the governing assumption of find classification. This approach, which has even more severely hampered the study of 'Merovingian' glass (see below, 84ff), has downplayed the evidence that whole vessels in their original completed state arrived on sites, as it clashes with the desire to see value-added exchange. The amphora stopper was 'reworked', but in the east *before* the amphora was filled to send to the west.

The peculiarities of this epsiode are heightened by the fact that any possibly associated imports are so far small in number. The eastern Mediterranean origin of glass fragments from Tintagel awaits detailed proof. A censer of cast copper alloy from Glastonbury has been noted as being of definite eastern Mediterranean origin (Rahtz 1991, 33), but such finds are few and far between. The distribution of sixth-century Mediterranean pottery, where found in Britain, Ireland and Portugal, is as close to indicating a typical 'historic' event as archaeology can come. It is, firstly, an intrusive outlier of a new, but short-lived, Byzantine presence in the west. Secondly, its context in Britain and Ireland is mostly on very high status sites, more so than is the case for the later imports. Fulford's attempts to locate it in the context of historical evidence for Byzantine interest in the Atlantic are hence far more appropriate than continued attempts to create a long-term *floruit* for the wares on the basis of the variety present, or attempts to attribute to the 'economy' of the imports any role in social or political change. That the contacts which brought in the imports may have had a political role is an entirely separate matter—so far unproven, but worthy of further consideration.

Chapter Five

Gaul and the Western Sealanes in the Sixth Century

It can probably be assumed that migrant populations along the western sealanes had consolidated their settlements and lessened their piratical activity by early in the sixth century. The conquest of the Aquitaine by the Franks, in 507, would have facilitated Frankish naval control of the coasts of Brittany and of the Saxon settlements in the Bessin and Loire-Atlantique regions. Frankish control in western Gaul doubtless also accounts for the appearance of direct maritime contacts between western Gaul and the Channel ports. The take-over of south-west Gaul from the Visigoths by the Franks may for a time have diminished links between that region and Spain, where Visigothic control remained. We cannot be sure how much such political change affected commerce, though we may observe that sixth century references to maritime links between western Gaul and Spain are mostly in the context of political exchange concerning the Galician Suevi, who were under threat from their Gothic neighbours. This may have encouraged a special link between Suevic Galicia and Frankish Gaul on the commercial front. After the Sueves were conquered, late in the 500s, such direct maritime links seem to disappear from the record. In the seventh century, overland contact of a military nature is all that is mentioned in sources such as the *Chronicle of Fredegar* (e.g. IV.5, IV.10 & LXXIII, ed. Wallace-Hadrill 1960, 5, 8 & 60-62). Around this time, imports of *paléochrétienne grise* pottery and of Gaulish lapidary formulae of very distinctive type, suggest important continental links, which precede the substantial flourishing of Gaulish links, more Ireland-focused, in the seventh century. Where we may be clear on the commercial content of the latter, however, we cannot be so sure that trade was the backdrop to the sixth-century voyages.

The Atlantic Orientation of Western Gaul in the Sixth Century

The insecurity of the western coasts of Gaul in the fifth century, in the face of piracy and migration, may have made the coastal ports and islands something of an economic backwater. As we have seen, though there are reports of naval activity, there is no mention of maritime trade. In the sixth century however, with western Gaul under Frankish domination, we see commerce in the coastal towns and travel from the coastal ports to offshore islands and foreign lands.

The offshore islands may have been pirate bases in the fifth century and this is certainly true of those around Angers where the Saxons had colonies (see above, 30). These Saxon settlements may have persisted in a distinct form in the sixth century, as Gregory of Tours seems to have been patron to a group on the Loire in 584 (*HF* VIII.18, ed. Krusch 1885a, 402). In some cases islands were centres for production. Leudast, the rebel count of Tours, was born on an unidentified island in Poitou called Gracina, where vineyards were tended. In the seventh century some of the islands were to house monasteries, Noirmoutier for example, which was also a commercial or production centre (see below, 67).

Around 570 Waroch, the count of Brittany, was shipwrecked while trying to sail from Vannes to the offshore islands around the coast of Morbihan (see above, 20). Waroch escaped, but with loss of cargo. This episode makes clear the easy availability of ships in ports in and around Brittany. We cannot assume these were all 'Gaulish'. The proximity of Saxons and Bretons to Nantes and Saintes could have made ships of these peoples available to carry cargoes, especially if the maritime Saxons had always relied on maritime activity for basic communication.

The classes of ceramics known as *sigillées paléochrétiennes* offer some pointers to the geographical pattern of the seaborne and river traffic in and out of the ports of sixth- and seventh-century Gaul. These are fine orange wares and black-washed grey wares found in France in fifth- through seventh-century contexts. They are also found in western Britain, where finds of the ware are generally labelled 'D ware' (Thomas 1981b, 19-20), and in increasing numbers in Spain. On French sites the range of forms includes bowls, shallow dishes, mortaria and pitchers (bowls, dishes and mortaria are found in insular contexts). Decoration ranges from elaborate stamped flowers and hatching, to very simple scored lines. Several major groups of the ware are isolated, though the ware does not yet have a fully refined chronology. Three basic Gaulish groups are defined by the Rigoirs as 'Languedoc', 'Provençal' and 'Atlantic' (Rigoirs and Meffre 1973). The Languedoc group has a very much higher proportion of orange vessels (about 50%) than the other two and these, in conjunction with the presence of palm stamps and other motifs from Africa, have led Hayes to suggest that this group is the earliest and a direct derivative of ARS (Hayes 1972, 402-4). Less than 10% of the Provençal and Atlantic groups are orange wares and this, along with the spread of stamped decoration to the sides of the pot, and a generally fifth-century and later horizon, has led Hayes to put these at the end of a line of descent from the Languedoc group (Hayes 1972, 402ff). On this basis, the Atlantic group may be the latest in development and this is consistent with the chronology of western Gaulish sites as currently known (Randoin 1981, 103-112). The Atlantic group is of most interest to the present study. It is unresolved which centres actually produced the Atlantic group. The Rigoirs favour Bordeaux (Rigoirs and Meffre 1973, 207ff), but this is questioned by French scholars (Santrot, *pers. comm.).* There are also local variants, for example in the Touraine (Randoin, *pers. comm.).*

The distinction between the Atlantic and the other *paléochrétienne* ceramic groups argues for a lack of easy exchange over the Aude-Garonne watershed—though the industry spreads at some point, the actual wares are not carried across the watershed. The Atlantic group is appositely named, as it is found in a coastal distribution and up the rivers of western Gaul. It spreads into the Channel, from where it is found at Rouen, and to Britain, where all the known finds are of the Atlantic group (Randoin 1981, 211). Campbell would hint at the presence of regional variants from western Gaul, but this is as a *caveat,* not on the basis of actual identifications (Campbell 1994).

James (1980, 237-8) has mustered the strongest arguments for the decline in overland traffic through western Gaul to the Atlantic, which he tentatively would date to around 507 (the Battle of Vouille). In particular he concentrates upon the spread of stone sarcophagi (James 1977, 234ff), which certainly represent the sorts of bulk objects which are unlikely to be carried by private, lightweight traffic. The dating of these objects is still equivocal—it not being certain whether they are fifth or sixth century in date. James' arguments, though convincing, depend heavily upon typological criteria. The south-west Gaulish sarcophagi, whatever their date, certainly indicate a developing distribution province focused on the seas. Examples went both through Bordeaux and Narbonne, but the distributions are clearly inland along the river valleys from the sea and not overland (James 1980, 229ff). The same pattern is seen in the distribution of the capitals of Pyrenean marble which, like the sarcophagi, only have a limited distribution outside the Aquitaine and Narbonne, but spread by sea to Nantes and to the Seine (James 1977, 236).

James would conclude that *paléochrétienne grise* finds support this pattern. Recent research by Jacques Lapart and the Rigoirs, however, has indicated that finds in the Gers département, roughly equidistant along this route from the Mediterranean and the Atlantic, include examples from both groups (Lapart and Rigoirs 1986, 111-24). While, as they observe (Lapart and Rigoirs 1986, 123), this must modify James' conclusions, it does not demonstrate overland communication between the two seas. A total exclusion of traffic along this route is not likely: a lack of *through* traffic is demonstrated. A territory midway between both seas will receive goods from both. But the occupants of the shores do not receive goods from each other.

All of the above still does not explain the absence of down-the-line commerce, but there is not much indication that through-traffic existed. Through-traffic was occurring in east Francia. Why not here then? If ceramics could reach the Département du Gers from both directions, it was physically possible for down-the-line exchange to occur The sorts of political boundaries postulated by James might more restrict the movement of large objects such as sarcophagi than the exchange of lightweight ceramics though, as observed above, the bronze bowls and other lightweight eastern Mediterranean objects moving northward along the Rhine corridor (Werner 1961, 307-46) do not make their way over the watershed to western Gaul (James 1980, 239). Werner's study of the values of coins in eastern and western Francia may be significant in this regard (Werner 1961; James 1988, 200ff). Werner has proposed a model for the use of currency in south and west Francia which supposes a face value for the exchange of currency, as opposed to east Francia, where coin was used primarily as bullion. The argument rests upon a distributional study of mints, with the additional indicator of the presence of balances as grave finds. The presence of balances alone is commonest in Germany, England and the Pyrenees. In the area east of the Seine and in the Alps the proportion of balances is still high. West of the Seine, however, the number of mints increases, but only one balance has been found. At the very least this evidence indicates some economic, as well as political, difference between western and eastern Gaul. If, for example, exchange in currency was more restricted in western Gaul this would be a considerable reason for the establishment of local ceramic industries, rather than direct exchange for ceramics manufactured elsewhere. If exchange systems in east Francia depended on weight value of currency it might be natural that western Gaulish commerce looked inward. Western Gaul also exchanged with western Britain and Ireland, but those regions did not use coin.

We will conclude that the western zone was a province the connections of which were with the Atlantic sealanes. Even there, however, our evidence is scanty and while there is a temptation to make a little go a long way, a lot depends on how much isolated events are indicative of broader patterns and how they can be related to patterns which are much more clearly visible in the seventh century: Ian Wood's study of the North Sea in the same period tackles precisely the same problems. We will now examine the routes for which we have evidence.

Relations Between Gaul and Galicia

Maritime contact between Gaul and Spain in the latter part of the sixth century is recorded in the context of the conversion and conquest of Suevic Galicia. In *De Virtutibus Sancti Martini* a ship carries some relics of St Martin of Tours to a harbour in Galicia, arriving, Gregory says, on the same day as Martin of Braga from the Mediterranean (Gregory of Tours, *De Virtutibus* 1.12; ed. Krusch 1885b, 144-6; Thompson 1980b, 83 for discussion). It is alleged that, even though the relics travelled from Tours *'navigio prospero...velociter',* they and Martin of Braga had set out to travel to Galicia on the very same day. The idea that a traveller from anywhere in the Mediterranean could journey to Galicia in the same space of time that it takes to travel from Tours to Galicia is preposterous—even allowing for contrary winds! The coincidence is no doubt a hagiographic embellishment making a link between the contemporary Martin and the missionary and spiritual ethos of his earlier namesake. At the very least the story might be taken to indicate that a sea voyage from Tours to Galicia occurred at sometime around 550-565.

The missions to the Suevi, their subsequent conquest by Leuvigild and Visigothic princesses marrying Frankish royalty all occasioned much coming and going of noteworthy people between Gaul and Spain. The death of Chilperic and his rivalry with Guntram also seem to have been of interest to the Spanish kings. Whether these people went by sea in any or all cases, and whether they would have travelled on regular voyages of commerce which in the normal way went unrecorded, is unclear.

King Mir of Galicia sent ambassadors to Guntram just after 580. They were arrested, however, in 'the neighbourhood of Poitiers' at the orders of Chilperic and imprisoned for a year *(cumque per Pectavum terminum praeterirent, quod tunc Chilpericus rex tenebat, nuntiata sunt ei. At ille sub custodia sibi eos exhibere praecepit et Parisius custodire: HF* V.41, ed. Krusch 1885a,248). Just prior to this we hear of the death of the Frankish bishop Elafius while on a mission in Spain *(HF* V.40, ed. Krusch 1885a,247). Leuvigild sent an ambassador to Chilperic (hence prior to 584: the death date of Chilperic) called Agilan, who had occasion to dispute with Gregory as 'Tours lay on his route' *(Leuvichildus vero rex Agilanum legatum ad Chilpericum mittit. Quem cum via Toronus detulisset...: HF* V.43, ed. Krusch 1885a,249). We also hear of ambassadors to Guntram from Spain in 586.

A more specific maritime reference is in 585 when the conquest of Galicia by Leuvigild saw the subsequent looting of ships travelling between Gaul and Galicia (see above, 21). Had these ships been making the same voyage unmolested for a long time? Or is it more likely that their presence was accountable to the same political/ religious exchange highlighted above: perhaps traffic with Gaul escalated as relations became more strained with Visigothic Spain? If the latter, Leuvigild's actions might seem more easily explicable. A conquering king may do as he pleases, but such actions directed by a king smack of politically motivated intervention. On the other hand the episode refers to the 'possessions' *(res)* being taken. This certainly might suggest commercial voyages, though the word *res* is not specific to commercial cargoes. The looting is unambiguously of ships.

The routes taken by the ambassadors are hinted at, but it is not specified whether they travelled any of the way by sea. A voyage to Nantes would seem to be implied by the route taken by Agilan and thence via the Loire valley to Paris or Soissons. A journey by sea to Bordeaux and thence via Poitiers would also be on a straight line, however, so neither can be said to be a certain candidate. Galswinth, however, making the same journey from Toledo to Neustria, seems to have gone from Poiters to the north by *sea*. Venantius, an eyewitness (George 1992, 97-8), writes of her progress from Poitiers:

> Excipit inde repens...Liger algidus...pervenit qua se piscoso Sequana fluctu in mare fert, iuncto in Rotomagiense sinu.
>
> (The cold Loire suddenly accepted her...she arrived where the Seine flows into the sea, the fishy flood which joins with Rouen: Venantius, *Opera* VI.5, ll. 233-4, ed. Leo and Krusch 1961,142).

It is clear in this case that the voyage is not up the Loire to Nevers and overland, but *down* the Loire to Nantes and by sea to the Seine mouth. The route taken by the ambassadors of King Mir is less easy to disentangle. Presumably they were headed to Guntram's court at Orléans, not to Burgundy, so a land-based route was probably used all the way. We should accept that the embassies between the Visigoths and the Franks went by land from Spain to Gaul. The Visigothic capital and heartland were in the central Meseta, to journey north to a Galician port to take ship for Bordeaux or Saintes would be unlikely as it was not safe terrain, lying too near to the Suevic kingdom, nor were the geographical obstacles much less than for the fully overland route to Gaul. Embassies between the Sueves and the Franks, however, doubtless went by sea from Gaul to Spain, to avoid travelling through the Visigothic territory and because it was the more convenient route. As we cannot imagine the latter political exchange to be on a very large scale, we would assume that the reference to the ships sacked by Leuvigild is almost certainly to ships whose primary purpose was commerce, not politics.

An archaeological dimension to traffic along this route is largely lacking. A south-west Gaulish sarcophagus found at Villaneuva de Lorenzana in Galicia might be evidence of exchange with this route (James 1977, 235), but Galicia is yet to produce definite finds of Atlantic group *paléochrétienne grise*. A few finds have been reported from Conimbriga and other Portuguese sites (Hayes 1980, lxvii), which may indicate that increasing Portuguese investigation will reveal more. These do not seem to be of the Atlantic group, however, though published literature is not clear on this point and it is worth observing that familiarity with the various fabrics is the only real guide with fragmentary examples. Excavation in Spain has been patchy by comparison with France, though Spanish archaeologists have been conscious of the likely occurrence of *sigillata paleocristiana.* A look at the distribution as recorded in 1979 demonstrates that the *gris* form, where it is so far found, occurs so far as a distribution related to Mediterranean-oriented traffic (Blasquez and Molina 1979, 240-2). Examples of *paleocristiana gris* in the very north, without accompanying orange wares, may suggest distribution across the Pyrenees, but may also be from the Mediterranean, along the Ebro. From the map we may also note that the Guadiana is again highlighted. Here the valley may be being used to disperse material which could have been brought overland from the Mediterranean. On the other hand, Galicia may have encouraged contact with western Gaul, on account of its hostility to the Visigothic kingdom, which itself enjoyed more frequent exchange with southern Gaul. Hence we may find that exchange in the Atlantic was limited to a western Gaul-Galicia model,

Fig. 5 Iberian distribution of Paleocristiana pottery (after Molina)

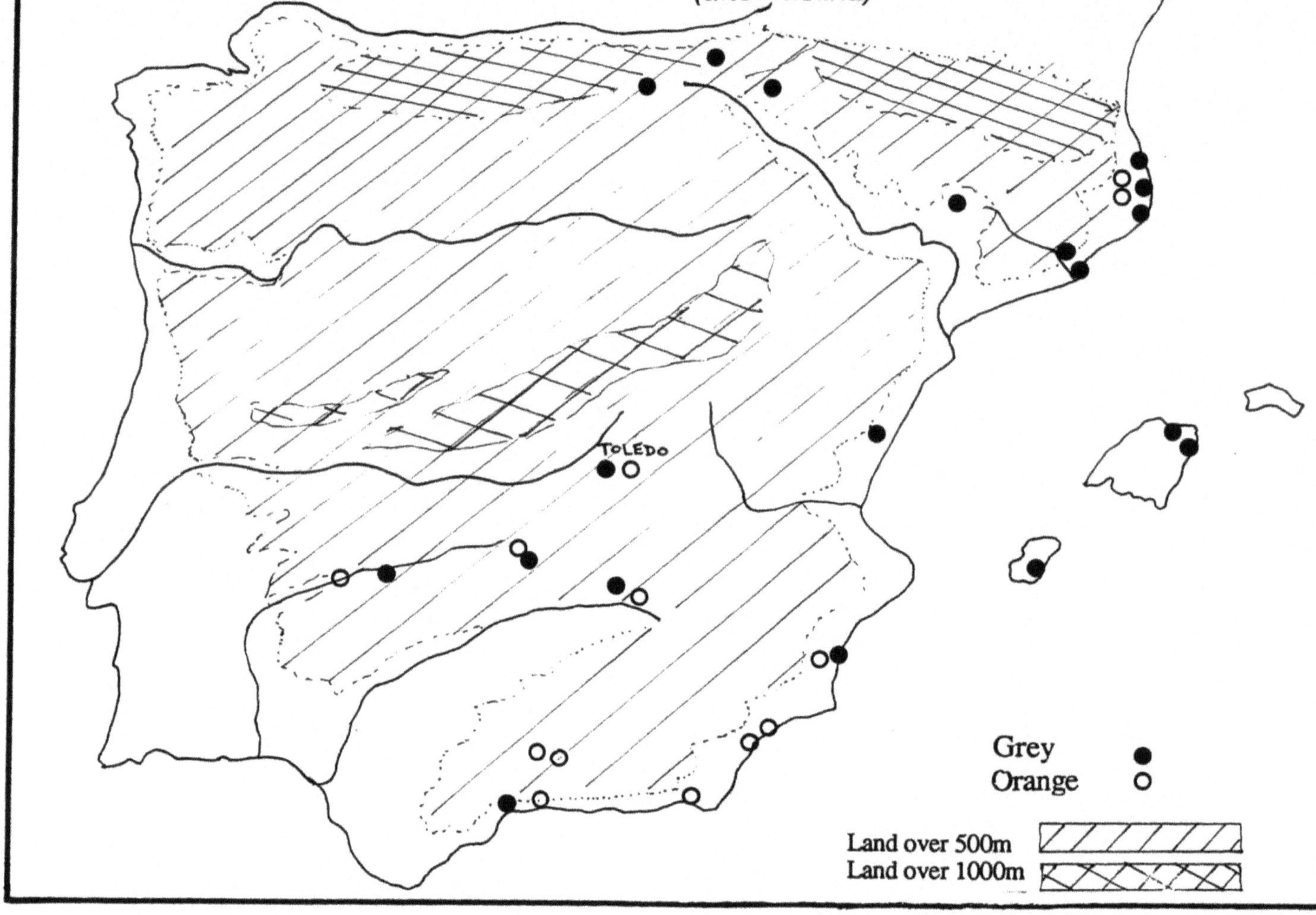

rather than between western Gaul and Spain in general. Leuvigild's hostility to the Frankish ships in Galicia would be hard to explain if they were ships that also called at his own ports.

Connections Between Spain and Britain

Evidence for links between Galicia and Britain can be seen in the late sixth-century focus upon church affairs in the Suevic kingdom. A sixth-century *parochiale* has survived, in more than one version, listing thirteen sees of the kingdom. The final entry of the list refers to the 'see of the Britons' *(Ad sedem Britonorum)* comprising churches 'which are among the Britons' and a monastery *(ad sedem Britonorum ecclesias que sunt intro Britones una cum monasterio Maximi et que in Asturiis sunt*: to the see of the Britons: 'the churches which are among the Britons together with the monastery of Maximus and [the churches] which are in the Asturias', ed. David 1947, 44). This is in all probability the town of Bretoña and its hinterland, in the vicinity of Lugo. Corroborative evidence is found in the notes on the second council of Braga, in 572 (see Thompson 1965, 201-5; L. Olson, *pers. comm.)*. In the lists of signatures of the various bishops the bishop of *Britonensis ecclesia* is one Mailoc. Kenneth Jackson has declared this to be an undeniably British Celtic name (Jackson 1953, 464). Neither the see nor its bishop are appended to the first Council of Braga of 561: a Maliosus signed that document, but this is philologically far from being identifiable with Mailoc. No other name among the signatories could conceivably have been Celtic. The bishoprics are not listed at all at the first council. The *parochiale* documents the parishes of all the sees except Bretoña, for which it simply makes a sweeping inclusion *(ecclesias que sunt intro Britones)*. The implication of this might be of a community apart, about which the writer of the *parochiale* knew little. This would be logical if Bretoña had been a Catholic pocket in the Arian Suevic kingdom. This might have encouraged, also, the persistence of a British identity and, doubtless, the continuation of their dialect.

Clearly what is described is a British community which migrated down the western sealanes sometime in the fifth or sixth century. The other alternative, Bretons, is hardly likely. The idea that a community from the Brittany settlements (themselves only recent) would be in Galicia in 572 (and most probably earlier) seems unnecessarily complex. If so, it might be disputed that they should be termed 'Bretons', anyway. The Britons of Galicia are best explained as a comparable migration as that of the Britons to Brittany. The idea that the church was established as a missionary centre, however, should also not be ruled out: in such a case the interest of the church at Tours in Martin of Braga's mission may be suggestive that these colonists are Bretons relocated from Gaul by Frankish authorities (see above, 30). Whether any continuing contact with Britain was maintained is not recorded.

Ireland, Western Britain and Gaul

For the sixth century we possess no unquestionable textual evidence for travel between Gaul and the Irish Sea basin. The *Vita Kyarani,* a Latin life of the founder of Clonmacnois, talks of how 'merchants with wine of Gaul come to St Ciaran and fill a large vessel' *(mercatores cum vino Gallorum venerunt ad sanctum Kiaranum, et impleuerunt ingentum vas...: Vita Kyarani* XXXI, ed. Plummer 1910, 214). The problems of this text and its evidence have been discussed by a range of authors. At face value it would represent evidence that a ship from Gaul sailed to the Shannon around 550 AD. The manuscript from which it comes, however, is probably of no earlier than fifteenth-century date (ed. Plummer 1910, xlviii). In this case it becomes highly likely that the incident as described represents a familiar medieval scene. By as early as the twelfth-century wine trading with France was a widespread activity. A possibly earlier Irish version of the life contains the same story, with the exception that the merchants are there specifically described as Franks (ed. Macalister 1921, 92; discussion at 154). This second fact is probably of little importance: the word in an Irish context is a common counterpart to Latin 'Gaul'. The agreement between the two recensions is more significant as it argues for at least a slightly earlier prototype of the *vita* containing the same incident. Even so, no amount of argument can support the use of this text as evidence for sixth-century activity. Where the date of the earliest textual tradition is medieval, the evidence must be suspected of referring to a medieval view of trading activity, though it is quoted still as the cornerstone of the idea that wine traders from Gaul visited Ireland in the early medieval period (O'Neill 1987. 44 is a typical recent example: 'In the Life of St Ciaran of Clonmacnois, there is mention of wine from Gaul being brought up the Shannon to the monastery).

The reference to British ships in the harbour of Bordeaux in the *Vita et Virtutes Eparchii* (ed. Krusch 1896b, 562) is in a similar position as evidence to the *Vita Kyarani*, being from a late text with no obvious early text-tradition. Reliable references to links between the Irish Sea basin and western Gaul are not found before the seventh century. This obviously raises the question whether the appearance of reliable references in the historical record must be taken to give any real guide to the beginnings of contact between the two regions. The archaeological evidence of E ware increasingly suggests, however, that the *seventh* century was at the centre of contacts between Gaul and the Irish Sea basin.

One, generally reliable, text does purport to depict 'Gaulish sailors, from the provinces of Gaul' visiting Dalriada in the period 563-597 (the time of Columba). The episode relates to Columba's prophesy of a disaster abroad to Lugbe saying: 'before the year is out...Gallic sailors arriving from the provinces of Gaul will tell you the same'. Adomnán, *Vita Columbae* I.28, ed. & trans. Anderson and Anderson 1961, 262). Perhaps the redundancy in this statement is a gloss to distinguish the generic Gaelic *gall* ('foreigner') from 'Gaul' i.e. an actual Gaul; if the word had acquired this generic use by Adomnán's time. Though the text is Latin, the Iona monks would have been native Gaelic speakers. In the context it is useful, as there is no doubt as to whom Adomnán is describing. That there might be evidence in this episode for the seasonal character of voyages may be noted. The identification of this disaster, in which an Italian city was consumed in sulphurous fire, is not possible, though volcanic eruptions in Italy are not uncommon (Thomas 1990, 2). The *caput regionis* to which Lugbe travelled was probably Dunadd. From Dunadd come finds of D and E ware pottery which are sixth or early seventh-century imports from Gaul. The lack of a specific location for the *caput regionis* might indicate a fictional basis, or a lack of memory of where the event took place. Most likely, however, is that such ships would be seen by a seventh-century writer to be common visitors to Dalriada, not to Iona but to a secular site some distance away which was controlling exchange (i.e. Dunadd). There is no certainty, however, that the episode is accurate for the *sixth* century, as it is written late in the seventh.

In Britain, the classification D ware was first set up by Radford (1956, 67) to cover a series of mortaria and grey-slipped bowls among the Tintagel material. Fragments from the early twentieth-century excavations at Dunadd and the Mote of Mark were soon identified as being of the same type. The discovery of a considerable quantity of the ware at Dinas Powys in Glamorgan (Alcock 1987, 120-1) in the late 'fifties, exhibiting a range of forms, allowed most D ware to be soon after be identified as belonging to the Atlantic group. The agreement between the Rigoirs' choice of Bordeaux for an origin point and the accepted historical wisdom of a wine trade emanating from Bordeaux was, of course, immediately observed (Alcock 1987, 120-1). The matter has largely rested at this point. New finds were added to the British corpus by excavations at Congresbury and Cadbury, both in Somerset, and Clogher in Tyrone (the Clogher find is no longer accepted as D ware). Since the publication of the 1981 catalogue new finds have come from Whithorn (Hill 1989, 9) and from the resorting of find bags from an old excavation at May's Hill, Isles of Scilly (Thomas 1983, 78-80). The finds from Somerset (from Cadbury and Congresbury) have been held to suggest that the ware is largely sixth-century in date and that its range is different to that of E ware.

Some confusion and doubt has subsequently sprung up regarding D ware. No petrological study has been made of the known finds. However many of the finds correspond clearly to the Gaulish typology, while a few clearly do not. Others are so uncertain in fabric that they can be excluded from consideration. There was a tendency to include any mortaria found in this class, as well a belief that the class only contained mortaria (R. Warner, P. Hill *pers. comms.).* Both of these ideas have led to confusion. The listed find from Clogher has, on examination by Charles Thomas (R.Warner, *pers. comm.*) and subsequently by the present writer (1987-8), been found to be unlike D ware in form and fabric. The finds from Tintagel, ironically the origin of the designation, have also been found not to be *paléochrétienne grise.* Charles Thomas and the author re-examined these pieces in 1988 and found no definite correspondences with the *paléochrétienne grise* corpus. The fabric of a few plain pieces was not sufficiently preserved to allow any judgement to be made. The only piece to bear a strong (though not exact) resemblance to a *paléochrétienne grise* form was darker and harder in the fabric than normal vessels of the class (CAU excavation, 1988, stratified with amphorae of classes 43 and 44 — Thomas 1988c, 59). The only piece largely similar in fabric to *paléochrétienne grise* was a beaded mortarium more like a late-Roman vessel in form. An identical fragment in the British Museum (also from Tintagel, accession number 1949,5-1,4) was examined there by a Roman specialist and seen to be unlikely to be anything other than Roman (S. Youngs, *pers comm.).* This is perfectly consistent with the character of the Tintagel assemblage, which contains late-Roman pieces (Thomas 1981b, 16). It need hardly be said that this information does not invalidate the notion of D ware as a class, even though the label was coined with Tintagel assemblage in mind. The label is a post-Roman classification and remains attached to the post-Roman pieces within the corpus from other sites.

Because *paléochrétienne grise* remains the least numerous of imported types in western Britain it seems to have been given the least attention in studies of British trade and communication. Its evidence has seemed to offer little opportunity for expansion—even the finding of a kiln site would not add significantly to what is already known, unless to refine the dating. Some possibilities are opened up, however, to refine the evidence on the strength of work both in Britain and in France. A few general observations might first be made. Evidence from French sites has been coloured by varying scales and standards of excavation in different parts of the country. The strongest links of the British material have so far been seen to be with pieces from the Garonne basin. There are several ways in which this conclusion might be premature. The Rigoirs' report is not much use in this regard as it publishes mostly only pieces from the Aquitaine for comparison. An examination, for example, of the collection of the ware in Nantes shows that only a limited series of stamped pieces are preserved (personal observation 1988—I would like to thank Jacques Santrot for his assistance in showing me this material and discussing it with me). These come from nineteenth-century excavations in the Centre de Ville. Almost certainly other, less ornate, pieces were discarded (cf. Knight 1984, 359). If there were good parallels for the British finds in Nantes they could have been in the discarded group.

All of this has a strong bearing upon the subject of western sealanes traffic. The evidence of *paléochrétienne grise* has been increasingly held up as the one definite example of a direct Irish Sea link with Bordeaux (Alcock 1987, 89). New evidence from Tours must cast some doubt upon this point. Excavations of the Chateau and Monastery of St Martin sites in Tours have unearthed a wide range of *paléochrétienne grise* forms (Randoin 1981, 107-110 and *pers. comm.).* Included amongst these are several of the forms found at Dinas Powys (a decorated beaker, context no. 3.1091-14, from the Chateau site is almost identical to the vessel illustrated in Alcock 1987, 120, Fig 6.4, no. 8; also see Rigoirs and Meffre 1973, 240). What is important is that, considering the quantities in the Loire basin, the vessels to be taken to Britain need not have been obtained in Bordeaux. The textual evidence for the seventh century favours contacts with the Loire basin over the Aquitaine, as far as it goes (see below, 65ff).

The excavations in Tours have refined the dating of the Atlantic group to a broadly sixth and seventh-century horizon (Randoin 1981, 107-110). The site at Whithorn in Scotland, in a well preserved sequence south of the priory, produced a piece of *paléochrétienne grise* in hill wash with E ware and Merovingian glass (observed by the author in 1987): both broadly of seventh-century date. The ware has only once been found at a British site which did not produce Mediterranean wares, namely Dunadd. There the absence of Mediterranean wares is not likely to suggest an absence of sixth-century occupation (Lane 1984, 45). *Paléochrétienne grise* is found at sites which do not produce E ware, namely Congresbury and Cadbury. This is seen (along with other hints) as precluding seventh-century occupation at these sites and by implication putting the start of *paléochrétienne grise* importation slightly earlier than that of E ware. This is probably true, though it should be noted that the fact that E ware is uncommon in south-west Britain (and not found at all on the north coast, east of the Kelsies) may mean that the ware simply never reached Somerset. On the other hand, the fact that it is found in Glamorgan, almost on the same longitude of the Bristol Channel as Congresbury should suggest that it at least could have travelled the short distance further to Somerset if required and there is other evidence to show that Somerset finds are probably sixth century.

In general, however, the evidence suggests a ware imported at a slightly earlier date than E ware, its importation continuing perhaps into the period of E ware. The fact that the two wares could have been imported from the same region (which will be explored further below), might suggest that the activity which brought in E ware existed before E ware began to be imported. Again, as with the questions surrounding the Mediterranean wares, the archaeological discontinuities might not represent discontinuity of the related activities. Other possibilities should also be entertained, however. The total absence of *paléochrétienne grise* from Ireland to date (indeed it is almost totally confined to British-speaking areas: Dunadd and, maybe, Longbury Bank being exceptions) may indicate importation by way of some British agency.

Paléochrétienne grise is a puzzling artefact. The distribution of the Atlantic group outside of western Gaul is extremely limited so far: only a handful of finds coming from northern Gaul, Brittany and Britain. No site has produced more than the nine vessels from Dinas Powys: no more than three at any other site; at Whithorn, Cadbury and May's Hill the number is one vessel only.

Some doubt may also attach to other identifications apart from Tintagel. The Cadbury piece is very small, but is convincing as D ware. The Congresbury pieces are badly discoloured and not easily matched and the Somerset pieces are fairly crucial in assigning a sixth century date and separating E ware from D ware.

On an economic level the differences between D ware and E ware are fundamental. Whereas E ware is clearly evidence of a regular commercial contact between Gaul and the Irish Sea, nothing about the D ware finds necessitates a definite commercial context. How did these pieces travel to the sites where they are found? The May's Hill piece draws Scilly into the picture and makes a direct maritime link between Britain and Gaul likely. Western Gaul is the obvious launching point as Atlantic group pottery is certainly from western France. A focus on the Severn estuary is indicated, as the Scottish finds are numerically likely to be secondary. Along with the glass finds, also very limited in Ireland, we seem to be looking at objects which are more 'British' in distribution than E ware, which is overwhelmingly associated with Ireland and Scotland. That little evidence of such a British province exists may be accountable to the lack of a durable import good such as E ware. On the other hand there is the possibility that these goods are not part of a trading province in the way that E ware undoubtedly is. The small quantities involved in the movement of D ware might reinforce this idea. The glass finds present other problems, which will be discussed in the following chapter. We may conclude that very little may be regarded as proven in the case of D ware. The context is probably separate from E ware, however, and oriented more toward the British shore of the Irish Sea. The fact that the distribution excludes Ireland for the moment seems suggestive of this, although a find of D ware in eastern Ireland would not be incompatible with the picture of redistributive routes indicated by the Mediterranean wares, which is different from that of E ware.

In the Irish Sea basin we should note the appearance of centres of maritime trade in the sixth century which will be discussed further in Chapter Seven. Any conclusions on these must be tentative in the light of our poor knowledge of function of crucial sites, but two at least allow some potential to identify the focuses of exchange. Dalkey Island, Co. Dublin, a small island with an enclosed settlement at the northern end, has figured in most discussions of trade in the early medieval Irish Sea (Mytum 1992, 262-3; Griffiths 1992a, 63; Thomas 1990, 21). Both Hodges and Mytum have seen this site as a likely 'gateway community' (Hodges 1989, 51; Mytum 1992, 262), the island location and the enclosure of the settlement during the seventh century being taken as indications of commercial neutrality and political regulation, respectively (Hodges 1989, 51). The former seems a better indication of commercial significance than the latter as we would have to look to anachronistic comparisons with enclosed ninth century *emporia* to find parallels. Thomas would doubt the importance of Dalkey Island in the distribution pattern which he proposes for E ware: seeing the more politically important centres as central to the distribution of E ware (Thomas 1990, 21). This may be a reasonable argument for E ware, which we will see is imported by voyages from the continent as far north as Scotland. The sixth-century role of Dalkey Island might be quite another question. Dalkey Island is the only site near the coast between Co. Cork and Co. Tyrone to produce finds of Mediterranean pottery in any quantity, which as we have seen is likely to be brought north by secondary voyages out of the south-west British peninsula (see above, 51ff). It is also the only site in the same region to produce more than one sherd of imported glassware, which we will see may also be a sixth-century import. Both these sets of imports are rarer in Ireland than in Britain, unlike E ware. Is Dalkey Island a stopping point, a neutral port outside of Irish society, in a 'British'-oriented trading network linking the north and the south of the Irish Sea? The distributional evidence is superficially suggestive, but further excavation may very well change this picture. The typology of an island emporium is also very questionable in an Irish Sea context. In the sixth century the settlement seems to have been unenclosed and this may represent a change in function from the sixth to seventh century. Does this reflect a change in function as new networks emerge, which seem to involve landfalls in Meath, unlike those of the sixth century?

Other sixth century British sites clearly enjoy long-distance links. The most interesting of these is Whithorn, where an unenclosed settlement five kilometres from the nearest harbour shows occupation over several hectares: an authentically urban settlement with a wide range of local and imported goods, including 17+ glass vessels and amphorae of three different Mediterranean classes (unusual outside of Cornwall and Somerset). It remains unclear whether the site is primarily religious in function.

In both these cases (as well as with Tintagel) we have sites with assemblages of unusual size and some clues to strategic or historical importance, which we may set against the rich assemblages at Dinas Powys and the Mote of Mark, where the focal status of the site is not obvious in maritime terms, or historically recorded.

The context of D ware in Wales, south-west Scotland and Somerset takes in the areas in which Latin memorial stones are found. It is not found in Ireland, where Latin inscriptions in early formulae are rare. The evidence of stones along the shores of the Irish Sea with Latin lapidary inscriptions in continental formulae has been seen to imply contact with Gaul in the fifth century and continuing into the sixth. The evidence should be treated critically as it is in need of substantial revision (see now Thomas 1994). The Llantrisant stone, on Anglesey, for example, used to be thought to commemorate a bishop from Andecavi on the Loire (Nash Williams 1950, 63-4, no. 33), but this is now held to be a misreading. The possible reading 'ANDOCO NATIONE', upon which the identification with the Andecavi is suggested, is incorrect. Particularly of note is the missed letter, (Nash Williams suggests G or S, but clearly it is G) which precedes NATIONE and renders the reading: 'AU (ligature: U or N) DOCO GNATIONE', probably *audo cognatione*. (L. Olson, *pers. comm.*). It is sufficient to say that the reading into this inscription of a connection with the Loire, or any part of Gaul is not worthy of the credence which frequent citation has lent it.

At Penmachno, in Gwynedd, a stone is very precisely self-ascribed to the reign of Justinus (*In Tempore Iustini*), the consul of 540 (Nash Williams 1950, 93, no. 104; Knight 1981, 62; Miller 1978-80, 316). Knight's argument that this is a dating formula imported from Gaul, where it is limited in use to Lugdunensis I, is more convincing than Johnstone's attempt to tie it to supposed broader uses of consular dating (such as in the *Historia Brittonum*: Johnstone 1962, 102-9). This formula, which would probably only be used by an individual who had been resident in Gaul (whether British or Gaulish of birth we cannot tell), is good chronological evidence for a continuation of the sort of dialogue between the British and Gaulish churches which the travels of Riochatus and Faustus and the *hic iacet* formula indicate in the previous century (see above, 35). We should note that a date no earlier than the fifth century should be accepted for the latter, as the early to mid-fifth century is the *floruit* of this formula in Gaul. McManus (1991, 62), follows Nash-Williams in accepting the Italian *floruit* of the fourth century as a *terminus post quem*, but these is no reason to believe that the insular occurrences lie outside the Gaulish use of this formula. *Paleochretienne grise* may well enter Britain in this sort of context: it is an urban pottery of limited cultural affinity in Gaul, not connected with typically Frankish groups and might well be a symptom of a phase of British church activity which the seventh century links of the Irish Sea basin have obscured.

A traveller who voyaged within the 'British province' in the sixth century is St Samson of Dol. The evidence of the *Vita Samsonis* is controversial and may or may not be reliable witness to the sixth or seventh century (the former the era of the saint, the latter the postulated earliest date for the *vita*). The author's reference to having traced the path of the saint through Cornwall and Wales adds weight to his testimony as to routes of travel used in the early middle ages (*Vita Samsonis* XLVIII, ed. Fawtier 1912, 144; Olson 1989, 9ff; Hughes 1981, 4ff; Thomas 1994, 224ff).

The *vita* describes several incidents of voyaging. St Samson sailed to Ireland from *Ynys Pyr* (almost certainly Caldey Island, Dyfed) and back. On his return journey he was forced to wait for a northerly wind at a port nearby *Arce* (*Vita Samsonis* XXXVIII, ed. Fawtier 1912, 134). Several manuscripts read this as *Arce Etri*, read by Loth (*Vita Samsonis* XXXIII, ed. Fawtier 1912, 134 & note A; Taylor 1925, 40, note 1) as 'Dun Etair' (Howth). In a characteristically exemplary episode the sailors leave without him, but are forced to bend to the saint's will. Though the incident is a *topos*, we should observe that the maritime detail is at least consistent with real conditions. The need for a northerly wind would certainly indicate somewhere northward of Rosslare on the Irish east coast. The chance of a north or north-easterly wind (a north-westerly would make rounding South Wales very difficult) in summer from Dublin is only around 25-30%, so this delay fits the evidence quite well. The fact that the sailors would depart without the saint might indicate that Dublin(?) to south Wales was a normal commercial route, not a special commission, but it is too much a stock incident to be reliable.

All such hagiographic episodes must be read with care. How much might this story be based on genuine detail? The story of Samson's voyage to and from Ireland might be considered more doubtful than the detail of his journey between Wales and Brittany: in the light of the importance of the ethos of St Columbanus in Gaul in the seventh century we cannot be sure that a journey to Ireland didn't become a necessary embellishment to the saint's story. Archaeological evidence, however, does suggest strong links between South Wales and Ireland in the sixth/seventh century (see below, 101).

The episode where St Samson of Dol travelled from Wales to Brittany is also of relevance. He took ship to Cornwall, walked across the peninsula by way of St Kew (*Vita Samsonis* XILV, ed. Fawtier 1912, 142) and then took ship on the other side to Brittany (*Vita Samsonis* LII, ed. Fawtier 1912, 147). Crawford's explanation of the choice of this route as being due to a desire to avoid a voyage around Land's End is tenable only to the degree that, for a journey from South Wales to Brittany, the latter would be a very round-about route.

Other problems confront us when considering Brittany. Very little is known of the typology of early medieval sites in Brittany. We may make some obvious observations about the existence of links between Brittany and other regions. The south-west peninsula of Britain was certainly in contact and Samson of Dol's is surely only one of thousands of such voyages made between the two peninsulas. Likewise, local traffic must have frequently been in contact with western Gaul. In the seventh-century setting of the *Vita Filiberti, naves Brittanici* are seen at Noirmoutier (XLII, ed. Levison 1910, 602), though the rarity of *paléochrétienne grise* from Brittany should be noted. Whether contacts with Ireland existed is uncertain, but there is probably no reason to see these any earlier than the seventh century. In the ninth-century *Vita Winwaloei* the saint expects to be able to sail directly between Brêhat (North Brittany) and Ireland (*Vita Winwaloei* I.19, ed. De Smedt 1888, 205-6)—even though he ultimately does not do so. Breton glosses of the eighth century and later testify to contacts with Ireland, Wales and Cornwall (Fleuriot 1984). With the example of St Samson's travels to all these lands, but reaching Brittany overland through Cornwall, we cannot be absolutely certain any of the glossators came directly by sea from Ireland (Fleuriot 1984, 223, where he notes the disharmony with Thomas's theories). Likewise, followers of Columbanus were residing in Brittany and are the addressees of his 610 letter from Nantes. Most probably they had come with him to Nantes, before making their way into Brittany from the south (see below, 65).

Historical Models for Sixth-Century Western Sealanes Traffic

The picture of events in the sixth century is very uneven and there is little doubt that our evidence is not representative of the whole picture. We have seen that there is reason to doubt that our evidence indicates the use of the same routes over the entire century. The Visigothic conquest of Suevic Galicia probably saw an end to maritime links between Gaul and Spain. There is no definite evidence yet to see links between Gaul and Ireland and absence of *paléochrétienne grise* from Ireland should be noted. The Mediterranean wares at most indicate a few decades of activity. Archaeological clues do not give anything more than a very patchy picture. This contrasts sharply with the evidence of the use of the western sealanes in the seventh century, which will be shown to give a much more regular picture of activity.

Archaeological and historical sources give odd clues which we might be tempted to draw into a more harmonious picture. Ian Wood asserts that Frankish politics intruded into the affairs of most of their neighbours and also notes the Byzantine interest in this Frankish hegemony (Wood 1983, 10ff). Byzantine agents in the west, commercial or political in intent, may be seen approaching Britain from different directions, in both cases largely avoiding Gaul, though there may have been maritime reasons why the voyages which came to Britain via the Straits of Gibraltar avoided a landing in western and, probably, southern Gaul. That Byzantine authorities were interested in what lay beyond Frankish Gaul is not unlikely, however—an interest that they might not have liked the Franks to be aware of. In the following century, Ebroin's suspicion that Theodore of Tarsus was an agent of the emperor may show the continuity of a suspicion of such interest (see above, 21) in Frankish Gaul.

We should not be carried away by other influences. Zimmer was inclined to highlight the importance of the cult of Martin in the spread of monasticism to Ireland, on account of the seemingly early manuscript traditions of Sulpicius's *vita* in Ireland (Zimmer 1909c, 593-610), but James (1982, 367-8) has rightly stressed the incompatibility of the organisation of the Irish church with Martin's model. Nonetheless, we are tempted to observe that early dedications to St Martin at Whithorn and Canterbury coincide with finds of sixth/seventh century north-western Gaulish artefacts: at Whithorn, pottery and glass; at Canterbury, coins of western Gaulish origin (Rigold 1975, 655). The name of Martin of Tours also crops up in connection with the establishment of Martin of Braga in Galicia. The strongest historical connection of the British churches in the fifth century is with Auxerre (Knight 1981, 56-7), most likely operating via the overland routes through western Britain (see above, 35-6). The Saxon conquest of the west country in the sixth century, however, may have forced such connections between the Gaulish and British churches to use the maritime routes through western Gaulish ports. The situation in Galicia seems to have stimulated activity through the western ports also. Does this bring the Loire connection and the cult of St Martin into greater prominence? In 680 John the Archcantor, abbot of the monastery of Martin at Rome, travelled via Tours to Britain (Bede, *HE* IV.18, ed. Colgrave and Mynors 1969, 390-1), stopping at the shrine *en route* before making a crossing of the 'Ocean' (*Oceanum transitum*), which would seem to indicate an Atlantic voyage, rather than simply a Channel crossing (though Tom O'Loughlin, *pers. comm.*, suggests that Bede is consistent in his use of 'Ocean' to describe all the seas around Britain). St Columbanus followed the same route down the Loire to the sea in 610. Networking through the *familia* of Columbanus will be shown to be important in the western sealanes activity of the seventh century: we cannot afford to overlook potentially important links of a similar nature in the sixth. The Loire begins to emerge as a focal point for much maritime activity in the sixth century and this connection may repay more investigation.

Chapter Six

Cargoes and Commerce between western Gaul and Ireland in the Seventh Century

Zimmer's model assumed that contacts between western Gaul and Ireland had existed at least since the Roman period (Zimmer 1909a, 363-400a) and that when Irish *peregrini* sought to go abroad, they took ships to Gaul which were already regularly making this voyage. James, in reassessing this thesis, does not make an issue of the question of pre-existing commerce, except to make admirably clear the non-committal character of Jonas's evidence on this point (James 1982, 375-7). He also notes that the predominant theatre of Irish mission on the continent was east Francia, not western Gaul (James 1982, 380) and therefore stresses the likelihood that, as Anglo-Saxon England was Christianised in the seventh century, the Irish may increasingly have chosen to travel to the continent by way of England, rather than by way of the western Gaul.

In re-examining the sources we thus need to resolve, firstly whether there is any solid evidence of actual voyages by churchpeople; secondly, their relationship to trading activity; and thirdly, how much the changing directions of travel may be seen in terms of long term patterns. For example, does the greater instance of travel through Anglo-Saxon England after the mid-seventh century indicate a shift in general terms to what would, all things being equal, be the preferred route, or does this simply indicate a growth of personal contacts between the two churches and a greater involvement of the Irish in English affairs? In other words, were the seaways only drawn upon for communication when paths through Britain were closed? And does trade between Ireland and Gaul pre-exist monastic travel, or is it even possible that the late-sixth/early-seventh century flourishing of church links actually stimulated the growth of long-distance exchange?

When did voyages between western Gaul and Ireland begin? If no certain evidence for sixth-century links is forthcoming, attention must focus upon the reliability of the testimony of Jonas (c.639) that Irish commerce was found in Nantes as early as 610. The detail as to how St Columbanus reached Gaul, around 590, is less exact than for the episode in Nantes in 610: Jonas writes of Columbanus going to the shore with his companions, where he embarked on a ship, and went with a calm sea and favourable winds for the dangerous voyage to *brittanicis sinus* (*Carinamque ingressi, dubias per freta ingrediunter vias mitemque salum, prosperantibus zepherorum flabris, pernici cursa ad Brittanicos perveniunt sinus:* Jonas, *Vita Columbani* I.4, ed. Krusch 1902a, 71). From there they proceeded into Gaul. This *brittanicis sinus* has been taken to suggest that Columbanus landed in and made a transit of Cornwall, though Zimmer, more logically, assumed a direct sea voyage (Zimmer 1909a, 395ff). More likely *brittanicis sinus* is the western or southern coast of Brittany, rather than Britain itself. When Columbanus is ordered to return to Ireland, Bertechar tells him to go to Nantes to 'return by the route along which you first came to this place' (*pergas eo itinere quo primum his aduentasti in locis:* Jonas, *Vita Columbani* I.20, ed. Krusch 1902a, 91) and he then took a boat on the Loire so that he might come again to *brittanicis sinus* (Jonas, *Vita Columbani* I.21, ed. Krusch 1902a, 93).

It is clear from the above that Jonas is suggesting that Columbanus's exit point from Gaul was intended to be the same as his entry point (unless we read Bertechar's words as simply 'return whence you came', in which case the phrase might be held to be needlessly elaborate). Columbanus' own letter from Nantes in 610 observes that his companions are 'here in the region of the Britons' (*hic in vicinia Brittonum sunt: Epistulae* IV, ed. & trans. Walker 1957, 36). James (1982, 376) has, further, observed that Venantius Fortunatus (*Opera*, ed. Leo and Krusch 1961, 29) describes the seas off Poitou as *oceanus britannicus*. There is no obstacle to this terminology implying an initial arrival of Columbanus in the vicinity of the Loire estuary. In the 610 journey it is clear that Nantes was always Columbanus' destination. Walker, among others, confused this by implying that Nantes was only chosen as an alternative destination—that the party diverted to the Loire through a desire to avoid Neustria (Walker 1957, xxvii). This is not explicitly stated in the text, however, and Walker evidently was acting on the assumption that anyone who wished to travel from Gaul to Ireland would simply by preference travel to the Channel coast rather than the Atlantic. Walker's general preoccupation with overland routes becomes clear with his suggestion that the St Columb dedications in western Cornwall indicate a transit of Cornwall *en route* to Gaul (Walker 1957, xix; but see Padel 1988, 71).

At Nantes a ship involved in commerce with Ireland was found (*quae Scottorum commercia vexerit:* Jonas, *Vita Columbani* I.23, ed. Krusch 1902a, 97). Jonas was writing some decades after the event and from Italy. This obviously does not make him a first hand observer, but he certainly knew men who had travelled with the saint. The corroborative value of the *Epistulae* of the saint himself may further render the core of the episode reasonably certain. In his letter of 610 Columbanus writes that 'a messenger has reached me, saying that the ship is ready for me, in which I shall be borne unwilling to my country'. He goes on to say, however,

> Sed si fugiero, nullus vetat custos; nam hoc videntur velle, ut ego fugiam. Si in mare proiciar more Ionae, qui et ipse in hebraeo columba dicitur, orate, ut vice ceti sit quidam felici revocans remigio tutus celator:
>
> (But if I should escape, there is no guard to prevent it; for they seem to desire this, that I should escape. If I am cast into the sea like Jonah, who himself is called Columba in Hebrew, pray that someone may take the place of the whale to bring me back in safe concealment by a happy voyage: *Epistulae* IV.8, ed. & trans. Walker 1957, 34-5).

In a later epistle he talks of 'Jonah, whose shipwreck I have also almost undergone' *(Ionae...cuius et pene subivi naufragium: Epistulae* V.16, l.21, ed. & trans. Walker 1957, 54-5). The fact that the first reference is to being 'cast into the sea' and the second, to 'almost' being shipwrecked is at least different enough in reference for the earlier to be coincidental. This seeming foreshadowing of subsequent events in the first of these references to Jonah must, however, raise some interesting questions. Columbanus' comments make rhetorical use of the fact that his name means 'dove', just as does *jonah* in Hebrew. Hence the hagiographic episode of the boat being stranded until he is cast ashore parallels the legend of Jonah. Several possibilities are raised. One is that Jonas based the incident of Columbanus' release on the reference in the letter. Alternatively the letter may be a forgery—though it is not one of the works listed by Walker as being of doubtful authorship. If it is a forgery it is an elaborate one. Columbanus elsewhere talks of being a 'fearful sailor' *(timidus nauta: Epistulae* V.3, ll. 19-20, ed. Walker 1957, 38) and frequently uses maritime metaphors such as tides, ocean swell and pilotage *(Epistolae* V.3, V.8, V.11, V.15, ed. Walker 1957, 44-5, 48-9, 54-5), perhaps indicating earlier experiences at sea. One can only comment in all this that the idea of his expecting to take ship at Nantes is not in doubt, nor is there any reason to especially doubt the commercial context of such ships, though the latter point must be regarded as unproven. The Jonah conceits, however, must always give pause to anyone wishing to read these episode at face value.

As in the case of Adomnán's reference to 'Gallic sailors', the *Scottorum commercia* of the *Vita Columbani* may be a detail of Jonas's time, c.639. Columbanus describes a ship prepared for him *(navem parari: Epistulae* IV, ed. Walker 1957, 34), which is not the same thing as commerce. Trading ships would be likely to be chartered even for commercial voyages, as we will see below. There is no evidence that an infrastructure for trade existed and each commercial voyage may have been a more or less separate event. Jonas does not then conclusively prove that direct, independent, contacts pre-existed Columbanus.

Even more vague is any evidence for Irish *peregrini* being active in Gaul prior to Columbanus. Kenney is correct to dismiss examples such as Fridolinus, an Irishmen who is said to have come to Poitiers in the time of Clovis and later to preach in Germany. The story was 'reconstructed' in the tenth century by Balther of Säckingen (the monastery founded by Fridolinus) from memories of a 'lost' original. It is accordingly vague and fabulous—Kenney convincingly shows that the core of the story is genuine, but concerning the time of Clovis II, in the seventh century, not Clovis I (Kenney 1929, 497-80). The reference in it to relatives of Fridolin being involved in the mission to Northumbria seems to confirm this *(Vita Fridolini* XV, ed. Krusch 1896a, 361) and fits him firmly into the regular seventh-century pattern of links between Ireland, Northumbria, western Gaul and Germany.

It must be admitted, however, that evidence for Irish activity in western Gaul is rare enough at any time. A will of Ansoald, Bishop of Poitiers, mentions a Romanus, described as 'an Irish pilgrim', whom he places in charge of the monastery at Mazerolles (Tardif 1898, 789-90). The same Romanus seems to appear earlier, as signatory of the *donatio* of Ansoald to Noirmoutier in 677, where he is described as a 'bishop' (Tardif 1898, 786). 'Thomeneus' is a fellow witness, perhaps the same Tomianus of Angoulême who appears in the Acts of the Council of Modogarnomo Castro (CAM I, ed. Maasen, 216). Tomianus is a name known in Ireland in this period. The Bishop of Armagh addressed in the letter of Pope John in 540 (Bede, *HE* II.19, ed. Colgrave and Mynors 1969, 200), for example, bears this name. However this parallel alone should not be regarded as conclusive proof by any means that the Bishop of Angoulême was Irish.

A couple of cases apart, the evidence for contact between western Gaul and Ireland is thus distinctly circumstantial. This is also true of the archaeological evidence, where the western Gaulish connection rests on a few definite parallels and, for the greater part, on negative evidence for other Gaulish connections. We must not fall into the diffusionist assumption, however, that the Irish *peregrini* were necessarily likely to be most active in the region where they made their initial landfall. Even Columbanus, presumably one of the earliest *peregrini*, did not stay in western Gaul, though a number of his followers were in Brittany (possibly the region around Nantes) at the time of his letter of 610. That some western Gaulish church centres maintained connections with Ireland may be another matter. Poitiers and Noirmoutier are mentioned more than once in connection with Irish traffic. In the case of figures such as Dido of Poitiers and Philibert of Noirmoutier, however, we know that the churchmen maintaining such connections were not Irish by birth, but cultivated an Irish connection, perhaps on account of the prestige of the Irish monastic ethos in Gaul. That churchmen from Ireland arrived in Gaul through such connections is only logical. But they need not have remained where they landed and therefore the evidence of their activity in western Gaul is not directly visible.

The complexities of these relations may be seen in the story of the abduction of Dagobert II. The *Liber Historiae Francorum* (c.727) states that, following the demise of Sigibert III, Grimoald the *maior palatii* had the king's young son tonsured and sent into the care of Bishop Dido of Poitiers, with instructions that he be sent on to Ireland. Grimoald then put his own son on the throne *(Liber Historiae Francorum* XLIII, ed. Krusch 1888a, 43; Picard 1991; Gerberding 1987, 47-66, 80ff; Ó Cróinín 1987, 40-3). The *Vita Wilfridi* (written between 711 and 731) also gives an account of the story:

> Nam supradictus rex in iuventute sua ab inimicis regnantibus in exilium perditionis pulsus, navigando ad Hiberniam insulam, Deo adiuvante pervenit.
>
> (For this king Dagobert when he was a young man had been driven into exile and ruin by his enemies who were then reigning, and sailing away, came to Ireland by God's help: Eddius, *Vita Wilfridi* XXVIII, ed. and trans Colgrave 1927, 54-5).

The chronology and circumstances of this episode are probably the most controversial in Merovingian history, though the details relevant to the present study are not especially doubtful. The episode is usually dated to 656, although Gerberding has argued for redating it to 651 (Gerberding 1987, 66). This is now questioned by Picard (Picard 1991, 28-31, 37-8).

Dido was at Nivelles at the time, not Poitiers, having arrived there in the 16th of January (*Additamentum Nivialense de Fuilano*, ed. Krusch 1902b, 451), as Ó Cróinín (1987, 40) has noted. We might speculate that, to avoid suspicion from Dagobert's relatives and in the likelihood of Poitou being in regular maritime contact with Ireland, it was most likely that Dido returned with Dagobert to Poitiers and from there sent him by river and sea to Ireland, but there is simply no evidence to confirm this. Grimoald's entrusting of Dagobert's exile to Dido, however, may presuppose established links with Ireland, or at least that Grimoald thought that the Bishop of Poitiers was well placed to carry out such a task. We have already seen that Ansoald, Dido's successor as Bishop of Poitiers, had Irish connections (see above, 65). To send Dagobert directly to Ireland by sea would have been convenient, as there would always be the possibility that in taking him by way of Anglo-Saxon England some power would interrogate a Frankish entourage and discover Dagobert's lineage.

The *Vita Wilfridi* continues the story,

> Post annorum circulum amici et proximi eius, viventem in perfecta aetate florentem a navigantibus audientes, miserunt nuntios suos ad beatum Wilfrithum episcopum, petentes, ut eum de Scottia et Hibernia ad se invitasset et sibi ad regem emisisset.
>
> (In the course of years his friends and kinsmen heard from some travellers that he was alive and flourishing in the prime of manhood. So they sent messengers to the Bishop Wilfred asking him to invite Dagobert across from Scotland and Ireland and to send him out to them as king: Eddius, *Vita Wilfridi* XXVIII, ed. and trans. Colgrave 1927, 54-55).

This was duly done, around April-June 676. The 'travellers' who informed Dagobert's relatives are described as *navigantibus*, which *might* imply that they were seafarers. Perhaps the news was acquired in western Gaul from seafarers who had contacts with Ireland, but no locations are given.

That Dagobert used different routes to travel to and from Ireland should not be regarded as odd, however—in fact, this story serves to underline the point that between Ireland and the continent neither the route through England, nor the direct route by sea ought to be regarded as more 'natural'. A lot might depend upon political/religious connections. The same point may be seen with regard to where a person might move after landing on the continent. Such personal connections also very likely governed where goods would be transported. Dagobert's return through North Britain might be taken to suggest that travel by sea from Ireland to Austrasia was not possible and that he would not risk travel through western Gaul. On the other hand, it is far more likely that this was a matter of Wilfred's own political connections. Since the mid-660s Wilfred had enjoyed close personal ties with Agilbert, Bishop of Paris (cf. *Vita Wilfridi* XII, ed. Colgrave 1927, 26), who had been present at the Synod of Whitby. More than likely it was this connection which was exploited to bring Dagobert home. In other words, Dagobert's return was facilitated by links of the Gaulish church which had sprung up *since* the time of his exile. I would suggest that this at least makes the idea that the earlier journey was direct rather more likely. *Pace* James we may say that the use of the route via England was less on account of its directness, but due to personal relationships which grew up between Irish, English and Gaulish clergy after 660.

Agilbert is another who may have followed the western Gaul-Ireland connection from Gaul earlier in the seventh century. Agilbert, who became the Bishop of Wessex around 640, is said by Bede to have been 'a Gaul by birth, who had spent a long time in Ireland for the purpose of studying the Scriptures'*(natione quidem Gallus sed tunc legendarum gratia scripturarum in Hibernia non paruo tempore demoratus:* Bede, *HE* III.7, ed. & trans. Colgrave and Mynors 1969, 234-5). It is quite probable that this may be taken to mean that he had not previously been to England at all, suggesting a direct voyage to Ireland from Gaul. His lack of knowledge of English *(barbarae loquellae)* was certainly considered worthy of note at the time of his Wessex episcopacy (Bede, *HE* III.7, ed. Colgrave and Mynors 1969, 234). Agilbert took the part of the 'Roman' party of Wilfred at Whitby, which must suggest that he spent his time in the south of Ireland, Ó Cróinín would suggest among the Anglo-Saxon community there (Ó Cróinín 1983, 245). Agilbert has attracted surprisingly little scholarly attention (though this is now rectified to some extent by Richter 1991), despite his obvious significance as a figure who moved easily between Ireland, Gaul and Anglo-Saxon England. Or perhaps this is the very reason why: Agilbert's movements sit awkwardly with those who defend an 'isolation' model of western insular culture. His family had links with St Columbanus and with the latter's monasteries in the Paris region and this must be seen as the probable origin of his Irish connection. These were the sort of familial connections which characterised Irish activities abroad (Angenendt 1982, 52-79). Agilbert later became Bishop of Paris where, for example, Theodore of Tarsus stayed with him in 668. Despite the known antagonism of Wilfred and Ebroin, he may have been an intimate of both. On his death, he was buried at Jouarre, where his sarcophagus still survives and is one of the only sarcophagi in Merovingian Gaul to have extensive figure sculpture—which it has been claimed to owe to both Irish and Northumbrian inspiration (for illustration see Lasko 1971, 101).

This unusual feature, like the Irish references in some Frankish saints' lives, is a conscious underscoring of Agilbert's links with an insular ethos and spirituality. Agilbert may have played a causal role in the involvement of English and Irish churchmen in the continental politics of king-making between Austrasia and Neustria. This in itself might not be seen as apposite in a study of overseas communication, except where we must consider the central role played by personal contacts in the causation of overseas links.

Western Gaulish churchmen, such as Amandus, Remaclus, Eligius and Nicetius, were involved in the conversion of Germany (Wallace-Hadrill 1985, 143ff). The presence of such a series of missionaries from this distant region is striking, particularly if we add the Irish missionaries arriving by way of western Gaul (who may be then as much 'western Gaulish' recruits as 'Irish'). The Arnulfing leaders encouraged this link, but its beginnings may be traced to Dagobert I. The policy pursued by Dagobert I and his son Clovis II involved the establishment of monasteries within Neustria, often by monks born outside of Neustria. A second field of activity involved sending others on missionary activity abroad: certainly to Germany and Wood would also suggest to East Anglia (Wood 1991, 9ff).

The crucial aspect of this activity for our purposes is that these movements established continuing relationships. Churchmen moved from the centre to the periphery, but they maintained links with their origin points. Some monasteries in Neustria were granted control of estates in western Gaul. Perhaps these were claimed by the monks through family connections, or perhaps the Neustrian and Austrasian rulers were seeking to appropriate territory in western Gaul to increase their personal *dignitas* (Picard 1991, 32-3). Whatever the pattern, much movement of people and goods seems to have been accomplished through these relations around the periphery of the Neustrian heartland of the Frankish kingdom in the seventh century.

A charter of Sigibert III, but linked with Grimoald, granted control of two monastic ports to the monastery of Stavelot-Malmédy, near Aachen—namely *Sellis* (Champtoceaux on the Loire) and *Vetraria* (Port-Saint-Père—Halkin and Roland 1909, 12-13). Such arrangements would have been attractive to monasteries in the north-east, who would benefit from the produce of the south-west, in particular wine and oil. That a northern monastery was given control of the ports is significant in that it implies an involvement of the monastery in western maritime traffic. These are admittedly river ports, and traffic could have travelled up the Loire and overland. Jonas indicates that Nevers was a port for overland travellers to embark on the Loire (Jonas, *Vita Columbani* XXI, ed. Krusch 1885a, 93) and we may recall Gregory of Tours's testimony to the use of the Loire Valley to bring goods west from Orléans (see above, 31). St Philibert shipped olive oil direct by sea from Bordeaux to Jumièges, however, for the lighting of the church (*Vita Filiberti* XXXVII, ed. Levison 1910, 602). The abbey of Saint Wandrille also held estates in the Angoumois and Saintonge (James 1977, 223). We cannot be certain whether this would have involved seaborne shipment of goods back to Saint Wandrille, though this would be a logical inference.

One of the most interesting texts to discuss links around the periphery of Gaul is the *Vita Filiberti*, which survives in a ninth-century text, from a probable eighth-century original (Kenney 1929, 495). The personal connections of St Philibert, whose espousal of a commercial ethos will be examined below, provide an example of the way the western-eastern Gaul interface relates to the western Gaul-Ireland connection. Born in Gascony, Philibert became a follower of the cult of Columbanus (*Vita Filiberti* V, ed. Levison 1910, 587; James 1982, 377), first founding a monastery at Jumièges, before moving to Noirmoutier, where he founded a monastery under the patronage of Ansoald of Poitiers, whose Irish connections have already been discussed. The *Vita Filiberti* suggests that a conflict with St Ouen of Rouen forced his exile to the west—Philibert and Ansoald both following Dagobert II's party against Ebroin (Kenney 1929, 497; James 1982, 377). At this distance we have difficulty in assessing whether this was the actual reason, or a reflection of the conventions of hagiography in the time of the writing of the *vita* (perhaps of contemporary politics). The fact that Philibert was active both in northern and western Gaul, however, is consistent with seventh-century events.

Often cited is an epilogue to chapter 42 of the *Vita Filiberti:*

> Nec multum post Scothorum navis diversis mercimoniis plena ad litus adfuit, qui calciamenta ac vestamenta fratribus larga copia ministravit.
>
> (Not much later an Irish ship with a diversity of goods on board put into shore and supplied the brethren with an abundance of shoes and clothing: *Vita Filiberti* XLII, ed. Levison 1910, 603).

This episode is obviously intended to underscore Philibert's adherence to the ethos of Columbanus. This does not, however, invalidate the details of a ship from Ireland putting in at a site in the Loire estuary, or the presence of shoes in its cargo, which were a product for which the Irish were well known. The detail of an Irish ship is a factor of interest to contrast with the predominant evidence for Gaulish vessels involved in such traffic (see below 97ff). In the context of the need to stress the Irish links of Philibert's monasticism it may have suited the hagiographer to have Irish ships involved in such traffic—but there may also have been Irish ships making this voyage. The fact that Noirmoutier is the likely site of the composition of the *vita*, however, may be taken to add weight to the idea that the author describes a scene which was likely to be found at Noirmoutier.

We will summarise the picture identified so far. The monasteries which grew up on the periphery of the Frankish heartland seem to have established economic networks which brought the western sealanes into contact with east Francia. Dagobert's policy was to move missionaries from one periphery to the other—the diversion of Amandus to work on the frontier mission may be taken as characterising his recruitment of missionaries to his personal service (*Vita Amandi* XVII, ed. Krusch 1910, 440-1; also see Wood 1991, 9). Presumably economic freedoms were allowed as a reward for the participation of the monastic founders in the settlement of the terrain acquired through expansion. It is clear that the Frankish conquest and conversion of Germany was a focus of overseas contact in which Irish and English clerics were heavily involved, probably by virtue of a model of insular political involvement in Frankish affairs stretching back earlier into the seventh century and especially linked to the legacy of Columbanus (Angenendt 1982, 64ff; James 1982, 377-81; Wallace-Hadrill 1985, 68ff, 143).

The personal links of the mission of Willibrord to Germany also indicate an underrated western maritime link. The story begins with Egbert, a Northumbrian living in Ireland (Bede, *HE* V.9, ed. Colgrave and Mynors 1969, 478). The miraculous events of the story may cause us to treat it with suspicion, though the actual routes of the voyages are plausible enough. While a ship is being prepared, Egbert disregards the message of a vision that he should sail to Iona and not Germany. Before it leaves harbour, the ship is driven aground by a storm, which leaves the ship 'lying on her beam ends in the waves'. The possessions of Egbert and his companions are saved, but the ship's stores lost (Bede, *HE* V.9, ed. Colgrave and Mynors 1969, 478). This could be interpreted as contradicting the earlier impression that the brethren were the sole proprietors of the voyage, but it may simply imply that the punishment did not include the personal possessions of the brethren, but only those stores needed to make the voyage possible. It can only be assumed (though there is no plausible alternative) that the route of this voyage was intended to have been around Cornwall and up the Channel. If Egbert was still at this time living at Rath Melsigi (Bede, *HE* III.27, ed. Colgrave and Mynors 1969, 312), which is thought by Ó Cróinín and Fanning to have been just east of the River Barrow, near Carlow (Fanning 1984, 43), the port at which these events occurred would have been probably somewhere in south-east Ireland, perhaps Waterford or Wexford. A southerly gale and floodtide in the Barrow estuary could disable a ship in just this way, but it is unwise to read to much into Bede's maritime detail, which may be wholly imaginary.

A series of Northumbrian exiles in Ireland took up the task which Egbert abandoned. Wictibert 'took ship and arrived in Frisia', but meeting no success, returned to Ireland (Bede, *HE* V.9, ed. Colgrave and Mynors 1969, 478-80). In 692 Willibrord followed. His visit to see Pippin *en route* is specifically described as a detour (Bede, *HE* V.9, ed. Colgrave and Mynors 1969, 480). The latter's intervention in their mission is suggestive: 'supporting them with his imperial authority so that none should interfere with their preaching, and granting many favours to those who wished to embrace the faith' (Bede, *HE* V.9, ed. & trans. Colgrave and Mynors 1969, 480). In another, perhaps confused, episode, two more Northumbrian exiles in Ireland, both called Hewald, go to Saxony and are martyred (Bede, *HE* V.10, ed. Colgrave and Mynors 1969, 483).

These voyages seem to be constituted by the churchmen in question and presumably take them up the English Channel, from a starting-point somewhere in Ireland. There is no suggestion that Northumbria lay on their route. As Bede was writing about events in his own lifetime it may be accepted that the routes described are correct at least on this point. This evidence raises important issues for the understanding of the basis of seventh century exchange between Gaul and Ireland. It emerges as most likely that Irish voyagers would still travel by way of the Atlantic sealanes (just as Willibrord did) even though their destination was Germany. The sea is a much less labour-intensive transport medium than travel overland and if travellers were going directly to Gaul the sea route would be more efficient—if they could afford the charter of a ship. We may contrast then travellers such Willibrord and Columbanus, whose destination seems to have been the continent all along, to a traveller such as Fursa (Bede, *HE* III.19: ed. Colgrave and Mynors 1969, 276), who had specific connections with a monastery in Anglo-Saxon England (see James 1982, 380) or St Samson of Dol who may well have landed in Cornwall without any specific intention of going on to Brittany (see below, 107). It is hard to be precise as to detail in any of these cases, but we must at least make the attempt to distinguish the potentially different motivations of travellers.

Cargoes and Commerce Between Gaul and the Irish Sea Basin

There is no doubt at least that ships were coming and going between Ireland and the continent in the seventh century and on the basis of the archaeological evidence we may make some firm speculations as to the routes and destinations of maritime commerce. These will be discussed in Chapter Seven. The documentary evidence suggests that a diversity of goods might be found in a ship's cargo. It does not suggest a traffic dominated by a single, regular commodity. We have seen, anyway, that the 'wine trade' model rests on no appreciable evidence. A regular range of goods involved in commerce might be identified, of which wine was one element, but there is no evidence to suggest that it was the principal, or even a major, element.

Surviving passages from the early Irish *Muirbretha ('Sea Judgements')*, provide considerable detail on the possible contents of cargoes. We can be sure that a text or texts bearing this title formed a part of the corpus of Irish law at a date earlier than the tenth century, covering the topics of flotsam, jetsam, ownership of the strand and the maintenance of stranded mariners. We are now, however, dependent for an idea of its contents on a few quoted lines in other tracts. Passages relating to the maintenance of shipwrecked mariners are quoted in *Di Chetharšlicht Athagabála* (e.g. ed. Binchy, *CIH* 1978, 369.2-369.8—these are specified as being *muirbretha* at 388.18, whether this means that they are taken from a text by that name is unclear). In *Bretha Étgid* is discussion of the ownership of goods brought from inside and outside of territorial waters (e.g. ed. Binchy, *CIH* 1978, 314.17-315.28, named as from the *Muirbretha* at 314.17). Some of the same material is also to be found in the *Heptads* (MacNiocaill 1971) and the range of topics covered in the *Muirbretha* are also briefly listed in a section of *Tecosca Cormaic* (which is probably citing the *Muirbretha):*

> Bárca do thocor i port | Allmaire sét | Murchuirthe dílse
>
> (Bringing barks into harbour, treasures from overseas; sea-waifs forfeited: *Tecosca Cormaic* I.25-8: ed. Meyer 1909, 2-3, my translation).

Of central interest to our discussion of cargoes are the passages concerning the ownership of goods 'which have been brought over nine waves of the sea': in *Bretha Étgid* (in Trinity E 3.5—ed. Binchy, *CIH* 1978, 315.26-8), in other passages in Rawlinson B 506 (ed. Binchy, *CIH* 1978, 139.32-4), Trinity H 5.15 (ed. Binchy, *CIH* 1978, 2155.16-22) and entries in the glossaries of Cormac and O'Davoren. These, though evincing some differences, are clearly all quoting variants of the same original text which spelled out the likely contents of the cargoes of wrecked ships.

This discussion in the commentaries provides two details of vital interest. The first of these is that cargoes may be made up of a variety of elements, in which wine is not accorded any special status:

> IS ann ata .s. ui screpal uaithi no .s. foraici uingi: in tan tainic fo thomus duine airithi hi, 7 ni 'na lesc lama-sin fein dorala iat s a ferann duine aile 'na comocus, 7 .s. ui screpal do ar connad 7 uisci do lecad di masa seichida 7 iarann 7 saland ata indti, no .s. foraici uingi masa cno gnae 7 cuirnd, 7 escup fina no mela ma ta fin (no) mil indti.
>
> (That [case] when a *sét* of six *screpals* from her [is due], or a *sét* worth an ounce of silver, is where she came directed to a particular person, and it was not onto his land which she happened to be driven, but into the land of another person in his vicinity; and a *sét* of six *screpals* to him [the other person] for allowing her firewood and water, if it be hides and iron and salt are in her; or to a *sét* worth an ounce of silver, if it be exotic nuts and goblets; and an *escup* of wine or of honey, if wine or honey be in her: ed. Binchy, *CIH*, 1978, 315, ll.24-8).

Secondly, cargoes may be 'directed to a particular person', or, as stated earlier in the same passage, to a particular *tuath (in tan tainic fo tomus tuaithi airithi hi:* ed. Binchy, *CIH*, 1978, 315.17). While there is a danger in talking in evolutionary terms, we may observe that this sort of model would fit the idea of a society in which external commerce played a fairly limited role and where goods from outside entered under very precise terms.

The variety of goods listed here carries important implications for those who would see single-element cargoes as the norm in early medieval western sealanes traffic. Where wine is mentioned, it is not given any special priority and the *escup*—in *Sanas Cormaic* simply a 'wine measure'—is here used to measure honey as well. The recension of part of the same passage in Rawlinson B 506, puts honey ahead of wine in the reference, as well as adding further goods:

> RAWLINSON B 506
> masa or (no) airget (no) allmhaire set 7 set foraicce se scripla do masa iarand (no) sechedha 7 escub meala (no) fina ma ta mil (no) fin indte.
>
> (if there be gold or silver or overseas treasures and a *sét* equivalent to six *screpals* if there be iron or hides or a *escup* of honey or wine if there be honey or wine in her; ed. Binchy, *CIH*, 1978, 139, ll.32-4).

Another recension, in Trinity H 5.15, adds *clúman:* 'feathers or 'furs' (ed. Binchy, *CIH*, 1978, 2155, l.20). *O'Davoren's Glossary* adds 'British horses':

> GAILLTI .i. laire breathnacha no cno g[n]ae 7 cuirnd 7 buabhaill... *(O'Davoren's Glossary*, ed. Stokes 1862, 95).

In *Sanas Cormaic ('Cormac's Glossary')* the *Muirbretha* is explictly cited in a context which gives valuable evidence for dating the passages concerning cargoes:

> EPSCOP FÍNA isna Muirbrethaib .i. escra tomais fina le cennaigib Gall 7 Frangc.
>
> *(Epscop Fína [sic]* in the *Muirbretha* i.e. vessels for the measurement of wine amongst the merchants of the Gauls or Franks: ed. Stokes 1862, 19).

It is clear that variant forms of this list of currency items formed the basis of various commentaries in the corpus of Irish law. They may have formed a regular set of interpretations to the statutes relating to the law of distraint regarding flotsam and jetsam—perhaps under the title *Állmuire Sét*, which is used in *Tecosca Cormaic* (see above). That the phrase *escup fina* is quoted by Cormac may be taken to indicate that such a list was an early part of the *Muirbretha* proper—even though it now only appears in the commentaries—or, alternatively, it may indicate that the text had commentaries even in the Old Irish period. Binchy was prepared to accept that some commentary material on texts regarding distraint was on linguistic grounds as early as the ninth century (Binchy 1973, 72-80). Cormac's obit of 908 provides a *terminus ante quem* for both the name and one phrase now only found in the commentaries. *Tecosca Cormaic* (c. ninth century) also may be quoting this list of cargoes when it notes that mead and wine are amongst the treasures which a king will attract to his court *(Tecosca Cormaic* I.44, ed. Meyer 1909, 4-5). We may not be so certain as to the early date of the other references to cargoes, but there is a strong possibility that these, too, are early medieval references.

The fact that the *escup* has here become purely a wine vessel *(epscop fína)* carries no implications that the *escup* was principally for use with wine, when considered in the light of these variants. We may accept Zimmer's conclusion that the malapropism *epscop* is a play on words with the word for bishop (Zimmer 1909b, 441) and assume that the abbreviation of the *Muirbretha's* full reference is a convenience to this end. The *Muirbretha*'s reference to measuring vessels would tally best with the idea of the wine being imported in casks, which would stay on board the vessel, with the wine being sold in small quantities during the voyage from port to port. Despite Cormac's ascription of the *escup* to a Gaulish context, however, we need not see the use of *escup* vessels as limited to Gaulish goods. The word *escup* is ultimately from Latin *scopa*, but where we find it here, *scup* itself is likely to be a local word, not a Gaulish borrowing (though ultimately a loan-word through British: see Binchy 1958, 291; O'Rahilly 1942, 43).

In the *Muirbretha* wine is cited as a possible cargo. The phrase 'if wine be in her', implies that it was not a ubiquitous cargo. Wine was probably imported in casks, though skins are another possibility. We may discount ceramic vessels as these would leave archaeological traces. Thomas' reference to Adomnán's metaphor of 'wine oozing from a cask' (Thomas 1976, 252-3), is actually to nothing more specific than 'cracks' *(rimulas)* in a 'large vessel' *(pleni vassis:* Adomnán, *Vita Columbae* epilogue to Book I, ed. Anderson and Anderson 1961, 322), which could just as easily be ceramic. His much quoted reference to remains of casks at the (inland) sites of Lagore and Lough Faughan (Thomas 1976, 252—most recently in Mytum 1992, 265) proves little, as there is no evidence that the casks are Gaulish. These comments by Thomas are in any event to be seen in the context of his argument for a link between E ware and wine. This approach is also particularly seen in the studies of Hodges. The only possible connection would be in terms of a common origin area—E ware itself can have no conceivable connection with wine, unless we take the far-fetched step of imagining E ware pitchers (Eiv) to be the *escup* vessels. It is worth stating categorically that no other E ware vessel could even remotely be imagined as a carrying container for wine.

Let us now consider the other cargoes mentioned in the *Muirbretha* or its commentaries. Honey was the only sweetener available in the early middle ages and the principal ingredient of mead, which was a valued drink for regular secular consumption in early medieval Celtic society (Jackson 1961, 35-6). That honey was marketed in Gaul is suggested by charter evidence of the tenth century (see below, 72). Clearly it should be regarded as a good which would have a high exchange value, especially if the role of wine consumption is diminished. Ireland was a producer of honey (e.g. *Bechbretha* XXI, ed. Charles-Edwards and Kelly 1983, 62-3), which may render its presence in the *Muirbretha* as being either that of an object of local exchange, or an export good. Malt was doubtless also an object of exchange, for use in alcohol production, in which context it finds mention in other Irish laws *(Cáin Aicillne,* ed. Binchy *CIH* 1978, 481, ll. 9ff), though not in the *Muirbretha.*

Ireland was a major producer of hides and these are also mentioned in the *Muirbretha* commentaries. Export of leather goods is also attested in the *Vita Filiberti*'s reference to shoes (see above, 67). It should be noted for the unwary that the evidence of the *Vita Filiberti*'s reference has been somewhat inflated by repetition. Hodges (1989, 127) would have Mediterraneans returning with leather to Byzantium, wine being exchanged for leather by 'Irish monks' (actually Irish sailors) in the 'Loire valley' (actually Noirmoutier) and, on another occasion, carried there along with hunting dogs (Hodges 1989, 38). Despite his pluralistic use of this reference, however, we might take note of Hodges's point as to its singularity: that the *Vita Filiberti* is a rare text in referring to leathergoods as an early medieval export good (Hodges 1989, 127). Early medieval Irish shoes were of a very high quality (Mytum 1992, 245). Sites such as Ballinderry II and Iona have produced debris from shoe making (Hencken 1942; Barber 1982, 103-6; Lucas 1956, 367ff; Waterer 1968, 70-82; Neill 1991, 14-15; O'Rourke 1991, 22-3) and the finished products from the latter site are similar to pictorial evidence from insular manuscripts, for example the Book of Durrow (Henderson 1987, 51). It may be that only Ireland treated leathergoods as an object for export, or perhaps only those of Ireland were of a quality sufficient to command a market abroad. Hides were certainly a major element of Ireland's export trade in the high-medieval period (O'Neill 1987, 77-83). The reference to 'clothing' as an export from Ireland in the *Vita Filiberti* also finds a parallel in later Irish trade (O'Neill 1987, 68-89).

Feathers, noted in one variant of the commentaries, are also a likely enough Irish export, gathered from offshore islets. Certainly they were commercially traded for the making of matresses and pillows in more recent times (Mac Conghail 1987, 32).

Iron, carried as a raw material and as a value-added product, is likely to have been a common cargo. Material for intensive study of the iron industry is being uncovered at Whithorn, for example, where extensive evidence of on-site smelting exists, utilising ore brought from a source at some distance (Hill 1992a, 21-3), probably from coastal trade. Iron objects are also another possible import from abroad. This will be discussed below. Gold and silver are mentioned in Rawlinson B506, and are logical enough materials to be shipped at any time.

'Exotic nuts' *(cnoe gnáe)* would appear to be self-explanatory. A commentary on *Bretha im Fhuillema Gell* (ed. Binchy *CIH* 1978, 472.l.16) describes these as 'eastern' in origin. Kelly would suggest these are West Indian nuts brought by the Gulf Stream, but it is not clear on what grounds (Kelly 1988, 249, n. 37; Mac Cana 1994).

The evidence for a salt trade has not attracted much discussion. Salt has a clearer consumer context than wine, as the early Irish Laws make reference to salted meat. It may in time be possible to trace changes in eating and cooking habits in early historic Ireland, with communal killing and immediate consumption of meat giving way to killing and storing of individually owned beasts, for which salt would be necessary (Wooding 1988a, 15). The references to salted meat *(Críth Gablach* ll. 270, 300, 350, 381, ed. Binchy 1940) in a text such as *Críth Gablach* (early eighth century) might suggest this. Salt referred to individually is 'sea salt' *(Críth Gablach* XV, l. 190, ed. Binchy 1940): *murlúaith:* lit. 'sea ash', the name possibly coming from the extraction process involving the heating of brine over a fire, or perhaps the analogy that salt is the residue of the sea, where ash is the residue of the fire (cf. Adomnán, *De Locis Sanctis,* II 15-16—though Smyth 1996, 263-5 makes a case that salt from seaweed is what is referred to). Adomnán's extensive discourse on rock salt and its origins may be taken as an indication that only sea salt was known in Ireland:

> Aliter uero sal in quodam Siculo monte haberi solet. Nam illius montis lapides de terra euulsi naturaliter salissimum sal esse gustu conprabantur, quod proprie nominatur sal terrae. Aliter ergo sal maris atque aliter sal terrae uocitari solet:

(There is another way of getting salt in a mountain in Sicily. The stones of this mountain, when torn away from the earth, are found on tasting to be genuinely the purest natural salt, which is properly called salt of the earth. Thus it is customary to distinguish the names sea salt and salt of the earth: Adomnán, *De Locis Sanctis* II.17-18, ed. & trans. Meehan 1963, 88-9).

This seems to imply that sea salt in its extracted form, and not simply seaweed brine, was familiar to the Irish. Is there a case for salt having been imported? The western coasts of France and Brittany are major salt producers (LeFond 1969, 183; Gaillou and Jones 1991, 95-6) and the Loire valley was central to salt trading by the eighth century (see below, 72). The monastery of Noirmoutier, for example, was involved in salt trading. In the case of Ireland it might seem logical that it would simply produce its own salt—but an historical sense is necessary here. Ireland may have been less likely to initiate subsistence extraction of salt if large quantities of salt only became necessary for the first time in the early Christian period. Viking Age Ireland imported salt from Anglo-Saxon England *(Salann Saxanach: Aislinge Meic Conglinne,* ed. Meyer 1892, 62) and Irish place-name elements associated with salt production (e.g. 'Saltpan, Saltworks') are all English, being completely absent from the Gaelic stratum (Scott 1981b, 115-6). This would suggest that salt production was a late-Medieval or later development: probably later. Salt production is not mentioned in the Irish Laws, even where there is reference to ownership of the strand. Whether salt was produced elsewhere around the Irish Sea is hard to determine. Certainly it was an Iron-Age activity in Wales (where it is attested by Very Coarse Pottery) and Cornwall (Peacock 1969). Nothing in the nature of early medieval *briquetage,* however, has been discovered. The case is not as clear in the place-name elements for Britain as for Ireland. Charles Thomas *(pers.comm.)* has observed that the Cornish for salt is *hile,* easily confused with *hely* ('hunting'—*viz* Goonhilly Downs which is definitely a hunting, not a saltworking, name). Early names for saltworkings could well be hidden behind this sort of similarity of elements. If Ireland did not possess salt industries from prehistory, early medieval economic structures may not have accommodated the founding of them. Do the place-names suggest that this waited upon the much later arrival of an English bourgeoisie? At least we should remain aware that salt was traded, and more than one source might be accommodated in exchange processes.

The reference to goblets is not clear as to the class of vessel involved, though a related gloss in H 5.15 reads *cuirn buabaill:* 'drinking horns' (ed. Binchy *CIH* 1978, 2155, l.22), which may be indicative of the original reading, though *O'Davoren's Glossary* (see above) reads *cuirnd 7 buabhaill.* Mac Cana (1994 81-93) has discussed this phrase in a recent note. As we will see in the following chapter, there is a likelihood that long-distance cargoes carried both ceramic and glass vessels. We can only say that the evidence of the *Muirbretha* for the movement of small consumption vessels over a long distance is supportive of this model.

These then are the goods described in the *Muirbretha.* Both this text and the *Vita Filiberti* stress the variety of goods which might be on board a ship operating in and out of Ireland. They are probably many other goods involved in such traffic. The making of quern stones *(Vita Brigidae* XXXI, trans. Connolly and Picard 1987, 24-5) was certainly an activity for which suitable stones were brought from quite a distance (Campbell 1987, 105-17; Jope 1966, 131; Proudfoot 1961, 94-122; Hodges 1989, 124). Over short-distances we have references to the movement of timber (see above, 9) and reed-cutting (Adomnán, *Vita Columbae* II.39, ed. Anderson and Anderson 1961, 434-5). Fishing industries were doubtless involved in short-distance traffic. A traffic in very small fragments of Samian ware, which could be imports from the continent or from local Roman period sites, also existed though its consumer context is unknown (Bradley 1981-2; Warner 1976, 285-8; Lynn 1984, 28). We should not push speculation on goods involved in such exchange beyond the limits of the evidence. Further items involved in exchange will be identified as further sites with well-preserved sequences are excavated and little-known texts, such as the Irish laws, are translated and dated.

The idea that exotic pigments and decorative stone were long- and short- distance trade goods in the early middle ages has been indicated by recent excavations. Hill has suggested that a traffic in lime from the eastern Solway, for decorative use, is evinced by datable finds from Whithorn (Hill 1992, 22). Lime traffic has certainly followed this route in more recent times (Donnachie 1971, 146-7). The early medieval traffic along this route might be best dated to the Anglian period at Whithorn, which brings Cumbria and the eastern Solway into closer contact with the rest of the Irish Sea. Colouring matter is also a very likely exchange good, though where it is known from western sealanes contexts, however, it is not absolutely clear whether it was a seaborne arrival. Colouring matter used in insular gospel decoration includes (Roosen-Runge and Werner 1960, 262-7; Fuchs and Oltrogge 1994, 135-148) orpiment (yellow), lapis (blue), kermes (from the pregnant *kermoccus vermillo,* a Mediterranean insect, this was available in Spain: Strabo, *Geographica* III.2; ed. Jones 1949, Vol. 1, 33) and *crozophora tinctoria* (maroon). Where such colouring is used in unprovenanced manuscripts such as the Book of Durrow and the Book of Kells, obviously the question of the routes by which such colouring matter was imported cannot be inferred with any precision. Alcuin, in a letter from Northumbria to his student Joseph in Gaul in 790, asks to be sent 'plenty of paints of fine sulphur and dyes for colouring' (see below, 96). A piece of orpiment was discovered at Dunadd in 1981 (Campbell 1987, 113), however, showing perhaps that it was not confined to the ecclesiastical network only and this find has at least a strong likelihood of having arrived by the western route from the continent. Ewan Campbell (1996 forthcoming) has made much of the case for madder *(rubia tinctorum)* as a trade good, which will be discussed in the next section.

The commerce which was associated with Dagobert's monastic foundations in Gaul provides some interesting parallels for the range of goods involved in the long-distance insular traffic. At St Denis in 634-5, Dagobert's foundation charter, now lost but cited in a later source, granted the monastery the right to hold a fair on October 9 (*Gesta Dagoberti* XXXIV, ed. Krusch 1888b, 413). The insular focus of the fair is highlighted in the forged foundation charter (probably tenth century) which describes the market (*mercato*) of St Denis in 629 and the ports of Rouen (*Rothomo*) and Quentovic (*Wicus*), where there are 'those coming from over the sea to buy wines, honey and madder' (*qui veniunt de ultra mare pro vina et melle et garantia emendum: Diplomata Spuria* No. 23, ed. Pertz 1872, 140). This is not good evidence to support a connection with western sealanes traffic, but Campbell reasonably suggests that it does give some notion of the value accorded to these particular commodities in the commercial networks of northern Gaul. Hatcher (1973, 16) would argue that the Abbé Raynal in 1782 had access to a lost charter of Dagobert, establishing markets in seventh-century Gaul where Saxons brought lead and tin from Britain. This might well indicate contact involving Cornwall, but it is a doubtful reference.

The collection of charters from St Denis, authentic and otherwise, is exceptional, but we find clues in other sources that this type of traffic would have existed in earlier contexts, and in foundations on the Atlantic seaboard. In the *Vita Filiberti*, the monastery's commitment to commerce, using surplus production from its estates, is made into a religious ethos where the saint pronounces on 'holy commerce' (*Vita Filiberti* XXIII, ed. Levison 1910, 596) and the need to 'give more than lay merchants give' (*Vita Filiberti* XXIII, ed. Levison 1910, 596). The ninth-century *Miracula* of the saint describe the salt production of the monastery and the exchange of this with British mariners (Doehaerd 1978, 156), maybe Breton, who had brought wheat to La Furca. Wine is also sold at fairs at Noirmoutier (Doehaerd 1978, 156) and the use of the Loire as a distribution route for salt and wine from various centres, with Noirmoutier and Orleans as focal points, is indicated in sources such as the ninth century *Miracula* of St Benedict (Doehaerd 1978, 156). Doehaerd would suggest that Dagobert offered incentives to encourage monastic groups to settle more marginal areas: citing examples such as the clearance of scrub to found the monastery of St Wandrille in 649 (Doehaerd 1978, 33-4), though he goes on to link this with the *desertum* ethos, also. That there was a direct benefit to the crown to be gained from encouraging this economic development in monastic settlement is clear: comparable to that which the secular *emporia* were to confer. We should not discount the possibility that these networks played a part in the establishment of the late-sixth through eighth century networks which sent goods between Gaul and Ireland and western Britain.

If monasteries in Gaul provided opportunities and markets for trade, we may see this neither as indicating that all trade was under monastic control, nor that all commerce at the British and Irish end reached monastic ports. Traders such as worked in and around Noirmoutier may have responded to orders conveyed via the monastic networks, or monastic figures with royal connections in Ireland may have sent goods to their families back home. That monasteries ultimately attained prominence in the growth of a market economy of Ireland after the eighth century may suggest that the commercial/monastic ethos in Gaul could have been inspirational in this process, with Dagobert's model being adopted in Ireland.

We should remain relatively open-minded as to the types of sites which were landfalls for ships from Gaul. Thomas favours the view that imported goods were channelled through secular centres at the British and Irish end, which would tally with the eighth-century text *Tecosca Cormaic* in which a king is defined as 'inviting barcs into port, with overseas treasures' (see above, 69). Campbell, too, has discussed the means by which he sees local exchange mechanisms used to generate surplus for the purchase of the imports by local potentates. Even if the secular dominance of the landing places is shown to be definite, we do not know if all cargoes were destined for secular consumption. If secular authorities dominated the landing places, monastic purchases might have to pass through them. That Dunadd evinces a wider range of imports than Iona, for example (Lane 1994, 112), may simply be matter of its convenience as a terminus for ships from abroad (see below, 107) and we should be wary of seeing this as carrying any implication for a general royal 'control' of imports.

Let us summarise the important points regarding our picture of seventh-century traffic. Undoubtedly goods were now being carried directly by sea between Gaul and Ireland. Terms such as *commercia* and *cennaigi* indicate that the activity could be commercial, stepping aside for a moment from whatever causal links existed with political/ecclesiastical activity. Adomnán confirms that continental ships sailed as far north as Dalriada. Two of the more specific references indicate a connection between the Loire estuary and Ireland, in particular, rather than the Bordeaux connection favoured by Zimmer. The episode of 610 AD, in which St Columbanus was taken to Nantes to be put on board a vessel (*Vita Columbani* I.23, ed. Krusch 1902a, 97), would still seem to be a classic illustration of Zimmer's model. It should be noted, however, that this connection cannot be shown to exist much prior to 600 AD, if at all. The poverty of evidence for the fifth and sixth centuries must be admitted, but this, although it fails to disprove Zimmer's long term continuity model, it also does nothing to confirm it. It is also worth repreating that at no time is there evidence for a large scale wine trade, though wine *was* traded among other goods.

The seventh and eighth century sources all suggest that a diversity of goods was involved in western sealanes commerce, quite a similar diversity and range of goods to that which typified Gaulish coastal commerce of the seventh and eighth centuries.

Gaulish Artefacts in Ireland and Western Britain

The Gaulish/Frankish link with the Irish Sea basin in the seventh century is confirmed by a range of archaeological indicators found on sites in western Britain, Ireland and Scotland: running through objects of Gaulish manufacture such as ceramic and glass vessels to objects which show strong Gaulish/Frankish stylistic influences, such as decorative metalwork, sculpture, iron weapons and horse trappings. These will now be discussed at length and their evidence fully integrated into the historical picture. Though the glass of 'Merovingian' type is possibly also relevant to the sixth-century pattern, it will be discussed in more detail here on account of the comparative value of considering its research problems in conjunction with those of E ware.

The items of more definite foreign manufacture, the mostly homogeneous collection of tablewares known as 'E ware' and the collection of glass types putatively identified as 'Merovingian' have attracted the most research interest on account of their widely accepted diagnostic role in sixth, and especially seventh, century site chronology, though beyond this point there is much disagreement as to both the finer points of their chronology and the social context of their importation and use (Thomas 1990, 1-26; Campbell 1988a; Alcock 1987, 89-90, 122; Wooding 1996). The distributions of these wares follow generally identifiable maritime paths and so offer great potential for identifying the origins, routes and destination points of commerce. There is a lack of agreement on many basic points regarding the character and significance of the 'Gaulish' finds, however, especially E ware. Some scepticism has also been expressed as to the value of research undertaken into them (Duncan 1988, 70-1; Laing 1985, 169; Griffiths 1992b, 9-10; Campbell 1984, 35-8). It is, accordingly, important that we now make clear definitions of the following: the value of the research questions so far asked of these finds; their probable date and geographical range, and their social and economic context.

E ware and Related Types

E ware is the most numerous of the imported ceramics: found on more than 60 insular sites. E ware is a much less prepossessing ware than either the Mediterranean wares or *paléochrétienne grise* and this fact makes it a more complex problem in terms of locating its origins and identifying its social context. E ware is a coarseware pottery: unglazed, fired in a reducing atmosphere. Basic forms have been well documented, but will be briefly listed here (a full *corpus* is expected soon from Ewan Campbell). Some forms found in Britain and Ireland, not the full range, are illustrated in my Figures 6 & 7, to aid in comparative discussion of continental finds.

Ei: the commonest form of E ware, a jar seemingly in two basic sizes, around 15 and 20 centimetres in height. The rim diameters are around 13 and 15 centimetres and the shoulder diameter between 15 and 18 centimetres. It is common, but not ubiquitous for there to be a simple horizontal scored shoulder mark, just above the widest point, running right around the vessel. The rim forms show the greatest variety: one type is sharply everted and flattened on top; others are flattened, but more horizontal than everted; others everted, but not at a sharp angle.

Eii: a distinctive style of carinated beaker around 8 centimetres at the shoulder. Virtually every example is slightly different to the others.

Eiii: a distinctive bowl, again with slight variety from piece to piece. Examples from Whithorn evince a light brown slip.

Eiv: a pitcher form which can have either a simple lip or a trefoil spout. The handle has two parallel grooves. Otherwise they resemble Ei jars. The lipped vessels seem to have the less everted rim forms, while the trefoil pieces have sharply everted rims.

Ev: lids for larger Ei jars in standard fabric.

Evi: a small 'unguent pot'. One example identified by M. O'Donnell out of the collection of miscellaneous sherds from Ballycatteen—these are not listed as E ware in Thomas's 1981 catalogue.

Despite minor variations of form from pot to pot, E ware is a homogeneous class. All pieces have large sub-angular quartz inclusions and a red grog with a high iron content. Fabric colour varies considerably, but fairly consistently, between light grey, pink and brick red. In many cases it would appear that pink is the original colour, other colours being the result of heating and post-depositional discolouration. The amount of iron grog may vary, however, and this could cause differing degrees of pink colour at the time of firing. Suggestions by O'Kelly (1963, 105) that this grog is absent from some pieces are erroneous (they were based on exaggerated expectations arising from the literature).

E ware is often not finely finished. Some from Garryduff are so poor in form as to inspire O'Kelly to the view that they were wasters, or crude copies made on site (O'Kelly 1963, 107). Most E ware bases have string marks indicating that they were cut from a moving wheel. A piece from Derrynaflan lacking this mark may simply be the last of a batch, cut off after the wheel had become stationary. This seeming speed of production may again account for some slight dissimilarities. These differences do not indicate a lack of homogeneity in class E. The fabric of E ware is almost identical from piece to piece and a tendency not to fully update the *corpus* has perhaps obscured this. It has been argued that the fabric is close in character to a later Scottish ceramic, known as 'East Coast Gritty Ware' (ECG), but this not correct and stems from comparison of ECG with pieces which are erroneously identified as E ware on formal similarities, but which are actually ECG. A number of the latter are still listed in Thomas' (1981b) catalogue and his 1990 map (Thomas 1990, 15): for example, the supposed E ware from Craig's Quarry in east Lothian (Thomas 1981b, 21, now in the National Museum of Antiquities, Edinburgh) and the finds from Abercorn, also in Lothian. Laing has argued that ECG forms may be copied from E ware pieces (Laing 1973, 185ff), but this must remain an open question. Williams's (1982) petrological comparison, for example, between pieces from Saint Christoly (a site within the *urbs* of Bordeaux), and British finds of E ware, seems to have used the Abercorn finds for comparative purposes: the identification of which as E ware Thomas has doubted for some time (*pers. comm.* 1988—on examination, in 1988, they were clearly not E ware). In time it may be possible to identify individual batches of E ware, but as we have seen in the case of the Mediterranean wares there is no reason to accept any slight variety of this sort as indicating change across time (any more than variety between broadly contemporary batches).

Identifying a Source for E ware

That E ware has attracted a great deal of scholarly attention may be seen to reflect an appreciation of its potential in solving chronological and cultural problems of the early middle ages in the Celtic West—too often, however, with sharp echoes of the 'wine trade' fixation and its attendant *sapientes* (Hillgarth 1984, 15; Thomas 1981a, 271; Hodges 1977, 241). The seeming intractability of its problems has also proved a lure to researchers. Hodges for example has seen a definite solution to the problem of its exact origins as tantalisingly just over the horizon (Hodges 1977, 240; 1984, 40), citing Giot's forthcoming petrological analyses. Professor Giot *(pers. comm.)* and Ewan Campbell (1984, 35-41), however, have convincingly questioned the ability of such analysis to answer these questions in the way they have been used so far. It is important then that we re-examine the process of research into E ware, to establish what questions have been asked and why the answers have not been more precise. This is also an important process to pursue in the case of the glass finds.

E ware, not being present in the Tintagel assemblage which formed the core of Radford's study, was a later addition to the alphabetical typology of imported wares: hence it is somewhat grotesque to occasionally see it referred to as 'Tintagel ware E'. Before Thomas proposed it as a homogeneous class of early Christian imports under the label 'E' ware in 1957 (Thomas 1957, 15), it had been known in considerable quantity from sites such as Lagore, Dunadd and Garranes for some decades.

The reasonable assumption has been that the British and Irish finds of E ware are a tiny subset of a mass of such undecorated coarsewares in France, begging the question of why such a plain domestic pottery would be imported to a zone where pottery use was previously almost non-existent (Thomas 1990, 8; Wooding 1988a, 14-16). Research initially proceeded on the assumption that E ware belonged to the well-known sub-Roman Rhenish groups and had arrived overland via Anglo-Saxon England. The expertise of scholars such as Wheeler and Dunning, who had done very early work on the Rhenish wares, was enlisted (Hencken 1950, 124; 1942, 49-50). In historical terms, we may thus view the early models as a consequence of the better publication of the Rhenish material and of the fact that a number of British researchers had worked on them, mostly as a byproduct of Roman and high medieval period interests. The same pattern is also true of the study of early medieval glassware, where the Rhenish products are still better known (see below). The researches of Wailes (1963, 142, Fig. 102-58; Peacock and Thomas 1967, 36) established that comparable, and largely closer, parallels for E ware existed in Northern French assemblages, while macroscopically similar fabrics existed in western France, usually from later wares. For the most part these latter parallels were collected un-systematically (Thomas, Giot, Warner, Bruce-Mitford *pers. comms.*—examples are the pieces from Camp-du-Chaillot and Pépiron). Through the work of Hodges (1981), Brown and Timby (1988; D. Gaimster, *pers. comm.)* the Northern French wares have become better known, while the western finds have not seen such extensive reanalysis.

The forms of the Ei-iii, and some E iv, vessels are indeed best paralleled among northern and western Merovingian assemblages. Exact parallels have been hard to locate in France, however, leading to doubts in the minds of many scholars regarding this identification. It is arguable, however, whether any short term identification of the exact origins of E ware can be expected—the problem on the continental side is of the needle-in-the-haystack variety. Comparatively little excavation has been done. Random searches amongst known western French collections have turned up a bare minimum of parallels outside of Brittany: from early excavations such as Herpes and Chadenac (Giot & Querre 1985, 99) and the Chateau excavations at Tours in the 1970s (Randoin 1981, 106-7).

The problem may not be solved by the simple adoption of a waiting brief. Such a policy has been effective in the case of the sixth century Mediterranean imported wares, but there the research interest abroad has been fuelled by the western insular debates. This is clearly evinced in the use of the narrow insular terminology Bi, Bii, etc. in the Mediterranean context (Thomas 1982, 23). And there are obstacles to easy identification of E ware. Munsell colours, for example, are of little use in identifying wares with the wide range of discolouration of E ware. That some of this is caused by weathering on site is clear from the variation of colour from sherd to sherd on pieces from the same vessel (O'Kelly 1963, 103). Discolouration is also caused by the heating of the pots, often again varying from sherd to sherd depending on the closeness of portions of the vessel to the heat source. The colour may vary from dull grey to the original pinkish-orange—both colours being seen, for example on a beaker from Herpes (acc. no. British Museum 1905 5-20 176).

Only certain rim forms, emergent grains, striations and basal string marks studied in combination allow exact identification. As coarsewares have not generally been crucial to archaeological chronology, fabric based research methods accordingly are not well adapted to the problems of locating sources for these wares.

We turn now to a second methodological issue. Research into E ware has been heavily influenced by historical paradigms. While this is somewhat contrary to accepted notions of the objectivity of archaeological study, it must be accepted that such analyses have been made—and *post facto* are part of the individual history of E ware scholarship. They are, moreover, fully defensible in methodological terms. For vessels imported in a clearly limited series of events it is likely that a historical context *can* ultimately be established. The formula for such research proposed by Rahtz (1985; for an example of this approach: Mytum 1986, 375-8) would suggest that the historical data are best introduced after the completion of the manual search for parallels. But is this necessary? If the search for parallels may be aided by the testing of an historical model, this does not prevent the gradual testing of the model by further publication and study of the material.

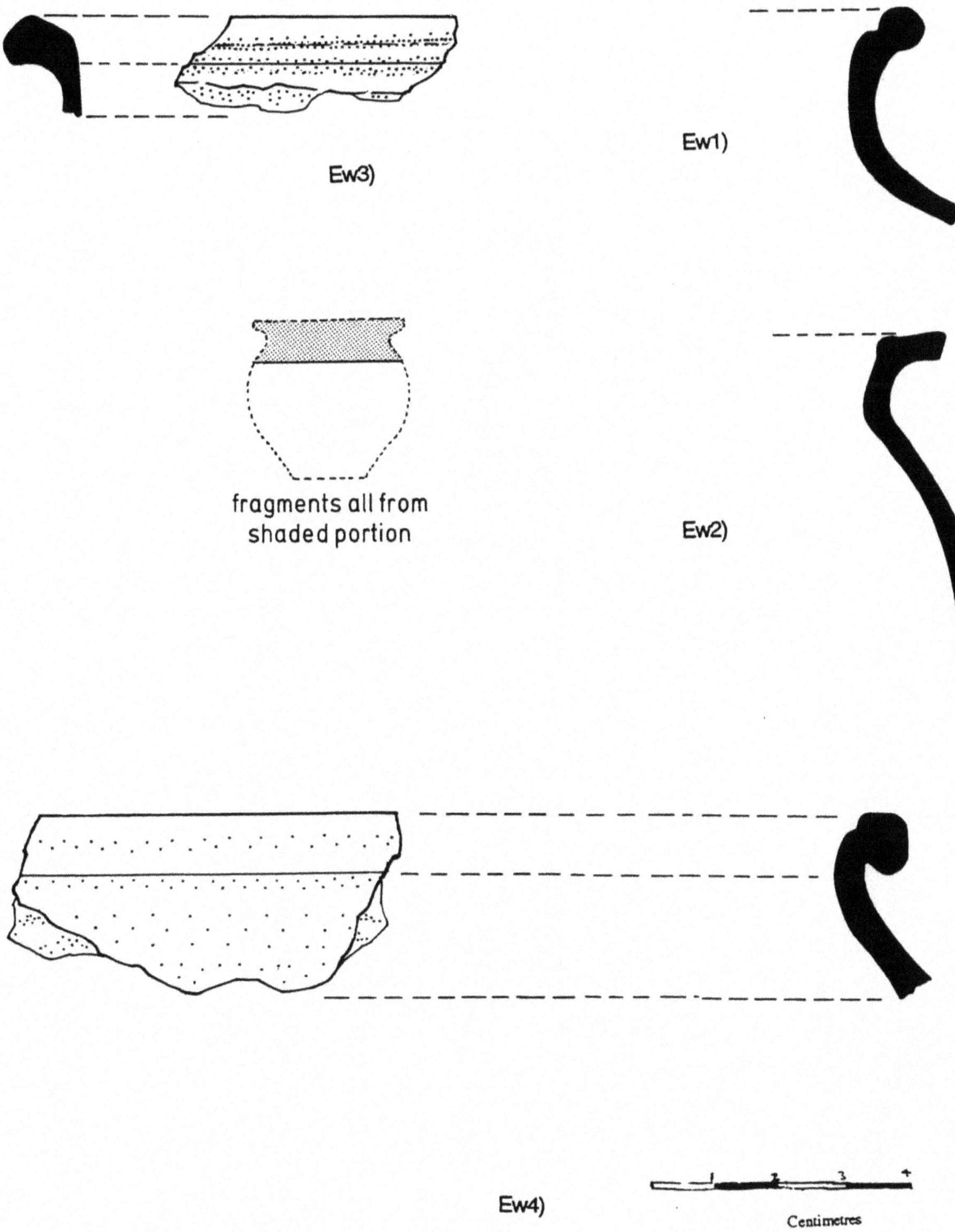

Fig. 6
E1 rim forms
Ew1) Large E1: Garryduff, 401
Ew2) Large E1: Garryduff, 336 and 456
Ew3) Large E1: Whithorn, +88/8420
Ew4) Large E1: Whithorn, +88/8444

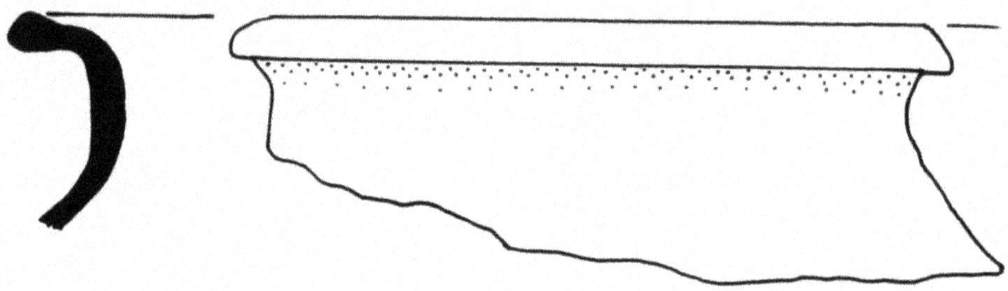

Ew5)

Ew6)

Fig. 7 E ware Rim Forms
E ware Vessel Fo

Ew5) Large E1: Whithorn, +88/8440
Ew6) Small E1: May's Hill

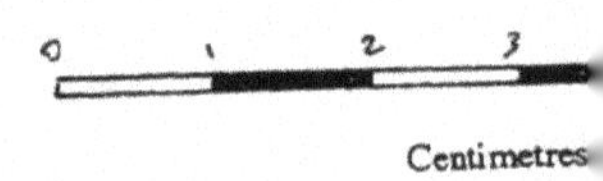

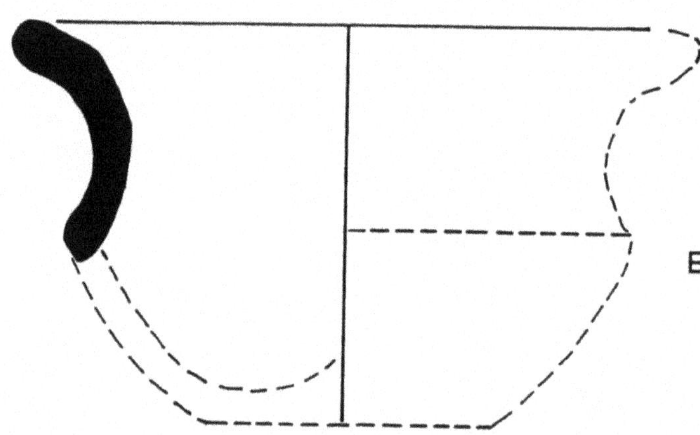

Ew7)

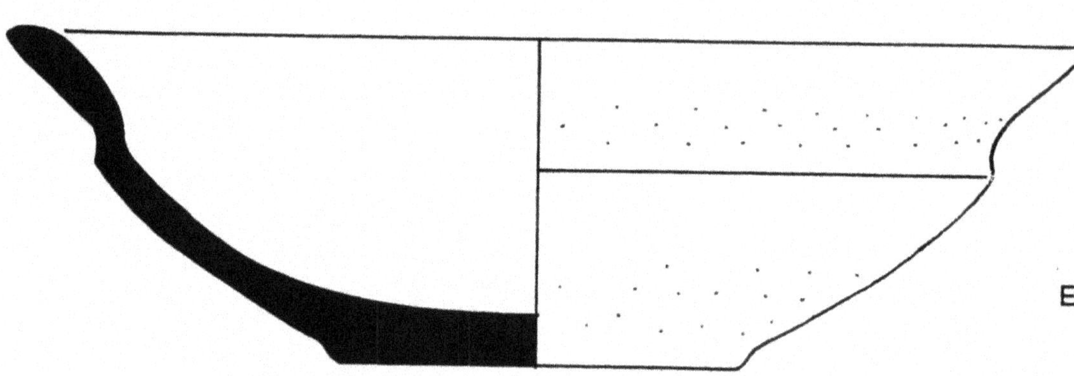

Ew8)

Ew7) E2 beaker from Whithorn, +88/7439
Ew8) E2 Bowl from Whithorn +87/4545-1/2 & +87/4541 1

The posited link between the early medieval Irish Sea basin and the Rhineland had no historical basis. Perhaps doubting the likelihood of an overland link through Anglo-Saxon England, Thomas found an archaeological comparative model in the importation of the 'Bar-Lug' ceramic form into Cornwall from the Rhineland at the end of the first millennium AD (Hutchinson 1979, 81ff). In strictly historical terms, however, the maritime links of the period of Bar Lug pottery are of a wholly different character to those of the sixth and seventh centuries. E ware is also rare in Cornwall—hence invoking the Bar-Lug model is scarcely apposite to explain the forces behind its importation to the Celtic West.

In 1967 Thomas and Peacock abandoned the idea that E ware was primarily Rhenish in origin. The principal evidence mustered was from heavy mineral analysis of the tempering sands, which were identified as post-Triassic and most probably Tertiary in character. Such sands are rarer in the Rhineland and not found in Rhenish wares (Thomas, *pers. comm.*; Peacock and Thomas 1967, 43). The conclusiveness with which these analyses have been accepted has been questioned by Campbell (1984, 38). First of all must be noted the failure of non-petrologists to appreciate the methodology of petrological studies: a similar problem to the way in which the work of philologists and numismatists is accepted by non-specialists. The heavy minerals present are not unique to Tertiary mineral assemblages. Tertiary and post-Triassic sands themselves are known from a number of parts of Europe (Giot *pers. comm.*) and we should also note that such is their suitability for ceramic tempering that small pockets might be sought out in areas where they are less common. Peacock's point is still reasonable: that the assemblage present is more likely to reflect activity in one or two areas where kyanite and andalusite are present in Tertiary sands. Identification of likely sources, however, is still something of a shot in the dark. It is clear from the 1967 study that the historical link of Ireland with Aquitaine, and at least western and Northern Gaul, influenced greatly the new choices of likely areas to test. As Thomas observed in his 1967 study: '...there is no real link between the Rhineland and Western Britain', while: 'On the historical side, Bordeaux and the mouth of the Garonne are wholly relevant to the idea of links between post-Roman Gaul and post-Roman Britain' (Peacock and Thomas 1967, 39). In fact, as we have seen, Bordeaux is less relevant than the Loire, though this does not detract from Thomas' basic point about historical likelihood. Doubts raised by the then recent fieldwork of Wailes (1963; Peacock and Thomas 1967, 36) and the identification of Gaulish Atlantic group *paléochrétienne grise* with the insular class D seemed to support the likelihood of a link, but the work of Zimmer and the 'western seaways' researchers was clearly also causative (Thomas 1981a, 271; Thomas 1976, 252-4; Thomas 1990, 10, 16-17).

E ware in France

In more modern contexts E ware would be described as the product of a rural industry rather than an urban (where in modern Brittany, for example, there were broadly similar pots to the Ei type, termed *pot à lait* and *pot à beurre*, cf. Pillet 1980). This distinction may mean little for the early middle ages, though the excavations at the urban centre of Tours produced only a couple of sherds of a ware which might be E ware, amongst a great amount of *paléochrétienne grise* while, conversely, E ware is found in Frankish cemeteries in western France from which *paléochrétienne grise* is almost totally absent (e.g. Herpes and Chadenac: see above, 74). *Paléochrétienne grise* is also absent from Ireland, where there is less obvious influence of the urban Gallo-Roman church than in Wales, where both types occur. This question may deserve more attention, though chronological differences in the occurrence of these wares could also be responsible.

Some intermittent attempts to locate E ware in France have been carried out during the last decade by Mary O'Donnell, Ewan Campbell, Alan Lane and the author. These have concentrated on Poitou and have been, understandably, founded on a wider understanding of the range of form and fabric variants found in Britain and Ireland than Wailes was able to obtain in the 1950s and '60s. We are now clear that the production area will be a small one: the uniformity of E ware forms and fabric indicate a likely single source for all the British and Irish finds.

The first priority of fieldwork has been to clarify if E ware actually was a Gaulish product and to gain a clearer idea of its likely cultural context in western Gaul. These researches have not been systematic investigations, however, and mostly only an adjunct to attempts to fully understand the British and Irish distributions.

The situation on the continent is hardly comparable to that in Britain. French archaeologists do not depend upon coarsewares as a cornerstone of chronology. The fact that parallels for E ware are rare is not at all surprising and suggestions of searches in the less-likely terrain of Spain or Portugal are perhaps premature (Campbell 1984, 36; Hodges 1984, 40).

Distribution maps with limited continental distributions have been confusing to the viewer and have led to suggestions of a British origin for E ware, but there is little reason why a British-made coarseware would be exported to Gaul, except perhaps from Cornwall to Brittany, which received few imports from Gaul.

E ware *has* been found in continental assemblages to the south of Brittany. Three recent finds from Poitou and the Touraine fit with the historical link with the Loire estuary. In Poitou, 'an Eiii bowl' was a surface find from a churchyard at Chadenac (Campbell, *pers. comm.*; on the site: Barrière-Flavy, n.d., 201ff). The context is unknown, though a major early medieval cemetery was excavated there last century. From the collection of the British Museum, three beakers of Eii type are from a sixth- to seventh-century assemblage in an enormous cemetery at Herpes, excavated in the last century by P. Delamain. The exact context is unknown, but recent doubts as to the reliability of the site attributions for pieces in the Delamain collection are in this case dispelled by published illustrations (D. Kidd *pers. comm.*). Accession numbers are 176, 178 and 179. Wailes and Campbell list 176 as E ware, but don't seem to have seen the other two. 176 is not precisely a common Eii form, being elongated above the carination and having an atypical rim. Its fabric is of the dull grey discolouration typical of the E ware from Garranes and Lagore, though one patch is of the brighter orange which is suspected to be the original colour. 179, however, is extremely convincing as E ware (see below). It is of parallel form to British Eii vessels and is of an orange/brown fabric with 'pimply' emergent quartz grits and odd red inclusions. The string cut-off base is identical to E ware base-marks.

From Tours a good parallel to E ware is an Ei style rim and shoulder from the Chateau site (sixth- to seventh-century context). The form is closely but not exactly paralleled at Whithorn in Scotland. The fabric is hard, greyish-white and has rounded, unsorted quartz and odd iron (probably haematite) inclusions. Randoin describes it as 'Paté gris beige clair, fine, avec inclusions de quartz et de feldspath' (sighted by B. Randoin, E. Campbell, M. O'Donnell, P-R. Giot, J. Wooding). From the Monastérie de Saint Martin, there is an Eii type beaker with collar from a sixth- to seventh-century context. The fabric would be again acceptable as E ware, as it has the pinkish tinge which is lacking from the other find. It is not paralleled in decoration on British sites (though such a collar is common on Ei pots), though form is acceptable as E ware and the collar is of the type found on many Ei vessels (sighted by B. Randoin, E. Campbell and J. Wooding). Also worth noting at Tours is a local variant of *paléochrétienne grise* (No. 3.2063.27) with trefoil spouts very similar to Eiv.

These finds add to the pieces from Brittany already accepted as E ware. Of these, the Guisseny piece is exactly paralleled on British sites (cf. my Figure 6, Ew4). Unfortunately the Morbihan and Les Cléons pieces have been mislaid. The Les Cléons pieces are particularly of interest as they are from the Loire estuary, which has an historical link with Ireland. Some of Wailes's drawings of the pieces from this site seem to represent good E ware pieces and some do not (Wailes 1963, Fig. 104—he notes that this vessel is paler and more finely gritted than most E ware). A report from Professor Giot *(pers. comm.)* of a find from the Louvre excavations in Paris has yet to be confirmed by other observers and should not be taken at face value.

The author's studies in France in 1987 and 1988 were conducted on a consciously limited scale, so only those collections already identified were examined, along with comparative visits to Paris, Rouen, Evreux, Nantes, Beauvais and Orléans (circumstances prevented access to material at Poitiers and some at Orléans). Extensive use was also made of the work of Wailes and Hodges. There were, in 1987, very few scholars who were convinced that any exact parallels to E ware existed outside of Britain and this evidence was vital to a critical use of E ware as historical evidence.

There is certainly E ware in western-French contexts. This is not a claim to be made lightly. Often there have been reports of E ware being found on the continent which have a long life in oral history (perhaps in the process becoming more conclusive than their claimants intended them). Examples are Swan's finds from Saint-Christoly (Warner, *pers. comm.;* Williams, unpublished), Giot's from Île Lavret (Giot and Querre, 1985, 98-9 and examined by the author in 1988: they are thin, ribbed sherds in a hard, whitish fabric, clearly not E ware) and also finds from Orléans (Hodges 1977, 241), most of which are not very like E ware at all. Bélier in a recent note (Bélier 1995, 261-5) has also suggested that E ware is an Aquitanian type, but her discussion offers no evidence or up-to-date information. There are various features of the finds from Tours which make them inconclusive: the best fabric parallel is not convincing in form and the better form is less certain in fabric. The Guisseny piece is exactly matched by Irish finds in form and fabric, but northern Brittany is not western France. The conclusive proof comes, ironically not from French collections, but from the British Museum. The previously unsighted Herpes 179 is a matched Eii form, macroscopically identical to British E ware in fabric and colour and with the string cut-off base exactly like other E ware finds. It awaits closer fabric comparison with British finds.

A good deal of emphasis in refining the origins of E ware has been placed upon comparisons with later, western French ceramic traditions. Peacock and Thomas' 1967 study included analysis of a piece from Camp du Chaillot, near Saintes (Peacock and Thomas 1967; Campbell 1984, 36-8). A piece from Saint Christoly, provided by Leo Swan, was examined in 1982 by David Williams. These have both evinced fabric similarities to E ware, but are not identical. A piece in the possession of P-R. Giot, from an assemblage of medieval wares from a cave mouth at Grotte de Villebors (Poitou) is so like in form and fabric to pass as E ware (if it is not a genuine piece, out of context: Fig. 9, Ew13; cf. Fig. 6, Ew6). All of this may seem to add to the likelihood of E ware being a Poitou product, but it is circumstantial evidence at best.

The earlier distribution might have suggested an origin in Brittany—however this is not likely on geological grounds. The heavy minerals in E ware are rare, if not unknown, in Brittany. The finds so far point to the regions of the Touraine, Saintonge and Poitou, though there is a danger of exaggerating the evidence of such a small number of finds. This makes sense in terms of an historical model of links between the Irish Sea basin and the Loire valley, such as has been argued in the present study. That there is no E ware from the Bordeaux region, slightly further to the south, is logical enough in this connection. Refinement of the historical evidence has rejected the earlier model which led Thomas to argue for the link with the Garonne mouth, cited above. We would expect to find the origin point of E ware somewhere in the Loire region or Poitou on present historical expectations. If not, however, there seems no need to follow Thomas in attributing E ware to a residual Roman ceramic tradition in the very south-west of Gaul—indicated by sites such as Pépiron (Thomas 1981b, 24-5; Gabet 1969; Santrot 1986, e.g. 141). Finds from sites such as St Pierre de Vauvray and Orléans are suggestive of similar ceramic traditions in northern Gaul close to the Loire, which are relevant in the light of the known traffic along the Loire valley.

As E ware is now identified confidently on some western French sites (Tours, Chadenac, Herpes), even though the number is small and some finds (Herpes) are more convincing than others (Tours), looking westward of the Rhineland for a source seems more likely to be

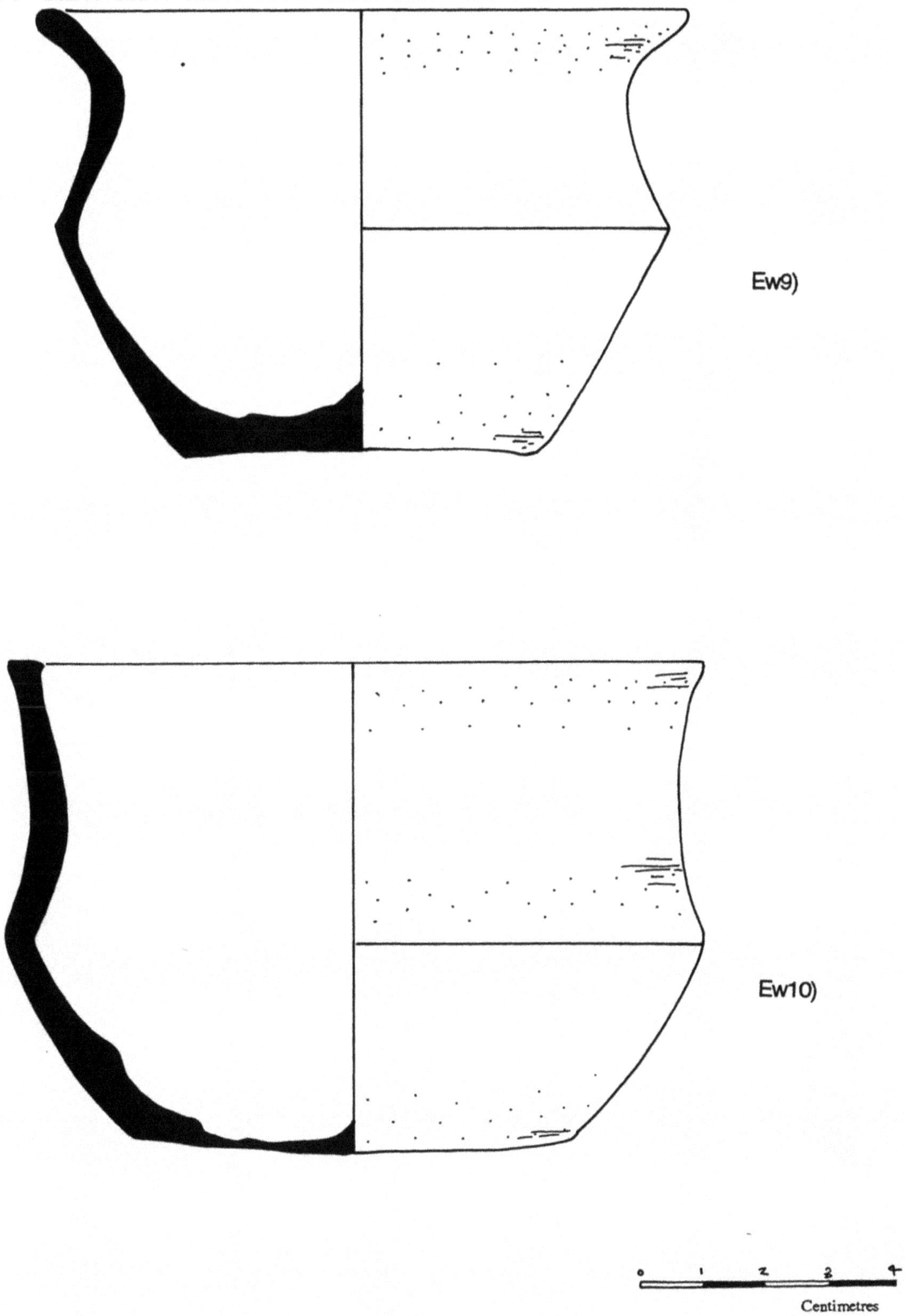

Fig. 8 E2 beakers from Herpes (Charente)
Ew9) British Museum, 1905 5-20 179
Ew10) British Museum, 1905 5-20 176

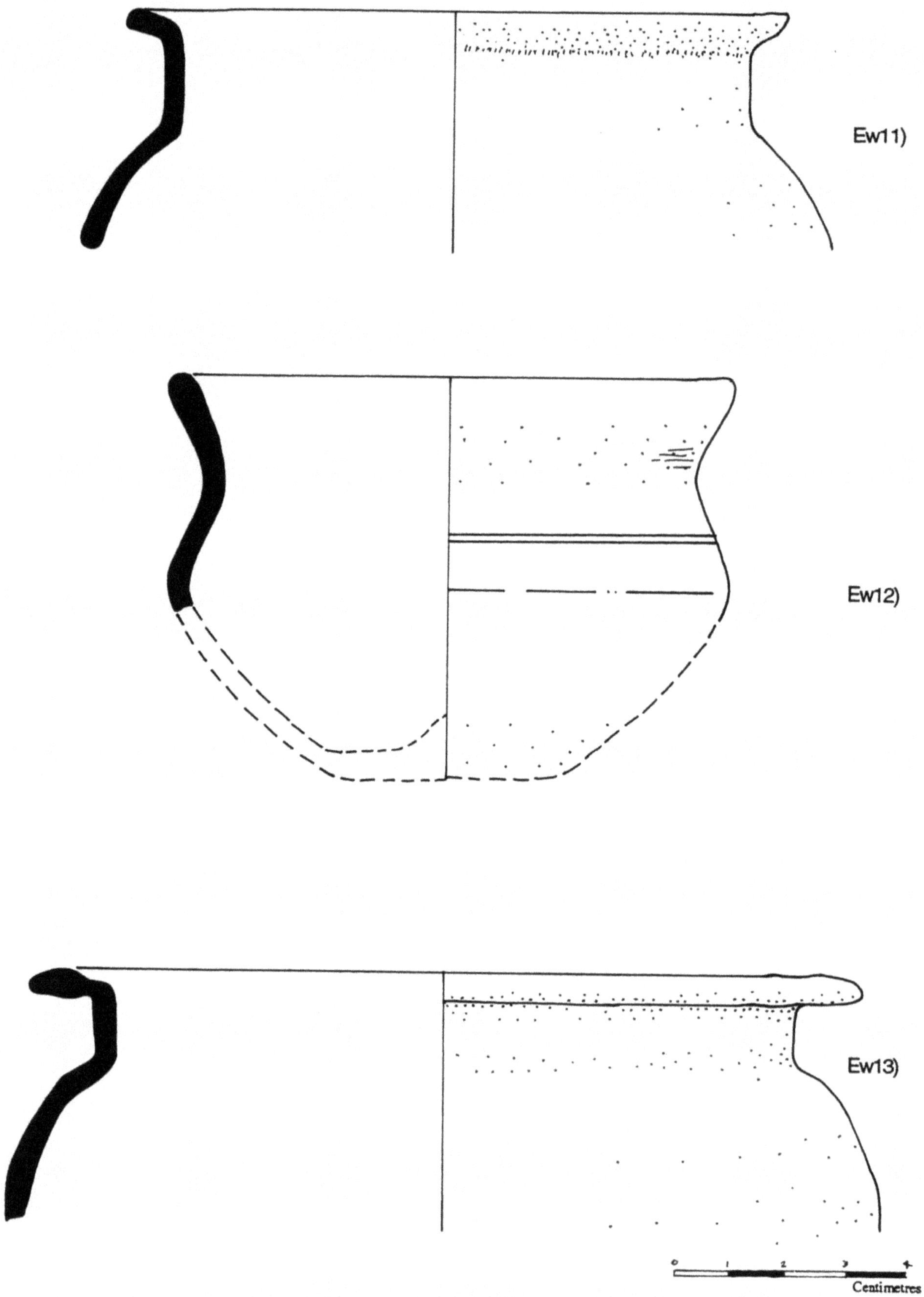

Fig. 9 Possible E ware vessels from western France
Ew11) Small E1: Tours, Chateau 3.1968
Ew12) E2: Tours, Monasterie d'Saint Martin 7.546
Ew13) Large E1 style vessel, Grotte de Villebors, Lavalette, Charente

effective than the earlier approach. Ironically, if anything slowed down the investigation it was Thomas' adherence to the Bordeaux link over the better-attested historical links with the Loire estuary which prevented more attention being given to Poitou and the Touraine.

Historical research has led to the narrowing down of the principal *floruit* of Irish *peregrini* to the continent to the seventh century, with St Columbanus seen as a pioneer, rather than continuing a trend of the sixth century. This assists in assessing the likelihood of the broadly seventh-century horizon proposed in recent studies (see below).

The Social and Economic Context of E ware

In assessing the possible consumer use of E ware, there are some basic points which can be made. The Irish Sea basin, and especially the parts of Ireland and Scotland where E ware is found, had no domestic pottery at the time of the importation of E ware (Wooding 1988).

Ewan Campbell (1996; also Lane 1994) has argued that the E ware vessels are containers—and hence evidence for the vascular systems of commerce. He has used both E ware and the Mediterranean wares as evidence for an evolving exchange model—in which these ceramics are suggestive of sites for *emporia*. That E ware vessels were containers, however, seems extremely unlikely. Ei and Eii types could have had covers bound over them—Ei in particular usually having a sharply everted rim. But they would be makeshift containers at best. This is not to say that they would have been packed into a ship empty as the dry space inside the jars would have been useful for storage. At best, however, we might imagine a situation where the jar was a bonus offer with the contents: such as one finds in Chinese grocery shops today, where preserved fruit is sold in lidded jars of equal value to the contents. Any attempt to see E ware as regular containers for goods, and hence direct evidence for exchange in commodities in the same way as the amphorae, must explain why these 'containers' are in the same fabric as vessels (Eiii and Eiv) which are more obviously serving vessels. Lane (1994, 110) is correct to question the constant references to E ware as 'kitchen ware', but, in the absence of any evidence that similar vessels were containers in any continental context, the case that they were imported as containers remains to be proven, rather than disproven.

Ewan Campbell has disputed the idea that E ware was used to cook in, noting the irregularity of soot-staining of the fabric, which is often internal as well as external (Campbell 1996). It is difficult to be conclusive on this, however, and much discolouration could have been caused by damage sustained after the pots were broken. Campbell has also suggested that there is a possible association between E ware and the use of madder. The Ei vessel from Teeshan, in County Antrim, contains a thick deposit of madder (Warner, forthcoming; Lynn 1985/6, 51). Other pieces from Ireland (Ballinderry Nos. B E6 347; A E6 547, now in the National Museum of Ireland) and Scotland (in the possession of L. Alcock) also have purplish stains which may be madder deposits. However none of these show staining of anything like the same quality as the Teeshan piece and it is hence doubtful that this can be held to prove that E ware was ubiquitously used to import madder. The logical supposition is that the Teeshan jar was used to *heat* madder, after which it was discarded as useless on account of being set with madder beyond the point where it could be cleaned. Interestingly, it is the most completely preserved (approximately 40% of the vessel: all the lower part of the jar) of all Irish or British finds of E ware, which may further suggest that the vessel was, unusually, abandoned before being broken in use. All this evidence implies was that these were all-purpose vessels, occasionally used to heat dye. We should be cautious of giving any suggestion that E ware directly related to a sort of value-added exchange, involving dying, which may be anachronistic.

Identifying a universal usage pattern for E ware may prove difficult, as any consumer may have found their own use for it. In a region where no other pottery was used it can have no established use-pattern to fit into. Subsequent developments might be noted. Caroline Earwood has suggested that wooden vessels from Loch Glashan are modelled on E ware forms (Earwood 1990, 85: also Lagore vessels are similar to Eiii: Mytum 1992, 247, Nos. 1 & 4). The emergence of Souterrain Ware pottery, very dissimilar in form to E ware, in Northern Ireland at the beginning of the Viking period may suggest at least some continuity of a social receptivity for pottery. If wooden vessels *were* made in imitation of E ware it might suggest that the function of E ware in such regions was not one where external heating of the pot was required. In Northern Ireland, on the other hand, the emergence of Souterrain ware might suggest that the ceramic character of vessels was the most desired characteristic.

The economic context of E ware is a puzzle, but it is too easy to take the view that it can only be explained as a throwaway addition to a lucrative trade in more valuable items. In this madder is no more defensible a choice than wine. Other attempts have been made to prove that E ware was a luxury good in Irish society. In a very doubtful argument Harold Mytum has interpreted an incident in the ninth-century text *Bethu Brigte* to a servant inspiring the wrath of the king for dropping a valuable vessel (Mytum 1986, 375-6) as being to an E ware vessel:

> Do-rigenæ at[h]ech a tigh ind ríg bet mar. Du cer airi airit[h]ech logmar ind ríg co mmebaid frisin meis ara belaib ind ríg. Ba ingnad a lestar, ba dia [s]etaib ingantaib ind rig.
>
> (A churl in the king's house had done a terrible thing. He let fall a valuable goblet belonging to the king so that it smashed to pieces against the table in front of the king. The vessel was a wonderful one, it was one of the rare treasures of the king: *Bethu Brigte* XXX, ll. 324-6, ed. & trans. Ó hAodha 1978, 10, trans. 27-8).

Mytum's argument depends on the detail that the vessel was breakable. He assumes then that the vessel is E ware and concludes that E ware vessels could hence be termed a 'rare treasure' (Mytum 1986, 377). This is wholly unconvincing. *Lestar* ('vessel') is an ambiguous term in Irish (as it is in Welsh—see below, 92). It could imply metal vessels, which might still be fragile enough to shatter, or might also be used of glass. Mytum contends that it cannot here be a glass vessel, on account of Harden's thesis that no intact glass vessels were in use in this period (Mytum 1986, 376). There is no basis for Harden's thesis, as we will see below and Mytum's expectations of identification must anyway be considered highly optimistic.

If we may use textual sources to find any context for E ware in Celtic society it must be in broader terms. Texts such as the eight century Irish status-law tract *Críth Gablach* show a wide range of vessels used in the sorts of small households which characterised the complex society of seventh through ninth century Ireland (*fidlann*, l.139; *ian*, ll.74, 184; *cúad*, ll.116, 176; *coire*, ll.174-5, 338, 549; *lestar*, ll. 141, 338, 364, ed. Binchy 1940). We should seek the value of E ware in this sort of context: perhaps imported to aid in cooking on a more individual basis than was done before; or perhaps to introduce a greater range into the vessels available, so that each rank of nobleman might have a cooking pot of a value apposite to his rank.

The Date of E ware

The chronology of E ware has been another cause for debate. Thomas, in the 1960s and '70s, was prepared to accept a date as early as the fifth century, in which connection he associated it with Zimmer's thesis. Much of his argument depended upon the sequence at Gwithian, which has never been completely published. Warner's discovery of E ware in a ditch-fill at Clogher, where it is consistently separated from Mediterranean wares by a sterile 'yellow' layer, tended to confirm a growing view that E ware was mostly separate in distribution and date to the Mediterranean wares. It has become increasingly clear from Mediterranean sites that the Mediterranean wares were very unlikely to be arriving in Britain later than the mid-sixth century. This would imply that E ware was largely a seventh-century phenomenon, or later.

The potential dating of E ware rests on several foundations which should be treated critically. Firstly, one may highlight the historical evidence for seventh-century links with Gaul, but not for much earlier than 600. This point, oddly enough, was not taken up in work on E ware prior to the 1980s, most archaeologists working on E ware following the older (not entirely superseded) view that links as far back as the fifth century were evinced by the sources. The better evidence for the seventh century, on the other hand, should not be accorded very much weight in dating E ware as, firstly, it reflects a much broader distinction between sixth and seventh-century sources, with Britain and Ireland having few sixth-century historical sources of any reliability and, secondly, the total lack of references to the Mediterranean links evinced by the sixth-century pottery finds warns us that there could equally have been sixth-century Gaulish links which have left no trace.

A second foundation for the dating of E ware is the pattern of distribution. The evidence for the separation of the E ware distribution from that of the Mediterranean wares is beyond doubt and must certainly imply a separate importation context. The exclusion of the Mediterranean wares from E ware distributions on the continent has been discussed above and seems conclusive. E ware is totally absent from at least two British regions which have produced the Mediterranean wares in some quantity. In one of these cases, North Wales, the comparatively small amount of excavation of early medieval sites may be noted (though, in part, this is a circular argument, as the finding of E ware is often diagnostic in the interpretation of a site as early medieval). The fact that it is not found on any sites in Somerset, and only in minimal amounts in Cornwall, is more pertinent. Cornwall has been at the centre of study of the imported wares since the 1960s. The recent identification of finds of imported wares from an old excavation at May's Hill may indicate the possibility of finds being overlooked even there, but in general it must be said that the chances of any recently-excavated material being incorrectly identified are very small.

The dating of E ware is yet to be refined by any continental data. Only the pieces from Tours were found in context on a site with a long sequence: in a seventh-century pit. Our problem, then, is principally one of relating the occurrence of E ware to the *datum* line provided by the Mediterranean wares, and other reliable dating evidence. The writer, along with other archaeologists, has held the view for some time that E ware is a largely seventh-century phenomenon, but on analysis this bears some re-consideration. The finds from Abercorn, with its conveniently narrow historical floruit, are not E ware (I am grateful to Professor Thomas for allowing me to re-examine the Abercorn finds with him in 1988). Sites such as Dunadd, with a broadly seventh-century historical floruit, have yielded radiocarbon dates which suggest sixth-century activity (A. Lane *pers. comm.*). Recent experience, in any event, should warn against attempts to associate occupation phases on historic sites with actual historic events, at least for dating purposes. This has been seen in the case of Conimbriga with regard to the dating of ARS, and is also demonstrated by Warner in a reassessment of Lagore (Warner 1985-6, 76). There are problems also with the separation of the distribution. The absence of E ware from sites in Somerset must be considered in the light of the general rarity of E ware in Cornwall and Devon. As no finds of E ware have been made east of the Kelsies (near Newquay) on the northern coast, there may be no especial reason to think they would have reached Somerset in the normal course of events, though we should not forget E ware is found as far east as Glamorgan, on the opposite shore of the Bristol Channel. The Clogher sequence must similarly be considered in the light of its location. Clogher itself is well inland and, though an important royal site, may have received only intermittent and unrepresentative imports.

Our discussion of E ware dating is best informed by those sites with complex sequences containing both E ware and the Mediterranean wares: good examples are sites such as Whithorn, Clogher, Dalkey Island and Dinas Powys. Other sites such as Garryduff, Garranes, Derrynaflan, Randalstown, Dumbarton, Iona, Bantham, May's Hill, Caldey and Longbury Bank all have produced both types of wares, but not in a stratified context. Campbell (*pers. comm.*) suggests that the Dinas Powys sequence shows a distinction between the Mediterranean wares and E ware. Two provisionally-published sequences support this chronological distinction between the wares.

At Whithorn the large number of E ware and Merovingian glass finds are mostly from the waterlogged southern sector at the base of the hill. Peter Hill, the excavator, now interprets the Gaulish material as 'rubbish strewn on the fields of the sixth? century monastery', perhaps for manuring. This is an area which was heavily trampled and ploughed in later centuries. The recent interim reports evince little doubt that the Mediterranean wares from the site are associated with earlier features than the Gaulish find-deposits (Hill 1990, 4-5; 1992b, 4-7 and personal observations). Sherds of amphorae were found in a rubbish pit, the upcast from another pit and a ditch-fill from phase 3a (Hill 1992b, 4). This phase is associated with a series of round gutters and other features, distinctly earlier in the sequence than the colluvial phase which produced the Gaulish material. Hill is tempted to see the field wash as sixth century, but we should note that this is probably only on the basis of the c.560-720 date range which seems posited for E ware in his report (Hill 1992b, 5). Likewise, he is willing to accept a late fifth-century date as possible for the Mediterranean wares (Hill 1992b, 4). If my redating of these wares, suggested above, is accepted, this could make his E ware phase more recent.

A second aspect of importance is the relationship of the phase of timber buildings in the southern sector. This phase Hill would associate with the Northumbrian activity further north on the site, on the basis of a dendrochronological date for one of the buildings; the presence of one or two Northumbrian artefacts (such as a cresset); and the generally harmonious alignment with the Northumbrian stone buildings immediately to the north (Hill 1992b, 14-18). That all the buildings are Northumbrian is not certain, though they appear to be built from a slightly later context than the finds of pottery and glass. Strictly speaking, the building phase does not fully seal the trampled hillwash phase of the Gaulish finds, but they are clearly later than the phase 3b, which is a distinct horizon. Of the 'Northumbrian' phase, some debate might attach to one building, No.11, which gives the dendrochronological date c.687-732 AD from its second phase (Hill 1992b, 14). The non-conformity of the alignment of this structure with the Northumbrian monastery buildings might suggest that the earliest phase of this building is earlier than the 'probably early eighth century' date that Hill cites (Hill 1992b, 17)—certainly he puts its earliest phase earlier than the surrounding structures and their shale floors.

How much does the association of the E ware and glass with a phase earlier than the buildings matter? We may note that the imports in question have generally 'Celtic', rather than Anglo-Saxon associations, but this does not imply there would be a cessation of importation during a Northumbrian presence. Much could depend on the nature of the takeover, however: it is possible that under a new power the ships which brought them would no longer be safely able to put in near to Whithorn. The layer of shale which seals the clearest building phase is indeed overlain with eighth-century coins which are the signifiers of a new economic order.

At Clogher, primary interest has focused on the construction sequence of the ditch, which seems clearly to put the Mediterranean wares and E ware to either side of the construction phase of a reveted ringfort (Warner 1979a, 37-40). A phase of yellow boulder clay consistently seals deposits of Mediterranean amphorae over a silted Iron Age ditch. This boulder clay layer runs under the revetment at some points and may have been part of the rebuilding process of the fort (Warner 1979a, 38). E ware is found consistently stratified above this layer, in layers which sit against and run under the revetment. The virtue of this evidence is its quantity: in Trench X alone sherds of some 3 or more E ware vessels overly some 22 amphora sherds (at least 4 vessels: Warner 1979a, 38-9). There is no possibility that the E ware could be upcast from the same layer as the Mediterranean wares, which is the most significant point. The dating of the upper phases is more complex. We would like to be clearer on whether the revetment actually seals any E ware sherds. This is suggested in earlier interim reports, though not explicated in the 1979 discussion (Warner 1972, 28). The E ware sherds may be upcast from the building phase of the revetment. If so (as Warner suggests), their chronology might not be far removed from that of the Mediterranean wares. In any event, the separation is unquestioned.

At these sites, the chronology of E ware and the amphorae is clearly separated. If there is good reason to put the Mediterranean wares as no later than the 560s, E ware would seem to be a c.600 or later import. This corresponds very closely with our earliest textual evidence for contacts between Ireland and Gaul. Charles Thomas has clung strongly to the idea that E ware occurs in early sixth-century contexts in Cornwall, suggesting that it came first to Cornwall, of all parts of the British Isles. Though this model fits the importation of the Mediterranean wares, its application to E ware must be considered doubtful. So little E ware occurs in Cornwall that doubt might be cast upon the idea that E ware was ever directly imported there, though this might only reflect a failure to find the west Cornish centres. The distribution might be secondary from Scilly or Ireland. In the light of the Gwithian sequence being only one sample, and not fully published, we perhaps should not attach such weight to its testimony as does Thomas.

The distributional pattern of E ware will be discussed in chapter Seven. For the moment we will conclude that the ware is most likely a Gaulish import from a single source, the floruit of which is probably measurable in decades, centred on the seventh century.

Imported Glass

Fragments of glass vessels occur on some thirty-odd western insular sites. The greater part of these vessels are of putatively 'Merovingian' type, so they are also likely to be direct imports from Gaul to the Irish Sea basin, though this idea has only been given consideration since the mid-1980s, before which importation overland through Britain was considered more likely. The glass vessels are of a distinctive character, though there is some variety of form and colour, and only a few are as yet paralleled by finds either from the continent or from Anglo-Saxon sites in England. The general features of the assemblage may now be established, however, and some progress made in defining the possible place of glass in maritime exchange. Recent discoveries which are not yet fully published have added greatly to our understanding of the topic, most notably finds from Whithorn in Scotland and Longbury Bank in Wales, though prior to these discoveries it had been suggested that there was already sufficent evidence to doubt the prevailing orthodoxy (Campbell 1989a; 1989b; Wooding 1988a). It is to be hoped that a full catalogue of the western British and Irish finds will soon be published, which are mostly listed in unpublished theses by Ewan Campbell and Edward Bourke (which were unavailable for consultation at the time this study was conducted—Bourke's thesis is now summarized in Bourke 1994). The following discussion is based upon my own fieldwork conducted in 1987-9 (though I would like to thank Ewan Campbell for much helpful discussion).

The study of the vessel glass has been dominated by the views of Harden and acceptance of his theories served to discourage comprehensive study of the vessel morphology of the glass, which would appear worthy of the same character of attention as the imported ceramics. Harden and Alcock argued that the imported material from the west represented a selection of fragments brought in as 'cullet', i.e. as a trade in scrap glass for use in metalworking (Harden 1956b, 154; 1987, 142-3) and hence implied that reconstruction of the forms of the vessels would be pointless. Doubt has also been cast upon the possibility of reconstructing the forms of vessels from fragments (Hunter 1975, 79). Harden's erroneous view has only been questioned in print in recent times (Campbell 1989b, 244; Wooding 1988a, 14; Alcock and Alcock 1990, 113-15), so before proceeding to discussion of the import types, we must first re-examine this thesis and its bases.

Harden's Thesis

The vessel forms from which the glass fragments from western British and Irish sites derive are of several types. By far the most common is a cone of pale yellow/green metal, decorated with white marvered trails. Study of this form (and its misinterpretation) was central to the formulation of Harden's model. In seeking to reconstruct the forms of the western British and Irish vessel finds, which are all in fragmentary form apart from atypical finds of flasks from Mullaroe, Co. Sligo (Warner 1979b, 124-5; also now Moynagh Lough, Co. Meath—Bourke 1996, 168-70), the decorative forms on the *eastern* British finds of cones of 'Merovingian' type were accepted as providing the most likely model. The eastern British finds, mostly from Anglo-Saxon graves, are trailed principally in a spiral below the rim and sometimes in a band of combed festoons at the waist (Harden 1956b, 146, 160; Harden 1987, 146). These festoons rarely reached the upper or lower extremes of the vessel, however, and did not explain the stubs of trails finishing close under the sub-rim spiral trails on fragments from Dinas Powys (Harden 1987, 143: Fig 9.1, Nos 26 & 29). The trailed proportion of the eastern British cones was considerably less than the ratio of trailed to untrailed fragments in the Dinas Powys and other collections (Harden 1987, 143). This allowed the theory to emerge that trailed pieces had been selectively collected for secondary use. The finding of molten droplets at Dinas Powys served to support the idea that scrap glass was melted down for decorative use. The fact that pale yellow glass, trailed or untrailed, was not amongst the re-used pieces, however, should have been given greater attention (Harden 1987, 149).

The correct conclusion is that many western British cones are trailed over a much larger proportion of their surface than those from Anglo-Saxon and Rhenish sites. The 'festooned chevron' and 'feathered festoon' are the commonest types (I owe these terms to Ewan Campbell). These often run the full length of the vessel from the base, sometimes to merge with the sub-rim spiral. A *small* number of western insular glass finds, however, do genuinely form a subset of the assemblage on Saxon sites. These include fragments of two claw beakers and other Saxon pieces from Dinas Powys (Campbell 1989b, 239-45) and some clear-trailed vessels from Whithorn. A few other fragments, which show engraving with a sharp wheel, are found at such sites as Dalkey Island and Whithorn may represent an assemblage shared between Anglo-Saxon England and the Celtic West, as the Whithorn piece seems to be very closely matched by the well-known vessel from Holme Pierpont in Nottinghamshire (Harden 1956b, 136). These parallels are the exception, however, rather than the rule and Harden was otherwise in error to suggest that the western British finds were a subset of the eastern British distributions.

Research has undoubtedly been hampered by the very small portions of glass found, but this too easily led to the suspension of formal approaches after the 1960s. Substantial proportions of vessels can be reconstructed. Campbell has been able to do this for some of the Dinas Powys vessels *(pers. comm.)*. At Whithorn a number of rim pieces were able to be fitted together by the author (See Fig. 12, H1 & H2). These attempts have been made principally by following decorative patterns. Undecorated pieces present more problems, but we may observe that the colour and thickness may vary considerably along the length of a cone, which again may have encouraged belief in a greater number of vessels being present than was actually the case. Finally, Harden made much of the lack of bases amongst the Dinas Powys assemblage. These have been found at Whithorn and Armagh, however, and as these are the most obtrusive parts of the vessel, being the thickest and sharpest fragments, they may have been most thoroughly disposed of on site.

The failure to recognise the western insular assemblages as mostly separate from the eastern was also the consequence of too easy acceptance of an 'industrial' model for glass usage. It stands to reason that glass vessels should be studied as objects with a functional use. This is contrary to common archaeological recording practice, however, where much research focuses on the technical question of glass manufacture. It is pleasing to see my Australian colleague Frank Broeze (1990, 126) taking issue with the same question in reviewing a recent shipwreck site report. We may contrast the expected role of pottery to

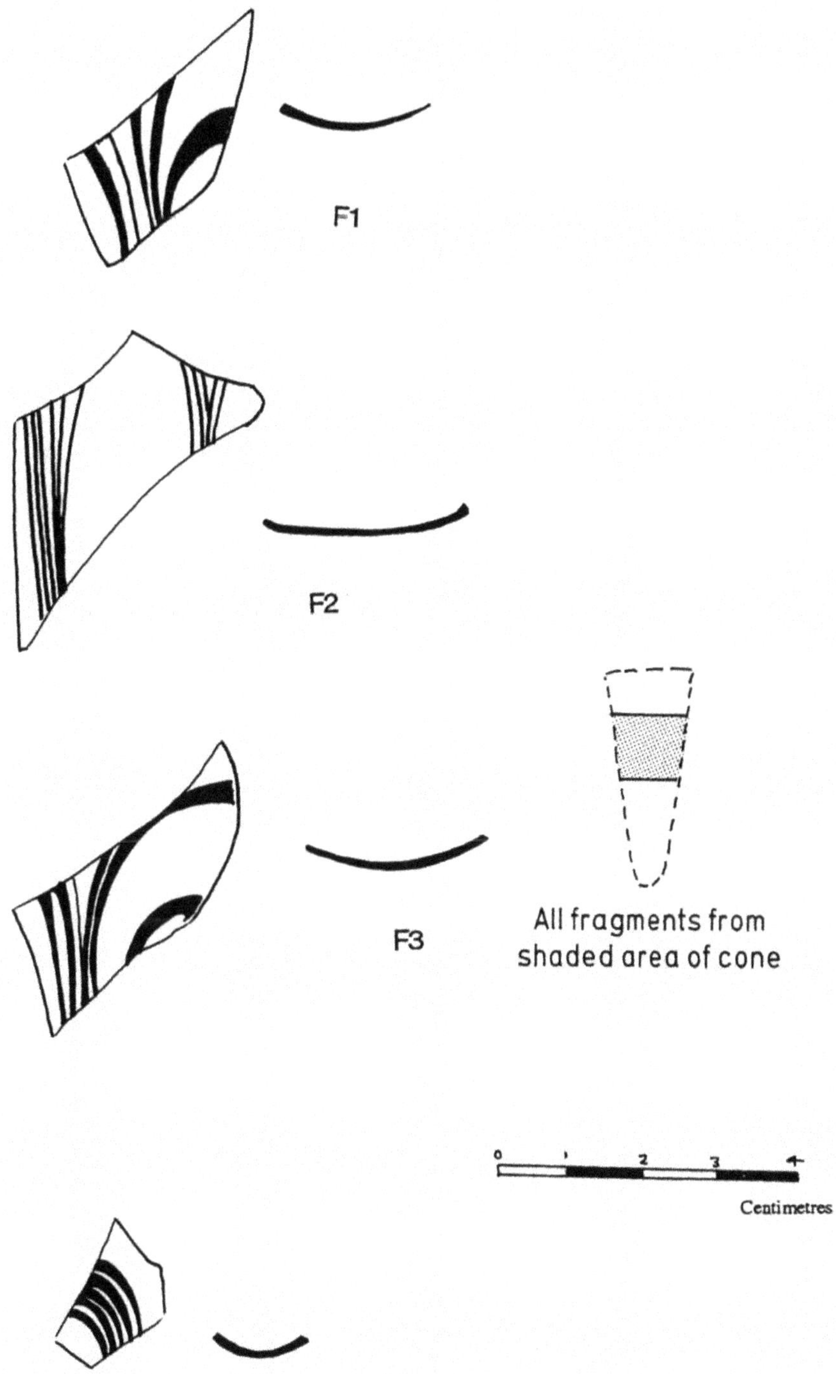

Fig. 10 Glass vessels with combed decoration
F1) Whithorn, +89/9850
F2)Whithorn, +89/10095
F3) Whithorn, +89/9845
F4) Whithorn, +89/1049

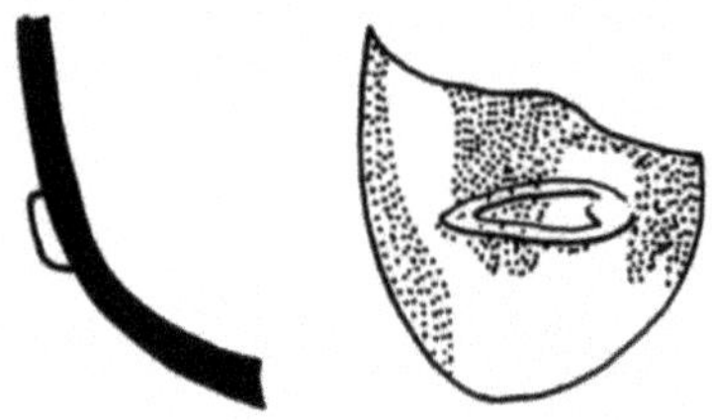

F5

F6

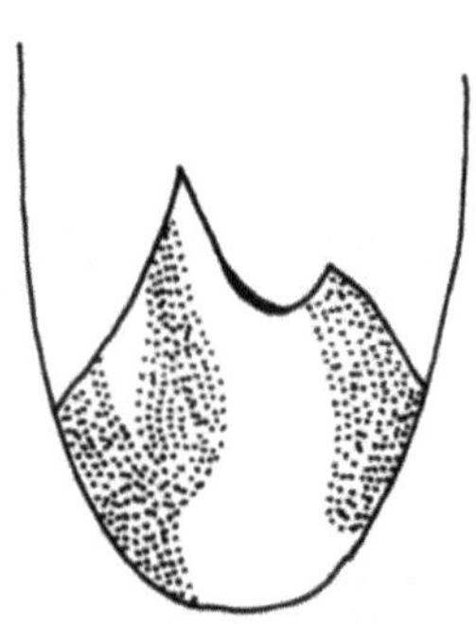

F7

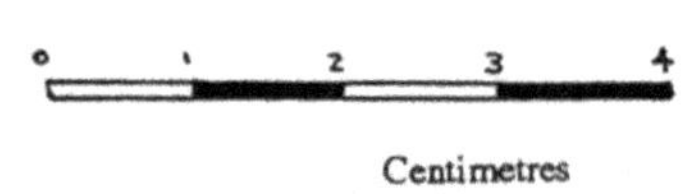

Fig. 11 Glass vessels with 'chevron' decoration
F5) Armagh
F6) Whithorn, +89/10000
F7) Dinas Powys, No. 93

that of vessel glass. The diagnostic value of glass is controversial. Unlike pottery, glass is not indestructible, though the reputation for poor survival of glass with a high potash content is often falsely carried over to the western insular assemblage. The imported glass from Celtic Britain and Ireland is mostly of the durable soda-lime-silica type. The working lifespan of glass may be much the same as that of pottery—the glass may have been treated with more care as it was more highly valued, but it was also more fragile and easily broken. The primary point, anyway, is that fragments of vessels with an identifiable morphology turn up frequently on western insular sites and may play an equally important diagnostic role to that of the imported ceramics. It is frustrating then that the fragmentary state of the assemblages has been being taken to invalidate certain types of typological analysis (Sanderson, Hunter and Warren 1984, 53). There is no need to argue the exclusive value of scientific approaches over typological in this way.

Henderson and Ivens (1992) have tackled further questions relating to the role of cullet in Irish decorative glass and enamel work. In the light of the small numbers of vessel finds, they conclude that detritus from a continuing glass usage is more likely to be the major contributor to metalwork decoration, rather than significant importation of cullet (Henderson and Ivens 1992, 61).

Types of Glass Present

The glassware falls into three definite decorative categories, with hints at further groupings.

Class One is pieces of putatively Mediterranean origin. **Class One (a)** is pieces from Tintagel which are listed by Harden as likely to be of Mediterranean origin. Both Campbell (1995; forthcoming) and the author have doubts about the Mediterranean ascription of these pieces, but the matter awaits further analysis. **One (b)** is the pieces with wheel-engraved decoration, which are of likely Mediterranean origin. Pieces of this type are from Dalkey Island, Congresbury (Price 1995, 139, no. 11) and Whithorn (no. +88/8362—Harden 1966, 193-5; cf Grave 49 at High Down: Welch 1983, 145). These may also be an assemblage shared between the eastern and western zones of the British Isles (see above).

Class Two is pieces which are likely imports from or through Anglo-Saxon England. These include the cobalt blue squat jars from Dinas Powys and Chew Stoke and the claw beakers from Dinas Powys (Campbell 1989b, 239-45). Various pieces from Congresbury also fall within this group. Congresbury (Price 1992, 139-41, no. 14-19) and Cadbury (Price and Cottam 1995, 101, no. 21-3) have also produced 'Kempston' style beakers and pieces from Whithorn (no. +88/8484) with similarly transparent trails may also be in this group.

Class Three is cones and bowls of pale yellow, yellow/green (very many examples of both these colours) green (e.g. Margam, Armagh) or yellow/amber (Whithorn +88/7707; Sanderson 1987, fiche 71—this colour is explained as an imperfection in the metal) or pale blue (e.g. Ballycateen) metal. Some appear to be undecorated. In others, decoration includes white marvered sub-rim trails in a spiral. Other pieces have hairline trails under the rim (e.g. Whithorn +87/4100; Mote of Mark Fig. D—Harden, 1956, 150). Very often they have white marvered trails on the body in festooned chevrons and feathered festoons. Other body decoration may be a form of thick loop trailing, uncertainly related to the chevron (e.g Dumbarton 71: Alcock and Alcock 1990, 113-15). All this glass I propose to call the 'Atlantic' type, as it is not yet paralleled further east in Anglo-Saxon England or Merovingian Gaul. This is by far the predominant type. Other types include pale amber (e.g. Fig. 12 H1 & H2) and iron blue cones (e.g. Mote of Mark Fig. F—Harden 1987, 150) with white marvered spiral trails under the rim, which are probably part of the 'Atlantic' group also. Some other pale yellow vessels have optic bulges (e.g. Whithorn No. +89/9898; Mote of Mark Fig. J—Harden 1956b, 150), others are plain and very thick at the rim (Mote of Mark Fig. A—Harden 1956b, 150; Dinas Powys No. 46—Harden 1987, 143 & 147). These latter two are not definitely cones and may be bowls or palm cups.

The basic 'Atlantic' cone and bowl forms and colours are found at the following sites, in some cases along with blue and amber pieces of the 'Atlantic' class—as most finds are not fully published at time of writing the following is not a comprehensive catalogue (references are given for discoveries made since the publication of Harden 1956):

Armagh (Harden 1984, 135-6).
Ballinderry
Ballycateen
Cadbury (Price and Cottam 1995, 101)
Castlehill (*PSAS* 53 [1918-19] 123—cf. Whithorn +88/7705 +89/10149).
Clogher (Bourke 1994, 170).
Congresbury (Price 1992, 140-2)
Dalkey Island (Harden 1966, 193-5).
Dinas Powys (Harden 1987).
Dumbarton (Alcock and Alcock 1990, 113-115).
Dunadd (National Museum of Antiquities of Scotland. Not listed in Harden 1956b).
Garranes
Garryduff
Gwithian (rim sherd in pale yellow/green. In the Royal Institution of Cornwall).
Longbury Bank (1 pale amber, 19 pale yellow-green. Campbell and Lane 1988).
Margam Deer Park (Campbell 1989b, 63-4).
Mote of Mark (Harden 1956b, 150; D. Longley, *pers. comm.*).
New Pieces (Lane 1988, 97).
Trethurgy (Price 1988, 26).
Whithorn (author's observations 1987-9. 40+ vessels).

Odd pieces remain unclassified. Amber palm cup rims from Whithorn (see Fig. 14, PC3) and Lagore may be Carolingian. Flasks from Mullaroe, Moynagh Lough and Lough Gara seem undoubtedly to be from the seventh century (Bourke 1996, 168-70).

Campbell (forthcoming), has set up his own typology which more or less agrees with the above, but not so closely that it would be convenient to adopt it here. Campbell's group A is the Mediterranean types (Wooding class One), his class B is 'Merovingian' types shared with Anglo-Saxon England (Wooding class Two), his groups C and D are plain and trailed 'Merovingian' types respectively (Wooding class Three includes both of these together) and his group E includes pieces, of a type only found at Whithorn, which he suggests might be local attempts at imitating the imported types—but this seems unable to be proved. I also prefer not to adopt his distinction between plain and decorated types as it does not seem likely to reflect any real distinction in importation (and Campbell himself suggests this by making this more or less a combined class 'C/D'). These are very minor disagreements, however, and our researches are fundamentally in agreement.

The dating of the groups all falls between the years 400-800 and a date between the mid-sixth and early seventh would be likely for all but the 'Kempston' types (possibly fifth century) and the ninth-century Mullaroe flask (Harden 1956b, 154). The cobalt blue jars of class 2 would be dated by Campbell to the early 600s (Campbell 1989b, 244) and the claw beakers are a sixth-century type (Harden 1987, 145). Class 3 is unknown outside of the Irish Sea zone and can only be dated by association with imported pottery. A broad contemporaneity with E ware seems likely from associations at Whithorn, but Hill *(pers. comm.)* would suggest that the glass appears earlier in the sequence than E ware, though it continues into the same period. Whether the glass fragments from earlier and later periods on site are of the same group needs further investigation. For example, a beaker in pale yellow metal with combed festoons (CF1: found in a trench opened in a field north-west of the main area in 1987), as opposed to feathered festoons or festooned chevrons, was found in an otherwise sterile context at Whithorn, away from the main sequences. It is very similar to, but not the same as, most Atlantic group pieces. When these sorts of fine distinctions are made, if they are indeed important, we might observe a narrower dating range for individual imported glass groups. Campbell (forthcoming) suggests that festooned vessels are earlier than those with chevron decoration. Pending further investigation of this question, and the discovery of other site sequences, we may only observe that the glass importations, on site chronology alone, seem likely to span a wider chronological range than E ware pottery. That glass appears on the hillfort sites of Somerset and western Cornwall, is again suggestive of sixth-century importation and trailed glass of post-Roman type is found in the same contexts as Mediterranean amphorae at some sites (Alcock 1995, 39; Bourke 1996, 167-8). At Congresbury the glass assemblage is both 'Saxon' (class 2) and 'Atlantic' (class 3), with several pieces being of the 'Kempston' type (P. Rahtz, *pers. comm.)*, while previously noted pieces from Cadbury and Tintagel are not demonstrably similar to the best-known types. The more recent find from Tintagel is of more normal 'Atlantic' type, however, with white horizontal trails (Price 1988, 26). A seventh-century context is unlikely at Tintagel. We will return to the distributional questions later in this chapter.

The Source of the Glass Imports

In searching for an origin for the glass imports, we may straight away observe that scholarship has followed a very similar pattern to that followed in investigating E ware. The different methods of research considered normal for these finds, however, have regrettably seen the E ware and glass distributions only rarely compared to each other—after an initial comparison which went a long way to inspiring the Rhineland origin theory for E ware (Peacock and Thomas 1967, 36). The likely source identified was the Rhineland and the assumed entry path was overland by way of Britain. This was somewhat contrary to historical likelihood. Again, as in the case of E ware, the fact that the closest parallels were in the Rhineland was reflective of the intensity of research and excavation work in that region and the paucity of such work further west in France. The incidence of cones with white marvered festoons is seen as more of a Belgian/northern French trait (Van Lith 1988, 67)—just as the northern French parallels for E ware are superior to the Rhenish. A cone in greenish metal with white marvered festoons was found at Herpes in Charente-Maritime (British Museum 1905 5-20 61)—matched exactly by a find from Highdown in Sussex (Welch 1976, 15). These pieces are not close to the western British finds in decoration, but are close enough to suggest that there are more westerly trailed cone traditions (of coastal distribution) than the Rhenish which offer potential for placing the 'Atlantic' group.

Museum collections in France do not contain wide ranges of glass vessels from late-sixth/seventh century contexts. Probably this simply reflects a past lack of interest in collecting fragments from domestic refuse. Two palm cups in the collection at Saint Germain-en-Laye (see Fig. 14) suggest that the same colours and marvered trailing as found on British sites also existed in the Marne region in the late-sixth century, but these are only vague clues and only systematic study of new glass discoveries is likely to reveal the source for the British finds.

The Cultural and Commercial Relations of the Glass

Two textual sources demonstrate that the use of glass vessels was known to literary audiences in the Celtic West. In the *Gododdin*, the hero Bleiddig mab Eli drank wine from brimming glass vessels *(Bleidic mab eli ervisset gwin gwydyr lestri llavn: Gododdin* XCII, ed. Williams 1961, 45). Drinking wine from glass vessels is also used as a metaphor for the ease with which a hero picks up his spear *(hut arolli wayw mal gwin gloew o wydyr lestri: Gododdin* LXV, ed. Williams 1961, 32). This text is of indeterminate date, however, and though it establishes a courtly context for the drinking of wine we should not place too much value upon it in the light of our conclusions upon the value of the heroic literature of Ireland (see above, 34). A reference in Adomnán also depicts the use of a glass vessel in the Pictish court at Inverness, when the saint prophesies:

> 'Nunc Broichanus fortiter concussus est; nam angelus de caelo misus graviter illum percutiens vitream in manu ejus de qua bibebat confregit in multa biberam fragmenta...' Adhuc sancto haec loquente verba, ecce sicuti praedixit duo a rege misi equites adveniunt; omnia quae in regis munitione de Froichano juxta sancti vaticinium sunt acta enarrantes.

> ('Now Broichan has received a hard blow. For an angel

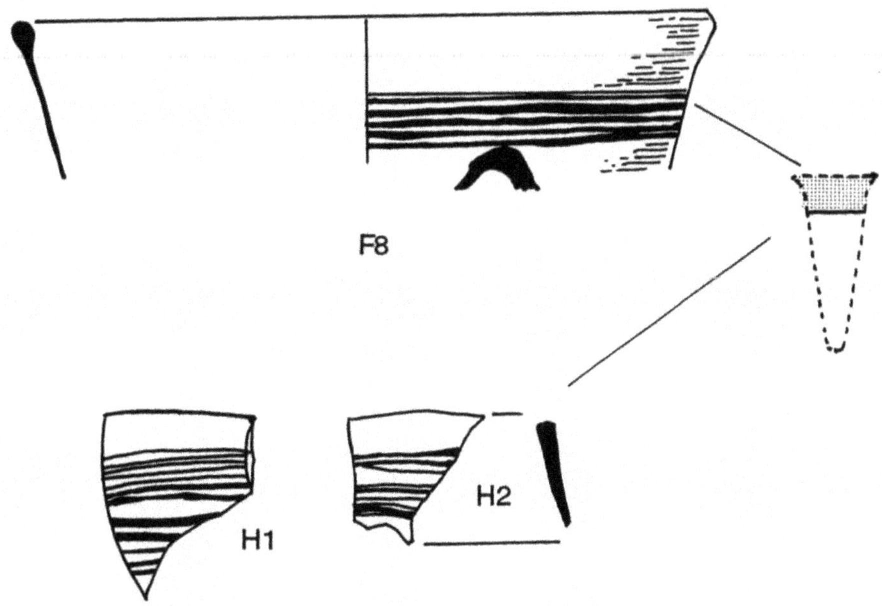

Fig. 12 Glass cones:

with horizontal sub-rim trailing

F8) Dinas Powys, No. 26 (with tip of chevron)
H1) Whithorn, +87/4032
H2) Whithorn, +88/8318 (joins with H1)

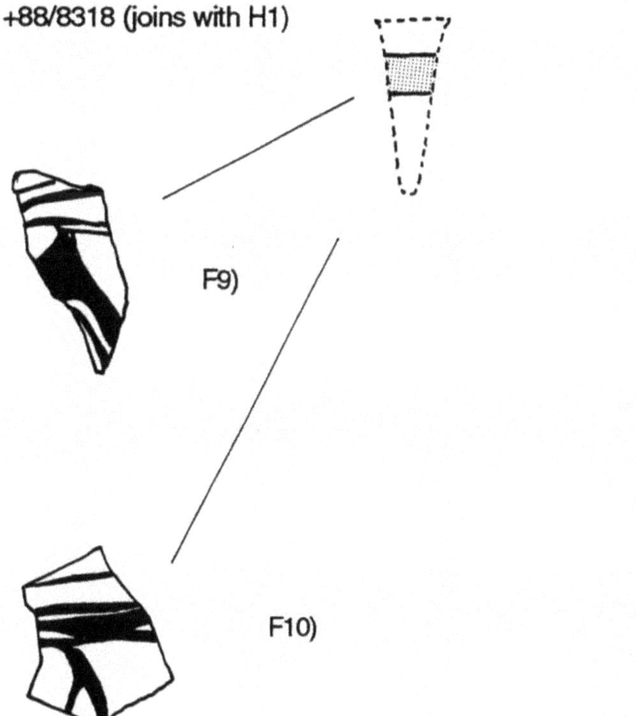

with combed festoons

F9) Whithorn +88/8442
F10) Mote of Mark (Harden, p. 150, 'M').

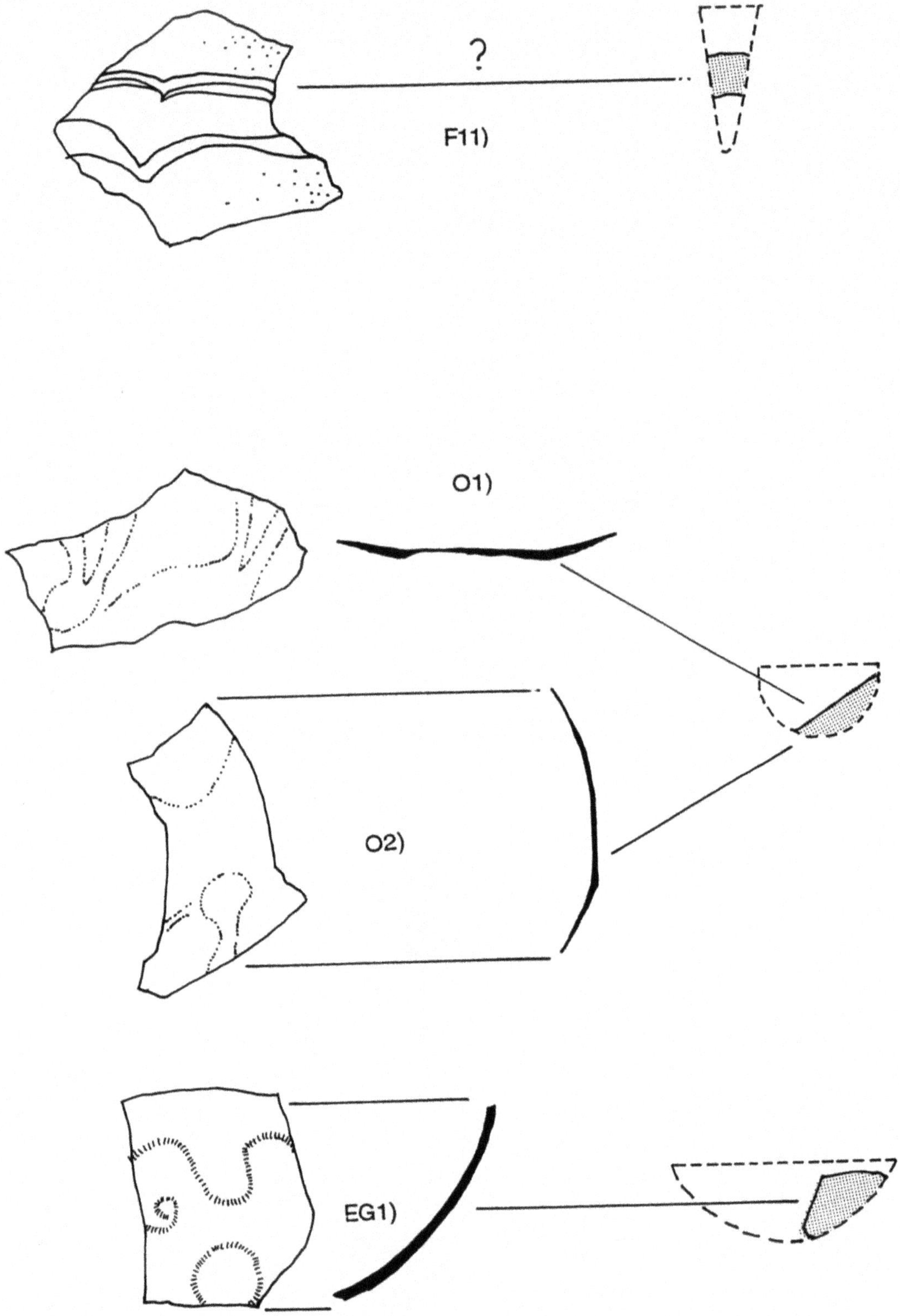

Fig. 13 Glass vessels:

with combed festoons

F11) Whithorn +87/4273

with optic decoration

O1) Whithorn +89/9898
O2) Mote of Mark (Harden, p. 150, 'J').

with engraved decoration

EG1) Whithorn +88/8326

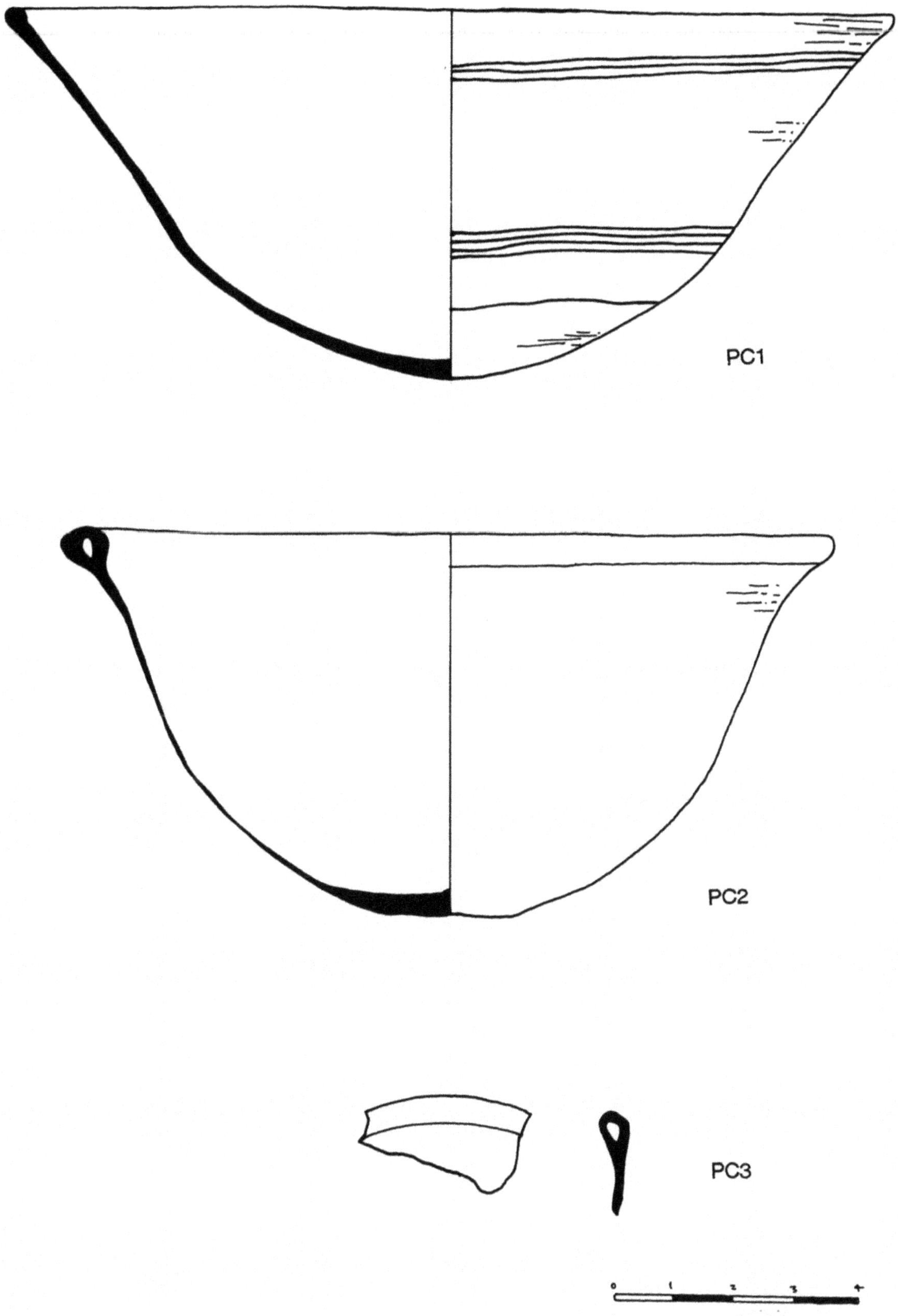

Fig. 14

Possible parallels from the continent:

PC1) Pale yellow palm cup from Chaouilly-sur-Marne (collection: St Germain-en-Laye)
PC2) Amber palm cup with folded rim (collection: St Germain-en-Laye)

For comparison:

PC3)Amber palm cup with folded rim: Whithorn +87 4216

> sent from heaven has struck him heavily and broken into many pieces in his hand the glass vessel from which he was drinking...' While the saint was still speaking these words, behold, as he had predicted, two men on horseback, sent by the king, arrived, and told all that had happened concerning Broichan, in the king's fortress, in accordance with the prophecy of the saint: Adomnán, Vita Columbae II.34, ed. & trans. Anderson and Anderson 1961, 400-1).

There are no definite Irish references, though the indefinite word *lestar* (the same lexical item used in the *Gododdin* reference) might sometimes be describing glass vessels. The context is evidently 'courtly' and this is reflected also in the archaeological distribution: which is more confined to high status sites than that of E ware. Adomnán does not specify wine as the contents of the glass, though the *Gododdin* does, so we should not assume that such vessels were only used for wine (see *Gododdin* LXXXIII, where a hero drinks mead from a glass: *tavloyw ac ysgeth tavlet wydrin*, ed. Williams 1961, 40).

The evidence of metalwork, especially iron objects of supposedly Frankish origin in Ireland and Scotland is of interest, in the light of the definite ceramic evidence for Gaulish links. Thomas has returned debate to this evidence in his recent reassessment of the Gaulish material (Thomas 1990, 18-19). Finds of such objects have been sporadic, with metal having a lower rate of post-depositional survival than pottery or glass—the largest collections being from crannóg sites such as Lagore and Buston, where an anaerobic context was present. This fact should be appreciated as yet another example of the ways in which the omnipresence of Frankish influence may be hidden behind the unrepresentative quality of the evidence. Nonetheless, it would seem easy to overrate the evidence of the metalwork—a Frankish origin is not proven for most pieces, both Anglo-Saxon or local manufacture cannot be ruled out. Beyond that, we can also only guess at the social context within which such artefacts might sit. Some objects are unique in insular contexts and are best explained as personal possessions of individual travellers. From a midden at Tean, Isles of Scilly, a bronze loop and a riveted openwork plate are definitely Merovingian imports. Thomas interprets the former as part of a *châtelaine*, or *gürtelgehänge* (Thomas 1990, 18; Thomas 1985, 195-7). The riveted openwork plate is in fact also almost certainly part of a *châtelaine* as sixth/seventh century examples are characterised by such studding on an openwork plate (Renner 1970 provides a typology for round types only, but the relationship between these and the Tean piece is clear). An object such as this in Scilly is testimony to a maritime link with somewhere. Most other supposed finds of Frankish metalwork in Ireland and western Britain (James 1982, 385-6) are uncertain evidence of trade or even direct travel. A variety of beads, brooches, horse trappings and iron weapons may all be of Frankish origin (Thomas 1990, 19-20; Hencken 1950, 93ff): for some, however, no more than a 'Germanic' origin can be held as certain and Anglo-Saxon may be as likely as Frankish. Those which are of Frankish origin may be best explained as personal possessions. Thomas' suggestion, on the strength of later usages of the word *ffranc* in Welsh (Williams 1944, 31), of a presence of Frankish mercenaries seems overly ingenious (Thomas 1990, 6) and must be balanced against Rowland's reinterpretation of the word as more likely to mean 'freeman' (Rowland 1993, 23; also Breeze 1991a; Breeze 1991b). Also possible is the idea that arms might be traded (Doehaerd 1978, 163).

Certainly unlikely to be trade goods are two Frankish coins from Ireland, both from the Sarthe département: one, at Port Laoghaise, minted in Le Mans; another, from Trim, minted at Beaufay (Rigold 1975, 660). It is of interest in this connection that Picard would suggest that Slane, very near Trim, figures in the Frankish machinations of the seventh century—being where Dagobert II was sent into exile (Picard 1991b, 27-52). These compare with Rigold's coinage phases I and II in Britain—made up of coins from the period pre-625 AD including 3/4 of the Sutton Hoo assemblage and the pre-Augustinian coins in the Canterbury cemetery, which contains a strong western and northern Gaulish element (Rigold 1975, 653-77; Grierson and Blackburn 1986, 122-7). The 625 date must be regarded as somewhat arbitrary: being obtrusively based upon the desired historical association with Redwald (see also Wood 1991, 4). Later Frankish coin imports to England are from east Francia exclusively (Rigold 1975, 655). The association of these coins with trade by both Peacock and especially Hodges in discussions of E ware are totally unjustifiable (Hodges 1984): quite clearly the Canterbury and Sutton Hoo assemblages are personal collections, rather than anything to do with economics. The offshoots in Ireland are likely to be personal possessions, also, as Ireland did not use coin in this period—*contra* Hodges this non-use of coin reflects more than a shift in western Gaulish monetary policy which saw coinage less often traded.

In conclusion, we may be much less optimistic concerning the potential of the metalwork and related imports, unless further finds show repeated patterns of contact with one or two sources. Where even less tangible evidence is concerned, such as the Gaulish sculptural influences postulated by Henry, Hamlin, James (1982, 384-6), Warner (*pers. comm.* who observes a further strong link between Poitou and the slabs of the Rathmichael/ Glencolumcille group) and Sheehan (1994), transmission of ideas via the western sealanes might not be unlikely, but is so far unprovable. Both the E ware and glass offer better possibilities for refining patterns of contact otherwise only vaguely indicated by textual sources and for resolving questions of site chronology which are themselves crucial for our understanding of economy. The glass emerges as potentially the more interesting group of artefacts. We should note, along with the Alcocks (1990, 113), that the glass is more numerous than the pottery at sites, for example Dinas Powys and Whithorn, where there are large assemblages of both. The glass is probably of less limited chronological range than E ware, as we have seen, which may ultimately make E ware a more useful finite *datum*, while the varieties of glass may be individually and relatively datable to different periods.

Chapter Seven

Routes of Maritime Trade in the Late-Sixth through Eighth Centuries

Where objects are found distributed along a coastline and are also found inland from that coast, and where we have accounts of travel by sea and inland from the sea, we are confronted with a number of possible explanations of their distribution. Are all the seaside sites regular landfalls for ships from outside the region, or are some sites primary landfalls from which secondary voyages distribute goods through 'coastal' traffic? Where objects are found inland from the sea we need to explain from which coastal points they have travelled inland. We also need to explain the mechanics of the distribution. Is trade responsible for most movement of goods? Or are we looking at complex models of exchange within kinship or political networks, to secure political and social prestige for those who control the source of imports? A crucial question here is whether the primary landing site is hence more a commercial or a political centre. This has implications for many parts of the western sealanes, where we are unclear as to the status of various sites and where a standard typology for settlements is often lacking. It also has implications for the degree to which the needs of the political authorities and the degree to which the needs of the mariner are taken into account when a site is chosen for a harbour. If the harbours are not the primary exchange sites, where are the major points of exchange? All of these questions affect our ability to determine the existence of long-distance traffic.

Short-distance and Coastal Traffic

From earliest prehistory short distance travel and exchange must have occurred on a local basis, for the purpose of gathering raw materials and food gathering. Such activity may have operated both overland and across short distances of sea. The latter is often termed 'coastal' exchange. 'Down-the-line' exchange occurs when a series of short-distance exchange links, often initially set up for local exchange, are used to distribute goods over a longer distance. Redistributive exchange may occur when short-distance links are utilised to distribute goods which have arrived at a primary importation site from a long distance away—the routes and ships involved in transit to the secondary sites in the network may be the same as are used in local, 'coastal' exchange in raw materials and produce.

Long-distance maritime exchange involves the use of the sea as a more direct means of travel, bypassing short-distance exchange mechanisms until a primary landfall is reached. In making a case for the existence of long-distance voyages, much importance must be attached to evidence which specifies the presence of ships which have unquestionably travelled over a long distance. Sometimes such evidence may be an unambiguous literary reference, sometimes distributional evidence leaves little doubt. At a certain point, however, the long-distance voyage will cease and secondary networks will take over. This is not a simple matter. A combination of factors may provide a lack of incentive for continuation of the voyage.

Long-distance traffic has received the greater attention in western sealanes studies, and recent critiques have seen this as a result of the tendency to attribute to identifiable long-distance links the role of a cultural *deus ex machina*, at the expense of an understanding of already existing cultural forces (Mytum 1992, 7ff). On economic questions, David Griffiths would single out for criticism those, such as Hodges (1989, 67; 1978, 11), who have applied the typology of the *emporium* to the western zone of Britain before 800AD, as implying the existence of a type of trading network which did not exist in the early medieval period. He questions the emphasis placed upon the study of the imported ceramics in terms of the likely minor *economic* role of long-distance exchange in the Irish Sea basin:

> Coastal sites show every indication that they depended more on fishing, farming and local redistribution than on long-distance trade routes with exotic, but occasional, imports....the existing political role of the royal sites (and their relationship to sites within their territories) can be said to be far more important than their long-distance trading links (Griffiths 1992b, 10).

Peter Hill has raised some similar objections in a study of the early economy of Whithorn, though more clearly noting the degree to which previous studies lacked the clear evidence to make studies of middle- and short-distance exchange (Hill 1992). Where the imported ceramics are concerned we must be clear that the issue of overemphasis is so far an archaeological rather than an economic one. That imported ceramics have a major role to play in identifying routes and ports of maritime exchange would seem to be taken for granted in a range of studies of the Irish Sea basin, as well as in the study of North Sea and related exchange (Griffiths 1992a, 63; Alcock and Alcock 1990, 119, 130-8). Arnold, however, has expressed strong criticism of Hodges's implicit corollary between ceramic distributions and commercial networks (Arnold 1983, 80-1). Marx (thinking in terms of tool-making industries and the Three-Age system: Marx 1930,

172) suggested the superiority of archaeology was that it emphasised the importance of production through its focus on the 'osseous systems' (tools) not the 'vascular systems' (containers). In early medieval archaeology, however, the need to establish firm *datum* lines for insular chronology has seen the vascular systems brought to the fore. As firmly datable finds, the imported ceramics provide the framework for dating other production and exchange activities. As Mytum says 'they can be of significance because they can be provenanced, their distributions plotted and the mechanics of trade and distribution suggested' (Mytum 1992, 252). The short-term nature of their importation makes the *datum* they provide especially finite.

All this may serve to defend an approach initially informed by long-distance imports. However, it is certainly time we reconsidered the relationship between long- and short-distance traffic in historical study. Does one grow directly out of the other? Though the identifiable goods seem to have arrived in the Irish Sea basin in foreign vessels, there is some potential to see this traffic as having a link with Gaulish coastal traffic (see above, 68ff). The ability to absorb imports may indicate a level of demand for goods acquired through internal exchange. Coastal networks in the Irish Sea may have been stimulated by inclusion in foreign import processes.

How does a landing site relate to regional commerce and exchange? McGrail's definition of the likely relations of a landing site is worth quoting as a starting point:

> The [landing] site should ideally be at the centre of the regional economy or with good access to it. The natural economic and political centres for many regions lie away from the coast and in these cases the trader's ideal site would be inland, up a river and possibly at a ford as at Dublin.....The political authority requires a well-defined, possibly defended, site, preferably near the coast (i.e. as near the common frontier as practicable), where traders can be segregated, protected and supervised, justice imposed and tolls collected. Settlements in coastal zones on promontories or islands are suitable locations for these activities (McGrail 1983, 311-12).

The crucial question for the western sealanes is whether we would see sites with these criteria as purely trading sites, or whether sites with imported goods which fit these criteria may have other political or religious functions. McGrail's criteria are derived from an extensive theoretical discussion in prehistoric archaeology, which is in turn founded in comparative anthropology—defining sites which are usually purely for exchange. The classic typology of *emporia* (market sites where locals are resident to service the needs of commercial visitors) and 'gateway communities' (boundary sites where traders can be isolated and the movement of goods into society regulated) has intruded into western sealanes studies. Dalkey Island has been described as a 'gateway community' (Mytum 1992, 262-3). Longbury Bank and Whithorn are suggested as possible *emporia* (Campbell and Lane 1988; Alcock and Alcock 1990, 121). Various sites along the western sealanes have features which superficially fit McGrail's criteria: Tintagel and Dumbarton are defended promontories; the Scillies, Dalkey and Caldey are islands which have produced evidence for overseas exchange in the form of imported pottery. The tenuousness of this evidence is demonstrated by the fact that Nendrum, cited more than once by Mytum (1993, 262-3; 266) as an example of an island trading site, has actually produced no E ware, despite earlier reports (M. O'Donnell, E. Campbell, *pers. comms.).* In most cases we may note that actual evidence for hinterland relations is mostly lacking, and that these indentifications depend on slight similarities to the accepted typology and on a handful of imported pottery sherds.

Thomas has suggested that this debate is only marginally relevant to the traffic of the western sealanes in our period (Thomas 1990, 10)—though it has played a major role in the interpretation of the Frisian and Viking commercial networks in the early middle ages (Hodges 1989, 13-25). Thomas, with Alcock, would see the coastally-located import centres as seats of *political* power, using wealth derived from levies and tributes to acquire prestige goods to be redistributed through family networks and levelling mechanisms.

The exchange economy of the Irish Sea zone is still something of a mystery. The fact that many high-status sites were selectively drawing upon large agricultural economies is becoming clear from the studies of animal bones from sites such as Dinas Powys (Gilchrist 1988, 50-62) and Whithorn and Irish texts (e.g. Gerriets 1987; also *Críth Gablach* (ed. Binchy 1940). The data would suggest that select foods, for example choice cuts of meat, were brought from the hinterland to sites which controlled manufacturing and exchange of prestige goods, which in turn were redistributed back down the line. Into this process also fits the gathering of prestige imports through international trade and the gathering of raw materials for manufacturing of brooches, combs, beads and other items. We must proceed carefully with this model, however, as the conjuring up of images of many small vessels going every which way with local goods and materials is dangerously unspecific and unfounded, whatever its likelihood, and inclined to leave us with a picture no less chimerical than that of Bowen's multiplicity of saintly seafarers. We have also questioned some of the industrial models involved in the interpretation of finds such as pottery and glass (see above, 84-7).

Zimmer and his contemporaries do not seem to have been in any doubt that trade of a large-scale, commercial nature was predominant on the western sealanes and this model underpinned interpretation of the distribution of imported ceramics until the early 1980s. Studies of exchange systems in prehistoric societies underwent a revolution in the 1930s, however—as anthropological fieldwork by Malinowski (1922) and Mauss (1954) provided models of alternative processes to trade to explain circulation of imported goods in early societies. These are explained in terms of such methods as prestige gift-giving and exchange at neutral points, external to the society, with non-commercial social networks used to redistribute goods. A specialised terminology has been developed by those who consider formal economic terms to be inappropriate to anterior economies: with such terms as the 'port-of-trade' and 'gateway community' introduced to explain sites set aside for landing and trading of goods. The strongest use of this terminology (known as 'substantivist') in western sealanes studies has been by Hodges (1989, 67; Hodges 1978, 115) and Doherty (1980, 67-70).

Doherty and Hodges have attempted to explore the theoretical paradigm in the case of Ireland—beginning with enclosed trading and assembly sites on the boundaries of kingdoms, and running through to the development of trading leases in connection with monasteries in the eighth century onward (Doherty 1980, 80ff). Attempts to identify the earlier style of market site have been inconclusive, however, with Hodges's (1975) example of Knockdhu depending too much on formal comparisons and Dark's investigation of Arrallas in Cornwall, resting too much on the suggestive character of a name (from *arghans *lys*: 'silver court': Padel 1985, 244; Preston-Jones and Rose 1986, 138). The latter name is of indeterminate, perhaps pre-medieval, date—being of a class of names which Padel would date as an earlier stratum than the average, on account of the generic/qualifier elements being in the reverse of the usual order (Padel 1985, xv). Location near a boundary may have been significant at later dates, but for reasons unique to the early medieval period, not as an indicator of an anterior form of market. Tintagel is located near an ancient boundary (Thomas 1964, 70-9). Orléans is on the boundary between Neustria and Burgundy and there are implications for its involvement in economic activity. We may also note that gateway community model is applicable in some modern contexts, such as Hong Kong, where it is scarcely in an evolutionary context. Alcock has recently warned against application of external paradigms to post-Roman societies which display complexities which belie the models (Alcock 1988, 22) and Peter S. Wells has further suggested that the evidence of historic archaeology must be held to show that some exchange models, taking input from anthropology, are too simplistic for even the Iron Age contexts which they were developed to interpret (Wells 1992, 43-9 & *pers. comm.*). We may note in conclusion the need for discrimination in the use of the substantivist terminology and models, which carry a baggage of evolutionary debate which has not been adequately comprehended in the Atlantic context.

Much exchange was probably non-commercial in nature, at least at some point. The *Muirbretha* appear from the commentaries to have stated that a cargo would be 'consigned to a certain person' *(in tan tainic fo thomus duine airithi hi*, ed. Binchy CIH 1978, 315, ll. 24-5), or 'to a certain tuath' *(in tan tainic fo thomus tuaithi airithi hi*, ed. Binchy CIH 1978, 315, l. 17), but if washed onto another's land a portion would be forfeit. Does this imply then that goods would not be brought into Ireland unless they were earmarked for an individual customer? Alcuin has goods purchased in Gaul with his own money by a follower there and shipped to him in York *(Epistolae* VIII, ed. Dümmler 1895, 33). This may also imply that commercial purchase is only possible in Gaul, not in Britain, though there may be other explanations. St Filibert receives oil from Bordeaux by prior arrangement *(Vita Filiberti* XXXVII, ed. Levison 1910, 602), but there may be difficulties in taking the information of saints' lives literally. The *topoi* of hagiography require fortuitously arriving mariners with gifts or delayed orders to demonstrate the omniscience and patience of the saint, but these examples may still be drawn from the everyday activity of the time of the hagiographer. Consignments of goods from abroad may be gifts, which presumably prompted reciprocal gifts. Alcuin *(Epistolae* VI, ed. Dümmler 1895, 32) sends gifts of roofing tin and wine to Eanbald of York. There are accounts of high-status gift-giving in Gregory of Tours (Gregory of Tours, *HF* VII.1, ed. Krusch 1885a, 370), Bede *(HE* III.5, ed. Colgrave and Mynors 1969, 226) and a range of other sources. This sort of exchange may range from gifts given by an outsider to facilitate social intercourse, or to cultivate a powerful visitor, through gifts of a reciprocal nature amongst high-status equals (kings, churchmen and the like), or gifts from a ruler to a client —the latter taking the form of ritual feasting as an affirmation of the political relationship. Imported goods may be passed down the line in this way, from a central place to quite humble holdings. Such redistributive exchange systems serve to explain the range of sites where objects such as the imported ceramics are found on western British and Irish sites. These objects were passed on along with prestige items manufactured in the distribution centres.

The growth of a market economy in the Irish Sea basin is another matter. Whether the tribal assembly *(óenach)* was actually used as a market place is a debatable point. Certainly, however, monastic assemblies took on this role in the eighth century or later (Doherty 1980, 81). In view of the existence of monastic fairs in Gaul, however, and movement between Gaulish and Irish monasteries, it is possible that this was an idea carried over from Gaul to Ireland.

Gaulish exchange systems in the period AD400-800 were more sophisticated than those operating in Britain. Coin was in extensive use—Werner would suggest more in western Gaul than elsewhere (Werner 1961). A reference in Gregory of Tours to merchants selling food at exorbitant prices (in coin) in time of famine suggests sophisticated commercial exchange even at the level of basic necessities (Gregory of Tours, *HF* VII.45, ed. Krusch 1885a, 365). Cargoes of wine and oil being imported into Gaul (Gregory of Tours, *HF* VII.29, ed. Krusch 1885a, 348), which was already a primary producer of these items, suggests a market economy where supply and demand might be met through competing sources, providing different quality of goods. The provision of a loan by the crown to the businessmen of Verdun (Gregory of Tours, *HF* III.34, ed. Krusch 1885a, 129-30) implies that we should beware of importing any but the most sophisticated interpretative models to explain the Gaulish economy in our period.

Where did shipping fit into this picture and how was it operated? This is a much less discussed topic than the question of redistribution. In the Mediterranean at this time sources such as the *Rhodian Sea Law* give evidence of the transition to owner-operated ships, mostly using their own capital to buy and sell cargoes. The poignancy of the position of the sea-captain who must accept a cargo from the church in *The Life of St John the Almsgiver* (see above, 46) shows that the independence of these operators was a matter of some pride. In the western sealanes we must also presume the existence of owner-operated vessels. We find ships working regularly for monasteries, such as in the *Vita Filiberti* (see above, 72). In the *Vita Columbae*, Libran is refused passage by in a ship's crew in Derry, who 'repelled him and would not receive him because they were not of the monks of Saint Columba' *(sed ipsi non suscipientes refutaverunt eum quia non erant de monacis sancti Columbae*—*Vita Columbae* II.39, ed. & trans. Anderson and Anderson 1961, 428-9). Whether the sailors were actually monks is ambiguous.

In 1986 the writer (Wooding 1987, 1-17) , following the suggestion of my colleague John Pryor, discussed the idea that the modern 'tramp steamer' provided a model to assist in explaining the nature of western sealanes shipping. This term has been used by others recently in a slightly different sense to my use and requires clear definition. A 'tramp steamer' is a vessel which travels from port to port, wherever a cargo is available. It may sail one route regularly, but does not rely on doing so. Its cargo may vary from a single element, to a composite of elements, maybe consigned to more than one destination. Some elements may have cartage pre-paid, some may be ordered in advance and the operators may also have bought goods on a speculative basis. If the price was right a passenger might be all that is carried, though one would suspect that goods for sale would be carried on the chance that extra profit might be made. There is little doubt that western sealanes traffic was mostly on this model. Most references to ships imply independence from either ecclesiastical or royal control: at least ambiguity on this point. The model has validity in helping to explain trade in various goods in recurrent patterns and can offset the monolithic image of established trade conditioning the movement of travellers. In the case of royalty and important clergy, who are almost our only recorded passengers on voyages over long distances, it is possible that commissions to carry passengers made viable longer-distance voyages and that trade goods were carried initially only as a sideline. The tramp steamer might go to ports in a different order on different voyages and might sometimes take coastal traffic as well as international.

Archaeological use of the 'tramp steamer' model has been too limited in the western sealanes context: with Thomas and Campbell citing the term only in a polemical response to those who would accept a minimal number of cargoes as being responsible for bringing imported ceramics to western Britain and Ireland. This suspicion of reductionism is typical of archaeological approaches to assemblages which are far from fully known—Alcock's recent discussion of the problem of estimating the number of amphorae from sherd quantities is making the same point (Alcock and Alcock 1990, 138-9). These are arguments against the imposition of single-element, bulk cargo models. The tramp steamer model has little to offer these arguments, however, as the likelihood is that a tramp steamer would *not* have repeatedly made the same long voyage over many years. In the case of both the amphorae and E ware pottery the evidence does not suggest importation over a long period.

Routes of Traffic

Artefacts which demonstrate a maritime distribution offer potential to identify the paths of maritime exchange and to locate the ports where ships landed. In the following discussion, centering on the distribution of E ware, we will look at possible routes into and within the Irish Sea and the maritime considerations of voyages. It is contended here that more and less probable speculations as to use of these sealanes can be made from critical use of archaeological and literary sources, along with input from marine data.

First we must consider the distribution patterns of the imported artefacts and how much these patterns may represent the original paths of importation and redistribution. The quantity of E ware seems far too great to be explained by one, speculative cargo—nor is it the type of good (unlike the Mediterranean amphorae and their contents) which would be likely to form the bulk of a single cargo. The overall E ware forms are very uniform and there appear to be no grounds for claiming that we have a diversity of continental wares in this class—except perhaps in the case of the numerically small class of Eiv (where there are two distinctly different forms of spout). Any demand for pottery in western Britain and Ireland at this time was being filled by imports from one continental centre. Either we must imagine that regular voyages from Ireland were only converging on one continental centre to obtain pottery or, far more likely, that the impetus for the imports was Gaulish and that one set of 'sailors from Gaul' were bringing in their local pottery.

The fact that the largest concentrations of E ware are in the north of the Irish Sea basin suggests that foreign vessels carried the wares into the north of the zone—like Adomnán's *gallic nautae* going as far north as the Clyde estuary and adjacent waters. This is not to say that all discoveries of the ware at coastal sites are primary importations. We may indeed distinguish a primary voyage from secondary distributions, though the secondary voyages were probably over a shorter distance than the redistributive voyages which carried the Mediterranean wares northward—as the latter are concentrated in the south of the Irish Sea zone and the primary voyages seem likely to have stopped there.

A look at a simple distribution map of E ware is largely a reflection of archaeological enterprise, however, rather than a basic guide to maritime routes. We may offset this problem by discussion of the character of some of the individual sites. In the earliest discoveries of E ware, clusters of dots appeared on the map through individual events such as the Harvard archaeological mission and concentrated work on the early medieval period by O'Kelly, Alcock, Thomas, Lane and Campbell in different places and decades. Most of the earliest research was on obviously high-status sites such as Garranes, Garryduff, Lagore, Dunadd and Dinas Powys. Finds from a more economically diverse range of sites have only been added with more systematic excavation work: for example in Northern Ireland, since 1950 (e.g. Armagh, Co. Armagh, Ballyfounder, Downpatrick and Lough Faughan, Co. Down, Lisdhu Co. Fermanagh, Scrabo, Co. Derry, Teeshan, Co. Antrim); and the Republic of Ireland since 1970

(Derrynaflan and Killededadrum, Co. Tipperary, Killucan Co. Westmeath, Randalstown, Co. Meath, Reask, Co. Kerry). This is also seen most recently in Scilly, where the number of find-sites of E ware has doubled as a result of Thomas' focus on these islands since 1980. The greatest concentration of E ware finds is in Northern Ireland and southern Scotland, though the fact that many sites were abandoned in Northern Ireland at the end of the early Christian period has aided in the recovery of much data in that region.

E ware finds as listed in Thomas, *A Provisional List*, pp. 20-24. Additions and Deletions are given here in Thomas' format. Forms present are noted where known. A new, complete, catalogue is expected shortly from the work of Ewan Campbell. Identifications by: LA = Leslie Alcock, EC = Ewan Campbell, MOD = Mary O'Donnell, CT = Charles Thomas, JW = Jonathan Wooding.

Additions

South-west Britain

Bryher, Isle of Scilly (Thomas, 'Bryher') CT
Dial Rocks Hill, Isle of Scilly (Thomas, 'Bryher') CT
May's Hill, Isle of Scilly (Thomas in F. Turk, 'A Study', pp. 78-80) 1/ Ei CT JW

Severn—South Wales

Caldey Island, Dyfed (Campbell, 1989a). 1/ Ei EC

Isle of Man

Port e Candas, German, Isle of Man EC

Scotland

Ardifuir, Argyll (in National Museum of Antiquities, Edinburgh) 1/ Ei JW LA
Lochspouts, Argyll (Laing, 'Cooking Pots', pp. 185-92) Ei EC JW
Whithorn, Wigtownshire (Hill, *pers. comm.* and author's observations) 10/ Ei, 1/ Eii, 4/ Eiii, 1/ Eiv JW EC

Ireland

Clonmacnois (4 sherds, Heather King, *pers comm.).*
Derrynaflan, Co. Tipperary 1/ Ei JW EC
Kedrah, Co. Tipperary EC
Lisleagh, Co. Cork MOD
Marshes Upper, Co. Louth EC
Moynagh Lough Crannóg, Co. Meath EC

Deletions:

South-west Britain

Hellesvean, Cornwall CT JW

North Wales

Dinas Emrys, Gwynedd EC JW

Scotland

Abercorn, West Lothian EC CT JW
Craigs Quarry, East Lothian EC JW
Dún Ardtreck, Skye EC
Elie, Fifeshire EC
Little Dunagoil, Bute EC
Luce Bay, Wigtownshire EC

Ireland

Nendrum, Co. Down MOD

Growth of the distribution in last two decades has followed a distinct pattern, however: new finds have been from areas where E ware was already found, or in areas closely linked. Odd finds in areas otherwise bare of E ware have been gradually recognised as misidentified: such as Dinas Emrys in Gwynedd (inspected by the author in the National Museum of Wales in 1988), finds from Lothian (Craigs Quarry, Abercorn) and one from Skye (Dún Ardtreck). Some areas remain uncertain, however, owing to a lack of ability to identify early medieval sites. Lane and Campbell, with persistence, have identified a number of early medieval sites in South Wales—in Dyfed two of these, both unfortified and only located by stray finds, producing E ware (Longbury Bank, Caldey Island). Brittany has similar problems, with none of its early medieval sites being identifiable by visible morphology (Giot and Fleuriot 1977, 110).

Some areas are now very likely to be excluded from the distribution. McPeake's suggestion that E ware existed in Chester (McPeake *et al.* 1980, 14-38) was inaccurate. Despite its Irish Sea outlook it was a relatively isolated port (Griffiths 1992a, 68ff). Somerset has seen enough archaeological endeavour to have turned up E ware if such were there. Central and western Cornwall remain a little more puzzling. Pieces of E ware from High Peak and Bantham, on the south coast of Devon, and Guisseny on the north Breton coast, seem to suggest that E ware could have been imported in cargoes brought into the English Channel, though, if so, the paucity of finds does not yet indicate whether such activity focussed on either shore in particular, or was primary or redistributive in character.

E ware occurrence will continue to increase, as it is clear that we have only found a small percentage of the amount imported, but the occurrences will probably now be more predictable. The largest totals of E ware at individual sites have been found at Dunadd, Whithorn, Dinas Powys and Garryduff. All of these sites have been the subject of sustained excavation over several years—in the case of the early twentieth century excavations at Dunadd the techniques used were primitive and likely to extract larger percentages of finds than would be the case with modern methods. The quantities found range from around 20 vessels at Dunadd and 16 at Whithorn to single vessels at the majority of sites. For comparison we may note that no single site contains as large a proportion of the entire insular assemblage of E ware as the Tintagel assemblage does for the Mediterranean wares. This is not a question of scale of excavation as at Tintagel the Mediterranean pottery is a ubiquitous surface find. All of this indicates that E ware was probably a subsidiary good, never forming the physical (let alone economic) core of a single cargo.

The finds of single vessels must be set in context with the region in which they are found. One vessel from a totally excavated site at Trethurgy in Cornwall is explicable in terms of the general rarity of E ware in the south-west peninsula. Single finds from sites on the Isle of Man must be seen in the light of comparatively little excavation—though the absence of E ware from recent major excavations at Peel is interesting to note (Freke 1983-7), even though it is found at the nearby site of Port e Candas (German). Odd finds through trial-trenching at Whithorn and Longbury Bank have expanded naturally along with the assemblages—in areas where E ware had previously been rare. On the other hand, a single find from Proudfoot's narrow trench at Downpatrick has not been significantly added to by later excavation, even though E ware is ubiquitous in Northern Ireland.

It can be seen that our pattern is achieving greater stability when we note that more finds are being made in the hinterland of the sites where the largest totals already exist. Around Dunadd, E ware finds identified from Ardifaur, Loch Glashan, Dunollie and Dumbarton in recent decades have helped in defining a hinterland province. Finds from Lisdhu in Co. Fermanagh are likely to be closely linked to the centre at Clogher, and finds in North Co. Cork and Tipperary extend the range of finds at major sites in South Cork. Routes in and out of Dinas Powys can be related to more recent finds at Lesser Garth Cave and in Dyfed.

The Distribution of Glass Vessels

With the dismissal of Harden's thesis from consideration, comparisons of the Atlantic glass and E ware distributions have again been made, though few discussions have appeared in print (Wooding 1992). Ewan Campbell *(pers. comm.)* considers the two to be related imports and this idea is worthy of discussion.

The glassware distribution is heavily weighted toward the eastern side of the Irish Sea, in contrast to the western and northern focus of E ware. Very large totals from Dinas Powys and Whithorn certainly reflect the larger scale of excavation at those sites. Differences in scale between excavations in Ireland and western Britain could account for differences. Very few of the humbler sites producing E ware have produced glass finds, either in Britain or Ireland. The high status sites in Ireland in general have not been excavated on the scale of Dinas Powys, Dunadd or Whithorn. This is certainly likely to make the distribution lopsided. The situation is not the same as with *paléochrétienne grise,* where there is no Irish distribution at all. Nonetheless, as noted previously, the glass finds compare interestingly with the redistributive pattern of the Mediterranean wares in being found in quantity at sites in western Britain and at Dalkey Island, but in lesser quantities elsewhere in Ireland—though glass is found at sites in Co. Meath, at Dunadd and at the Mote of Mark, whereas the Mediterreanean wares are not.

Routes of Maritime Traffic: The Severn and Southern Coasts of Ireland and Britain

The pattern of Bristol Channel traffic, which we have seen in the sixth century with regard to the distribution of the Mediterranean wares, is not replicated in the seventh. On the north side there may have been little change. The Welsh sites of Dinas Powys and Longbury Bank produce the full range of Gaulish import classes: E ware, D ware and 'Merovingian' glass, with further finds of E ware and glass in Glamorgan and Dyfed. The E ware at least can be explained by a landfall in Glamorgan, close to Dinas Powys (perhaps in Cardiff itself) and another at Caldey Island in Dyfed, near to Longbury Bank. There is good reason to see the Lesser Garth finds as linked to Dinas Powys. Campbell has suggested that iron ore sources at Lesser Garth supplied the iron-working activities at Dinas Powys (Campbell 1988b, 86-7). The Longbury Bank site was clearly in contact with the island monastery of Caldey (Campbell 1989a, 259ff).

The finds of earlier imports at Congresbury, virtually on the same longitude as Dinas Powys, suggest that the voyages, redistributive or primary, which took the Mediterranean wares to Dinas Powys, Coygan Camp, Longbury Bank and Caldey were likely to have been the same as brought the wares to Somerset. This pattern is not replicated in the seventh century finds. On the south side of the Bristol Channel E ware is found no further east than The Kelsies (near Newquay) and E ware is conspicuously absent from the heavily-excavated sites of Tintagel and Congresbury, where it is accordingly unlikely ever to be found. There are continental glass finds at Congresbury, but these contain a very substantial Saxon component.

We might suggest then that there is a real change to the pattern of contact in this area. The relocating of the *paléochrétienne grise* and much of the glass to a British-focused trading network of the mid-sixth century, proposed in Chapter Five, would see it separated from the E ware evidence, which may suggest that the Bristol Channel became less central after Saxon incursions into North Somerset and Devon. By the mid-seventh century imports into Dyfed and Glamorgan may have been coming from Ireland. The weight of the distribution of E ware is, after all, towards the north of the zone and the maritime incentives for a voyage north along the eastern shore of the Irish Sea are not as great as along the western shore.

Particularly interesting in this connection is the hagiographical evidence linking Caldey to Ireland, implied to be more than an isolated voyage (see above, 62). The links in metalwork finds between Glamorgan and Meath are also especially compelling. A penannular brooch fragment from Dinas Powys is of Kilbride-Jones Class C4, one of the only firmly-provenanced types, centring on County Meath (Graham-Campbell 1987, 122-4). This indicates either the presence of an Irish craftsman, or a direct import from Ireland. Graham-Campbell would favour the

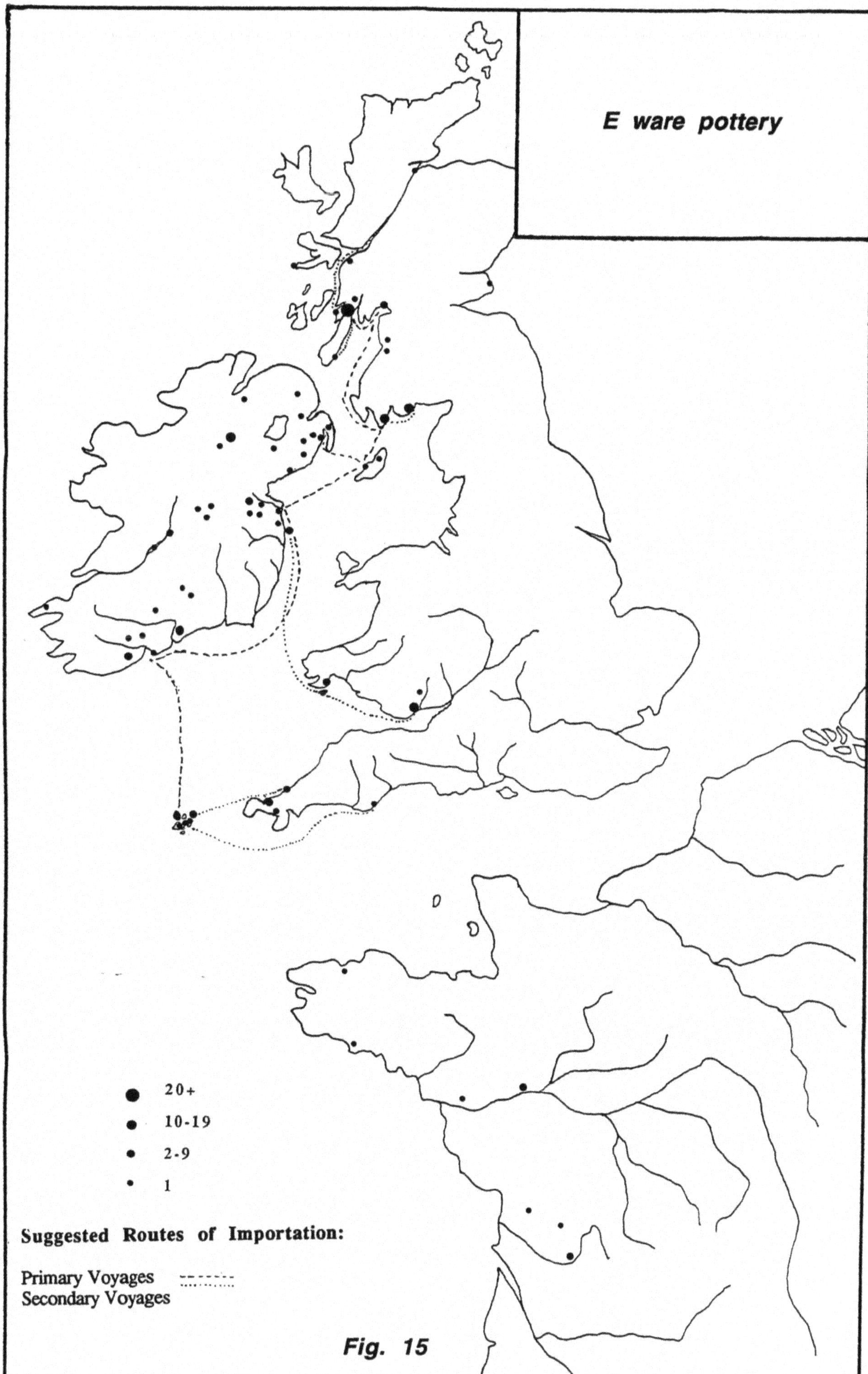
E ware pottery
20+
10-19
2-9
1
Suggested Routes of Importation:
Primary Voyages
Secondary Voyages

Fig. 15

Glass vessels of 'Atlantic' type: British and Irish distribution
- 30+
- 10-20
- 2-10
- 1

Fig. 16

latter (Graham-Campbell 1991, 224) and suggests a trade in scrap metal as the most likely explanation. This is plausible, though Irish style metalwork also occurs on an industrial site at Lesser Garth (Alcock 1959, 221-7). The E ware could easily be a secondary import from Ireland, also. Its absence from most other parts of the Bristol Channel make Dinas Powys less likely to have been primary importation point from the continent.

On the other hand, a primary landfall in Scilly is not unlikely. E ware pottery occurs there on some 6 sites (Bryher, Dial Rocks Hill (Tresco), Mays Hill (St Martins), Samson, St Mary's, Tean) and most of the other Cornish finds are in the very west of Cornwall, where they could be secondary distributions from Scilly. The maritime advantages of Scilly as a primary landfall from the continent have been outlined in chapter 4. The primary involvement of Scilly in voyages into the Irish Sea zone in the seventh century, however, could just as easily be en route to southern or eastern Ireland as to the Bristol Channel ports. Out of Scilly, E ware finds at Gwithian point to the natural harbour of St Ives Bay. Finds on an unenclosed site, washed by the tide, at Bantham, on the south coast of Devon point to a landfall there. In both cases this is likely to have been a coastal trading voyage out of Scilly.

The East Coast of Ireland and North Wales

The quantity of E ware pottery from Co. Cork would make it a likely a primary landfall by a foreign vessel. Indeed in view of the problems of the outfall of the mouth of the English Channel, a vessel setting on a northward voyage from Brittany might easily find conditions for landing in Scilly unfavourable and head instead for Munster, which may then have alternated with Scilly as a primary landfall from abroad. A cluster of sites within reach of Cork harbour might favour this as the principal landing point. From Munster it is possible to make a broad reach across the prevailing wind to the east or the west. Finds of E ware at Reask and Inishcealtra do not necessarily imply voyages from Gaul directly into the Shannon. The unreliable story in the *Vita Kyarani* (see above, 59) represents the commercial interests of a later age, when ships from France sought fish from the Shannon as part of restricted medieval commodity networks, which did not obtain in our period. That the Shannon played a secondary role in distribution of E ware seems undoubted (perhaps along with fish for local markets), but *(contra* Thomas) the trail of E ware to Westmeath from Dublin seems equally likely to have first brought the ware to the Shannon shores, only from there to be distributed southward to Iniscealtra and Reask. St Samson's voyage seems to indicate the presence of a port in Dublin Bay (see above, 62). Thomas, however, would suggest that a site in the Boyne estuary is more likely to be responsible for the E ware finds west into Meath (Thomas 1990, 21).

As we have seen, voyages up the Irish Sea to Ireland, Scotland and Wales are suggested by both literary and archaeological evidence. That these followed the western shores, i.e. the easy coast of Ireland, would seem most logical in maritime terms. Significant obstacles exist on the coast of Wales, especially Dyfed, which is heavily encumbered with shoals. At all times of the year, except Spring, south-westerly winds are most prevalent. In Summer the chances of a westerly or south-westerly in the Irish Sea are around 60%. The evidence of E ware pottery, present in greater amounts on the western shores of the Irish Sea, may reflect the maritime concerns of sailors from the continent favouring the safer western shore of the Irish Sea in the face of prevailing conditions which rendered the eastern shore less safe for northward navigation. That the glass and Mediterranean wares, otherwise rare in eastern Ireland, are found in quantity at Dalkey Island might suggest that even a British-focused network would proceed north via a leg toward the east coast of Ireland (see above, 52, 61-2).

There is no E ware in Gwynedd. Mediterranean finds, however, are reported from Dinas Emrys and Degannwy in Gwynedd, though both are problematical. The Dinas Emrys material of definite early medieval type is limited—even the Mediterranean pottery is ambiguous, being of Class 45, which can be of either Roman or post-Roman date—the very fragmentary Degannwy B ware has been impossible to locate for re-examination. Bede's testimony to Anglo-Saxon incursions into Gwynedd and Man in the 620s, which he claims 'brought the isles of Man and Anglesey under English rule' (Bede, *HE* II.9, ed. & trans. Colgrave and Mynors 1969, 162-3), may account for the absence of the sorts of connections which might have brought in E ware.

The Northern Basin of the Irish Sea

In the northern basin of the Irish Sea, tidal streams in the Solway are especially strong, as are those off the coast of Lancashire. On the Solway coast, no E ware occurs east of the Mote of Mark, while no imported ceramics are found at all in the Mersey area, though this is likely to reflect the boundary between Celt and Saxon as much as the dangerous tides and shoals.

Bowen highlights the role of the Isle of Man in Irish Sea traffic (Bowen 1969b, 26-7), though an early Anglian presence here is also suggested by Bede. The lack of excavation on Man renders its role uncertain. Certainly it is a likely stopping point and landmark for vessels operating around the significant region of Whithorn. Tidal streams divide around Man and from Man a ship can wait to pick up a tidal stream to almost any part of the region. A major slack water area is present off County Louth, between the Boyne mouth and Ulster and a detour toward Man is often necessary for a sailing vessel heading north along the Irish coast. The highest point of Man, Snaefell, is 620 metres and can be viewed from both Ireland and Scotland, though cloud envelops it much of the time. It should be noted in passing that excavation in the Isle of Man may have much to tell us about the possible divisions between 'British' and 'Irish' trading provinces.

Finds of E ware in Northern Ireland are very likely to have been from a primary voyage from the continent. A cluster of finds in Co. Down might highlight this coast as a primary landfall, rather than the treacherous conditions of Belfast or the Antrim coast. Unlike the Sound of Jura, the passage off the Mull of Galloway presents few dangers, though the tidal race is fierce. The Admiralty Pilot describes it as 'free from dangers, except in the vicinity of Craig Laggan' (Hydrographer 1974a, 28) and the same is generally true of the Ayrshire coast, except around Girvan. Hence it is arguable that continental shipping would have ventured at least as far as the Clyde estuary. At the head of navigation of the Clyde is a political centre where there is a wide chronological range of imports in Dumbarton Rock. This is the well-attested British fortress of *Alt Clut*—mentioned in Bede, Adomnán and later sources—doubtless commanding a harbour nearby and an ideal landmark for a ship approaching from the south or west.

A voyage into the seas around the Hebrides is an entirely different proposition to a voyage up the Clyde. Tidal streams are strong off the western side of the tip of Kintyre, owing to the funnelling between the landmasses of Northern Ireland and western Scotland. This renders both the Jura and Kilbrannan Sounds dangerous. South of the Isle of Mull the waters are very treacherous indeed with inequalities in the seabed causing possible tidal races, heavy surf at the change of tide and eddies. For the moment we may note the disincentives for voyages of ships travelling up the Irish Sea from abroad. If a vessel put into the Clyde estuary it would also have to backtrack to go on to Dunollie or Iona. There is no definite evidence that the route around Kintyre or along the Antrim coast was used in this period, though we should not overemphasise negative evidence when the sources are limited. E ware is rare in Antrim and Derry and not suggestive of a primary importation to Derry or any point west of Belfast Lough or Kintyre. The case for the intermediacy of Dunadd in the Dalriada importations has already been made (also see below, 107). Voyages between Ireland and Iona are of course known, but there is no evidence that any of these left Ireland from east of Kintyre / Derry. Libran, for example, sails for Iona from Derry (Adomnán, *Vita Columbae* II.39, ed. Anderson and Anderson 1961, 432-3) and though his general destination is stated as 'Britain', it is clear that the *island* of Britain is what is meant (i.e. in this case Dalriada). The familial and political links between Dalriada (in particular Iona) and Ireland were of a character which would be well served by maritime links with Derry.

Within the northern zone of the Irish Sea there have been a number of attempts to identify a range of movements of raw materials and produce between sites. The excellence of the fishing conditions off the west coast of Man and the south coast of Dumfries and Galloway may have been a motivation for the existence of regular contacts between these shores from an early date—along with the fact of the easy visibility of neighbouring landmasses, not a major issue in international trade, but probably crucial in the paradigm of coastal voyaging.

Whithorn has a range of finds suggesting long-distance traffic as well as a likely pattern of east-west trade along the south coast of Dumfries and Galloway. Whithorn itself is five kilometres from a harbour at the Isle of Whithorn, which Symson, in his *Description of Galloway* of 1684, described as 'a very advantageous port .....in which ships of great burthern were safe in any storm' (Graham 1979, 49ff). As with Grenville's estimation of Tintagel (see above, 52), we should put some weight in the testimony of early modern mariners who judged these harbours by the requirements of ships comparable in size and performance to those of the early middle ages, who saw these harbours before modern improvements were made upon the natural conditions. Whithorn clearly constituted a centre which brought in and processed materials from long and short distances. Discoveries in David Pollock's 1992 excavations have opened up an area on the north side of the church hill, with settlement comparable in extent to that covered by the site excavated in 1986-91, identifying it as a centre of considerable size by the seventh century. In the absence of evidence for the extractive industry in the immediate vicinity, and taking account of the centrality of Whithorn in the northern part of the Irish Sea, we may see the economic importance of Whithorn as predicated in a large degree upon location—though the political and religious contributions to the status of the site remain less clear. Whether the imported wares at Whithorn represent primary landfalls from abroad or, perhaps more likely in terms of a northward voyage to Dumbarton, Dunadd or beyond, secondary imports from Man or Ireland must remain for the moment unsolved.

In summary, the distribution of E ware offers evidence for a general north-south voyage pattern, with hypothetical landing-points at Scilly, Cork, Dalkey Island, Man, Isle of Whithorn, Co. Down, Dumbarton and Dunadd. These in turn may connect with identifiable coastal traffic out of Scilly to far western and southern Cornwall; out of Cork to Kerry and the Shannon; out of Dublin to South Wales; between Man, Whithorn and the Solway; and between Dunadd and Dalriada.

France

At the other end of the voyages, the finds of E ware from western Brittany may or may not represent maritime distributions. Certainly the three known find sites are on or near the coast. It is most logical to explain their presence as due to local traffic with the Loire estuary, such as the appearance of *Brittani* in the *Vita Filiberti* may represent (see above, 67). However, links between Brittany and western Gaulish ports remain something of a mystery: for example there is almost no *paléochrétienne grise* in Brittany (Giot and Fleuriot 1977, 110). The finds from Guisseny may be imports from Cornwall. The western coast of Gaul does not present ideal conditions for the mariner setting out. There is only a 30% chance of a fair wind for leaving Nantes or Bordeaux and such a wind continues to be necessary until one reaches a point west of Ushant. The estuaries of both the Loire and the Garonne are encumbered by shoals. The story of St Columbanus' ship being obstructed and stranded while setting out from Nantes, however miraculous, certainly presents a picture which fits the genuine maritime problems of Nantes. For a vessel voyaging out of Nantes, however, the chances of a favourable return wind are around 70% which might have encouraged local enterprise, which could wait for a fair wind to leave, knowing that their return could be relied upon. For foreign vessels arriving, the island of Noirmoutier, apart from its salt resources, might have represented a good place to obtain pilotage for the difficult entry of the

Port sites discussed
Dunadd
Dumbarton
Luce Bay
Isle of Whithorn
Meols
Dalkey Island
Waterford Harbour
Cork Harbour
Caldey
Cadbury Congresbury
Tintagel
Bantham
Scilly
Nantes
LOIRE
Noirmoutier

Loire—just as, on reaching Britain, the Scillies may have useful for the same reason.

Changes to the Maritime Routes in the Eighth Century

The E ware evidence centres on the seventh century. Clear definition of the eighth century in the western sealanes is lacking. In parts of the western sealanes the eighth century would have seen dramatic changes. That Spain fell to Islamic invaders in 711 might be expected to have stimulated the Atlantic connections of the Christian pockets remaining in the Asturias. The most logical target, southwest Gaul, however, was also conquered in the 720s. In the light of these disruptions it may not be surprising that clear evidence for Atlantic activity in western Gaul and Spain is lacking in the eighth century.

In the Irish Sea no definitely eighth-century artefacts show an identifiable maritime distribution. In Ireland, a few literary sources have been noted, such as *Sanas Cormaic* and *Tecosca Cormaic*, which suggest that foreign, and in particular Gaulish, links might not have ceased with the cessation of importation of E ware, but political changes would certainly have closed some ports and routes. Anglian conquest of Galloway had occurred by the early 700s, bringing measurable changes in the sequence of imports at Whithorn. Consolidation of other coastal holdings, such as in Anglesey, Man and Cornwall, would have seen greater Anglian naval control of the Irish Sea. An assault on Ireland is recorded in 684 (Bede, *HE* IV.26, ed. Colgrave and Mynors 1969, 426-7). How early Anglo-Saxon ports in the Mersey entered into the activity of the Irish Sea is unclear. Sites such as Meols in the Wirral (Griffiths 1992a, 68), and Luce Sands (Cormack 1965, 149-50) and Whithorn (Hill 1990, 8-14) in Wigtownshire produce eighth-century *sceattas* which at least show a new presence in coastal trading centres in the eastern part of the Irish Sea, even if we cannot show such coins to be the objects of maritime activity.

In Ireland the transition between the eighth and the ninth century AD coincides with changes in decorative techniques in insular metalwork art. Ninth-century brooches and other decorated pieces from Ireland use amber by preference to enamel and glass ornaments. The ninth century seems very early for such changes to be attributed to 'Viking influence' (Ryan 1983, 38-41)—in a period where raiding seems to have been the norm, it is hard to see Viking influences penetrating established Irish factories, such as those which produced the Ardagh and Derrynaflan chalices (the latter showing the shift to amber ornament). Some archaeologists are even prepared to see amber arriving in the seventh century (Youngs 1989, 208). This is a change which brings the far northern regions into contact with the western sealanes—prefiguring Viking period links and what Bowen was to describe as the 'seaways in reverse'—with Ireland and the Irish Sea receiving regular imports and settlement via the sealanes around northern Scotland to the North Sea and Iceland: the reverse of the pattern in AD400-800. *Did* this 'reversal' have a an earlier counterpart in Irish links with the far north? Irish voyages northward had begun in the late-sixth century, when the voyager Cormac explored north by sea and Columba, visiting the Pictish court at Inverness, negotiated protection for him from the King of Orkney if his voyage took him there (Adomnán *Vita Columbae* II.42, ed. Anderson and Anderson 1961, 440-1). Dicuil, writing early in the ninth century, provides clear evidence of the persistence of this coastal activity northward out of Iona. Though he describes 'Irish' voyages northward, he is a monk of Iona (this is evident from the reference to Suibhne, Abbot of Iona 766-72 as his 'master': Dicuil, *Liber de Mensura Orbis Terrae* XII, ed. Tierney 1967, 62; Smyth 1984, 167-9) and talks of having voyaged himself to some of the northern isles (Dicuil, *Liber de Mensura Orbis Terrae* XV, ed. Tierney 1967, 76-7). Irish activity in this region clearly overlapped with Norse activity and may be influential in the Norse settlement of the Faeroes and Iceland. It also may have opened up new sources of materials. The possibility that reindeer antler was arriving in Orkney in the eighth century has been canvassed (Weber 1992) and similar speculation has been made of the importation of amber to Orkney (Roesdahl 1992). These links may explain some changes in the orientation of Irish exchange, though sources via Anglo-Saxon England may also be considered for the amber imports.

In Chapters Four, Five, Six and Seven we have examined definite cases of overseas exchange which suggest that the economic impact of imports and long-distance overseas contact was less than is assumed in most studies. The evidence for cargoes shows no evidence for traffic having been supported by one central cargo or set of comsumer demands. The evidence of the Mediterranean ceramics and E ware, moreover, shows little sign of being part of sustained, long-term importation patterns. The assumption that they are the archaeologically-visible detritus of largely archaeologically-invisible, long-term, traffic has been shown to less likely than that traffic carrying such imports was intermittent and episodic. Future archaeological research will refine and correct the models sketched here—there is a great deal more to be done in defining activity, especially on a local level. The most important conclusions of the present study should be seen in the case for the abandonment of diffusionist perspectives and the need for greater attention to the details and mechanics of maritime communication events.

Appendix One: Two Unsubstantiated Cases of Seventh-Century Travel

The substantial evidence of E ware allows us to examine a definite continental connection and subsidiary routes within the Irish Sea. Obviously this should not lead us to overlook the possibility of other links and other routes which are not so tangible. Hillgarth has attempted to counter Zimmer's thesis by stressing the importance of the cultural links between Ireland and Spain in the seventh century (Hillgarth 1961; 1962; 1965; 1984). As Mayr-Harting rightly observes, however: 'one may search the text and voluminous notes of the learned articles of...Hillgarth, who seeks to establish such links, without finding a single piece of evidence of travel or written correspondence or direct communication of any kind between Ireland and Spain' (Mayr-Harting 1972, 127). There is nothing other than circumstantial evidence to support the existence of such contacts at *any* point in the early middle ages. Hillgarth's case is founded on the circumstantial evidence of strong influence of Spanish writings upon seventh-century Irish learning. Hillgarth's thesis obviously highlights questions as to the importance of the evidence of direct travel favoured by Zimmer and Levison to identify regular contact between regions. Hillgarth has recently shifted the emphasis of his debate by observing that, in cultural terms, the route by which influences arrive may be 'secondary to the question of reception' (Hillgarth 1984, 16). But *both* are important in their own right.

Do we assume, then, following Zimmer, that commercial links have a determining role in the formation of cultural contacts? Can we, like Hillgarth, accept that definite cultural connections between two regions allow us to assume the existence of direct commerce for which there is no other substantive evidence? And does the fact that the majority of Irish churchmen travelling to Gaul worked in east Francia allow us, following James, to doubt the predominance of the western sealanes route? The answer is no to all of these questions. Hillgarth is correct to emphasise the importance of reception over routes of communication for cultural studies. Intellectuals, carrying texts, may have travelled on trading ships to western Gaul. Beyond this point, however, they enjoyed powers of movement beyond that of traders. The evidence for commerce suggests western Gaulish links were predominant. To seek the major influences on Ireland in western Gaul, however, is no more logical than looking for the sources of, say, contemporary English influences on Scottish culture in Kings Cross and Euston railway stations.

In a discussion of western sealanes traffic in the seventh century, we are also obliged to consider the story of Arculf, a bishop of 'Gaulish race' who visited the Near East, and who provided the details for Adomnán's book *De Locis Sanctis*. Adomnán only states that Arculf was a Gaulish bishop and that he dictated the account to him (Adomnán, *De Locis Sanctis*, Prologue, ed. Meehan 1963, 36-7). Bede furnishes us with the details as to how Adomnán came to meet Arculf:

> Patriamque navigio revertens, vi tempestatis in occidentalia Brittaniae littora delatus est: ac post multa, ad memoratum Christi famulum Adamnanum perveniens, ubi doctus in Scripturi sanctorumque locorum gnarus esse compertus est...cuncta mox iste litteris mandare curaverit.
>
> (Coming home by sea [Arculf] was driven by a mighty tempest to the west coasts of Britain; and after suffering many things he reached the aforesaid servant of Christ, Adomnan, and was found to be learned in the Scriptures and acquainted with the holy places...all these Adomnan by and by procured to be put in writing: Bede, *HE* V.15, ed. & trans. Colgrave and Mynors 1969, 506-8).

A similar account precedes Bede's own *De Locis Sanctis* (largely based on Adomnán) with no additional detail:

> Sed cum patriam revisere vellet, navis, que vehebatur, post multos, anfractus venti contrario in nostrum, idest Brittannorum isulam perlata est, tandemque, iste post nonnulla pericula ad prefatum virum venerabilem Adamnanum perveniens...(Bede, *De Locis Sanctis*, ed. Geyer 1975, 302).

Bede may have received this story from monks of Iona, though he also records a story whereby Adomnán presented Aldfrith with a copy of the book in Northumbria (Bede, *HE*, ed. Colgrave and Mynors 1969, 504-6; Meehan 1958, 4-5). From whatever source Bede received this information may also have come these further details regarding Arculf. What are the logistics of this story? The questions which have concerned most commentators have been why a traveller returning to Gaul from the Near East would have travelled by sea at all and how, having done so, he would be wrecked off the western coast of Britain.

It is tempting to see the story as confused or conflated by Bede. Certainly Adomnán's silence on the point is important in this regard. A storm-driven churchman is a likely *topos* in insular writing. Bede, or some intermediary between him and the events, may have felt this a more convenient explanation of Arculf's presence at Iona than a more lengthy, prosaic and less entertaining account of his presence there. Certainly the fact that he is implied to have travelled straight from the Mediterranean to Britain is suspiciously neat. On the other hand some details of the story are not implausible. Ships on the western sealanes may be driven by storm far off course by contrary winds (Bede's *venti contrario*). They may be forced to sail long distances in the opposite direction to their course, where the alternatives would be a dangerous head sea or a reach, broadside on to the prevailing swell. *If* Arculf were travelling to western Gaul via the Straits of Gibraltar, for example, it would not be impossible for him to fetch up in western Britain. In summer the south westerly winds would be quite likely to drive a ship into the western channel of Britain. Another point is that Arculf might well have planned a voyage *via* Britain. There is no assurance that Arculf would have owned his own vessel or could have ordered a ship to change its route of travel to set him ashore any more than a modern traveller can ask an express train to put them down at a rural halt. When we consider a case like that of John the Archcantor, travelling to Britain via Tours, it is implicit that coastal voyages around Brittany and up the English Channel may have been contemplated as an alternative to overland travel through Neustria. If we were to speculate that Arculf was from the north-east of Gaul (Meehan 1958, 5-6), the hostility between Neustria and Austrasia in this period (679-686) provides an adequate reason why sea travel might be considered as an alternative to crossing Neustria: which explanation might also suffice for the route of John Arch-Cantor (680). Finally, Arculf's ship may have been wrecked well to the south of Iona. Bede simply says *in occidentalia Brittaniae littora,* which may imply anywhere between Cornwall and the Hebrides. Conceivably Wales or Cornwall may not be unlikely. We should also note that there is the possibility that Adomnán did not meet Arculf at Iona, perhaps meeting him in Ireland before coming to Iona (this may make little practical difference, as Adomnán would still most likely have been in the *north* of Ireland).

The best explanation of this story is that it is a conflation, or simple fantasy. The detail of a churchman travelling by a roundabout route is believable enough in the context of the late seventh century, but the chances of the case for this being a direct voyage from the eastern Mediterranean must regarded unproven in the absence of any supporting evidence. The likelihood that Arculf was making a voyage off western Gaul is more likely.

In Britain, whether by accident or by design, Arculf may have found a return via Iona the most convenient route. This may seem illogical to the modern traveller. A lack of east-west contacts between Anglo-Saxon England and Celtic Britain south of Scotland in this period is implicit from a variety of sources. Iona had links with Northumbria which would assure Arculf a safe journey and Northumbria likewise with Gaul. It should be noted that Dagobert returned to Gaul from Ireland via the same route around the same time (see above, 66).

All of the above is simply speculation. It raises questions, however, which are fundamental to study of historical assumptions regarding early medieval travel. Both mariners and churchmen were limited by political and economic considerations in respect of where they could safely put into shore and across whose land they could safely travel. The sea is more neutral ground. Likewise, early medieval commercial voyages may have been rare and roundabout routes explicable in the context. The details of Arculf's voyage, however, are difficult to reconcile with the other evidence for western sealanes usage in the seventh century. Likewise it must be held to be unlikely that Mediterranean ships were arriving in Britain along the same lines of commerce as in the mid-sixth. That Werner and Nordenfalk have seen this supposedly 'direct' traveller arriving conveniently laden with the many manuscript exemplars required to underpin their theories of insular art (Werner, forthcoming; Nordenfalk 1977, 22) must be regarded as quite unacceptable in terms of the quality of the evidence.

Appendix Two: The 'Peninsular Road' Model

In looking at the question of distribution, Crawford (1936, 185), Bowen (1969b, 14) and Miller (1978-80, 317) placed considerable emphasis on the existence of 'peninsular roads', a model which Crawford imported from a Mediterranean context: most particularly inspired by the isthmus of Corinth (Crawford 1936, 185) and first applied to prehistoric distributions around the Irish Sea. In his seminal study of the early medieval use of the western sealanes, however, he integrated his prehistoric data with historical evidence which he took to demonstrate the validity of this model. Distributions of artefacts and the locations of monuments in Wales have been invoked to support the existence of peninsular roads across the tips of Dyfed, Gwynedd, Cornwall, the Mull of Galloway and Kintyre (Bowen 1969b, 19). This model and its relevance must be regarded as dubious in the extreme. That peninsulas were fearsome zones to the mariner is undoubted. This does not imply that traders would have unloaded their ships and carted goods overland to avoid them. The cost of land transport is massively greater than that of sea-travel. The Corinth case also needs to be understood in the context of the *distance* of the voyage around the Peleponnese, leaving aside the unreliable seas of the Southern Aegean. The voyage around, say, Dyfed is of nothing like the same length. If landing sites exist at the ends of paths that cross the peninsulas, this presumably implies the existence of central places straddling these paths and requiring links to each shore.

The example of St Samson of Dol, though an example of a person who travelled overland across Cornwall, does not aid the 'peninsular road' theory. In his *vita* he sets out to be 'a pilgrim, and beyond the sea, great in the church' *(Vita Samsonis* XLV, ed. Fawtier 1912, 141). Landing in the estuary of the Fowey *(Vita Samsonis* XLV, ed. Fawtier 1912, 142), he appears quite willing to make his home in Cornwall and when he crosses to the continent 'according to his promise' *(Vita Samsonis* LII, ed. Fawtier 1912, 147), the promise in question was simply to travel across the sea until he found a place to settle. In other words, the hagiographer believed that Samson left Wales *without* the explicit intention of travelling as far as Brittany. There is no case then to argue that he travelled across Cornwall to avoid the seas off Land's End.

Quite different circumstances may be found in Scotland, where at least two likely 'peninsular' roads existed, across Kintyre and between Loch Ness and the Moray Firth. The site of Dunadd commands the Crinan isthmus and its hinterland relations clearly extend into the Clyde estuary, as well as further west in Dalriada (Nieke and Duncan 1988, 16ff; Campbell 1987). Here we must be conscious of the likelihood of a peninsular transit from the evidence of E ware pottery. The maritime conditions between Fairhead and Kintyre are truly intimidating (see above, 8) and this seems to be reflected in the lack of finds of E ware at distribution points which necessarily reflect use of this channel. The furthest south find-site in Dalriada on the west side of Kintyre is Ardifuir, which must certainly be in overland contact with Dunadd. Nieke and Duncan convincingly explain finds near the tip of Kintyre on the east side as secondary from Dunadd (Nieke and Duncan 1988, 17-18).

Very relevant here is the much discussed episode in the *Vita Columbae* where the saint prophesying a disaster in Italy, tells a man that 'before the present year is ended (the) Gallic sailors from the provinces of Gaul will tell you the same' *(et antequam praesens finiatur annus gallici nautae de Galliarum provinciis adventantes haec eadem tibi enarrabunt:* Adomnán, *Vita Columbae* I.28, ed. & trans. Anderson and Anderson 1961, 262-3) and the man duly goes to the 'chief place' where he hears the news from Gaulish sailors, as prophesied. The identification of the 'chief place' *(caput regionis)* has been discussed at length several times (Watson 1926, 92; Campbell 1987, 114; Thomas 1990, 3; Alcock and Alcock 1987, 143), most discussions favouring Dunadd, though rejecting the possibility that *caput regionis* is a calque of Old Irish *cenn tire* (Kintyre). Alcock has argued that Dunollie is the 'chief place' of the 'Iona district' (Alcock and Alcock 1987, 143) and it is certainly true that Dunadd's claim to be the capital of Dalriada as a whole rests on ambiguous evidence (Lane 1984, 43). There are certainly good reasons why a ship might only come as far as the good harbour at Dunollie to land goods, maritime conditions around Iona being much less predictable. On the other hand, if we are to imagine Dunadd to be the *caput regionis,* the fact that ships from abroad must stop so far from Iona would be more worthy of mention.

In the north-east of Scotland, the Inverness region commends itself as an obvious peninsular road. A Pictish capital at Inverness in the sixth century opened up links with Dalriada, by boat along Loch Ness south to the east coast forts such as Dunottar and Clatchard Craig (Close-Brooks 1986) and by sea along Moray Firth (Adomnán, *Vita Columbae* II.34, ed. Anderson and Anderson 1961, 404-7); and north to the Orkneys, as is seen in the *Vita Columbae* (II.42, ed. Anderson and Anderson 1961, 440-1), when the saint sought assurances from the king of Orkney, who had come to Inverness, that monks of Iona, exploring the western sea routes, would be safe if they came to Orkney by this new route.

In both the above cases we are dealing with peninsular roads which should be regarded, not as part of the western sealanes, but as traversing peninsulas which isolate generally separate thalassocracies from the western sealanes (Armit 1990, 2-3; Harding 1990, 7). When Crawford proposed his 'peninsular road' model there had been little theoretical discussion of redistributive networks in the spatial arrangements and location of landing sites. We would now be inclined to see the same evidence as indicating redistribution of goods by inland routes and coastal traffic.

Abbreviations

AA	*Auctores Antiquissimi.*
BAR	British Archaeological Reports.
BBCS	*Bulletin of the Board of Celtic Studies.*
CBA	Council for British Archaeology.
CMCS	*Cambridge Medieval Celtic Studies* 1-25;*Cambrian Medieval Celtic Studies* 26-.
IJNA	*International Journal of Nautical Archaeology.*
LCL	Loeb Classical Library.
MGH	*Monumenta Germaniae Historica.*
PL	*Patrilogia Latina.*
PRIA	*Proceedings of the Royal Irish Academy.*
JCHAS	*Journal of the Cork Historical and Archaeological Society*
JIA	*Journal of Irish Archaeology*
JRGZMM	*Jahrbuch Römisch-Germanischen Zentral-Museums Mainz*
JRSAI	*Journal of the Royal Society of Antiquaries of Ireland.*
PSAS	*Proceedings of the Society of Antiquaries of Scotland.*
SLH	*Scriptores Latini Hibernici.*
SS rer. Merov.	*Scriptores rerum Merovingicarum.*
SAR	*Scottish Archaeological Review*
TDGNHAS	*Transactions of the Dumfriesshire and Galloway Natural History and Archaeological Society*
UJA	*Ulster Journal of Archaeology*
ZCP	*Zeitschrift für Celtische Philologie*

Bibliography

Abrams, L. and Carley, J.P. 1991 (edd.): *The Archaeology and History of Glastonbury Abbey,* Woodbridge.

Adelson, H. 1960: 'Early Medieval Trade Routes', *American Historical Review* 65, 271-87.

Airlie, S. 1989: Review of Driscoll and Nieke 1988, *SAR* 2, 133-7.

Alarcao, J. 1988: *Roman Portugal,* Warminster.

Alcock, L. 1959: 'Dark Age Objects of Irish Origin from Lesser Garth Cave, Glamorgan', *BBCS* 18, 221-7.

Alcock, L. 1959-60: 'Post Roman Sherds from Longbury Bank Cave, Pembrokeshire', *BBCS* 18, 77-9.

Alcock, L. 1963: *Dinas Powys,* Cardiff.

Alcock, L. 1969: 'Was there an Irish Sea Culture Province in the Dark Ages?', in Moore 1969, 55-64.

Alcock, L. 1972: *'By South Cadbury is that Camelot...',* London.

Alcock, L. 1973: *Arthur's Britain,* Harmondsworth.

Alcock, L. 1975-6: 'A Multi-Disciplinary Chronology for *Alt Clut* Rock, Dumbarton', *PSAS* 107, 103-113.

Alcock, L. 1982: 'Forteviot: A Pictish and Scottish Royal Palace', in Pearce 1982, 211-39.

Alcock, L. 1981: 'Early Historic Fortifications in Scotland', in Guilbert 1981, 150-81.

Alcock, L. 1987: *Economy, Society and Warfare among the Britons and Saxons,* Cardiff.

Alcock, L. 1988: 'The Activities of Potentates in Celtic Britain AD 500-800: A Positivist Approach', in Driscoll and Nieke 1988, 22-39.

Alcock, L. *et al.* 1995: *Cadbury Castle Somerset: the early medieval archaeology,* Cardiff.

Alcock, E. and Alcock, L. 1987: 'Excavations at Dunollie Castle, Oban, Argyll, 1978', *PSAS* 117, 119-147 and fiche.

Alcock, E. and Alcock, L. 1990: 'Excavations at *Alt Clut,* Clyde Rock, Strathclyde, 1974-5', *PSAS* 120, 119-30 and fiche.

Anderson, A.O. and M.O. 1961 (edd.): *Adomnán's Life of St Columba,* Edinburgh.

Anderson, W.B. 1936 & 1965 (ed.and trans.): *Sidonius, Poems and Letters* (LCL), New York and London, 2 vols.

Andrews, P. 1988 (ed.): *Southampton Finds, Volume 1: The Coins and Pottery from Hamwic,* London.

Angenendt, A. 1982: 'Die Irische Peregrinatio und ihre Auskwirkungen auf dem Kontinent vor dem Jahre 800', in Löwe 1982, 52-79.

Armit, I. 1990 (ed.): *Beyond the Brochs,* Edinburgh.

Arnold, C. 1982: *The Anglo-Saxon Cemeteries of the Isle of Wight,* London.

Arnold, C. 1983: Review of Hodges, *Dark Age Economics,SAR* 2, 80-81.

Arnold, C. 1988: *An Archaeology of the Early Anglo-Saxon Kingdoms,* London.

Ashburner, W. 1909 (ed.): *The Rhodian Sea Law,* Oxford.

Ashe, G. 1963: *Land to the West,* London.

Aubet, M.E. 1993: *The Phoenicians and the West: politics, colonies and trade,* trans. M. Turton, Cambridge.

Bannerman, J. 1974: *Studies in the History of Dalriada,* Edinburgh.

Barber, J. 1982: 'Observations on Early Irish Footwear', *JCHAS* 86, 103-6.

Barley, M.W. and Hanson, R.P.C. 1965 (edd.): *Christianity in Britain* 300-700, Leicester.

Barrière-Flavry, C. n.d.: *Études sur les Sepultures Barbares du Midi et de l'Ouest de la France,* Toulouse/Paris.

Bass, G. 1966: *Archaeology Under Water,* London.

Bass, G. 1972 (ed.): *A History of Seafaring based on Underwater Archaeology,* London.

Bass, G. and Van Doorninck, F. 1982: *Yassi Ada: A Seventh Century Byzantine Shipwreck,* College Station, Texas.

Bateson, J.D. 1973: 'Roman Material in Ireland: A Reconsideration', *PRIA* 73C, 21-97.

Bateson, J.D. 1976: 'Further Finds of Roman Material from Ireland', *PRIA* 76C, 171-80.

Baumgarten, R. 1984: 'The Geographical Orientation of Ireland in Isidore and Orosius', *Peritia* 3, 189-203.

Bélier, A-C.: 'Note sur la céramique E (E-ware)', in Picard 1995, 261-264.

Bennett, I. 1994 (ed.), *Excavations 1993,* Bray.

Bieler, L. 1963 (ed.): *The Irish Penitentials,* Dublin.

Binchy, D.A. 1940 (ed.): *Críth Gablach* (Medieval and Modern Irish Series 2), Dublin.

Binchy, D.A. 1958: Review of Jackson *Language and History in Early Britain, Celtica* 4, 288-92.

Binchy, D.A. 1962: 'St Patrick and his Biographers: Ancient and Modern', *Studia Hibernica* 2, 7-173.

Binchy, D.A. 1973: 'A Text on the Forms of Distraint', *Celtica* 10, 72-80.

Binchy, D.A. 1976: 'Irish History and Irish Law', *Studia Hibernica* 16, 1-36.

Binchy, D.A. 1978 (ed.): *Corpus Iuris Hibernici,* Dublin, 6 vols.

Binchy, D.A. 1981: 'Brewing in Eighth-Century Ireland', in Scott 1981a, 3-6.

Bird, J. 1977: 'African Red Slipware in Roman Britain', in Dore and Greene 1977, 269-77.

Bischoff, B. 1976: 'Turning Points in the History of Latin Exegesis in the Early Middle Ages', in M. McNamara (ed.), *Bibilical Studies: the Medieval Irish Contribution,* Dublin, 74-160.

Blagg, T. *et al.* 1984 (edd.): *Papers in Iberian Archaeology* (BAR International Series 193), Oxford.

Blazquez, J.M. 1979 (ed.): *Castulo 2 (Excavaciones Archaeologica Espana).*

Blazquez, J.M. and Molina, F. 1979: 'La Villa Urbana del Olivar', in Blazquez 1979, 109-268.

Boissonade, P. 1916-18: 'Les Relations entre l'Aquitaine, le Poitou, et l'Irlande du Ve au IXe Siècle', *Bulletin de la Societé des Antiquaires de l'Ouest* 4, 181-202.

Bonner, G. *et al.* 1989 (edd.): *St Cuthbert, his Cult and Community to AD 1200*, Woodbridge.

Bourke, C. 1995 (ed.): *From the Isles of the North: early medieval art in Ireland and Britain*, Belfast.

Bourke, E. 1989: 'Stoneyford: a first century Roman Burial from Ireland', *Archaeology Ireland*, 56-7.

Bourke, E., 'Glass Vessels of the First to Ninth Centuries AD', *PSRAI* 24 (1994), 163-209.

Bowden, M. 1989 (ed.): *From Cornwall to Caithness* (BAR British Series 209), Oxford.

Bowen, E. G. 1944: 'The Travels of the Celtic Saints', *Antiquity* 18, 16-28.

Bowen, E.G. 1954: *The Settlements of the Celtic Saints in Wales*, Cardiff.

Bowen, E.G. 1969a: *Saints, Seaways and Settlements in the Celtic Lands*, Cardiff.

Bowen, E.G. 1969b: '"Britain and the British Seas"', in Moore 1969, 13-28.

Bowen, E.G. 1972: *Britain and the Western Seaways*, London.

Bowman, A. 1990: 'Underwater Survey at Tintagel Haven', in Morris 1990, 23.

Bradley, J. 1981-2: '"Medieval" Samian Ware: A Medicinal Suggestion', *UJA* 44 & 45, 196-7.

Breeze, A. 1991a: 'Old English *franca*, "Spear"', *Notes and Queries 236*, 45.

Breeze, A. 1991b: 'Hen Saesneg franca; Hen Gymraeg franc', *BBCS* 37, 98-9.

Brindley, A. and Lanting, J.N. 1990: 'A Roman Boat found in Ireland', *Archaeology Ireland* 4.3, 10-11.

Broeze, F. 1990: Review of J.N. Green, *The VOC Retourschip Batavia, The Great Circle* 12.2, 125-6.

Brøgger, A.W. and Shetelig, H. 1951: *The Viking Ships*, London.

Brown, P. 1971: *The World of Late Antiquity*, London.

Brown, T.J. 1972: 'Northumbria and the Book of Kells', *Anglo-Saxon England* 1, 219-46.

Bruce-Mitford, R. 1975 (ed.): *The Sutton Hoo Ship Burial*, Vol. 1., London.

Bruce-Mitford, R. 1989: 'The Durham-Echternach Calligrapher', in Bonner *et al.* 1989, 175-88.

Buchanan, R. 1989: 'The Irish Sea: the Geographical Framework', in McCaughan and Appleby 1989, 1-12.

Bullough, D. 1982: 'The Missions to the English and the Picts and their Heritage to c. 800', in Löwe 1982, 80-98.

Burrow, I. 1973: 'Tintagel - Some Problems', *Scottish Archaeological Forum* 5, 88-103.

Burrow, I. 1981: *Hillforts and Hilltop Settlement in Somerset* (BAR British Series 91), Oxford.

Bury, J.B. 1905: *The Life of St Patrick and his Place in History*, London.

Buxton, D. 1936 (ed.): *Custom is King: Studies in Honour of R. R. Marett*, London.

Byrne, F.J. 1971a: 'Ireland Before the Norman Invasion', in Moody 1971, 1-15.

Byrne, F.J. 1971b: 'Tribes and Tribalism in Early Ireland', *Ériu* 22, 128-66.

Byrne, F.J. 1980: 'The Lament for Cummíne Foto', *Ériu* 31, 111-122.

Byrne, M. 1932: 'On the Punishment of Being Set Adrift', *Ériu* 11, 97-102.

Cameron, P. 1982: 'Saxons, Sea and Sail', *IJNA* 11, 319-32.

Campbell, E. 1984: 'E Ware and Aquitaine: A Reconsideration of the Petrological Evidence', *SAR* 3, 35-41.

Campbell, E. 1987: 'A Cross-Marked Quern from Dunadd and other Evidence for Relations Between Dunadd and Iona', *PSAS* 117, 105-117.

Campbell, E. 1988a: 'The Post Roman Pottery', in Edwards and Lane 1988, 124-136.

Campbell, E. 1988b: 'Lesser Garth Cave', in Edwards and Lane 1988, 86-7.

Campbell, E. 1989a: 'New Finds of Post-Roman Imported Pottery and Glass from South Wales', *Archaeologia Cambrensis* 137, 59-66.

Campbell, E. 1989b: 'A Blue Glass Squat Jar from Dinas Powys, South Wales', *BBCS* 36, 239-45.

Campbell, E. 1995: 'New Evidence for Glass Vessels in western Britain and Ireland in the 6th/7th centuries AD', in Foy 1995, 35-9.

Campbell, E. 1996: 'The Archaeological Evidence for External Contacts: Imports and the Economy of Celtic Britain', in Dark forthcoming.

Campbell, E., forthcoming: 'A Review of Glass Vessels in Western Britain and Ireland AD 400-800', in Price, forthcoming.

Campbell, E. and Lane, A. 1988: *Excavations at Longbury Bank 1988*, Interim Report, Cardiff.

Canner, A.C. 1982: The *Parish of Tintagel*, Enfield.

Cardoso, G. 1978: 'Anforas no Museu do Mar', *Conimbriga* 17, 63-78.

Carney, J. 1971: 'Three Old-Irish Accentual Poems', *Ériu* 22, 23-80.

Carney, J. 1975: 'The Invention of the Ogam Cipher', *Ériu* 26, 53-65.

Carver, M. *et al.* 1992 (edd): *Maritime Studies, Ports and Ships, Medieval Europe 1992 Pre-Printed Papers, Vol. 2*, York.

Carver, M. 1992 (ed.): *The Age of Sutton Hoo*, Woodbridge.

Casey, P.J. 1979 (ed.): *The End of Roman Britain* (BAR British Series 71), Oxford.

Cassard, J-C., 'Les Saints bretons et la mer', *Mémoires de la Société d'histoire et archéologie de Bretagne* 64 (1987), 5-17.

Cederlund, C. 1985 (ed.): *Post-Medieval Boat and Ship Archaeology* (BAR International Series 256), Oxford.

Chadwick, N.K. 1954 (ed.): *Studies in Early British History*, Cambridge.

Chadwick, O. 1954: 'The Evidence of Dedications in the Early History of the Welsh Church', in Chadwick, N. 1954, 83-136.

Charles-Edwards, T. 1976: 'The Social Background to Irish *Peregrinatio*', *Celtica* 11, 43-59.

Charles-Edwards, T. 1986: '*Críth Gablach* and the Law of Status', *Peritia* 5, 54-73.

Charles-Edwards, T. 1993: 'Palladius, Prosper and Leo the Great: Mission and Primatial Authority', in Dumville, *et al.* 1993, 1-18.

Charles-Edwards, T. and Kelly, F. 1983 (edd.): *Bechbretha*, Dublin.

Childe, V.G. 1946: *Scotland Before the Scots*, Edinburgh.

Childe, V.G. 1958: 'Retrospect', *Antiquity* 32, 69-74.

Childe, V.G. 1973: *The Dawn of European Civilisation*, reprint of 1957 edition, St Albans.

Clarke, H. and Brennan, M. 1981 (edd.): *Columbanus and Merovingian Monasticism* (BAR International Series 113), Oxford.

Claude, D. 1980: 'Der Handel im westlichen Mittelmeer während des Frühmittelalters', *Untersuchungen zu Handel und Verkehr der vor-und frühgeschichtlichen Zeit in Mittel- und Nordeuropa*, Göttingen.

Close-Brooks, J. 1986: 'Excavations at Clatchard Craig, Fife', *PSAS* 116, 117-84.

Coles, K.A. and Black, A.N. 1970: *North Biscay Pilot*, London.

Colgrave, B. 1927 (ed.): *The Life of Bishop Wilfred by Eddius Stephanus*, Cambridge.

Colgrave, B. and Mynors, R. 1969 (edd.): *Bede, Historia Ecclesiastica*, Oxford.

Collins, R. 1980: 'Mérida and Toledo: 500-585', in James 1980a, 189-219.

Condamin, J. and Formenti, F. 1976: 'Recherche de Traces d'Huile d'Olive et de Vin dans le Amphoraes Antiques', *Figlina* 1, 143-58.

Connolly, S. 1987: 'Cogitosus's *Life of St Brigit*: Content and Value', *JRSAI* 117, 5-10.

Connolly, S. and Picard, J.M. 1987 (trans.): 'The Life of St Brigit', *JRSAI* 117, 11-27.

Coplestone-Crow, T. 1981-2: 'The Dual Nature of the Colonisation of Dyfed in the Dark Ages', *Studia Celtica* 16/17, 1-24.

Cormack, W. 1952: 'Northumbrian Coins from Luce Sands, Wigtownshire', *TDGNHAS* 52, 149-50.

Costa, D. 1958: 'Céramique Paléochrétienne Grise decouverte à Nantes', *Bulletin de la Societe Archéologique de Nantes* 97, 65-76.

Cotter, C.H. 1974: *The Atlantic Ocean*, Glasgow.

Craw, J.H. 1930: 'Excavations on the Poltalloch Estates, Argyll', *PSAS* 64, 111-27.

Crawford, B. 1994 (ed.): *Scotland in Dark Age Europe*, St Andrews.

Crawford, H. 1979 (ed.): *Subterranean Britain*, London.

Crawford, O.G.S. 1912: 'The Distribution of Early Bronze Age Settlements in Britain', *Geographical Journal* 40, 184-203.

Crawford, O.G.S. 1936: 'Western Seaways', in Buxton 1936, 181-200.

Crehan, J.E. 1976: 'The Liturgical Trade Route East to West', *Studies* 65, 87-100.

Crumlin Pedersen, O. 1978: 'The Ships of the Vikings', in T. Andersson and K.I. Sandred (edd.), *The Vikings*, Uppsala, 35-41.

Cullen, L.M. 1984: 'Establishing a Communications System: News, Post and Transport', in B. Farrell 1984, 18-29.

Cunliffe, B. 1973: Introduction to Childe 1973, iv-xiv.

Cunliffe, B. 1984: 'Relations between Britain and Gaul in the First Century BC and the First Century AD', in MacReady and Thompson 1984, 24-36.

Dansgaard, W. *et al.* 1975: 'Climatic Changes, Norsemen and Modern Man', *Nature* 255, 24-8.

Dark, K.R. 1985: 'The Plan and Interpretation of Tintagel', *CMCS* 9, 1-18.

Dark, K.R. forthcoming (ed.): *External Contacts and the Economy of Late-Roman and Post-Roman Britain*, Woodbridge.

David, P. 1947: *Études Historiques sur la Galice et le Portugal du VIe au XIIe Siècle*, Lisbon.

Davies, M. 1946: 'The Diffusion and Distribution Pattern of the Megalithic Monuments of the Irish Sea and North Channel Coastlands', *Antiquaries Journal* 26, 40-6.

Davies, W. 1983: 'An Historian's View of Celtic Archaeology', in Hinton 1983, 67-73.

Davis, R.H.C. 1976: *The Normans and their Myth*, London.

Dawes, E. and Baynes, N. 1948 (trans.): *Three Byzantine Saints*, London.

De Clercq, C. 1963 (ed.): *Concilia Galliae* A511-A695 (*Corpus Christianorum Series Latina* Vol. 148A), Turnhout.

De Courcy Ireland, J. 1987: *Ireland and the Irish in Maritime History*, Dublin.

De Courcy Ireland, J. and Sheehy, D. 1989 (edd.): *Atlantic Visions*, Dun Laoghaire.

de Paor, L. 1993: *St Patrick's World*, Blackrock, 38-45.

De Smedt, C. 1888 (ed.): 'Vita S. Winwaloei, primi abbatis Landevenecensis, auctore Wurdestino', *Analecta Bollandiana* 7, pp. 167-264.

Detsicas, A. 1981 (ed.): *Collectanea Historica: Essays in Memory of Stuart Rigold*, Maidstone.

Devoy, J.J. 1990: 'Controls on Coastal and Sea Level Changes and the Application of Archaeological-Historical Records to Understanding Recent Patterns of Sea-Level Movement', in McGrail 1990, 17-26.

Dewing, H.B. 1914-35 (ed.): *Procopius, Works* (LCL), New York and London, 7 vols.

Doehaerd, R. 1978: *The Early Middle Ages in the West: Economy and Society*, trans. W.G. Deakin, Amsterdam.

Doherty, C. 1980: 'Exchange and Trade in Early Medieval Ireland', *PRSAI* 110, 67-89.

Dolley, M. 1976: 'Roman Coins in Ireland and the Date of St Patrick', *PRIA* 76C, 181-90.

Donnachie, I. 1971: 'The Lime Industry in South-west Scotland', *TDGNHAS* 48, 146-56.

Dore, J. and Greene, K. 1977 (edd.): *Roman Pottery Studies in Britain and Beyond* (BAR Supplementary Series 30), Oxford.

Drinkwater, J. and Elton, H. 1992 (edd.): *Fifth-century Gaul: a crisis of identity*, Cambridge.

Driscoll, S. 1988: 'The Relationship Between History and Archaeology: Artefacts, Documents and Power', in Driscoll and Nieke 1988, 162-87.

Driscoll, S. and Nieke, M. 1988 (edd.): *Power and Politics in Early Medieval Britain and Ireland*, Edinburgh.

Duff, J.W. 1969 (ed.): *Lucan, Pharsalia* (LCL), London and New York.

Duff, J.W. and A.M. 1932 (edd.): *Rutilius, De Redito Suo, Minor Latin Poets*, Vol. 2 (LCL), New York and London, 764-829.

Dümmler, E. 1895 (ed.): *Alcuin, Epistolae, in MGH: Epistolae Karolini Aevi*, Vol. 2, Berlin.

Dumville, D. 1977: 'Sub-Roman Britain, History and Legend', *History* 62, 173-92.

Dumville, D. 1984: 'Some British Aspects of the Earliest Irish Christianity', in Ní Chatháin and Richter 1984, 16-24.

Dumville, D. 1988: 'Two Approaches to the Dating of "Navigatio Sancti Brendani"', *Studi Medievali* 29, 87-102.

Dumville, D., *et al.* 1993: *St Patrick, AD 493-1993*, Woodbridge.

Duncan, A.A.M. 1988: Review of C. Thomas, *Celtic Britain*, *Scottish Historical Review* 67, 70-1.

Duncan, H. 1982: 'Aspects of the Early Historic Period in South-west Scotland', unpublished M. Litt thesis, Glasgow University.

Earwood, C. 1990: 'The Wooden Artefacts from Loch Glashan Crannóg, Mid Argyll', *PSAS* 120, 79-94.

Earwood, C. 1993: *Domestic Wooden Artefacts*, University of Exeter.

Edwards, H.J. 1917 (ed.): *Caesar, Bellum Gallicum* (LCL), New York and London.

Edwards, N. and Lane, A. 1988 (edd.): *Early Medieval Settlements in Wales*, Bangor and Cardiff.

Einar Ól. Sveinsson 1934 (ed.): *Laxdæla Saga (Íslenzk Fornrit* Vol. 5), Reykjavík.

Ellis Evans, D. 1987 (ed.): *Proceedings of the Seventh International Congress of Celtic Studies*, Oxford.

Ellmers, D. 1969: 'Celtische Shiffbau', *JRGZMM* 16, 73-122.

Ellmers, D. 1979: 'The Cog of Bremen', in McGrail 1979, 11-12.

Ericsson, C.H. 1984: *Navis Oneraria: the Cargo Carrier* of *Late Antiquity* Acta Academiae Aboensis, Series A: Humaniora 63, no. 3, Åbo.

Estyn-Evans, E. 1973: *The Personality of Ireland*, Cambridge.

Evison, V. 1974 (ed.): *Medieval Pottery from Excavations: Essays Presented to Gerald Clough Dunning*, London.

Evison, V. 1983: 'Some Distinctive Glass Vessels of the Post Roman Period', *Journal of Glass Studies* 25, 87-93.

Facts on File Series 1990: *Northern World*, New York.

Fanning, T. 1984: 'Some Field Monuments in the Townlands of Clonmelsh and Garryhundon, Co. Carlow', *Peritia* 3, 43-9.

Farrell, A.W. 1984: 'The Boat Motif on the Tintagel Slate Fragment: Its Implications', *Mariner's Mirror* 70, 71-2.

Farrell, A.W. and Penny, S. 1975: 'The Broighter Boat: A Reassessment', *Irish Archaeological Research Forum* 2, 15-28.

Farrell, B. 1984 (ed.): *Communications and Community in Ireland*, Dublin and Cork.

Farrell, R.T. and Neuman de Vegvar, C. (edd.), *Sutton Hoo: Fifty Years After*, Oxford, Ohio, 1992.

Fawtier, R. 1912 (ed.): *Vita Samsonis*, Paris.

Fenwick, V. 1972 (ed.): *Three Major Ancient Boat Finds in Britain*, Greenwich.

Filigueras, O. 1977: 'The Xavega Boat', in McGrail 1977, 77-114.

Filigueras, O. 1979: 'A Presumptive Germanic Heritage for a Portugese Boatbuilding Tradition', in McGrail 1979, 45-82.

Flanagan, L. 1975: 'Ships and Shipping in Pre-Viking Ireland', *Cultura Maritima* 1 1975, 3-8.

Flanagan, L. 1988: 'Irish Annals as a Source for Maritime History, 1400-1600 AD', in Mac Niocaill and Wallace 1988, 500-502.

Fleure, H. J. and Roberts, J. E. 1915: 'Archaeological Problems of the West Coast of Britain', *Archaeologia Cambrensis* 70, 405-20.

Fleuriot, L. 1984: 'The Old Breton Glosses and the Cultural Importance of Brittany in the Early Middle Ages', in Ní Chatháin and Richter 1984, 218-225.

Fox, A. 1955: 'Some Evidence for a Dark Age Trading Site at Bantham, near Thurlestone, South Devon', *Antiquaries Journal* 35, 55-67

Fox, C. 1922: *The Archaeology of the Cambridge Region*, Cambridge.

Fox, C. 1946: *The Personality of Britain* 4th Edition Cardiff.

Fox, C. and Dickens, B. 1950 (edd.): *Early Cultures of North-West Europe*, Cambridge.

Foy, D. 1995: *Verre de l'Antiquite Tardive et du Haut Moyen Age*, Musée Archéologique du Val d'Oise.

Freill, J. and Watson, W. 1984 (edd.): *Pictish Studies* (BAR British Series 125), Oxford.

Freke, D. 1983-7: *Peel Castle Excavations*, Interim Reports, Liverpool.

Frere, S.S. 1966: 'The End of Towns in Roman Britain', in Wacher 1966, 405-420.

Fuchs, R. and Oltrogge, D. 1994: 'Colouring Material and Painting Technique in the Book of Kells', in O'Mahony 1994, 133-171.

Fulford, M. 1977: 'Pottery and Britain's Trade in the Late Roman Period', in Peacock 1977, 35-84.

Fulford, M. 1978: 'The Interpretation of Britain's late Roman Trade: the Scope of Medieval Historical and Archaeological Analogy', in Taylor and Cleere 1978, 58-69.

Fulford, M. 1979: 'Pottery Production and Trade at the End of Roman Britain: The Case Against Continuity', in Casey 1979, 120-30.

Fulford, M. 1989: 'Byzantium and Britain: a Mediterranean Perspective on Post-Roman Mediterranean Imports in Western Britain and Ireland', *Medieval Archaeology* 33, 1-6.

Fulford, M. and Peacock, D.P.S. 1984: *Excavations at Carthage: The British Mission Volume 1. 2: the Pottery from the Avenue du Président Habib Bourguiba*, Sheffield.

Gabet, C. 1969: 'La Céramique Gallo-Romaine Recueille á Pépiron Charente Maritime', *Gallia* 27, 45-70.

Gaillou, P. Fulford, M. and Clement, M. 1980: 'La Diffusion de la Céramique à l'éponge' dans la Nord-Ouest de l'Empire Romain', *Gallia* 38, 185-206.

Gaillou, P. 1984: 'Days of Wine and Roses? Early Armorica and the Atlantic Wine Trade', in Macready and Thompson 1984, 3-23.

Gaillou, P. and Jones, M. 1991: *The Bretons*, Oxford and Cambridge MA.

Galinie, H. 1981 (ed.): *Recherches sur Tours*, Tours.

Garnsey, P. *et al.* 1983 (ed.): *Trade in the Ancient Economy*, London.

Garvin, J.N. 1946 (ed.): *Vitas Patrum Sanctorum Emeretensium* Catholic University of America, Studies in Medieval History, New Series 19, Washington D.C.

George, J.W. 1992: *Venantius Fortunatus*, Oxford.

Gerberding, R. 1987: *The Rise of the Carolingians and the Liber Historiae Francorum*, Oxford.

Gerriets, M. 1983: 'Economy and Society: Clientship According to the Irish Laws', *CMCS* 6, 43-62.

Geyer, P. 1975 (ed.): *Bede, De Locis Sanctis* in *Itineraria (Corpus Scriptorum Ecclesiasticorum Latinorum* Vol. 39), New York and London.

Gibbins, D. 1995: 'What Shipwrecks can tell Us', *Antiquity* 69, 409-11.

Gilchrist, R. 1988: 'A Reappraisal of Dinas Powys: Local Exchange and Specialised Livestock in 5th-7th Century Wales', *Medieval Archaeology* 32, 50-62.

Gildas, B. 1989: 'Ships, Harbours and Navigation between the Continent and the Celtic Islands during the early middle age', in De Courcy Ireland and Sheehy 1989, 155-157.

Giot, P-R. and Fleuriot, L. 1977: 'Early Brittany', *Antiquity* 51, 106-116.

Giot, P-R. and Querre, G. 1985: 'Le Tesson d'Amphorae B2 de l'Île Lavret, Bréhat, Côtes-du-Nord et le Problème des Importations', *Revue Archéologique Ouest* 2, 95-100.

Gisli Sigurdsson 1988: *Gaelic Influence in Iceland (Studia Islandica* 46), Reykjavík.

Godley, A.D. 1926 (ed.): *Herodotus, Histories*, Vol. 2 (LCL), New York and London.

Graham-Campbell, J. 1987: 'A Lost Zoomorphic Penannular Brooch from Kells, Co. Meath', *JRSAI* 116, 122-4.

Graham-Campbell, J. 1991: 'Dinas Powys Metalwork and the dating of Enamelled Zoomorphic Penannular Brooches', *BBCS* 38, 220-232.

Graham-Campbell, J. 1992: *Viking Treasure from the North West: The Cuerdale Hoard in its Context (Proceedings of the Vikings in the Irish Sea Province Conference)*, Liverpool.

Greenwood, L. 1976 (ed.): *Cicero, Verrine Orations*, (LCL), London.

Grierson, P. 1959: 'Commerce in the Dark Ages', *Transactions of the Royal Historical Society* 9, 123-4.

Grierson, P. and M. Blackburn 1986: *Medieval European Coinage: The Early Middle Ages 5th-10th Centuries*, Cambridge.

Griffiths, D. 1992a: 'The Coastal Trading Ports of the Irish Sea', in Graham-Campbell 1992, 63-72.

Griffiths, D. 1992b: 'Territories and Exchange in the Irish Sea Region 400-1100', in Hall, Hodges and Clarke 1992, 9-12.

Griffiths, D. 1994: 'Trade and Production Centres in the Post-Roman North: the Irish Sea Perspective', in Nielsen, *et al.* 1994, 184-8.

Guilbert, G. 1981 (ed.): *Hillfort Studies: Essays for A. H. A. Hogg*, Leicester.

Haddan, A.W. and Stubbs, W. 1869 (edd.): *Councils and Ecclesiastical Documents relating to Britain and Ireland*, Vol. 1, Oxford.

Halkin, J. and Roland, C.G. 1909 (edd.): *Recueil des Chartes de l'Abbaye de Stavelot-Malmedy*, Brussels.

Hall, R. *et al.* 1992 (ed.): *Exchange and Trade, Medieval Europe 1992, Proceedings, Volume 5*, York.

Hanson, R.P.C. 1968: *St Patrick his Origins and Career*, Oxford.

Harbison, P. 1994: 'High Crosses and the Book of Kells', in O'Mahony 1994, 266-9.

Harden, D.B. 1956a (ed.): *Dark Age Britain*, London.

Harden, D.B. 1956b, 'Glass Vessels in Britain and Ireland', in Harden 1956, 132-70.

Harden, D.B. 1966: Appendix 10: 'Note on Glass Fragments from Dalkey Island', in Liversage 1966, 193-5.

Harden, D.B. 1984: 'Enamel and Glass', in 'Excavations at Cathedral Hill, Armagh', *UJA*, 135-6.

Harding, D.W. 1990: 'Changing Perspectives on the Atlantic Iron Age', in Armit 1990, 5-16.

Harden, D.B. 1987: 'The Glass', in Alcock, 1987, 142-50.

Hardy, A.C., *Seaways and Sea Trade*, London, 1927.

Harrison, K. 1980: *The Framework of Anglo-Saxon History*, Cambridge.

Hart, J. 1989: 'Leprosy in Devon and Cornwall, Problems and Perspectives', in Bowden 1989, 261-9.

Hartgroves, S. and Walker, R. 1988: 'Excavations in the Lower Ward, Tintagel Castle, 1986', in Thomas 1988b, 9-31.

Harvey, A. 1985: 'The Significance of Cothrige', *Ériu* 36, 1-9.

Harvey, A. 1987: 'Early Literacy in Ireland: the Evidence from Ogam', *CMCS* 14, 1-15.

Haseloff, G. 1987: 'Insular Animal Styles with Special Reference to Irish Art in the Early Medieval Period', in Ryan 1987, 44-55.

Hatcher, J. 1973: *English Tin Production and Trade before 1550*, Oxford.

Hawkins, A.B. 1971: 'Sea Level Changes around South West England', *Marine Archaeology: Colston Papers*, Bristol, 67-88

Hawkes, C.F.C. 1977: *Pytheas: Europe and the Greek Explorers*, Oxford.

Hawkes, C.F.C. 1984: 'Ictis Disentangled and the British Tin Trade', *Oxford Journal of Archaeology* 3, 211-33.

Hayes, J. 1972: *Late Roman Pottery*, Rome.

Hayes, J. 1977: 'North African Flanged Bowls: A Problem in Fifth-Century Chronology', in Dore and Greene 1977, 279-283.

Hayes, J. 1980: *Supplement to Late Roman Pottery*, Rome.

Haywood, J. 1991: *Dark Age Naval Power: A Reassessment of Frankish and Anglo-Saxon Naval Activity*, London.

Hencken, H.O'N. 1932: *The Archaeology of Cornwall and Scilly*, London.

Hencken, H.O'N. 1942: 'Ballinderry Crannóg No. 2', *PRIA* 47C, 1-76.

Hencken, H.O'N. 1950: 'Lagore Crannóg: A Royal Residence of the 7th-10th Centuries AD', *PRIA* 53C, 1-247.

Henderson, G. 1899 (ed.): *Bricriu's Feast*, London.

Henderson, G. 1987: *From Durrow to Kells*, London.

Henderson, J. and Ivens, R. 1992: 'Dunmisk and Glass-Making in Early Christian Ireland', *Antiquity* 66, 52-64.

Henry, F. 1940: *Irish Art in the Early Christian Period*, Dublin.

Herbert, M. 1988: *Iona, Kells and Derry*, Oxford.

Herren, M. 1970: '*Bigerro sermone clefabo*: Notes on the Life of Virgilius Maro Grammaticus', *Classica et Medievalia* 31, 253-7.

Herren, M. 1979a (ed.): *Hisperica Famina*, Vol. 1, Toronto.

Herren, M. 1979b: 'Some New Light Upon the life of Virgilus Maro Grammaticus', *PRIA* 79C, 21-71.

Herren, M. 1980: 'The Earliest Irish Aquaintance with Isidore of Seville', in James 1981, 243-50.

Herren, M. 1989: 'Mission and Monasticism in the Confessio of Patrick', in Ó Corráin *et. al.* 1989, 76-85.

Hill, P. 1987: *Whithorn 1: Excavations 1984-6*, Interim Report, Whithorn.

Hill, P. 1989: *Whithorn 2: Excavations 1984-7*, Interim Report, Whithorn.

Hill, P. 1990: *Whithorn 3: Excavations at Whithorn Priory 1988-90*, Interim Report, Whithorn.

Hill, P. 1991: 'Whithorn: the Missing Years', in Oram and Stell 1991, 27-44.

Hill, P. 1992a: 'A Thousand Years of Contact: the Economy of Whithorn from 450-1450', Hall *et al.* 1992, 19-24.

Hill, P. 1992b: *Whithorn 4*, Interim Report, Whithorn.

Hillgarth, J.N. 1961: 'The East, Visigothic Spain and the Irish', *Studia Patristica* 4, 442-56.

Hillgarth, J.N. 1962: 'Visigothic Spain and Early Christian Ireland', *PRIA* 62C, 167-94.

Hillgarth, J.N. 1965: 'Old Ireland and Visigothic Spain', in McNally 1965, 200-27.

Hillgarth, J.N. 1984: 'Ireland and Spain in the Seventh Century', *Peritia* 3, 1-16.

Hillgarth, J.N. 1987: 'Modes of Evangelisation in Western Europe in the Seventh Century', in Ní Chatháin and Richter 1987, 311-32.

Hinton, D. 1983 (ed.): *25 Years of Medieval Archaeology*, Sheffield.

Hirth, K.G. 1978: 'Interregional Trade and the Formation of Gateway Communities', *American Antiquity* 43, 35-45.

Hitchner, R.B.: 'Meridional Gaul, Trade and the Mediterranean Economy in Late Antiquity', in Drinkwater and Elton 1992, 122-131.

Höckmann, O. 1986: 'Römische Schiffsverbände auf dem Öber- und Mittelrhein und die Verteidigung der Rheingrenze

in der Spätantike', *JRGZMM* 33, 369-415.
Hodges, R. 1975: 'Knockdhu Promontory Fort', *Ulster Journal of Archaeology* 38 1975 19-24.
Hodges, R. 1977: Some Early Medieval French Wares in the British Isles', in Peacock 1977, 239-262.
Hodges, R. 1978: 'Ports of Trade in Early Medieval Europe', *Norwegian Archaeological Review* 11, 97-117.
Hodges, R. 1981: *The Hamwih Pottery: Local and Imported Wares from 30 Years Excavations in at Middle Saxon Southampton and their European Context* (CBA Research Report 37), London.
Hodges, R. 1984: 'The Date and Source of E ware', *SAR* 2, 39-40.
Hodges, R. 1989: *Dark Age Economics*, London, 2nd Edition.
Hodges, R. and Whitehouse, D. 1983: *Mohammed, Charlemagne and the Origins of Europe*, London.
Hood, A.B.E. 1978 (ed.): *St Patrick: His Writings and Muirchu's Life*, London.
Hornell, J. 1936: 'British Coracles', *Mariners Mirror* 32, 5-21.
Hornell, J. 1946a: *Water Transport*, Cambridge.
Hornell, J. 1946b: 'The Role of Birds in Early Navigation', *Antiquity* 20 1946, 142-9.
Hughes, E. 1938: *Studies in Administration and Finance*, New York.
Hughes, K. 1981: 'The Celtic Church: is this a Valid Concept?', *CMCS* 1, 1-20.
Humphrey, J.H. 1981 (ed.): *Excavations at Carthage Conducted by the University of Michigan*, Vol. 6, Ann Arbor.
Hunter, J. 1975: 'Glasses from Scandinavian Burials in the First Millenium AD', *World Archaeology* 7, 79-86.
Hutchinson, G. 1979: 'Bar-Lug Pottery of Cornwall', *Cornish Archaeology* 18, 81-104.
Hutton, M. 1914 (ed.): *Tacitus, Agricola* (LCL), New York and London.
Hydrographer of the Navy 1970: *Mediterranean Pilot*, Vol. 1., Taunton.
Hydrographer of the Navy 1974a: *West Coast of Scotland Pilot*, Eleventh Edition, Taunton.
Hydrographer of the Navy 1974b: *West Coasts of England and Wales Pilot*, Eleventh Edition, Taunton.
Hydrographer of the Navy 1974c: *Channel Pilot*, Taunton.
Hydrographer of the Navy 1974d: *Admiralty Tidal Stream Atlas: Irish Sea and the Channel*, Taunton.
Ireland, C. 1991: 'Some Analogues of the O.E. *Seafarer* from Hiberno-Latin sources', *Neuphilologische Mitteilungen* 92, 1-14.
Isings, C. 1957: *Roman Glass from Dated Finds*, Gröningen.
Jackson, K. 1952: *Language and History in Early Britain*, Edinburgh.
Jackson, K. 1961 (trans.): *The Gododdin*, Edinburgh.
Jackson, K. 1963: *The Oldest Irish Tradition: A Window on the Iron Age*, Edinburgh.
James, E. 1977: *The Merovingian Archaeology of South-West Gaul* (BAR Supplementary Series 25, i-ii), Oxford, 2 vols.
James, E. 1980a (ed.): *Visigothic Spain: New Approaches*, Oxford.
James, E. 1980b: 'Septimania and its Frontier: An Archaeological Approach', in James 1980a, 243-50.
James, E. 1982: 'Ireland and Western Gaul in the Merovingian Period', in Whitelock *et al.* 1982, 362-86.
James, E. 1988: *The Franks*, London.
Jarrett, M. and Dobson, B. 1965 (edd.): *Britain and Ireland*, Kendal.
Johnstone, P. 1962: 'A Medieval Skin Boat' *Antiquity* 36, 32-37.
Johnstone, P. 1964: 'The Bantry Boat', *Antiquity* 38, 277-85.
Johnstone, P. 1974: *The Archaeology of Ships*, London.
Johnstone, P. 1980: *The Seacraft of Prehistory*, London.
Johnstone, P.K. 1962: ' A Consular Chronology of Dark Age Britain', *Antiquity* 36, 102-9.
Jones, H.L. 1949 (ed.): *Strabo, Geographica* (LCL), New York and London.
Jones, M.E. 1993: 'The Literary Evidence for Mast and Sail During the Anglo-Saxon Invasions', *Studies in Medieval and Renaissance History*, new series 13, 31-67.
Jónsson, G. 1953 (ed.): *Ari Thorgilsson, Libellus Islendorum/Islendinga Sögur*, Reykjavík, 1-20.
Jope, E., *et al.* 1966: *Archaeological Survey of Co. Down*, Belfast.
Jung, E. 1995: 'Ibères en Hibernie?', in Picard 1995, 221-23.
Keay, S.J. 1984: *Late Roman Amphorae in the Western Mediterranean* (BAR International Series 196, i-ii), Oxford, 2 vols.
Kelly, F. 1988: *A Guide to Early Irish Law*, Dublin.
Kendrick, T.D., *et al.* 1960 (edd.): *Evangeliorum Quattuor Codex Lindisfarnensis*, Olten, Vol. 2., 262-7.
Kenney, J.F. 1929: *The Sources for the Early History of Ireland: Ecclesiastical*, New York.
Kidd, D. 1989: 'The History of the Early Medieval European Collections in the British Museum', *Journal of the History of Collections* 1, 103-7.
Kilbride-Jones, H. 1980: *Zoomorphic Penannular Brooches*, London.
Killeen, J.F. 1976: 'Ireland in the Greek and Roman Writers', *PRIA* 76C, 207-215.
King, J.W. 1893: *The Pilot's Handbook for the English Channel*, London.
Knight, J. 1984: 'Glamorgan 400-1100: Archaeology and History', in Savory 1984, 315-64.
Knight, J. 1981: '*In Tempore Iustini Consulis:* Contacts between British and Gaulish Churches before St Augustine', in Detsicas 1981, 54-62.
Krusch, B. 1880: *Studien zür Christlich-mittelalterlichen Chronologie*, Leipzig.
Krusch, B. 1885a (ed.): *Historia Francorum (MGH: SS rer. Merov.* Vol. 1.1), Hannover.
Krusch, B. 1885b (ed.): *De Virtutibus Sancti Martini*, in *MGH. SS rer. Merov.* Vol. 1.2, Hannover, 135-211.
Krusch, B. 1888a (ed.): *Liber Historiae Francorum*, in *MGH: SS rer. Merov.* Vol. 2, Hannover, 238-328.
Krusch, B. 1888b (ed.): *Gesta Dagoberti* in *MGH: SS rer. Merov.* Vol. 2, Hannover, 396-425.
Krusch, B. 1896a (ed.): *Vita Fridolini*, in *MGH: SS rer. Merov.* Vol. 3, Hannover, 351-69.
Krusch, B. 1896b (ed.): *Vita et Virtutes Eparchi, MGH: SS rer. Merov.* Vol. 3, Hannover, 550-564.
Krusch, B. 1902a (ed.): *Jonas, Vita Columbani, in MGH: SS rer. Merov.* Vol. 4, Hannover, 64-108.
Krusch, B. 1902b (ed.): *Additamentum Nivialense de Fuilano, MGH: SS rer. Merov.* Vol. 4, Hannover, 449-451.
Krusch, B. 1910 (ed.): *Vita Amandi, MGH: in MGH: SS rer. Merov.* Vol. 5, Hannover, 428-449.
Laing, L. 1966-7: 'Linlithgow Palace Excavations', *PSAS* 99, 111-47.
Laing, L. 1973: 'Cooking Pots and the Origins of the Scottish Medieval Pottery Industry', *Archaeological Journal* 130, 121-5.
Laing, L. 1975: *The Archaeology of Late Celtic Britain and Ireland*, London.

Laing, L. 1985: 'The Romanisation of Ireland in the Fifth Century', *Peritia* 4 , 261-78.

Lamb, H.H. 1977: *Climate: Past, Present and Future, Vol. 2, A History of Climate,* London.

Lamb, H.H. 1992: 'Climate and the History of Europe and its Offlying Seas', Carver *et al.* 1992, 1-26.

Lane, A. 1980: *Excavations at Dunadd 1980,* Interim Report, Cardiff.

Lane, A. 1981: *Excavations at Dunadd 1981,* Interim Report, Cardiff.

Lane, A. 1984: 'Some Pictish Problems at Dunadd', in Freill and Watson 1984, 43-62.

Lane, A. 1988: 'New Pieces, Montgomeryshire Powys', in Edwards and Lane 1988, 7-8.

Lane, A. 1994: 'Fifth to Seventh-Century Trading Systems in western Britain and Ireland', in Crawford 1994, 104-115.

Langlotz, E. 1969: 'Beobachtungen in Phokaia', *Archaeologische Anzeiger* 25, 377-85.

Lapart, J. and Rigoir, J. and Y. 1986: 'Les Derivées-des-Sigilées Paléochrétiennes Decorées du Gers', *Societé Francaise d'Etude de la Céramique Antique en Gaule: Actes du Congrès du Toulouse,* 111-24.

Lasko, P. 1971: *The Kingdom of the Franks,* London.

Law, V. 1980: *Insular Latin Grammarians,* Woodbridge.

LeFond, J. 1969: *Handbook of World Salt Resources,* New York.

Lehmann, L. Th. 1978: 'The Flat-Bottomed Boat from Druten, Netherlands', *IJNA* 7, 239-67.

Leo, F. and Krusch, B. 1961 (edd.): *Venantius Fortunatus, Opera (MGH: AA IV),* Berlin, rpr.

Levison, W. 1910 (ed.): *Vita Filiberti, MGH: SS rer. Merov.* Vol. 5, *Hannover,* 568-604.

Levison, W. 1946: *England and the Continent in the Eighth Century,* Oxford.

Lewis, A.R. 1953: 'Le Commerce et la Navigation sur les Côtes Atlantiques de la Gaule du Ve et VIIIe Siècles', *Le Moyen Age* 59, 249-98.

Lewis, A.R. 1959: *The Northern Seas,* Princeton.

Lewis, A.R. 1978: 'Byzantine Lightweight Solidi and Trade to the North Sea and the Baltic', in *idem., The Sea and Medieval Civilisation,* Variorum, Section V.

Lewis, A.R. and Runyan, T. 1985: *European Naval and Maritime History, 300-1500,* Bloomington.

L'Hour, M. 1987: 'Un Site Sous-Marine sur la Côte de L'Armorique L'Epave Antique de Ploumanach', *Revue Archéologique Ouest* 4 , 113-31.

Lindsay, W.M. 1911 (ed.): *Isidore, Etymologiarum Siue Originum,* Oxford.

Liversage, G.D. 1966: 'Excavations at Dalkey Is. Co. Dublin 1956-9', *PRIA* 66C, 53-233.

Lorren, C. 1980: 'Des Saxons en Basse Normandie au VIe siècle', *Studien zür Sachsenforschung* 2, 231-69.

Löwe, H. 1982 (ed.): *Die Iren und Europa im Früheren Mittelalter,* Stuttgart.

Lucas, A.T. 1965: 'Footwear in Ireland', *Co. Louth Archaeological Journal* 13.

Luetjohann, C. 1887 (ed.): *Sidonius, Opera, MGH: AA* Vol. 8, Berlin.

Lynn, C. 1984: 'Some Fragments of Exotic Porphyry found in Ireland', *JIA* 2, 19-32.

Lynn, C. 1985-6: 'Some Early Irish Ringforts and Crannógs', *JIA* 3, 47-57.

Lyon, B. 1974: *Henri Pirenne: a Biographical and Intellectual Study,* Ghent.

Maarleveld, T.J. 1995: 'Type or Technique. Some thoughts on boat and ship finds as indicative of cultural traditions', *IJNA* 24.1, 3-7.

Macalister, R.A.S. 1921 (ed.): *The Latin and Irish Lives of Ciaran of Clonmacnois,* London.

Macalister, R.A.S. 1938-56 (ed.): *Lebor Gabála Érenn,* Dublin, 5 vols.

Macalister, R.A.S. 1945-9 (ed.): *Corpus Inscriptionum Insularum Celticarum,* Dublin, 2 vols.

Mac Cana, P. 1993: 'Ir. *Buaball,* W *Bual* 'Drinking Horn', *Ériu* 44, 81-93.

Mac an Bhaird, A. 1991-2: 'Ptolemy Revisited', *Ainm: Bulletin of the Ulster Place-name Society* 5: 1-20.

McCaughan, M. and Appleby, J. 1989 (ed.): *The Irish Sea, Aspects of Maritime History,* Belfast.

McCone, K. 1990, *Pagan Past and Christian Present in Irish Literature,* Maynooth.

Mac Conghail, M., *The Blaskets: an island library,* Dublin.

Mac Eoin, G. 1977: 'The Lament for Cuimine Fota', *Ériu* 28, 17-31, 21-22.

McGrail, S. 1977 (ed.): *Sources and Techniques in Boat Archaeology* (BAR Supplementary Series 29), Oxford.

McGrail, S. 1979 (ed.): *The Archaeology of Medieval Ships and Harbours in Northern Europe* (BAR Supplementary Series 66), Oxford.

McGrail, S. 1983: 'Cross-Channel Seamanship and Navigation in the Late First Millenium BC', *Oxford Journal of Archaeology* 2, 299-337.

McGrail, S. 1987: *Ancient Boats in NW Europe,* London.

McGrail, S. 1989: 'Pilotage and Navigation in the Times of St Brendan', in De Courcy Ireland and Sheehy 1989, 25-36.

McGrail, S. 1990a (ed.): *Maritime Celts, Frisians and Saxons* (CBA Research Report 77), London.

McGrail, S. 1990b: 'Boats and Boatsmanship in the Late-Prehistoric North Sea and Channel Region', in McGrail 1990a, 32-48.

Mackinder, H. 1902: *Britain and the British Seas,* London.

McLeod 1982: 'The Concept of Law in Ancient Irish Jurisprudence', *The Irish Jurist* New Series 17, 356-67.

McManus, D. 1983: 'A Chronology of the Latin Loanwords in Early Irish', *Ériu* 34, 21-71.

McManus, D. 1984: 'The So-Called *Cothraige* and *Pátraic* Strata of Loanwords in Early Irish', in Ní Chatháin and Richter 1984, 179-96.

McManus, D. 1991: *A Guide to Ogam,* Maynooth.

Mac Mathúna, S. 1994: 'The Structure and Transmission of Early Irish Voyage Literature', in Tristram 1994, 313-358.

McNally, R. 1965 (ed.): *Old Ireland,* Dublin.

MacNiocaill, G. 1971: 'Jetsam, Treasure Trove and the Lord's Share in Medieval Ireland', *The Irish Jurist* 6, 103-10.

MacNiocaill, G. and Mac Airt, S. 1983 (edd.): *Annals of Ulster,* Dublin.

MacNiocaill, G. and Wallace, P. 1988 (edd.): *Kemelia: Studies in Memory of Tom Delaney,* Galway.

McPeake, J.C., Bulmer, M. and Rutter, J. 1980: 'Excavations in the Garden of No. 1, Abbey Green, Chester', *Journal of the Chester Archaeological Society* 63, 14-38.

MacReady. S. and Thompson, F.H. 1984 (edd.): *Cross Channel Trade between Gaul and Britain in the Pre-Roman Iron Age,* London.

Malinowski, B. 1922: *Argonauts of the Western Pacific*, London.

Mallory, J.P. 1987: 'Silver in the Ulster Cycle of Tales', in Ellis Evans 1987, 33-65.

Marcus, G. J. 1953-4: 'Factors in Early Celtic Navigation', *Études Celtiques* 6, 312-27.

Marcus, G. J. 1955: '*Hafvilla:* A Note on Norse Navigation', *Speculum* 30, 601-5.

Marcus, G. J. 1980: *The Conquest of the North Atlantic*, Woodbridge.

Marsden, P. 1972: 'Ships of the Roman Period and After in Britain', in Bass 1972, 114-24.

Marsden, P. 1976: 'A Boat from the Roman Period found in Bruges, Belgium in 1899, and Related Types', *IJNA* 5, 37-45.

Marsden, P. 1990: 'A Reassessment of Blackfriars Ship 1', in McGrail 1990, 66-74.

Marx, K. 1930: *Capital*, trans E. and C. Paul, London.

Mauss, M. 1954: *The Gift*, trans. I. Cunnison, London.

Mayr-Harting, H. 1972: *The Coming of Christianity to Anglo-Saxon England*, London.

Meehan, D. 1958 (ed.): *Adomnán, De Locis Sanctis (SLH* Vol. 3), Dublin.

Meyer, K. 1890: 'The Oldest Version of *Tochmairc Emire*', *Revue Celtique* 11, 424-57.

Meyer, K. 1892 (ed.): *Aislinge Meic Conglinne*, London.

Meyer, K. 1909 (ed.): *Tecosca Cormaic* Todd Lecture Series, Vol. 15, Dublin.

Meyer, K. 1910: 'Gauls in Ireland', *Ériu* 4, 208.

Meyer, K. 1913a: *Learning in Ireland in the Fifth Century and the Transmission of Letters*, Dublin.

Meyer, K. 1913b: 'Aus dem Nachlass Heinrich Zimmers', *ZCP* 9, 87-120.

Migne, J. 1846 (ed.): *Prosper: Opera, PL* , Vol. 51.

Migne, J. 1860 (ed.): *Cogitosus, Vita Brigidae*, in *PL*, Vol. 72, 775-90

Migne, J. 1862 (ed.): *Isidore, De Viris Illustribus*, in *PL*, Vol. 83, Paris, 1082-1106.

Miket, R. and Burgess, C. 1984 (edd.): *Between and Beyond the Walls, Essays on the Prehistory and History of North Britain Presented to George Jobey*, Edinburgh.

Miller, M. 1978-80: 'Hiberni Reversuri', *PSAS* 110, 305-27.

Mommsen, T. 1892 (ed.): *Prosper, Chronicon*, in *MGH: AA* Vol.9, Berlin, 341-499.

Mommsen, T. 1894 (ed.): *Hydatius, Chronicon*, in *MGH: AA*, Vol. 11, Berlin, 1-36.

Moody, T.W. 1971 (ed.): *Irish History 1945-70*, Dublin.

Moore, D. 1969 (ed.): *The Irish Sea Province in Archaeology and History*, Cardiff.

Morris, C., *et al.* 1991: *Tintagel Castle Excavations*, 1990, Interim Report, English Heritage.

Morris, J. 1965: 'Dark Age Dates', in Jarrett and Dobson 1965, 145-85.

Morris, J. 1977: *The Age of Arthur*, Chichester.

Muhlberger, S. 1990: *The Fifth-Century Chroniclers*, Leeds.

Munn, M. 1985: 'A Late Roman Kiln Site in the Hermionid, Greece', *American Journal of Archaeology* 89, 342-3.

Munro, D. 1895 (trans.): *The Life of St Columban*, Philadelphia.

Murphy, J. 1977 (ed.): *Rufus Festus Avienus, Ora Maritima*, Chicago.

Murray, J. 1991: 'Megaliths Again: a View from the Solway', *SAR* 8, 26-32.

Musset, L. 1975: *The Germanic Invasions* trans. E. and C. James, London.

Mytum, H. 1986: 'High Status Vessels in Early Historic Ireland: A Reference in *Bethu Brigte*', *Oxford Journal of Archaeology* 5, 375-8.

Mytum, H. 1992: *The Origins of Early Christian Ireland*, London.

Nash-Williams 1950: *The Early Christian Monuments of Wales*, Cardiff.

Naval Intelligence Division 1941: *Spain and Portugal Handbook*, Vol. 1, London.

Neill, M. 1991: 'A Lost Last', *Archaeology Ireland* 5.2, 14-15.

Nenquin, J. 1961: *Salt: A Study in Economic Prehistory*.

Netzer, N. 1989: 'Willibrord's Scriptorium at Echternach and its Relationship to Ireland and Lindisfarne', in Bonner *et al.* 1989, 203-212

Neuman de Vegvar, C. 1995: 'Drinking Horns in Ireland and Wales: documentary sources', in Bourke1995, 81-87.

Ní Chatháin, P. 1995: 'Aquitaine in Early Irish Sources', in Picard 1995, 137-146.

Ní Chatháin, P. and Richter, M. 1984 (edd.): *Irland und Europa: Die Kirche im Frühmittelatler*, Stuttgart.

Ní Chatháin, P. and Richter, M. 1987 (edd.): *Irland und die Christenheit: Bibelstudien und Mission*, Stuttgart.

Nieke, M.R. and Duncan, H.B. 1988: 'Dalriada: the Establishment and Maintenance of an Early Historic Kingdom in North Britain', in Driscoll and Nieke, 6-21.

Nielsen, P.O. *et al.* 1994 (edd.): *The Archaeology of Gunde and Lundeborg Arkeologiske Studier* 10, Copenhagen.

Nordal, S. 1933 (ed.): *Egils Saga (Íslenzk Fornrit*, Vol. 2), Reykjavík.

Nordenfalk, C. 1977: *Celtic and Anglo-Saxon Painting*, London.

Novakowski, J. and Thomas, C. 1990: *Excavations at Tintagel Parish Churchyard*, Interim Report, Truro.

Ó Caoimh, T. 1989: 'St Brendan Sources: St Brendan and Early Irish Hagiography', in De Courcy Ireland and Sheehy 1989, 17-24.

Ó Cathasaigh, T. 1984: 'The Déisi and Dyfed', *Éigse* 20, 1-33.

O'Conner, A. and Clarke, D. 1983 (edd.): *From the Stone Age to the '45*, Edinburgh.

Ó Corráin, D. 1989 (ed.): *Irish Antiquity: papers in honour of Michael J O'Kelly*, Cork.

Ó Corráin, D. 1994: 'The Historical and Cultural Background of the Book of Kells', in O'Mahony 1994, 1-32.

Ó Corráin, D. and Breatnach, L. and Breen, A. 1984: 'The Laws of the Irish', *Peritia* 3, 382-438.

Ó Corráin, D. *et al.* 1989 (edd.): *Saints, Sages and Storytellers, Studies in Honour of James Carney*, Maynooth.

Ó Criomhthain, T. 1929: *An tOileánach*, Dublin.

Ó Cróinín, D. 1983: 'The Irish Provenance of Bede's Computus', *Peritia* 2, 229-247.

Ó Cróinín, D. 1984: 'Rath Melsigi, Willibrord and the Earliest Echternach Manuscripts', *Peritia* 3, 17-42.

Ó Cróinín, D. 1986: 'New Light on Palladius', *Peritia* 5, 276-283.

Ó Cróinín, D. 1987: 'Merovingian Politics and Insular Calligraphy: The Historical Background to the Book of Durrow and Related Manuscripts', in Ryan 1987, 40-3.

Ó Cróinín, D. 1989: 'The Augsburg Gospel Codex, a Northumbrian Manuscript', in Bonner, *et al.* 1989, 189-201.

Ó hAodha, D. 1978 (ed.): *Bethu Brigte*, Dublin.

O'Kelly, M.J. 1952-3: 'Three Promontory Forts in Co. Cork', *PRIA* 55C, 25-60.

O'Kelly, M.J. 1963: 'Two Ring-Forts at Garryduff, Co. Cork', *PRIA* 63C, 17-125.

Oldfather, C.H. 1939 (ed.): *Diodorus Siculus, Historical Library* (LCL), New York and London.

Olson, L. 1988: *Early Monasteries in Cornwall*, Woodbridge.

Ó Lúing, S. 1991: *Kuno Meyer 1858-1919: a Biography*, Dublin.

Ó Lúing, S. 1994: 'Celtic Scholars of Germany', *ZCP* 46, 249-71.

O'Mahony, F. 1994 (ed.): *The Book of Kells: Proceedings of a Conference held at Trinity College Dublin*, Aldershot.

O'Mahoney, T., *et al.* 1865-1901 (edd.): *The Ancient Laws of Ireland*, 6 vols, Dublin.

O'Meara, J.J. 1949: 'Giraldus Cambrensis in Topographia Hibernie', *PRIA* 52C, 113-178.

O'Meara, J.J. 1978: 'In the Wake of the Saint', *Times Literary Supplement* (14/7/'78).

O'Meara, J.J. 1982: *The History and Topography of Ireland*, Harmondsworth.

O'Neill, T. 1987: *Merchants and Mariners in Medieval Ireland*, Dublin.

O'Rahilly, T.F. 1942: *The Two Patricks*, Dublin.

Oram, R. and Stell, G.P. 1991 (edd.): *Galloway Land and Lordship*, Edinburgh.

Ó Riain, P. 1984 'Samson alias San(c)tan?', *Peritia* 3, 320-3.

Ó Riordáin, S.P. 1942: 'The Excavation of a Large Earthern Ringfort at Garranes, Co. Cork', *PRIA* 47C, 77-150.

Ó Riordáin, S.P. 1947: 'Roman Material in Ireland', *PRIA* 51, 35-82.

O'Rourke, D. 1991: 'First Steps in Medieval Footwear', *Archaeology Ireland* 5.1, 22-3.

Oskamp, H.P. 1970 (ed.): *The Voyage of Mael Duin*, Gröningen.

Outhwaite, L. 1957: *The Atlantic: A History of an Ocean*, New York.

Padel, O.J. 1981a: 'The Cornish Background to the Tristan Stories', *CMCS* 1, 53-81.

Padel, O.J. 1981b: 'Tintagel: An Alternative View', in Thomas 1981b, 28-9.

Padel, O.J. 1985: *Cornish Place-name Elements*, London.

Padel, O.J. 1988: *A Popular Dictionary of Cornish Place-names*, Penzance.

Parker, A.J. 1984: 'Shipwrecks and Trade in the Mediterranean', *Archaeological Review from Cambridge* 3, 99-114.

Peacock, D.P.S. 1969: 'A Romano-British Saltworking Site at Trebarveth, St Keverne', *Cornish Archaeology* 8, 47-65.

Peacock, D.P.S. 1977a (ed.): *Pottery and Early Commerce*, London.

Peacock, D.P.S. 1977b: 'Late Roman Amphorae from Chalk, Kent', in Dore and Greene 1977, 295-300.

Peacock, D.P.S. and Thomas, C. 1967: 'Class E Imported Pottery, A Suggested Origin', *Cornish Archaeology* 6, 35-46.

Peacock, D.P.S. and Williams, D. 1986: *Amphorae and the Roman Economy*, London.

Peake, H.J. and Fleure, H.J. 1927-36: *The Corridors of Time series*, Oxford, 9 vols.

Pearce, S.M. 1982 (ed.): *The Early Church in Britain and Ireland: Studies Presented to Ralegh Radford* (BAR British Series 102), Oxford.

Peate, I.C. 1974-6: 'The Antiquity of Leprosy in Wales', *BBCS* 26, 361-3.

Penhallurick, R.D. 1986: *Tin in Antiquity*, London.

Pentz, P. 1992: 'Changing Patterns of Late-Roman/Early Medieval Trade in the Western Mediterranean', in Hall *et al.* 1992, 1-7.

Pertz, K. 1872 (ed.): *Diplomatum Imperii*, Hannover.

Peskett, A. 1914 (ed.): *Caesar, Bellum Civile* (LCL), New York and London.

Philipsen, J. 1965: 'The Utrecht Ship', *Mariners Mirror* 51, 35-46.

Picard, J-M. 1991a (ed.): *Ireland and Northern France*, Dublin.

Picard, J-M. 1991b: 'Church and Politics in the Seventh Century: the Irish Exile of King Dagobert II', in Picard 1991a, 27-52.

Picard, J-M. 1995 (ed.): *Aquitaine and Ireland in the Middle Ages*, Dublin.

Pillet, M. 1980: *Potiers et Potiéries Populaires en France*, Paris.

Pirenne, H. 1939: *Mohammed and Charlemagne* trans. B. Miall, London.

Plummer, C. 1910 (ed.): *Vitae Sanctorum Hiberniae*, Oxford, 2 vols.

Plummer, C. 1921-2: 'Notes on Some Passages in the Brehon Laws', *Ériu* 9, 31-42

Plummer, C. and Earle, J. 1892 (ed.): *Two of the Saxon Chronicles Parallel*, Oxford.

Polanyi, K. 1963: 'Ports of Trade in Early Societies', *Journal of Economic History* 23, 30-45.

Pollard, S. 1966: 'Neolithic and Dark Age Settlements at High Peak, Sidmouth, Devon', *Procedings of the Devon Archaeological Exploration Society* 23, 35-59.

Pool, P.A.S. 1964: 'The Hermitage Chapel of St Michael of Brea, St Just in Penwith', *Annual Reports of the Cornwall Polytechnic Society* 101, 24-39.

Preston-Jones, A. and Rose, P. 1986: 'Medieval Cornwall', *Cornish Archaeology* 25, 135-85.

Price, J. 1988: 'The Glass Fragments from the Lower Ward', in Thomas 1988b, 25-6.

Price, J. *et al.* 1992: 'The Glass', in Rahtz *et al.* 1992, 131-144.

Price, J. and Cottam, S. 1995: 'Late Roman and Early post-Roman Glass', in Alcock 1995, 99-103.

Price, J. forthcoming (ed.): *Glass in Britain 350-800 AD*, London.

Prieto, N. 1984: 'Algunos datos sobre las importaciones de cerámica "Phocean Red Slip" en la peninsula Iberica', in Blagg *et al.* 1984, 540-8.

Proudfoot, V. 1961: 'The Economy of the Irish Rath', *Medieval Archaeology* 5, 94-122.

Pryor, J.H. 1988: *Geography, Technology and War*, Cambridge.

Pucci, G. 1983: 'Pottery and Trade in the Roman Period', in Garnsey *et al.* 1983, 105-117.

Quinn. B. 1986: *Atlantean: Ireland's North African and Maritime Heritage*, London and New York.

Rackham, H. 1942 (ed.): *Pliny, Naturalis Historia* (LCL), New York and London.

Rademacher, F. 1942: 'Fränkische Gläser aus dem Rhinelande', *Bonner Jahrbucher* 147, 240-65.

Radford, C.A.R. 1956: 'Imported Pottery found at Tintagel Cornwall', in Harden 1956a, 59-70.

Radford, C.A.R. 1966: 'Cultural Relationships of the Early Celtic World', in *Proceedings of the 2nd International Congress of Celtic Studies*, Cardiff, 3-27.

Raftery, B. 1994: *Pagan Celtic Ireland: the Enigma of the Irish Iron Age*, London.

Raftery, J. 1965: 'ExOriente.....', *JRSAI* 95, 193-204.

Raftery, J. 1989: 'Concerning Chronology', in Ó Corráin 1989, 82-90.

Rahtz, P. 1974: 'Pottery in Somerset, AD 400-1066', in Evison 1974, 95-126.

Rahtz, P. 1982: 'Celtic Society in Somerset AD 400-700', *BBCS*, 30, 176-200.

Rahtz, P. 1985: *Invitation to Archaeology*, Oxford.

Rahtz, P. 1991: 'Pagan and Christian by the Severn Sea', in Abrams and Carley 1991, 3-37.

Rahtz, P. *et al.* 1992: *Cadbury Congresbury 1968-73* (BAR British Series 223), Oxford.

Randoin, B. 1981: 'Essai de Classification Chronologique de la Céramique de Tours du IVe au XIe Siècle', in Galinie 1981, Vol. 1, 103-113.

Redknap, M. 1992: 'Sea and Lake Use in Wales, 400-1100 AD', in Carver, *et al.* 1992, 107-118.

Reith, E. 1985: 'Research on Nautical Archaeology and Traditional Boats in France', in Cederlund 1985, 413-20.

Renner, D. 1970: *Die Durchbrochen Zierscheiben der Merowingerzeit*, Mainz.

Reynolds, P. 1984: 'African Red Slip and Late Roman Imports in Valencia', in Blagg *et al.* 1984, 474-539.

Reynolds, R.L. 1957: 'Reconsideration of the History of the Suevi', *Revue Belge de Philologie et d'Historie* 35, 19-57.

Richards, M. 1960: 'The Irish Settlements in South West Wales', *JRSAI* 80, 133-62.

Riché, P. 1976: *Education and Culture in the Barbarian West*, trans., J.J. Contreni, Uni. of South Carolina, 320, n. 71.

Riché, P. 1981: 'Columbanus, his Followers and the Merovingian Church', in Clarke and Brennan 1981, 59-72.

Richter, M. 1991: 'The English Link in Hiberno-Frankish Relations', in Picard 1991a, 95-118.

Richmond, I.A. 1958a (ed.): *Roman and Native in North Britain*, Edinburgh.

Richmond, I.A. 1958b: 'Ancient Geographical Sources for Britain north of Cheviot', in Richmond 1958a, 131-155.

Rigoir, J. & Y. and. Meffre, J-F. 1973: 'Les Derivées Paléochrétiennes du Groupe Atlantique', *Gallia* 31, 207-264.

Rigold, S.E. 1975: 'The Sutton Hoo Coins in the Light of the Contemporary Background of Coinage in England', in Bruce-Mitford 1975, 653-77.

Riley, J. 1981: 'The Pottery from the Cisterns', in Humphrey 1981, 85-124.

Roesdahl, E. 1992 unpublished: 'Denmark, Scandinavia, Europe - Trade and Exchange 11-12th Centuries', lecture to the *Medieval Europe 1992* conference in York.

Roosen-Runge, H.E.A. and Werner, A.E.A. 1960: 'The Pictorial Technique of the Lindisfarne Gospels in Kendrick *et al.* 1960, 262-7.

Rowland, J. 1993: 'Old Welsh *franc*: an Old English Borrowing', *CMCS* 26, 21-5.

Russell, J.C. 1968: 'That Earlier Plague', *Demography* 5, 174-183.

Russell, P. 1988: 'The Sounds of a Silence: the growth of Cormac's Glossary', *CMCS* 15, 1-30.

Rule, M. 1990: 'The Romano-Celtic Ship Excavated at St Peter Port, Guernsey, in McGrail 1990, 49-56.

Ryan, M. 1973: Review of Bowen 1972,*Studia Hibernica* 13, 198-200.

Ryan, M. 1983: *The Derrynaflan Hoard*, Dublin.

Ryan, M. 1987 (ed.): *Ireland and Insular Art AD 500-1200*, Dublin.

Ryan, M. 1994: 'Review of Driscoll and Nieke *Power and Politics in Early Medieval Britain and Ireland*, *Peritia* 8 (1994), 246-8.

Sanderson, D. 1987: 'Analytical Results from Two Glass Sherds from Dunollie' in Alcock and Alcock 1987, fiche, 66-72.

Sanderson, D., Hunter, J. & Warren, S.E. 1984: 'Energy Dispersive X-Ray Fluoresence Analysis of First Millenium AD Glass from Britain', *Journal of Archaeological Science* 11, 53-69.

Santrot, J. 1986: *Céramiques Communes Gallo-Romaines d'Aquitaine*, Paris.

Sarauw, C. 1900: *Irske Studier*, Copenhagen.

Savory, H.N. 1973: Review of Thomas, *The Iron Age in the Irish Sea Province, Archaeologia Cambrensis* 122, 187-9.

Savory, H.N. 1984 (ed.): *Glamorgan County History*, Vol. 2, Cardiff.

Sawyer, P. 1975: *The Age of the Vikings*, rev. ed., London.

Scott, B.G. 1981a (ed.): *Studies in Early Ireland*, Belfast.

Scott, B.G. 1981b: 'Some Conflicts and Correspondences of Evidence in the Study of Irish History and Language', in Scott 1981a, 115-119.

Seeck, O. 1883 (ed.): *Symmachus, Opera, MGH: AA* Vol. 6, Berlin.

Selmer, C. 1939 (ed.): *Navigatio Sancti Brendani*, Notre Dame.

Severin, T. 1978: *The Brendan Voyage*, London.

Sharpe, R. 1984:'Problems Concerning the Origins of the Church in Early Medieval Ireland', *Peritia* 3, 230-270.

Sharpe, R. 1989: '*Quattor sanctissimi episcopi:* Irish Saints before St Patrick', in Ó Corráin *et al.* 1989, 376-99.

Sharpe, R. 1991: *Medieval Irish Saints' Lives, An Introduction to Vitae Sanctorum Hiberniae*, Oxford.

Shaw, R.C. 1967: 'Prolegomena to a re-appraisal of the Early Christianity of the Isle of Man Relative to the Irish Sea Province', *Proceedings of the Isle of Man Natural History and Antiquarian Society* 7, 1-15.

Sheehan, J.J. 1994: 'A Merovingian Background for the Ardmoneel Stone?', *JCHAS* 99, 23-31.

Simpson, W.D. 1940: *St Ninian and Christian Origins in Scotland*, Edinburgh.

Smyth, A.P. 1973: Review of K. Hughes, *Early Christian Ireland: An Introduction to the Sources, Studia Hibernica* 13, 168-71.

Smyth, A.P. 1984: *Warlords and Holy Men*, London.

Smyth, M. 1986: 'The Physical World in Seventh Century Hiberno-Latin Texts', *Peritia* 5, 201-34.

Smyth, M. 1987: 'Isidore and Early Irish Cosmography', *CMCS* 14, 69-102.

Smyth, M. 1996: *Understanding the Universe in Seventh-Century Ireland*, Woodbridge.

Stevens, C.E. 1933: *Sidonius Apollinaris*, Oxford.

Stevenson, J. 1989: 'The Beginnings of Literacy in Ireland', *PRIA* 89C, 127-65.

Stevenson, W. 1904: *Asser, Life of Alfred*, Oxford.

Stokes, W. 1862 (ed.): *Three Irish Glossaries*, London.

Stokes, W. 1887 (ed.): *Tripartite Life of Patrick with other Documents Relating to that Saint*, Dublin.

Synge, J.M. 1919: *In Wicklow, West Kerry and Connemara*, Dublin and London.

Tardif, J. 1898: 'Les Chartes Mérovingiennes de Noirmoutier', *Nouvelle Revue Historique de droit Français et Étranger* 22, 763-90.

Taylor, J. du P. and Cleere, H. 1978 (edd.): *Roman Shipping and Trade: Britain and the Rhine Provinces*, London.

Taylor, T. 1925 (trans.): *The Life of St Samson of Dol*, London.

Thomas, C. 1957: 'Some Post Roman Imported Sherds in Cornwall', *Proceedings of the West Cornwall Field Club* 2, 15-22.

Thomas, C. 1959: 'Imported Pottery in Dark Age Western Britain', *Medieval Archaeology* 3, 89-111.

Thomas, C. 1960: 'People and Pottery in Dark Age Cornwall', *Old Cornwall* 5 1960, 452-60.

Thomas, C. 1964: 'Settlement History in Cornwall', *Cornish Archaeology* 3 1964, 70-79.

Thomas, C. 1972a: 'The Irish Settlements in Post Roman Western Britain', *Journal of the Royal Institution of Cornwall* 6, 260-5.

Thomas, C. 1972b (ed.): *The Iron Age in the Irish Sea Province* (CBA. Research Report 9), London, 1972.

Thomas, C. 1976: 'Imported Post-Roman Mediterranean Pottery in Ireland and Western Britain, Chronologies and Implications', *PRIA* 76C, 245-55.

Thomas, C. 1979: 'St Patrick and Fifth Century Christianity: A Historical Model Explained', in Casey 1978, 81-101.

Thomas, C. 1981a: *Christianity in Roman Britain to 500AD*, London.

Thomas, C. 1981b: *A Provisional List of Imported Pottery in Post-Roman Western Britain and Ireland*, ICS Special Report 7, Redruth, 1981.

Thomas, C. 1982: 'East and West: Tintagel Mediterranean Imports and the Early Insular Church', in Pearce 1982, 17-34.

Thomas, C. 1983: note in F. Turk, 'A Study of the Vertebrate Remains from May's Hill, St Martins', *Cornish Studies* 11, 78-80.

Thomas, C. 1984: 'Abercorn and the *Provincia Pictorum*', in Miket and Burgess 1984, 331-7.

Thomas, C. 1985: *Exploration of a Drowned Landscape*, London.

Thomas, C. 1986: *Tintagel Castle* (English Heritage Guide), London.

Thomas, C. 1988a: 'The Context of Tintagel: a New Model for the Diffusion of Post-Roman Imports', *Cornish Archaeology* 27, 7-25.

Thomas, C. 1988b (ed.): *Tintagel Papers (Cornish Studies* 16), Redruth.

Thomas, C. 1988c: 'The CAU Excavations at Tintagel Island and their Implications', in Thomas 1988b, 49-60.

Thomas, C. 1988d: 'Minor Sites at Tintagel Island, in Thomas 1988b, 31-48.

Thomas, C. 1988e: 'Bryher', Note on finds from South-west Electricity Board Excavations.

Thomas, C. 1990: '*Gallici Nautae de Galliarum Provinciis* - A Sixth/ Seventh Century Trade with Gaul Reconsidered', *Medieval Archaeology* 34, 1-26.

Thomas, C. 1992: *Whithorn's Christian Beginnings: 1992 Whithorn Lecture*, Whithorn.

Thomas, C. 1994: *And Shall these Mute Stones Speak?*, Cardiff.

Thompson, E.A. 1965: 'Britonia', in Barley and Hanson 1965,201-5.

Thompson, E.A. 1980a: 'Procopius on *Brittia* and *Brittania*', *Classical Quarterly* 30, 498-507.

Thompson, E.A. 1980b: 'The Conversion of the Spanish Suevi to Catholicism', in James 1980a, 77-92.

Thompson, E.A. 1982: *Romans and Barbarians*, Madison.

Thompson, E.A. 1984: *St Germanus of Auxerre and the End of Roman Britain*, Woodbridge.

Thompson, E.A. 1985: *Who was St Patrick?*, Woodbridge.

Thomson, D.S. 1961: *Branwen uerch Llyr*, Dublin.

Thorpe, L. 1974 (trans.): *The History of the Franks*, Harmondsworth.

Tierney, J.J. 1960: 'The Celtic Ethnography of Posidonius', *PRIA* 60C, 189-275.

Tierney, J.J. (ed.) 1967: *Dicuil, Liber de Mensura Orbis Terrae (SLH* Vol. 6), Dublin.

Tierney, J.J. 1976: 'The Greek Geographic Tradition and Ptolemy's Evidence for Irish Geography', *PRIA* 76C, 257-65.

Timby, J.R. 1988: 'The Middle Saxon Wares', in Andrews 1988, 73-174.

Todd, M. 1987: *The South West to AD 1000*, London.

Tooley, M.J. 1990: 'Sea-Level and Coastline Changes during the Last 5000 Years', in McGrail 1990, 1-16.

Tranoy, A. 1974: *Hydatius* (Sources Chrétiennes no. 218), Paris, 2 vols.

Tristram, H. 1994 (ed.): *Text and Zeittiefe*, Tübingen.

Tutin, T., *et al.* 1976: *Flora Europaea*, Cambridge.

Unger, R. 1980: *The Ship in the Medieval Economy*, London.

Ussani, V. 1932 (ed.): *Hegesippus, Historiae (Corpus Scriptorum Ecclesiasticorum Latinorum* 66), New York and London.

Van Doorninck, F. W. 1972: 'Byzantium, Mistress of the Sea', in Bass 1972, 134-56.

Van Lith, S.M.E. 1988: 'Late Roman and Early Medieval Glass from a Settlement Site at Maastricht, Dutch South Limburg, Part 2', *Journal of Glass Studies* 30, 62-8.

Vendryes, J. 1920: 'Les Vins de la Gaule in Irlande et l'expression *Fín Aicneta*', *Revue Celtique* 38, 19-24.

Vlek, R. 1987: *The Medieval Utrecht Boat* (BAR International Series 382), Oxford.

Vogel, F. 1885: *Ennodius, Opera (MGH: AA* 7), Berlin.

Wacher, J.S. 1966 (ed.): *The Civitas Capitals of Roman Britain*, Leicester.

Waddell, J. 1991-2: 'The Irish Sea in Prehistory', *JIA* 6, 29-40.

Wailes, B. 1963: 'Some Imported Pottery in Western Britain AD 400-800', unpublished doctoral thesis, University of Cambridge.

Walker, G.S.M. 1957 (ed.): *Sancti Columbani Opera (SLH* Vol. 2), Dublin.

Wallace-Hadrill, J.M. 1960 (ed.): *The Fourth Book of the Chronicle of Fredegar*, London.

Wallace-Hadrill, J.M. 1985: *The Frankish Church*, Oxford.

Walton, K. 1974: 'A Geographer's View of the Sea', *Scottish Geographical Magazine* 90, 4-13.

Ward, J.O. 1968: 'Procopius' *Bell. Goth.* II. 6, 28: the Problem of Contacts between Justinian I and Britain', *Byzantion* 38, 460-71.

Warner, G.F. 1906 & 1915 (ed.): *Stowe Missal*, London, 2 vols.

Warner, R. 1972: 'Clogher Demense', *Excavations: Bulletin of the Association of Young Irish Archaeologists*, 28.

Warner, R. 1976: 'Some Observations on the Context and Importation of Exotic Material in Ireland from the First Century BC to the Second Century AD', *PRIA* 76C, 267-92.

Warner, R. 1979a: 'The Clogher Yellow Layer', *Medieval Ceramics* 3, 37-40.

Warner, R. 1979b: 'The Irish Souterrains and their Background', in Crawford 1979, 100-144.

Warner, R. 1981: 'The Broighter Hoard', in Scott 1981, 29-38.

Warner, R. 1982: 'A Case Study: Clochar macc nDaimini', *Bulletin of the Ulster Placename Society* 4, 27-31.

Warner, R. 1983: 'Ireland, Ulster and Scotland in the Earlier Iron Age', in O'Conner and Clarke 1983, 161-87.

Warner, R. 1985-6: 'The Date of the Start of Lagore', *JIA* 3, 75-7.

Waterer, J. 1968: 'Early Irish Book Satchels or Budgets', *Medieval Archaeology* 12, 70-82.

Watson, W. 1926: *The History of the Celtic Place-names of Scotland*, Edinburgh.

Webb, J.F. 1965 (trans.): *Lives of the Saints*, Harmondsworth.

Weber, B. 1992: 'Norwegian Exports in Orkney and Shetland during the Viking Age', in Hall *et al.* 1992, 159-167.

Welch, M.G. 1976: *Highdown and its Saxon Cemetery*, Worthing.

Welch, M.G. 1983: *Early Anglo-Saxon Sussex* (BAR British Series 112), Oxford.

Wells, P.S. 1992: 'Origins and Content of Early Medieval Trade: A Long Perspective', in Hall *et al.* 1992, 43-9.

Werner, J. 1961: 'Fernhandel und Naturalwirtschaft im Östlichen Merowingerreich nach archäeologischen und numismatischen Zeugnissen', *Bericht der Römisch-Germanischen Kommission* 42, 307-46.

Whitehouse, D., 'The Mediterranean Perspective', in Farrell and Neuman de Vegvar 1992, 117-124.

Whitelock, D. 1950: 'The Interpretation of the Seafarer', in Fox and Dickens 1950, 267-75.

Whitelock, D. *et al.* 1982 (edd.): *Ireland in Early Medieval Europe: Studies in Memory of Kathleen Hughes*, Cambridge.

Williams, D. c.1983: 'Petrological Examination of a Sherd from Saint Christoly', Southampton, unpublished report.

Williams, I. 1944: *Lectures on Early Welsh Poetry*, Dublin.

Williams, I. 1961 (ed.): *Canu Aneirin*, Cardiff.

Winterbottom, M. 1978 (ed.): *Gildas: The Ruin of Britain and other Writings*, Chichester.

World Atlas of Archaeology 1985, Cambridge.

Wood, I 1982: 'The *Vita Columbani and Merovingian Hagiography*', in Clarke and Brennan 1982, 63-80.

Wood, I. 1983: *The Merovingian North Sea*, Alingsås.

Wood, I. 1990: 'The Channel from the 4th to the 7th centuries AD', in McGrail 1990, 93-7.

Wood, I. 1991: 'The Franks and Sutton Hoo', in Wood and Lund 1991, 1-17.

Wood, I. 1992: 'Frankish Hegemony in England', in Carver 1992, 235-241.

Wood, I. and Lund, N. 1991 (edd.): *People and Places in Northern Europe 500-1600: Essays Presented to Peter Sawyer*, Woodbridge.

Wooding, J.M. 1987: 'Some Evidence for Cargoes in Trade on the Western Coasts of Europe 400-900 AD', *Sailing Ships and Sailing People, Proceedings, Section 3*, Perth, Western Australia, 1-17.

Wooding, J.M. 1988a: 'What Porridge Had the Early Irish?', *Australian Celtic Journal* 1, 12-17.

Wooding, J.M. 1988b: 'Saxons Who Furrow the British Sea with Hides', *The Great Circle* 10, 33-6.

Wooding, J.M. 1992: 'Gaulish Artefacts in the Celtic West: Some Problems of Approach', in Hall *et al.* 1992, 169-172.

Wooding, J.M. 1996: 'Cargoes and Trade along the Western Seaboard of Britain, 400-800 AD', in Dark, forthcoming.

Wright, E.V. 1972: 'The Boats of North Ferriby', in Fenwick 1972, 3-7.

Youngs, S. 1989 (ed.): *The Work of Angels*, London.

Zimmer, H. 1902a: 'Keltische Kirche in Brittanien und Irland', *Realencyklopädie für Protestantische Theologie und Kirche*, Leipzig, 1901 trans. A. Meyer as *The Celtic Church in Britain and Ireland*, London, 1902.

Zimmer, H. 1902b: *Pelagius in Irland*, Berlin.

Zimmer, H. 1909-10: 'Über direkte Handelsverbindungen Westgalliens mit Irland im Altertum und frühen Mittelalter', *Sitzungsberichte der königlich preussischen Akademie der Wissenschaften:*

Zimmer, H. 1909a: 'Zeugnisse für westgallisch-irischen Handelsverkehr von Giraldus Cambrensis, a. 1186 bis Tacitus, a. 98', 363-400.

Zimmer, H. 1909b: 'Der Weinhandel Westgalliens nach Irland im 1. bis 7 Jahrhundert n. Chr und sein Niederschlag in irischer Sage und Sprache', 430-76.

Zimmer, H. 1909c: 'Galliens Anteil an Irlands Christianisierung im 4/5 Jahrhundert und altirischer Bildung A: Allgemeine Gesichtspunkte, B: Einzelheiten', 543-613.

Zimmer, H. 1910a: 'Der Gascogner *Virgilius Maro Grammaticus in Irland*', 1031-1098.

Zimmer, H. 1910b: 'Westeuropäischirischer Handelsverkehr im ersten Jahrhundert v. Chr.', 1098-1119.

Index

Abercorn, Scotland, 73, 82, 97
Additamentum Nivaliense de Fuilano, 66
Adomnán of Iona:
  Cáin Adomnáin, 33
  describes breaking of glass vessel, 88-9
  De Locis Sanctis, 105-6
  gallici nautae in *Vita Columbae*, 59, 65, 96
  voyages in *Vita Columbae*, 20, 21, 102, 104, 107
  terminology for ships in *Vita Columbae*, 9-12, 16, 18
Aegean, 16, 42, 51
Africa, 9, 29, 41, 49, 51, 54
Agilan—Gothic ambassador to Gaul, 57
Agilbert—Bishop of Paris, 66-7
Aislinge Meic Conglinne, 71
Alans, 32
Albiones—Spanish people mentioned by Avienus, 26
Alcuin of York, 95
ale, 33
Alexander the Great—interest in north, 23
Alexandria, 51
Allmuire Sét—'treasures from overseas' in Ireland, 10, 69
Amandus—Gaulish missionary, 67
ambassadors, 29, 57
amber, 104
amphorae—see 'Pottery'
Angers, France, 30
Anglesey, Isle of, 62, 101, 104
Anglo-Saxon Chronicles, 10-11
Anglo-Saxon England, 5, 47, 64, 66, 68, 70, 74, 77, 84, 87, 106
Anglo-Saxons, 3, 83, 92, 101, 104
Annales Cambriae, 53
Annals of Ulster, 18, 20, 34-5, 53
Ansoald—Bishop of Poitiers, 65-7
Antrim—Irish county, 106
Aquitaine—French region, 24, 55, 60, 77
Arallas, Cornwall, 95
Arculf—Gaulish bishop who visited Iona, 105-6, 107
Ardifuir, Scotland, 107
Arezzo, Italy, 26
Arklow, Ireland, 8
Arles, 35
Armagh, Ireland, 33, 84, 87, 96
arms trade, 92
Asia Minor, 42
Asser—biographer of Alfred, 17
Asturias, Spain, 98, 104
Aude, River (France), 56
Aurelius Victor, 11, 24, 26
Austrasia—Frankish kingdom, 67
Avienus, 10, 24-6
Avitus—Roman Emperor, 14, 15
Ayrshire, Scotland, 102
Azores—Atlantic islands, 7
Baile na bhFionnúrach, Ireland, 50
balances, 56
Ballinderry II Crannóg, Ireland, 70, 81, 87
Ballycateen, Ireland, 87
Ballyfounder, Ireland, 96
Balther of Säckingen—biographer of St Fridolinus, 65
Bantham, Devon (England), 50, 82, 97, 101
Barrow, River (Ireland), 37-8, 68
Bayeux, France, 31
Bay of Biscay, 7, 29, 30, 52
Beacon hermitages, 17, 53
beads, 94
Beauvais, France, 78
Bechbretha, 70
Bede—author of *Historia Ecclesiastica* and *De Locis Sanctis:*
  on Agilbert, 66
  on Arculf, 105-6
  on conquest of Anglesey and Man, 101, 104
  on English in Ireland, 18, 20, 68
  on gift-giving, 95
  on John the Archcantor, 63
  on Papal letter of 540 to Ireland, 65
  on Theodore of Tarsus in Gaul, 21, 63
  on vines growing in Ireland, 33
Belgae—later prehistoric migrants to Britain, 3
Belisarius—Byzantine general, 47
Berlin—Zimmer appointed to Chair of Celtic in, 2
Bethu Brigte, 81
birds—as navigation aids, 17
Bordeaux, France, 29, 32, 37, 43, 56-60, 67, 73, 77-9, 81, 102
Boundaries—influence on location of exchange sites, 95
bowls, 40, 47, 56
Boyne, River (Ireland), 107
bracelets, 40
Brêhat, Brittany, 50, 63
Bretha Étgid, 68-9
Bretha in Fhuillema Gell, 70
Bretoña, Spain, 59
Breton glosses, 63
Bretons, 30, 55
Bristol Channel, 7-8, 17, 25, 31, 53, 61, 82, 98, 101
British abroad, 30-1, 59
brooches—see 'metalwork'
Bryher, Isles of Scilly, 97
Burgundy, France, 93
Byzantine interests in northern Europe, 20-1, 41, 45-8, 53-4, 63
Cadbury (Cadbury Castle), Somerset (England), 54, 60-1, 87-8
Caesar, Julius, 6, 10, 12, 23-4
Cáin Admanáin—see 'Adomnán'
Calais, France, 25
Caldey Island *(Ynys Pyr)*, Wales, 62, , 82, 94, 97-8
Camel, River (Cornwall), 19, 38
Camp du Chaillot, France, 74, 78
Cantabria, Spain, 17
Canterbury, England, 63, 92
Cape Cornwall, 52-3
capitals, marble—transported within Gaul, 56
Carthage, Tunisia, 42-3, 51
Cashel, Ireland, 50-54
casks, 69-70
'Cassiterides'—mythical 'tin isles' of antiquity, 23
Castlehill, Scotland, 87
cattle, 25
Celtic Sea, 52
censer, from Glastonbury, 54
Chadenac, France, 74, 77
chalices—see 'metalwork'
Channel Islands, 13
charters:
  forged, St Denis, 71-2
  of Sigibert III, 67
châtelaine—see 'metalwork'
Cheshire, England, 38
Chester, England, 97
Chew Stoke (Somerset), England, 87
Childeric I—King of Franks, 30
Chilperic—King of Franks, 57
Christianity—Irish sources of, 1, 2, 5, 32, 35-6, 64
Chronicle of Fredegar, 55

church councils,
in Gaul, 30, 59
in Spain, 30, 59
Modogarnomo Castro, 65
Cicero, 15
Classical learning in Ireland, 24, 33, 37
Clatchard Craig, Scotland, 107
'cliff castles'—supposed, in Ireland, 23
climate, 7
Clogher, Ireland, 60-1, 82-3, 83, 87, 98
Clonmacnois, Ireland, 59, 97
clothing—as trade goods, 67
Clovis I, King of Franks, 65
Clovis II, King of Franks, 65, 67
Clyde, River (Scotland), 8, 102, 107
Cogitosus, see *Vita Brigidae*
coins:
Anglo-Saxon, in Celtic West, 83, 104
Gaulish, in Britain, 92, 95
in western and eastern Francia, 56
lack of, in Celtic West, 41, 45-7
combs, 38, 40
Congresbury (Somerset), England, 49, 50, 53, 60-1, 98
Conimbriga (Coimbra), Portugal, 29, 43, 45, 57, 82
containers—E ware as, 81
cooking, 70, 81
Cork, Irish county, 23, 37-8, 98, 101
Cormac—monastic voyager from Iona, 10, 21, 104
Cormac of Cashel—author of *Sanas Cormaic*, 69
Cornwall 8, 16-18, 23, 25-6, 30, 52, 62-4, 68, 70, 72, 77-8, 82-3, 88, 95, 97, 104, 106, 107
Coruña, Spain, 6
Coygan Camp, Wales, 98
Craig Laggan, Scotland, 102
Craigs Quarry, Scotland, 73, 97
crannógs—character of finds from, 92
cresset—from Whithorn, 83
Crith Gablach, 33, 70, 82, 94
cross motifs—sources of for insular church, 54
cullet, see 'glass'
currents, 51, 52
Dagobert I, King of Franks, 67, 72
Dagobert II, King of Franks, 65-7, 106
Dalkey Island, Ireland, 50, 60, 82, 87 94, 101, 102
Dalmatia, 35
Dalriada—early Scottish kingdom, 4, 6, 30, 59, 60, 102, 107
Danube, River, 47
dedications—see 'saints' dedications'.
dendrochronology, 13, 83
Derry, Irish county, 96, 102
Derrynaflan, Ireland, 50, 73, 82, 97
Devon, English county, 50, 97
Dial Rocks Hill, Isles of Scilly, 97
Di Chetharslicht Athagabála, 68
Dicuil—Irish geographer, 9, 18, 23, 104
Dido, Bishop of Poiters, 65-6
diffusionism, iii, 1-3, 65
Dinas Emrys, Wales, 97
Dinas Powys, Wales, 43, 50, 53, 60-2, 82, 84, 87, 92, 94, 97-8
Diodorus Siculus, 23, 25, 34
dipinti—on Mediterranean amphorae, 51
distraint—Irish law of, 69
dogs—as a trade good, 25, 35, 36, 70
Donatus—Latin grammarian, 37
Douro (Duero), River (Portugal), 52
Downpatrick, Ireland, 96, 98
'down-the-line' exchange, 93
Dublin, Ireland, 8, 62, 101
Dumbarton, Scotland, 50, 87, 94, 98, 102
Dunadd, Scotland, 55, 60-1, 71-2, 74, 82, 87, 97-8, 102, 107
Dún Ardtreck, Isle of Skye, 97
Dunollie, Scotland, 18, 98, 102, 107
Dunottar, Scotland, 107
Durrow—Book of, 70-1
dyeing industries, 81
Dyfed, Wales, 24, 30, 37-8, 52, 97-8, 101, 107
East Anglia—Anglo-Saxon kingdom, 67
Ebroin—Frankish mayor, 63, 66-7
Egbert—Anglo-Saxon missionarie to Germany, 10, 68
Egils Saga, 19-20
Egypt, 42
Elafius—Frankish bishop in Spain, 57
Elie, Scotland, 97
embayment, 7
Emporia—theory of, 5, 62, 81, 93-4
enamel, 104
English Channel, 7, 7, 13, 20, 25, 29, 50, 52, 55, 64, 68, 101
escup vessel—measurement of currency items, 69, 70
Evreux, France, 78
Faeroe Islands, 6, 104
Fairhead, Ireland, 8
Faustus—British churchman in Gaul, 62
feathers, 69, 70
Fergus Mór, King of Scots, 30
fish, 101
mackerel, 8
Fishing, 21
flotsam—in Irish law, 68
Fowey, River (Cornwall), 107
Franks, 5, 9, 14, 20-1, 22-5, 29-30, 47, 51, 55, 57, 67-8, 72, 92
Fredegund, Queen of Franks, 31
furs, 69
gales, 7, 18
Galicia, 6-7, 17, 22, 26, 29-30, 48, 52, 55, 57, 59, 63
Galloway, Scotland, 38, 102, 104, 107
Garranes, Ireland, 5, 74, 78, 82, 87, 96
Garrone, River (France), 56, 60, 77-8, 102
Garryduff, Ireland, 73, 82, 87, 96-7
'gateway communities'—theory of, 61, 94, 95
Gaza, Near East, 42, 51
geography, 3, 8, 24
Gers, French department, 56
Gesta Dagoberti, 71
Gibraltar, Straits of, 6, 14-15, 20, 26, 29, 41-2, 47, 63
gifts, 93-95
Gildas, 14, 15, 25, 30-1, 40
Giraldus Cambrensis, 1, 34, 40
Glamorgan, Welsh county, 82, 98
glass, 4, 5, 54, 61-2, 72-92, 98, 104
'Atlantic' type, 87-8
bowls, 87
claw beakers, 88-9
cones, 87
cullet, 84, 87
engraved, 84, 87
'Kempston' beakers, 87-8
manufacture of, 84, 87
Mediterranean, 54, 87
optic decoration, 87
palm cups, 87
trailed, 84, 87
Gloucestershire, England, 25
goblets—as trade good, 69, 71
Gododdin, 88, 92

gold—see 'metals'
Goonhilly, Cornwall, 71
Goths, 14, 29, 32, 47, 55
Graffiti—on Mediterranean amphorae, 51
grain, 25, 26, 46
Greek explorers, 7
Greeks, 7, 51
Greenland, 7
Gregory of Tours, 10, 15, 20, 30-1, 47-8, 51, 53, 55-7, 95
Grimoald—Frankish mayor, 65-7
Grotte de Villebors, France, 78
Guisseny, Brittany, 78, 97, 102
Guntrum—Frankish king, 57
Gwithian, Cornwall, 82-3, 87, 101
Gwynedd, Welsh region/kingdom, 38, 101, 107
Hadrian, Bishop, 21
hagiography, see 'saints' lives'
Hamburg—compared by Zimmer with Bordeaux, 33
Hanging bowls, see 'bowls'
harbours/ports, 6, 8, 19, 24, 31, 36, 47, 50, 53, 69, 72, 93, 96
Hebrides, Scotland, 6, 106
Hellesvean, Cornwall, 97
Heptads, 68
Herodotus, 46
Herpes, France, 31, 74, 77, 88
Heruls, 29, 30
Hewald—English missionary to Germany, 68
hides, see 'leather'
Highdown, England, 87-8
High Peak, Devon, 50, 97
Hisperica Famina, 32
Historia Brittonum, 62
historiography, 2, 8
Holme Pierpont, England, 84, 87
Holyhead, Wales, 37
honey, 26, 51, 69
horses, 69
Howth, Ireland, 62
Huns, 32
Hydatius, 14, 29
hyper-diffusionism, 6, 10, 16, 21, 24
Iceland, 6, 8, 17, 30, 104
Ictis—unidentified Atlantic site in Roman sources, 23
Île de Beniquet, Brittany, 7
Île Lavret, Brêhat, Brittany, 50
Île d'Ouessant, Brittany, 7, 52
Immram curaig Máil-dúin, 9
immrama, 10
Inishcealtra, Ireland, 101
inscriptions:
  in Gaul, 35
  Latin, in Britain, 51, 62
  ogham, 24, 37, 30, 37-8
Inverness, Scotland, 88, 107
Iona, Scotland, 18, 70, 82, 88, 102, 104 , 106, 107
Irish law, 20, 34, 68, 70, 82
Irish Sea, 6, 16, 31, 38, 40, 50, 59, 61-2, 81, 88, 93-4, 96-8, 101, 104-5, 107
'Irish Sea Province', 3, 4, 40
iron—see 'metals'
Isidore of Seville, 10, 15, 24, 33, 47-8, 105
Italy, 31, 41
jetsam—in Irish law, 68
Jonah, 20, 65
Jonas—author of *Vita Columbani*, 19, 33, 64-5, 67, 72
Jouarre—tomb of Agilbert at, 66
Jumièges, France, 67
Justinian—Byzantine emperor, 46
Kedrah, Ireland, 97
Kells—Book of, 71
Kelsies, Cornwall, 82, 98
kermes—see 'pigments'
Kerry, Irish county, 38
Killadedadrum, Ireland, 97
Killucan, Ireland, 97
kinship networks, 93
Kintyre, Scotland, 6, 8, 102, 107
kitchenware, 81-2
La Furca, France, 72
Lagore, Ireland, 5, 22, 70, 74, 78, 82, 87
Lancashire, English county, 38
Land's End, Cornwall, 8, 23, 107
latitude reckoning, 17
Laxdæla Saga, 21
lead—see 'metals'
learning in Ireland, 32-4
leather, 25, 51, 69, 70
Leinster, 24, 37
Leinster Poems, 9, 10
Leo, Pope, 35
Leontius—author of *Life of St John the Almsgiver*, 46, 95
leprosy—in early medieval Europe, 53
Les Cléons, France, 78
Lesser Garth, Wales, 98, 101
Leudast—rebel count of Tours, 55
Leuvigild—Gothic king of Spain, 22, 29, 57
Leyden Glossary, 32-3
Liber Historiae Francorum, 65
Libran—Irish voyager in *Vita Columbae*, 96, 102
Life of St John the Almsgiver, see 'Leontius'
lime, 71
Lisdhu, Ireland, 97, 98
Lisleagh, Ireland, 97
Little Dunagoil, Scotland, 97
Llantrisant, Wales, 62
loan-words—into Irish and British, 9, 36, 37, 70
Loch Glashan crannóg, Scotland, 81, 98
Lochspouts crannóg, Scotland, 97
Loire, River (France), 4, 15, 16, 25, 30, 55, 60, 62-5, 67, 70, 77, 81, 102, 104
Longbury Bank, Wales, 61, 82, 84, 87, 94, 9798
long-distance travel, 1,8, 93
longshoremen, 8
Lough Faughan, Ireland, 97
Lough Gara, Ireland, 87
Loughshinney, Ireland, iv
Louth, Irish county, 101
Louvre, Paris—excavations at, 78
Lucan, 10
Luce Sands, Scotland, 97, 104
Lugbe—character in *Vita Columbae*, 59
Lundy Island, 17
mackerel, see 'fish'
madder—'pigments'
Mainz, 13
malt, 70
Man, Isle of, 17, 98, 101, 102, 104
manuscripts, 106
Margam Deer Park Farms, 87
Marinus, 24
Marne region, 88
Marshes Upper, 97
'Massiliote Periplus', 24
masts and sails, 6, 11, 13, 16, 18

May's Hill, Scilly, 60-1, 82
mead, 33, 70, 92
meat, 94
Meath, 62, 98, 101
Mediterranean, 6, 9, 13-16, 18-19, 22-3, 25, 31-2, 41, 46, 48-9, 51, 53
megaliths, 4, 7
Meols, 104
mercenaries, 1, 22, 92
merchants, 31
Mersey, River (England), 104
metals
    gold, 25, 34, 70
    iron, 25, 69, 70, 73
    lead, 25, 51, 72
    scrap metal, 101
metal vessels, 81
metalwork, 22, 92, 98, 101, 104
    brooches, 31, 40, 94, 98
    châtelaine, from Isles of Scilly, 92
    chalices, 104
    pins, 40
    rings, 40
Milesian legends, 4, 24
Mir—King of Galicia, 57
Miracula of St Benedict, 72
Miracula of St Philibert, 72
missions, 64, 67-8, 72
monasticism:
    spread of, 1, 53
monks:
    as *peregrini*, 65
    as travellers, 67-8, 96
    involved in commerce, 67-8, 95
    ships used by, 11
Morbihan, Brittany, 78
mortaria, 60
Mote of Mark, Scotland, 60-2, 87
Mounts Bay, Cornwall, 8
Moynagh Lough, Ireland, 84, 87, 97
Muirbretha, iv, 19-20, 33, 51, 68-71, 95
Muirchertach Mac Erca—death of, 34
Muirchú—biographer of St Patrick, 36
Mullaroe, Ireland, 84, 87-8
Munster—Irish region, 24
Nantes, France, 56, 60, 64-5, 72, 78, 102
Navigatio Sancti Brendani Abbatis, 10, 11, 12
navigation, 6, 8, 16, 17, 18, 19, 53
Nendrum, Ireland, 94
Neustria—Frankish kingdom, 64, 67, 95, 106
Nevers, France, 67
New Pieces, Wales, 87
Nicetus—Frankish missionary, 67
Noirmoutier, France, 31, 55, 65, 67-8, 70-2, 102
Normandy—French region, 30, 31
North Sea, 93, 104
Northumbria—Anglo-Saxon kingdom, 65, 68, 105, 106
Northumbrian presence at Whithorn, 83
nuts, 69-70
oak bark—use in tanning, 11-12
O'Davoren's Glossary, 69, 71
'Oestrymnides'—mythical islands mentioned in Avienus, 26
ogham—see 'inscriptions'
oil, 26, 38, 38, 40, 51, 54, 67, 95
Orkney, Islands, 6, 21, 104, 107
Orléans, France, 29, 43, 67, 78, 95
Orosius, 24
orpiment—see 'pigments'
pack ice, 13
Paenitentiale Cummeani, 34
Palladius, 35, 37
Pannonia, 47-8
Peel Castle, Isle of Man, 98
Pelagius, 35
peninsular roads, 1, 4, 62, 107
peninsulas, 7
Penmachno, Gwynedd, 62
Pépiron, Aquitaine, 78
Peregrinatio, 10, 65, 81
petrology—of ceramics, 74
Philemon, 24
Phoenicians, 2, 23
Picts, 30, 37
pigments, 5, 22
    kermes, 26, 71
    madder, 71, 81
    orpiment, 71
pilot manuals, 7, 16
pilots, 17, 53
pins—see 'metalwork'
Pippin, King of Franks, 68
piracy, 8, 14, 22, 29-32
Pirenne thesis, 2, 22, 41
pitch, 26
place-names—on map of Ptolemy, 24
plague, 53
Pliny, 10, 24
Po, River (Italy), 26
Poitiers, France, 57, 66
Poitou—French region, 81
Pontus, 9
Port e Candas, Isle of Man, 97-8
ports—see 'harbours'
'ports of trade'—theory of, 95
Portugal, 14-16, 18, 20, 22, 26, 29, 41-5, 47-8
Posidonius, 24
Positivism, iv, 2, 3
pottery:
    African, 31
    African tablewares, 31, 42, 48, 49, 51
    African Red Slipware (ARS), 29, 42, 43, 45, 55, 82
    Argonne ware, 25
    Bar Lug Pottery, 77
    Bi, ii, iv, v, see 'class 43, 44, 45, 49'
    Bvi, see 'class 34'
    Byzacena amphorae (Class 34), 43, 45, 49
    Class 43 amphorae, 42, 45, 48-50, 60
    Class 44 amphorae, 42, 45, 48-50, 60
    Class 45 amphorae, 42, 45, 49-50, 101
    Class 49 amphorae, 42, 45, 50
    Dite à l'éponge, 25, 31
    Dressel amphorae, classes 1-4, 25, 26, 34
    East Coast Gritty ware, 73
    Eastern Mediterranean amphorae, 29, 41-5, 48-51, 82-3, 96, 101
    E ware, 32, 59, 60-1, 70, 72-84, 88, 92, 96-8, 101, 102, 104-5, 107
    imported, 1, 3, 4, 15, 22, 40, 82-3, 107
    Italian finewares, 26
    Mediterranean (general), 32, 41-2, 46, 53-4, 61-2, 73, 81-3, 96, 98, 101
    Paleochretienne grise (D ware), 55-6, 60-3, 77, 98, 102
    Paleocristiana gris, 56
    Phocaean Red Slipware (PRS), 29, 42-5, 51, 57

Portuguese amphorae, 26
Rhenish, 74
Samian ware, 71
Souterrain ware, 81
Pozzuoli, Italy, 26
Procopius of Caesarea, 24, 30, 46-7
Prosper of Aquitaine, 22, 35
Pseudo-Jerome—author of *Commentary on Mark,* 11
Ptolemy, 24-5
Pytheas of Massilia, 23, 47
Quentovic, France, 13, 31
quernstones, 71
radiocarbon dates, 12
Randlestown, Ireland, 82, 97
Rath Melsigi—monastery in Ireland, perhaps in Co. Carlow, 68
Reask, Ireland, 97, 101
redistribution—of imports, 93
Remigius—Frankish missionary, 67
Rhineland, 9, 13, 47, 56, 74, 77-8, 88
Rhodian Sea Law, 95
rings—see 'metalwork'
Riochatus—British churchman in Gaul, 62
Roman Edict of 419, 14
Roman imports in Ireland, 37-40
Romans:
rule in west, 2, 31
influence on/reports of ships in Atlantic, 6-9, 11-13
cultural influence in Ireland, 37-8, 40
trade with Atlantic, 21-5, 34
Romanus, Irish churchman in France, 65
Rome—Monastery of St Martin in, 63
Rouen, France, 56
rowing, 18
Rutilius Namatianus, 17, 30, 32
sailing, 6, 7
sails, see 'masts and sails'
St Brendan of Clonfert, 10
Saint Christoly, Charente, 73, 78
St Columb, Cornwall, 64
St Columba of Iona, 59, 96
St Columbanus of Bobbio, 20, 33, 63-5, 67-8, 79, 81, 102
Saint Denis, France, 72
Saintes, France, 30, 55, 57
St Fridolinus, 65
St Germanus of Auxerre, 35
St Govans, Wales, 52
St Ives, Cornwall, 53
St Jerome, 35
St John of Alexandria, 46
St John the Archcantor, 63, 107
St Kew, Cornwall, 62
St Martin of Braga, 47-8, 52
St Martin of Tours, 47-48, 63
St Ouen of Rouen, 67
St Patrick, 22, 33, 35-6, 38
St Philibert of Noirmoutier, 65, 67, 72
Saint Pierre de Vauvray, 78
St Samson of Dol, 62-3, 68, 101, 107
saints' dedications, 4
saints' lives, 2-4, 9, 11, 95
Saint Wandrille, France, 67, 72
St Wilfred of Hexham, 66
St Willibrord, 68
salt, 69-72
salted fish, 26
Sanas Cormaic, 69, 104
sapientes—supposed exiles to Ireland in Leyden Glossary
sarcophagi:
transportation within Gaul, 56
sarcophagus of Agilbert at Jouarre, 66
Sarthe, France, 92
Saumur, France, 30
Saxons, 14-15, 19-21, 29-30, 55
Saxony, 68
Scandinavia, 14
Schleswig, 14
Scilly, Isles of, 16, 52-3, 61, 92, 94, 97, 101, 102
Scotland, 6, 9, 17, 24, 61, 92
Scrabo, Ireland, 97
sculpture, 92
sea-level, 7
Seine, 56
Sellis—port on Loire, 67
Senchus Fer nAlban, 9
Senchus Mar, 33
Shannon, River (Ireland), 6, 24, 59, 101, 102
Shetland, 6
ships:
British, 31
Blackfriars, 13
Broighter, 9, 12, 16, 18-19
Bruges, 13
carvel built, 12-13
clinker built, 9
curachs, 1, 6, 9-13, 15-16, 18-20, 26
dugouts, 10-11, 14, 26
Fos-sur-Mer, 13-14, 16, 19, 51
Gaulish, 13-14, 16, 59
Irish, 9, 10, 13, 18, 31, 67
logboats, see 'dugouts'
Lough Lene, 9, 12, 13
luggers, 10
Mainz, 13
Mediterranean, 4, 7, 9-10, 15, 17, 41, 46, 48-53
merchant ships, 9, 10, 35
mortice-and-tenon joined, 9, 16
Nydam, 14
Ploucmanac'h, 25
Roman, 12-13
'Seine boats', 10
St Peter Port, 13
Thames barge, 13
Utrecht, 9, 13
of Veneti, 6, 12, 13
Waterstraat, 13
Yassi Ada, 16, 19, 48-50, 54
shipwreck, 18, 20, 25, 49, 65, 69, 84, 105
shoes, 67, 70
Shropshire, 25
Sidonius, 10, 14, 15, 29, 30
silver, 25, 34, 46, 69, 70
Slane, Co. Meath, 92
slaves, 25
Solinus, 10
Somerset, 49, 52-3, 62, 88, 97
sounding leads, 17
Sound of Jura, 101-2
Spain, iii, 5-7, 16-18, 20, 29, 41-2, 47-8, 51, 55, 77
spices, 51
Stephanos of Alexandria, 46
stoppers—amphora, 49, 54
Stowe Missal, 33
Stoneyford, Co. Carlow, 37
Strabo, 11, 12, 14, 16, 23, 25-6, 40, 71

substantivism, 5, 21, 94
Suevi, 55, 57, 63
Suibhne, Abbott, of Iona, 104
Sulpicius Severus, 63
Sutton Hoo, East Anglia, 92
Symmachus, 35
Symson, 102
Tacitus, 24-5
tanning, 12
Tarragona, 9
Tean, Isles of Scilly, 53, 92
Tecosca Cormaic, 10, 33-4, 68-9, 72, 104
Teeshan, Ireland, 81, 96
temperature, 7
territorial waters—possible concept in early Irish law, 68
Tertullian, 38
'Theodimir', Spanish king, 48
Theodore of Tarsus—archbishop of Canterbury, 21, 63, 66
tides—as a factor in navigation, 8, 12, 53, 101
Timaeus, 24
tin, 23, 25, 35, 46, 50-1, 53, 72, 92, 95
Tintagel, Cornwall, 31, 42, 45, 48, 50-2, 60, 62, 74, 87-8, 95, 98, 102
Tipperary, Irish county, 37
Tochmairc Emire, 34
Toledo, 57
Tomianus of Angoulême—Irish churchman in Gaul, 65
Toulouse, France, 33
Touraine—French region, 81
Tours, France, 29, 43, 55, 57, 60-1, 63, 74, 77, 78
trade, see 'exchange'
'tramp steamer' model, 96
Trethurgy, Cornwall, 87, 98
Trim, Ireland, 92
Trobriand Islands, iii, 4
Tuy, Galicia, 29
typological analyses, 87
Ulster—Irish region, 17
Ulster Cycle tales, 34
Uraicecht Becc, 9, 10
Ushant, Brittany, 8, 102
Vandals, 14, 20, 29
Vannes, Brittany, 55
Venantius Fortunatus, 57, 64
Veneti, 6, 12, 13, 34
Verdun, France, 95
Vetraria—port on Loire, 67
Vikings, 12-13, 18-20, 70, 81, 104
Virgilius Maro Grammaticus—grammarian, probably Irish, 33
Visigoths—see 'Goths'
Vita Amandi, 67
Vita Brendani, 11
Vita Brigidae, 33, 71
Vita Columbae, see 'Adomnán'
Vita Columbani, see 'Jonas'
Vita et Virtutes Eparchi, 59
Vita Filiberti, 31, 63, 67, 70-2, 96-6, 102
Vita Kyarani, 59, 101
Vitas Patrum Emeretensium, 47, 48
Vita Samsonis, 18, 62, 68, 107
Vita Wilfridi, 20, 65-6
Vita Winwaloei, 63
Vouille, Battle of, 56
Wales, 17, 25, 62-3
Waroch—count of Brittany, 20, 55
Waterford, Irish county, 18, 37, 68
wax, 26
Wessex, 66
'Western Seaways', iii, 1, 3, 6, 37
Wexford, Irish county, 8
Whitby, Synod of, 32, 66
Whithorn, Scotland, iv, 50, 60-3, 71, 78, 82-4, 87-8, 92-4, 98, 101, 102, 104
Wicklow, Irish county, 38
Wicklow Mountains, Ireland, 17
Wictibert, English missionary to Germany, 68
winds—as a factor in navigation, 7-8, 12, 16, 18-19, 24, 57, 62, 101-2, 105
    Levanter, 7, 52
    Meltemi, 16
    Penientes, 7
    Vendevales, 7
wine, 26, 31-4, 38, 40, 51, 54, 59, 69-70, 72, 77, 92, 95
wine trade, iii, 1, 5, 22, 32, 60, 68, 74
wooden vessels, 81
wool, 12, 26
Yeo, River (Cornwall), 53

www.ingramcontent.com/pod-product-compliance
Lightning Source LLC
LaVergne TN
LVHW071219210926
848482LV00015B/854